COMMENTARIES

ON

THE PROPHET EZEKIEL

VOL. II

THE CALVIN TRANSLATION SOCIETY,

INSTITUTED IN MAY M.DCCC.XLIII.

FOR THE PUBLICATION OF TRANSLATIONS OF THE WORKS OF
JOHN CALVIN.

COMMENTARIES

ON THE

FIRST TWENTY CHAPTERS OF THE

BOOK OF THE PROPHET EZEKIEL

BY JOHN CALVIN

NOW FIRST TRANSLATED FROM THE ORIGINAL LATIN,
AND COLLATED WITH THE FRENCH VERSION:

BY THOMAS MYERS, M.A.
VICAR OF SHERIFF-HUTTON, YORKSHIRE

VOLUME SECOND

WIPF & STOCK · Eugene, Oregon

Wipf and Stock Publishers
199 W 8th Ave, Suite 3
Eugene, OR 97401

Commentaries on the First Twenty Chapters of the Book of the Prophet Ezekiel, Volume 2
By Calvin, John and Myers, Thomas
Softcover ISBN-13: 979-8-3852-1675-8
Hardcover ISBN-13: 979-8-3852-1676-5
eBook ISBN-13: 979-8-3852-1677-2
Publication date 2/14/2024
Previously published by Baker Book House, 2005

This edition is a scanned facsimile of the original edition published in 2005.

COMMENTARIES

ON

THE PROPHET EZEKIEL.

CHAPTER XIII.

Lecture Thirty-Fourth.

1. And the word of the Lord came unto me, saying,	1. Et fuit sermo Iehovæ ad me, dicendo,
2. Son of man, prophesy against the prophets of Israel that prophesy, and say thou unto them that prophesy out of their own hearts, Hear ye the word of the Lord;	2. Fili hominis, prophetiza contra prophetas Israel prophetizantes, et dic prophetizantibus ex corde suo, Audite sermonem Iehovæ.
3. Thus saith the Lord God, Woe unto the foolish prophets, that follow their own spirit, and have seen nothing!	3. Sic dicit Dominator Iehovah, Væ super prophetas stultos[1] qui ambulant post spiritum suum: et non viderunt.

HERE God directs his discourse against the impostors who deceived the people under pretence of exercising the prophetic gifts. He speaks of the exiled prophets, as will be evident from the context: for among the captives there were those who assumed the name of God, boasting themselves endowed with the prophetic spirit: but meanwhile they intruded into the office, and then vainly boasted in their deceptions. But the end which they proposed to themselves was to promise the people a speedy return, and so to win the favour of the multitude. For the captives were already almost broken-hearted by weariness: and seventy years was

---

[1] Or, "disgraceful."—*Calvin.*

a long period. When therefore they heard of returning after three years, they easily suffered themselves to be deceived by such blandishments. But although God is so vehemently enraged against those impostors, it does not therefore follow that when he charges them with their crime, he absolves the people, or even extenuates their fault. Nor could the people object that they were deceived by those falsehoods, since they willingly and knowingly threw themselves into the snare. They were not destitute of true prophets; and God had distinguished his servants from false prophets by well-known marks, so that no one could mistake except wilfully. (Deut. xiii. 3.) But in the midst of light they blinded themselves, and so God suffered them to be deceived. But that was the just reward of their pride, since they could not be subject to God and his servants. Then when they sought enticements, as is evident from many passages, God also gave the reins to Satan, that there should be a lying spirit in the mouth of all the prophets. Micah reproves them because they desired prophets to be given them who should promise large grape-gatherings and a plentiful harvest, (ch. ii. 11;) meanwhile, when God chastised them severely, they roared and were tumultuous. We see, therefore, that while God inveighs so sharply against false prophets, the people's fault was not diminished; but rather each ought thus to reason with himself—if God spares not our prophets, what better have we to hope for?

When therefore the Prophet turns his discourse to the false prophets, there is no doubt of his intention to reprove the whole people for attending to such fallacies while they despised the true doctrine, and not only so, but even rejected it with fury. *Say therefore to the prophets of Israel while prophesying, say to those prophesying out of their own hearts.* Here he concedes the name of prophets of Israel to those who thrust themselves forward, and rashly boasted that they were commanded to utter their own imaginations, or what the devil had suggested. For then indeed no others ought to have been lawfully reckoned prophets, unless divinely chosen. But because the wicked seized upon this title, they are often called prophets, though God's Spirit is a complete stranger to them: but the gift of prophecy can only flow from that one fountain. This great struggle then happened when the prophets, or those who assumed the title, engaged with hostility among themselves: for we are commanded to acquiesce in God's truth alone: but when a lie is offered to us instead of truth, what can we do but fluctuate and at length engage in conflict? There is no doubt, then, that weak minds were thus vehemently shaken when they saw contests and dissensions of this kind between prophets. At this day God wishes to prove the fidelity of his people by such an experiment, and to detect the hypocrisy of the multitude. For, as Paul says, there must be heresies, that those who are approved may be made manifest. (1 Cor. xi. 19.) God therefore does not rashly permit so much license to Satan's ministers, that they should petulantly rise up against sound doctrine: nor yet without a cause does he permit the Church to be torn asunder by diverse opinions, and fictions to grow so strong sometimes, that truth itself lies buried under them: he wishes indeed in this way to prove the constancy of the pious, and at the same time to detect the lightness of hypocrites who are tossed about by every wind. Meanwhile, if the contention which we now perceive between those who boast themselves pastors of the Church disturbs us, let this example come to mind, and thus novelty will not endanger our faithfulness. What we suffer the ancients have experienced, namely, the disturbance of the Church by intestine disputes, and a similar tearing asunder of the bond of unity.

Next, God briefly defines who the false prophets are; namely, *those who prophesy out of their own hearts:* he will afterwards add, *they have seen nothing, they only boast in the name of God,* and yet they are not sent by him. The same thing is expressed in various ways, but I shall treat other forms of speech in their own places. Here, as I have said, we may readily decide at once who are the true and who the false prophets: the Spirit of God pronounces every one who prophesies from his own heart to be an impostor. Hence nothing else remains but for the prophets faithfully to utter whatever the Spirit has dictated to them. Whoever, therefore, has no sure testimony to his vision, and cannot truly testify that he speaks from God's mouth and by the revelation of his Spirit, although he may boast in the title of prophet, yet he is only an impostor. For God here rejects all who speak from their own heart. And hence we also gather the extreme vanity of the human mind: for God puts a perpetual distinction between the human mind and the revelation of his Spirit. If this be so, it follows that what men utter of themselves is a perverse fiction, because the Spirit of God claims to himself alone, as we have said, the office of showing what is true and right. It follows—

Woe to the foolish or disgraceful *prophets.* נבל, *nebel,* signifies "a vile person," "a castaway," just as נבלה, *nebeleh,* means "foulness," "crime," "wickedness," although נבל, *nebel,* is oftener taken for folly, and I willingly embrace this sense as it is generally received. He calls the prophets foolish, because they doubtless fiercely insulted the true servants of God—just like upstarts puffed up with wonderful self-conceit; for the devil, who reigns in them, is the father of pride: hence they carry themselves haughtily, arrogate all things to themselves, and wish to be thought angels come down from heaven. And when Paul speaks of human fictions, he grants them the form of wisdom. (Col. ii. 23.) Hence there is no doubt that these pretenders of whom Ezekiel speaks were held in great esteem, and so, when swollen with bombast, they puffed forth surprising wisdom; but meanwhile the Holy Spirit shortly pronounces them *fools:* for whatever pleases the world under the mask of wisdom, we know to be mere folly before God.

Now he adds, *who walk after their own spirit, without seeing any thing:* that is, when no vision has been given them. Ezekiel explains himself more clearly, or rather the Spirit who spake through him. As, therefore, he has lately condemned all who prophesy out of their own mind or heart,—for the noun "heart" is here used for "intellect," as in other places,—as, therefore, the Spirit has lately condemned all such, so he says that those *who walk after their own spirit* wickedly abuse the prophetic office. He here alludes to the prophetic gift when he speaks of "spirit."

For, because they might object that false prophets did not speak from their own heart, but had secret revelations, he concedes to them the use of the word "spirit" by a rhetorical figure,[1] and thus refutes their boasting, as if Ezekiel had said that those fictitious revelations are mere fancies: they have indeed something in them more than common, but still they are fanatics. This then is the sense of the word "spirit." Meanwhile there is no doubt that he repeats what he lately saw, and the contrast removes all doubt. *Without seeing any thing*, says he: thus vision is opposed to the human heart and spirit; but what is vision but a supernatural gift? When, therefore, God raises his servants above the capacity of human ability, and makes them discern what no mortal power can bestow, that is a vision; and if a vision is removed, nothing will remain but the spirit or heart of man. Hence those who cannot really show that their utterance is evidently inspired, shall be compelled to confess that they speak of their own minds. It follows—

4. O Israel, thy prophets are like the foxes in the deserts.

4. Tanquam vulpes in locis solitariis prophetæ tui, Israel, fuerunt.

Hence Ezekiel exposes the snares of the false prophets. The ten tribes had been dispersed, just as if a field or a vineyard had been removed from a habitable neighbourhood into desert regions, and foxes held their sway there instead. For they have many hiding-places; they insinuate themselves through hedges and all openings, and so break into the vineyard or field, and lay waste its fruits. Such, as I have said, was the condition of the people from the time of its dispersion. While the Israelites dwelt at home, they were in some way retained within their duty, as if fortified by certain ramparts. At Jerusalem, too, the High Priest presided over spiritual trials, that no impious doctrine should creep in: but now, since the people were so dispersed, greater license was given to the false prophets to corrupt

---

[1] CALVIN uses the Greek word καταχρηστικῶς, meaning in rhetoric the use of a word in a sense different from its natural one. *Catachresis* is the grammatical term, implying the use of terms in their "non-natural" sense. The French has "neantmoins que ce soit improprement."

the people, since the miserable exiles were exposed to these foxes; for they were liable to injuries just as if desert regions surrounded them. Being thus destitute of protection, it was easy for foxes to enter by clandestine arts, and to destroy whatever good fruits existed. Meanwhile Ezekiel obliquely reproves the people's carelessness. Although they were dispersed, and were so open to the snares of the false prophets, yet they ought to have been attentive and cautious, and God would doubtless have afforded them aid, as he promises to his people the spirit of discretion and judgment whenever they need it. (1 Cor. xii. 10.) But when the Israelites were wandering exiles, and attention to the law no longer flourished among them, it came to pass that foxes, meaning their false prophets, easily entered. Whence it follows that the people were not free from faults, since they exposed themselves to the snares of these false prophets. It follows—

5. Ye have not gone up into the gaps, neither made up the hedge for the house of Israel to stand in the battle in the day of the Lord.

5. Non ascendistis ad rupturas[1] neque sepiverunt sepem super domum Israel ad standum in prælio in die Iehovæ.

Hence he pursues the same sentiment, but presses the false prophets harder. He has said generally that they were sacrilegious, making a false use of God's name when speaking entirely in their own. He now separates them by another mark from the approved and faithful servants of God, namely, *they had not gone up into the breaches, nor built up a hedge to protect the house of Israel, that they might stand in the battle in the day of Jehovah.* This verse is variously explained: some refer what is here said to prayer; others twist it according to different imaginations, but I restrict it to their teaching.[2] Ezekiel not only blames their inner and hidden perfidy, he not only strikes their minds, so as to convince them that they had no desire for piety, and no zeal for God's glory, but he shows that their teaching must be altogether rejected, because they did not propose to them-

[1] Or, " breaks."—*Calvin.*
[2] Œcolampadius takes a different view: he says, " principibus et prophetis juxta quadrat: eorum est animam ponere pro ovibus contra pseudoprophetas." He then quotes John, chap. x., " Vident lupum venientem et fugiunt." The remainder of his comment on this verse is worthy of perusal.

selves the right object. But what is the mark at which all God's servants ought to aim? Surely to consult the public safety; and when they see signs of God's wrath, to meet them, and prevent the urgent calamity. These impostors saw the people not only impious, but rebellious, so that there was no hope of their repentance. On the other hand, they saw God threatening; and although they were blind, yet they could behold the signs of God's approaching vengeance. Hence it was their duty to go up to the breaches. Hence, also, we understand what the Prophet means by "breaches," namely, as an approach is open to an enemy to storm a city when a breach is made in the wall, so also, when the iniquity of the people overflows like a deluge, a rupture is already made, by means of which God's wrath is able to penetrate immediately, and to lay everything waste till it is reduced to nothing.

As often, then, as we see God offended by the people's wickedness, let us learn that a breach has been made, as if we had been destined to destruction. Hence those who desire to discharge the office of teaching faithfully ought to hasten to the breach, to recall the people from their impiety, and to exhort them to repentance. Thus the wall becomes restored, because God is appeased, and we are able to rest in quietness and security. What follows has the same object—*they have not restored the hedge.* For when a people breaks through all rights, and violates God's law, it is just as if they laid themselves bare in every part from the protection of God, as Moses reproves them when speaking of the molten calf: Behold, says he, this day ye are naked; that is, because they had hurled themselves into destruction. (Exod. xxxii. 25.) So the Prophet says that these traitors did not run up to restore the hedge when the house of Israel was exposed to robbers, thieves, and wild beasts, because it was no longer protected by the hand of God. What follows has the same object, *that they should stand in the battle in the day of the Lord;* that is, to oppose themselves to God's vengeance. This relates to prayers, when mention is made of Phinehas, in Psalm cvi. 30, and also in the same psalm, verse 23, where it is said of Moses, Unless Moses had stood in the breach to turn away God's wrath. Here also, as I have said, the Prophet looks rather to doctrine. For here he sharply rebukes the folly of false prophets who had promised wonderful things. Now, when God approached in earnest, all their prophecies vanished: he says, therefore, *they stood not in the battle in the day of Jehovah;* for, if they had diligently exhorted the people to repentance, those sinners had reconciled God to themselves: for we turn aside his judgment beforehand when we turn to him in time, as Paul teaches. (1 Cor. xi. 31.) If, therefore, the people had been thus diligently advised, they had stood in the battle; that is, their teaching would have been a bulwark against the breaking out of God's wrath to destroy them utterly. Now, therefore, we see the meaning of Ezekiel, namely, to show how the fallacies of the false prophets could be perceived, since by their blandishments and flatteries they destroyed the people. Now it follows—

6. They have seen vanity and lying divination, saying, The Lord saith; and the Lord hath not sent them: and they have made *others* to hope that they would confirm the word.	6. Viderunt vanitatem, divinarunt mendacium, dicentes, dicit Iehovah, et non misit eos Iehovah: et sperare fecerunt[1] ad stabiliendum sermonem.

Here again he pronounces generally that those false prophets were vain, and this assertion depends upon the principle that they had spoken from their own heart or spirit, for nothing false or vain can proceed from God. It follows, therefore, that they are here condemned of vanity and lying, because they dared falsely to use the name of God when they uttered nothing but their own dreams. He now confirms what we saw in the last verse, when he says, *they hoped to establish their word.* Hence they puffed up the people with vain hope, when they said that God would not be so severe as to exact continual punishment of the holy and elect nation. True prophets also often recall sinners to the mercy of God, and magnify it so, that those who wrestle with despair may not doubt God's long-suffering, since he is said to be slow to anger, and inclined to reconciliation;

[1] Others translate, "to be hoped for;" but the word is here taken transitively.—*Calvin.*

and his pity endures for a life, while his anger passes away in a moment. (Numbers xiv. 18 ; Ps. ciii. 8, and xxx. 5.) True prophets indeed act thus ; but they join two members which must not be separated, otherwise God himself would be, as it were, dissipated.[1] Hence, when true prophets exhort sinners to hope and predict God's freeness to pardon, they likewise discourse about penitence ; they do not indulge sinners, but rouse them, nay, wound them sharply with a sense of God's anger, so as in some way to stir them up, since God's mercy is set before us for that end, that by it we may seek life. Hence we must be dead in ourselves ; but false prophets sever between the two, and divide God, as it were, in half, since they speak only of his freeness to forgive, and declare his clemency to be set before all, while they are profoundly silent about repentance. Now, therefore, we see why the Prophet here reproves these traitors[2] who abused the name of God, *since they made the people hope.* Without hope, indeed, the sinner could not be animated to seek God : but they promised peace, as he will say directly, when there was no peace. Therefore let us proceed with the exposition.

7. Have ye not seen a vain vision, and have ye not spoken a lying divination, whereas ye say, The Lord saith *it ;* albeit I have not spoken ?

7. An non visionem vanitatis vidistis ? et divinationem mendacii locuti estis ? Et loquentes[3] dicit Iehovah : ego non fueram locutus ?

Here God shows why he had formerly pronounced that they brought forward nothing but vanity and falsehood, namely, because they used his name falsely, and out of light created darkness ; for by the feint of speaking in God's name, they darkened men's minds. That sacred name is, as it were, a fount of splendour, so as far to surpass the light of the sun ; nay, whatever light exists, is made apparent and refulgent by it. But, as I have said, the servants of Satan turn light into darkness, because they audaciously boast that God has said so. This passage and similar ones show us how diligently we ought to guard against Satan's fallacies. This is their astounding boldness to bring forward

---

[1] *Dissipetur :* The French has " fust luy-mesme deschirè par picces."

[2] Calvin's Latin is *nebulones ;* the French translation " belistres ;" the familiar English " rascals."   [3] Verbally, that is, " by saying."—*Calvin.*

God's name while they so wantonly trifle with his judgments. For to boast that God has spoken is as if we wished, by impious profanation, purposely to draw him into a dispute. For how can God bear us to turn his truth into a lie? But there have been impostors in all ages who have thus thoughtlessly flown in the face of God. We are not surprised at the heathen doing so; but in the chosen people, it was certainly an incredible prodigy and an intolerable disgrace, when they had access to all heavenly doctrine for the guidance of their conduct, and when God was daily calling forth prophets, as he had promised by Moses, to see these impious dogs who barked so, and yet pretended so proudly to speak in God's name. (Deut. xviii. 15-18.) Admonished, then, by this caution, let us be on our guard when we see Satan's servants endued with such arrogance. It follows—

| 8. Therefore thus saith the Lord God, Because ye have spoken vanity, and seen lies, therefore, behold, I *am* against you, saith the Lord God. | 8. Propterea sic dicit Dominator Iehovah, eo quod locuti estis vanitatem, et vidistis mendacium,[1] propterea ecce ego contra eos, dicit Dominator Iehovah. |
| 9. And mine hand shall be upon the prophets that see vanity, and that divine lies: they shall not be in the assembly of my people, neither shall they be written in the writing of the house of Israel, neither shall they enter into the land of Israel; and ye shall know that I *am* the Lord God. | 9. Et erit manus mea contra prophetas qui vident vanitatem, et qui divinant mendacium: in consilio populi mei non erunt, et in scriptura[2] domus Israel non scribentur: et ad terram Israel non redibunt: et cognoscitis quod ego Dominator Iehovah. |

Here at length he begins to pronounce judgment against the false prophets. Hitherto, under the form of a complaint, he shows how wickedly they had corrupted and profaned his sacred name: then how impiously they had rendered prophecies contemptible by their lies, and how cruel they were to the people whose safety ought to be their first care, and how they drew on the miserable to destruction. For after God has so narrated their sins, he now denounces punishment; and, first, generally he says that he was their adversary. This clause is by no means superfluous, since such

---

[1] There is a change of expression here, since he had formerly said, "ye have spoken a divination of falsehood and have seen a vision of vanity."—*Calvin.*   [2] That is, " in the catalogue."—*Calvin.*

carelessness would not have besotted the impious, unless they thought themselves free from all dealings with God; hence they utterly reject all fear and sin with freedom. But this could not happen, unless they determined that God either sleeps, or does not behold human affairs or trifles as they do. Since, therefore, false prophets very licentiously corrupt God's word, when they pretend it to be a pleasant sport; God, on the other hand, pronounces himself their adversary; as if he said, your contest shall not be with men, but I will be the avenger of so wicked a profanation of my name.

Besides, he afterwards points out the punishment; *my hand,* says he, *shall be against the prophets.* For although God threatens to become an adversary to the reprobate, yet this is not sufficient to terrify them, they are so stupid. But it is necessary to use another stimulus, namely, that God should display his power. This is the reason why he now adds, *his hand should be against the false prophets.* The hand is sometimes taken for a blow: but because God sees the impious torpid amidst their sins, he says that he would not only be their enemy and an avenger of his glory, but he brings forward his own hand into the midst. It follows, *they shall not be in the counsel of my people.* Some explain the noun סוד, *sod,* more subtlely than they need for that experience of God which is offered to the elect for their salvation. But this explanation is forced, for they are deceived in thinking that the Prophet's meaning is different in the second clause, where he adds, *they shall not be written in the list of the house of Israel:* he repeats the same thing in different words: in the first place he had said, *they should not be in the secret of the people:* for סוד, *sod,* signifies a secret, but it is taken for counsel: *they shall not be* therefore *in the assembly of the people:* afterwards he adds, *they shall not be in the catalogue of the house of Israel.* He mentions a catalogue, because judges and others elected to any office were written in a list. We see, therefore, what the Prophet intends—for I am compelled to break off here—namely, that those impostors who wished to enjoy the prophetic title, were altogether without the Church, since God had cast them off.

PRAYER.

Grant, Almighty God, since we are so torpid in our vices that excitements are daily necessary to rouse us up, first, that our destined pastors may faithfully call us to repentance; then, that we in our turn may be so attentive to their exhortations, and so suffer ourselves to be condemned, that we may be our own judges: Grant also, that when thou chastisest us severely, the taste of thy paternal goodness may never be so lost to us, so that a way may always be open to us to seek reconciliation in Jesus Christ our Lord.—Amen.

Lecture Thirty-Fifth.

WE explained yesterday what the Prophet meant when he pronounces that the impostors who deceived the people *should not be in the counsel of the pious nor in their catalogue,* and we said that this was twice repeated. Now the question arises, did the Prophet speak of the secret election of God, or only of an external state? For although these traitors were at the greatest distance from the Church, yet we know that they boasted in a common title like Ishmael, who, until he was cast out of his father's house, proudly boasted in his right of birth. (Gen. xxi. 9.) And at this day, we see how the Papists claim to themselves the name of " the Church," since they pretend to the perpetual succession: and truly we are compelled to confess that the ordinary ministry is with them. But because they have tyrannically abused their power, and have altogether overthrown that method of governing the Church which the Lord had appointed, we may safely laugh at their boastings.[1] There was the same haughtiness in the false prophets of old, who asserted that they held no mean rank among the people, because they were created prophets by God. Hence, therefore, we gather that these words are not used of any external state, because a

---

[1] The subject of " the perpetual succession" being so fully discussed in the present day, this admission of Calvin's is worthy of notice. The Latin has *ordinarium ministerium:* the French, " le ministère ordinaire." The reasons which he gives for rejecting such pretensions would be deemed by many unsatisfactory.

place among the elect people was always conceded to them. Without doubt, then, we must understand the contrast between the true members of the Church and hypocrites, who pretend to the name of God. And for this reason it is said in Ps. xv. 2, as well as Ps. xxiv. 4, that not all who go up to the mount of God have a perpetual seat there, unless they are pure in heart and hand. The sum of the whole then is, although false prophets thunder forth their boasts with inflated cheeks, and claim the prophetic name, yet they ought not to be reckoned in that rank, as they are altogether without the elect people.

But a second question arises out of this. If the Prophet denies their right to be included in the council of the pious, he ought not to speak in the future tense: because as God's election is eternal, so his sons were written in the book of life before the creation of the world. But he says *they shall not be written*, and this seems absurd. But Ezekiel here accommodates his language to the usual custom of mankind. The language of the psalm is harsher: let them be blotted from the book of life, since they are not written among the just. (Ps. lxix. 28.) For it cannot happen that he who is once written in the book of life can ever be blotted out. But in the second clause the Prophet explains himself—that they be not written with the just; that is, that they be not written in the catalogue of the just. So also Ezekiel now says: *they shall not be in the secret of my people,* and they shall not be *written in the writing of the house of Israel:* because for a time they seemed to be in the number of the pious: hence a change of expression is here used, but only in accommodation to the rudeness of our mind.

This passage is useful in this sense. The Holy Spirit admonishes us that it is not sufficient to suppose men members of the Church because the greater number seem to excel others, just as the chaff lies above the wheat and suffocates it: thus hypocrites bury the sons of God whose number is small, while they shine forth in their own splendour, and their multitude makes them seem exclusively worthy of the title of the Church. Hence let us learn to examine ourselves, and to search whether those interior marks by which

God distinguishes his children from strangers belong to us, viz., the living root of piety and faith. This passage also teaches that nothing is more formidable than to be rejected from God's flock. For no safety is to be hoped for, except as God collects us into one body under one head. First, all safety resides in Christ alone; and then we cannot be separated from Christ without falling away from all hope of safety: but Christ will not and cannot be torn from his Church with which he is joined in an indissoluble knot, as the head to the body. Hence, unless we cultivate unity with the faithful, we see that we are cut off from Christ: hence I said that nothing was more to be feared than that separation of which mention is here made. On the other hand, it is said in Ps. cvi. 4, Remember me, O God, in thy good will towards thy people: visit me with thy salvation. When the author of the psalm prays in this way, he at the same time acknowledges that our true and solid happiness is placed in the Lord's embracing us with the rest of the faithful. For God's good will towards his people is that fatherly kindness by which he embraces his own elect. If, therefore, God thinks us worthy of that fatherly favour, then we have a sure confidence of safety.

Afterwards he adds, *And they shall not return to the land of Israel: and ye shall know that I am Jehovah.* Ezekiel here places an outward mark as the sign of reprobation, since, while a free return was permitted to others, these were excluded. Hence Ezekiel signifies that God's anger would be manifest in the case of false prophets by their exclusion from the benefits common to the people. For when God shall open the door, and promulgate an edict concerning a free return, they shall remain exiles, and shall never enjoy that native country to which they boasted that they should in a short time return. He confirms then by an outward symbol what he has already said about reprobation. For although many died in exile who were real members of the Church, as Daniel and his allies, and many others, yet, as far as these deceivers were concerned, it was a sure sign of their rejection that they boasted of their speedy return to their country. Since, therefore, they were deprived of that advantage, God openly shows that they were unworthy of being reckoned among the elect people. It follows—

10. Because, even because they have seduced my people, saying, Peace; and *there was* no peace; and one built up a wall, and, lo, others daubed it with untempered *mortar:*

11. Say unto them which daub *it* with untempered *mortar*, that it shall fall: there shall be an overflowing shower; and ye, O great hailstones, shall fall; and a stormy wind shall rend *it*.

10. Propterea et proptera[1] quod deceperunt populum meum dicendo, pax et non erat pax: et ipse ædificavit parietem, et ecce ipsi leverunt ipsum insipido.

11. Dic ad linentes insipido, cadet:[2] erit pluvia *vel imber* inundans: et dabo lapides grandinis,[3] et spiritus turbinum *vel tempestatum* scindet *vel disrumpet*.

Here Ezekiel pursues the same metaphor which he had used with a very slight difference, for there is such an agreement that the connexion is apparent between the former and the present sentence. He had said that the false prophets did not go up to the breaches, and did not restore the hedges of the house of Israel: we have explained these words thus—teachers who discharge their duties honestly and sincerely are like builders, who, if they see a breach in a wall, instantly and carefully repair it: they are like gardeners who do not allow either a field or a vineyard to be exposed to wild beasts. As, then, he had formerly said that these false prophets did not go up to the breach through their not being affected by the dispersion of the people, but knowingly and willingly betrayed the people's safety through open and gross perfidy; so also he now says, that they built a wall indeed, but without mortar. The word תפל, *thephel*, "untempered," is variously explained, but I doubt not the Prophet meant sand without lime. Jerome thinks it to be mortar without chaff; but my view is better, namely, that they built only in appearance; and in this the image which the Prophet now uses differs from the preceding one. He had said before, they did not go up to the breach; he now grants them more—that they really built; but it is easy to reconcile the two assertions: since they

---

[1] The repetition is emphatic.—*Calvin*.

[2] The copula is superfluous.—*Calvin*.

[3] Others translate " and ye hailstones shall fall;" others take it transitively, " ye shall cause to fall;" but we must explain it either " they shall fall," or " cause to fall."—*Calvin*.

did not go up to the breach to provide safety for the people; and yet they feigned themselves anxious, and seemed as if they wished to restore the ruins. But while the Prophet merely grants their intention, he adds that they were bad builders, just as if any one should heap together a quantity of sand, and moisten it with water, yet it would profit him nothing; for the sand disperses by itself, and grows solid by lime alone, and thus becomes cement. Therefore the Prophet means that those impostors accomplish nothing seriously; and when they show great anxiety and care, that is in vain, because they only heap up sand and dust when they ought to temper the mortar with sand and lime. We understand then how these two places mutually agree: *because, even because they have deceived my people:* this is without a figure. Now he adds figuratively, *they have built up a wall, but they have daubed it only with untempered mortar*, that is, sand.

The kind of fallacies are now mentioned: *because they said, Peace, when there was no peace.* We yesterday reminded you that impostors have something in common with God's true servants, just as Satan transforms himself into an angel of light. (2 Cor. xi. 14.) We know that all the prophets were always messengers of peace: now this agrees chiefly with the good news, How beautiful are the feet of those who preach the gospel of peace. (Isaiah lii. 7; Rom. x. 15.) Whenever God commends his own word, he adds its character of peace. For when he is justly at enmity with us, there is one way of reconciliation and remission of sin. This springs from the preaching of the gospel. The prophets formerly discharged this duty; and when these impostors strove to deceive the people, they stripped off their masks and deceived the simple through the difficulty of discerning between themselves and the true servants of God. And yet, as we said yesterday, no one could be deceived except through their own fault. For God, indeed, offers us peace, and invites us to reconciliation by his own prophets; but on this condition, that we make war with our own lusts. This, then, is one way of being at peace with God by becoming enemies to ourselves, and fighting earnestly against the depraved and vicious desires of the flesh. But how do false prophets preach peace? Why! so that miserable and abandoned men may sleep in the midst of their sins. We must diligently attend, then, to this difference, that we may safely embrace the peace which is offered us by true prophets, and be on our guard against the snares of those who fallaciously flatter us with peace, because under promise of reconciliation they foment hostilities between God and ourselves.

How, then, can it happen that we can be at rest while God is opposed to us? *Thou shalt say*, therefore, *to those who daub with untempered mortar, it shall fall.* Here the Spirit signifies that the false prophets should be subject to the greatest ridicule, when they shall be convicted by the event, and their lies shall be proved by clear proof. Hence, also, we may gather the utility of the doctrine which Paul teaches, that we must stand bravely when God gives the reins to impostors to disturb or disperse the Church. They shall not proceed any further, says he. (2 Tim. iii. 9.) He says elsewhere in the same epistle, (iii. 13,) They shall wax worse and worse; that is, as far as God pleases to be patient with them. But meanwhile the end is at hand, when the Lord shall shame all the impious false prophets, and detect their ignorance, rashness, and audacity, because they dared to use his name in offering peace to the reprobate. *Thou shalt say*, therefore, *the wall shall fall.* He speaks here of doctrine. *There shall be an overflowing shower*, says he—a desolating rain. Here the Spirit signifies that there shall be a violent concussion which shall disperse all the artifices of the false prophets, and detect their frauds, when the Lord should bring on the Chaldeans, and deliver the city to them. Hence the same meaning is intended *by the shower, by stones, by the rush of a whirlwind*, but it was necessary to express the same thing in many ways, because the Israelites had grown torpid through their fallacies, and willingly seized upon what the false prophets said—that God would be propitious to them. After he had mentioned the shower, he goes on to hailstones. The more probable reading is, Ye, O great hailstones, shall fall; unless perhaps it is better to take the verb תפלנה, *thephelneh*, transitively, as I am inclined to do, *ye shall make fall*. This apostrophe is emphatic, because God addresses the stones themselves, and thereby obliquely reproves the sloth of those who thought to escape in safety through their blandishments. When God, therefore, addresses the stones, he doubtless reproaches the Israelites for hardening themselves so completely. He adds *the violence of whirlwinds*, or of tempests, in the same sense. *The violence of the whirlwinds*, then, shall *break down* or overthrow *the wall*. In conclusion, Ezekiel teaches that the doctrine of the false prophets had no need of any other refutation, that the arrival of the Chaldeans, and their boasting, is like a storm and whirlwind to devastate the whole land: and thus he derides those praters who used their tongues so audaciously: he says that those strangers should come to refute these lies, not by words only, but by a violent attack. It follows—

12. Lo, when the wall is fallen, shall it not be said unto you, Where *is* the daubing wherewith ye have daubed *it?*

12. Et ecce cadet paries,[1] annon dicetur ad vos, ubi litura[2] quam levistis.

He confirms the last sentence, namely, that the false prophets would be a laughing-stock to all when their prophecies and divinations came to nothing, for the event would show them to be liars. For when the city was taken it sufficiently appeared that they were the devil's ministers of deceit, for they were trained in wickedness and boldness when they put forth the name of God. Now the Prophet teaches that a common proverb would arise when the wall fell; for by saying, *shall it not be said to them*, he signifies that their folly and vanity would be completely exposed, so that this proverb should be everywhere current—*where is the daubing with which ye daubed it?* It follows—

13. Therefore thus saith the Lord God, I will even rend *it*

13. Propterea sic dicit Dominator Iehovah. Cadere faciam[3] spiritum

[1] That is, "when the wall shall have fallen:" we must understand the adverb "when."—*Calvin.*

[2] Some translate *lenimentum* or *linimentum*: grammatically it ought to be *litio*; but although good Latin authors do not use the word *litura* here for "daubing," yet we express it *ubi litura*.—*Calvin.*

[3] This is the same word which he had formerly used, but it is here taken

with a stormy wind in my fury; and there shall be an overflowing shower in mine anger, and great hailstones in *my* fury, to consume *it*.	tempestatum in ira mea: et imbre inundans in ira mea: et erit imber inundans in ira mea,[1] et lapides grandinis in excandescentia ad consumptionem.

He still pursues the same sentiment; but he says he will send forth storms and hail, and a whirlwind. He formerly spoke of hail, and showers, and violent storms; but he now says, that those winds, storms, and showers should be at hand to obey him. We see, therefore, that this verse does not differ from the former, unless in God's showing more clearly that he would send forth storms, whirlwind, and hail to overthrow the empty building which the false prophets had raised. It follows—

14. So will I break down the wall that ye have daubed with untempered *mortar*, and bring it down to the ground, so that the foundation thereof shall be discovered, and it shall fall, and ye shall be consumed in the midst thereof; and ye shall know that I *am* the Lord.	14. Et evertam parietem quem levistis insipido, et projiciam in terram, et discooperietur fundamentum ejus, et cadet: et consumemini in medio ejus: et cognoscetis quod ego Iehovah.

This verse ought to be united with the other: God says, *I will throw down the wall.* For the false prophets had acquired so much favour, that their boasting was as much esteemed as an oracle. Hence the people were persuaded that what even these impostors dreamt was uttered by God. Since, therefore, they had so bound men's minds to themselves, the Prophet was obliged to inveigh vehemently against those impostures, since he would not have succeeded by simple language. This language, indeed, may seem superfluous; but if any one considers how greatly these miserable exiles were deluded by the false prophets, he will easily acknowledge that God does not repeat the same thing so often in vain: as in this place he brings forward nothing new; but he so inculcates what we have already seen as to confirm it. *I will pull down,* therefore, *the wall which ye have daubed*

---

in another sense: he had formerly said, "And the spirit of tempests shall break or cut;" but he now says, "I will make it cut or break forth;" so that the sense is clearer—"therefore I will make it break forth."—*Calvin.*

[1] The original words for *ira* are different. We may translate חמה, *chemeh*, "burning wrath"—"therefore in my burning wrath I will make the whirlwind break forth."—*Calvin.*

with untempered mortar, and I will lay it low on the ground, and its foundation shall be uncovered, or discovered. Here the Prophet signifies that God would so lay bare the fallacies of those who had deceived the people with vain hopes, that no disguise should remain for them, but their disgrace should be plain to every one. Now, such was the shamelessness of these impostors, that if they were convicted on one point, yet they did not desist on that account, but took credit to themselves if anything turned out more fortunately than they could expect,[1] as if they had not prophesied in vain, while a single thing came true. Since, therefore, the impious so turned their backs when God detected their folly, the Prophet adds, that the false prophets would have nothing left, because God will not only overthrow whatever they seemed to build, but he will uncover even the foundations, so that the people may understand that there was not a scruple or the least particle of truth in them.

And it shall fall, and ye shall be consumed in the midst of it. He had just said that it should be ruinously consumed: hailstones, he said, should fall to consume it; by which word he understood that the final slaughter should be so severe that no hope should be left. For as long as Jerusalem stood, the Israelites always look forward to a return. But when they saw the kingdom not only weakened, but utterly destroyed, the temple overthrown, and the city ruined, whenever they heard of their dreadful dispersion, not the slightest remnant of hope survived. Now this consumption is transferred to the false prophets. As that consumption was final, and without a gleam of hope, *ye shall be consumed,* says he, *in the midst of it, and ye shall know that I am Jehovah.* He does not inculcate this particular so often in vain; but he inveighs with indignation against the wicked audacity of the false prophets, who dared so petulantly to oppose themselves to the true servants of God, and to assume his name, and to trifle with him like children. Such is the prodigious madness of mortals who dare to set

---

[1] Calvin's Latin is very cramped here. The French translation paraphrases it thus: " Mais ils repliqueront qu'il se pourra bien faire qu'il leur sera eschappé quelque chose mal à propos."

themselves against God: for this reason, he says, they shall at length perceive with whom they have to do. It follows—

15. Thus will I accomplish my wrath upon the wall, and upon them that have daubed it with untempered *mortar*; and will say unto you, The wall *is* no *more*, neither they that daubed it.	15. Et complebo excandescentiam meam in pariete et linentem ipsum insipido: et dicam illis non est paries, et non sunt qui levarunt ipsum.

If the inveterate obstinacy of the people had not been known to us, Ezekiel would seem too verbose, since he might have said in a few words what he explains at such length. But if we bear in mind the perverse and refractory disposition of the people, we shall find that there was need of such continual repetition, *I will fulfil*, says he, *my burning wrath upon the wall;* that is, I will show how detestable and destructive to my people was this doctrine. Hence God filled up his anger on the wall, when he reduced to nothing all the lies of the false prophets: afterwards also he attacked them, since the mark of disgrace was attached to their characters, and this rendered their doctrine detestable: *afterwards*, says he, *I will say, There is no wall; those who daubed it are not.* When God speaks thus, he means that he will suffer the false prophets to triumph among the people for only a short time. For even to the destruction of the city and temple they always withstood God's servants with a bold forehead, as if they would thrust their horns against God and his announcements. Let us observe, then, that while Jerusalem was standing, the appearance of a wall existed; for there was the prop of false doctrine, and the people fed willingly on such deceits. Their daubing, therefore, stood till it vanished with the ruin of the city, and then their vanity was proved, for God took vengeance on these insolent triflers. It follows—

16. *To wit*, the prophets of Israel, which prophesy concerning Jerusalem, and which see visions of peace for her, and *there is* no peace, saith the Lord God.	16. Prophetæ Israel prophetarunt de Hierusalem, et viderunt ei visionem pacis, et non est pax, dicit Dominator Iehovah.

He now concludes this discourse, and shows what he had hitherto intended by a building badly cemented, by using sand without lime. *The prophets of Israel prophesied con-*

cerning Jerusalem. Here he does not mean false prophets, with whom Jeremiah was continually contending, but those who in exile still hardened the wretched. While they ought to make use of the occasion, and so to humble the people who had been so grievously wounded by the hand of God, they stirred them up to pride, as we have formerly seen. Our Prophet was obliged to strive with them for the comfort of his exiles, for he was peculiarly sent to the captives, as we have said, although the advantage of his prophecies also reached Jerusalem. *The prophets,* those *of Israel,* that is, the ten tribes dispersed in different directions, *prophesied concerning Jerusalem.* Why then did they not rather predict a happy result? For they were reduced to extremes, and meanwhile promised victory to the Jews. *And they saw a vision for it,* says he. This clause seems opposed to another, in which the Prophet says that they saw nothing. How, then, do these two things agree—to see a vision, and yet to see nothing? What he now says as to *seeing a vision* refers to their false boasting. For they were altogether without the Spirit of God, nor did they possess any revelation. Yet when they boasted themselves to be endowed with the Spirit, and many had faith in their words, the Prophet concedes to them the name of a vision, although there was none, by accommodation. He says, therefore, *that they saw a vision,* that is, that they boasted in one since they professed to be spiritual. As at this time the Papists deny that they utter anything out of their own minds, and say that they have all those fictions, by which they adulterate all piety, from the Holy Spirit; so these prophets said they were spiritual: and as far as the title is concerned, the Prophet grants what in reality he disallows when he adds, *there was no peace when they said there was peace.* Hence it appears that a vision was in their mouth united with sacrilegious boldness: yet there was no vision; because, if God had manifested anything by his Spirit, he would really have proved it as he says by Moses. (Deut. xviii. 22.) Since, then, there was no peace, but the final overthrow of the city was at hand, it is easily collected that they saw nothing, but made false use of that sacred name of vision to acquire confidence for themselves. As to his saying *there is no peace,* it extends to the future. They promised peace by saying that the siege of the city was to be raised, and prosperity to await the Jews. But God, on the other hand, pronounces *there should be no peace,* because it will shortly be evident that Jerusalem is devoted to utter destruction.

PRAYER.

Grant, Almighty God, since we do not cease to provoke thee by our sins, that we may at length consider our wretched condition, unless thou govern us by thy Spirit, and subject us to thyself in true obedience: and may we so desire to be reconciled to thee, that we may not flatter ourselves, but being altogether humbled and emptied of self, may we fly to thy mercy with a true feeling of piety: and so find what is prepared for us in Christ Jesus our Lord.—Amen.

Lecture Thirty-Sixth.

17. Likewise, thou son of man, set thy face against the daughters of thy people, which prophesy out of their own heart; and prophesy thou against them,

18. And say, Thus saith the Lord God, Woe to the *women* that sew pillows to all arm-holes, and make kerchiefs upon the head of every stature, to hunt souls! Will ye hunt the souls of my people, and will ye save the souls alive *that come* unto you?

17. Et tu fili hominis, pone faciem tuam contra filias populi tui, quæ prophetant ex corde suo: et propheta contra eas.

18. Et dices, sic dicit Dominator Jehovah, Væ consuentibus pulvillos super omnes cubitos manus, et facientibus pepla[1] super caput omnis staturæ ad venandum animas: in animas venabimini a populo meo,[2] et animas quæ vobis sunt[3] vivificabitis.

WE may gather from this passage that Satan's lies were not spread among the people so much by men as by women. We know that the gift of prophecy is sometimes though rarely allowed to women, and there is no doubt that female prophets existed whenever God wished to brand men with a mark of ignominy as strongly as possible. I say as much as possible, because the sister of Moses enjoyed the prophetic gift, and this never ceased to the reproach of her brother.

---

[1] Or, " veils."—*Calvin.*
[2] That is, " ye hunt the souls of my people."—*Calvin.*
[3] That is, " yours."—*Calvin.*

(Exod. xv. 20.) But when Deborah and Huldah discharged the prophetic office, (Judges iv. 4, and 2 Kings xxii. 14,) God doubtless wished to raise them on high to shame the men, and obliquely to show them their slothfulness. Whatever may be the reason, women have sometimes enjoyed the prophetic gift. And this is the meaning of Joel's second chapter, (ver. 28,) Your sons shall see visions and your daughters shall prophesy. There is no doubt that the Spirit transfers to the kingdom of Christ what had been customary among the ancient people. For we know that Christ's kingdom is described, or rather depicted, under the image of that government which God formerly held under the law. Since, then, certain women were gifted with the prophetic spirit, Satan, according to his custom, abused this under a false pretence. We know that he always emulates God and transforms himself into an angel of light, because if he were to show himself openly, all would instantly flee from him: hence he uses God's name deceptively, to ingratiate himself among the simple and incautious. And he not only sends forth false prophets to scatter abroad their lies and impostures, but he turns even females to the same injurious use.

Here we see how anxiously we ought to guard against any corruption which may creep in to contaminate the pure gifts of God. But this contest seems not to have been sufficiently honourable to the servant of God; for it was almost a matter of shame when they engaged with women. We know that those who desire praise for their bravery do not willingly engage with unequal antagonists who have no strength to resist; since there is no praise in a victory when it is too easy: so also Ezekiel could put away from him this undertaking, since it was unworthy of the prophetic office. Hence it appears, that God's servants cannot faithfully discharge the duties assigned to them, unless they strive to remove all impediments. This then is the condition of all those to whom God assigns the office of teaching, that they may oppose all false doctrines and errors, and never consider or wish for great praise from their victory: it should suffice them to assert God's truth against all Satan's devices. Thus we see Paul strove with a workman (Demetrius), (Acts xix.

24,) and that was all but ridiculous: and truly he might seem not sufficiently to regard his dignity; for from the time when he saw secret things which it was not lawful for him to utter, and was carried up to the third heaven, (2 Cor. xii. 4,) when he engages in a contest with a craftsman, he seems to forget that dignity to which God had raised him. But we must remember the reason which I have mentioned, that as the duty of teaching is assigned to God's servants, so they are appointed as his avengers and defenders of the doctrine of which they are heralds. Hence if, so to speak, fleas were to come out of the earth and rail at sound doctrine, none who are influenced by a desire of edification will hesitate to contend even with those fleas. Thus the Prophet's modesty is conspicuous, because by God's command he turns to these weak women to refute even them.

It is said, then, *woe to those who sew pillows or cushions;* it is the same thing—*to all armholes, and to those who make coverings for the head of every stature.* There is no doubt that by these tricks they deluded the minds and eyes of the simple. It is evident from the law that some ceremonies are useful, since God commands nothing superfluous; but Satan by his cunning turns everything useful to man's destruction. Meanwhile we must remark that false prophets were always immoderately fond of outward signs; for since they have nothing substantial to offer, they have need of ostentation to dazzle all eyes. This then is the reason why men and women who intend to deceive, always heap together a number of ceremonies. Hence Ezekiel says, *that those women had sown together pillows,* and he adds, *for all armholes.* Whence it appears that they laid them under the armpits of those by whom they were consulted, although he afterwards seems to hint that they themselves reclined upon these pillows. But now he is treating of the people. The ancients were accustomed when they reclined at table to have cushions under their arms, though this is not our habit. But there is no doubt that they wished to represent a kind of sleep, like the foolish who consult oracles, and think themselves in ecstasies, and snatched away beyond all thoughts of this world.

Then they had veils or coverings which they put over their heads. In this way imposture flourished with the Roman augurs; for they veiled their head when they wished to begin their incantations. Livy says, that the augur stood at the threshold with his head covered, and uttered these words, "O Jupiter, hear;"[1] so that it is probable that veils covered the heads of those who wished to consult God, that they might be as it were separated from the world, and no longer look upon human things, but have only spiritual eyesight. With this view these women used such ceremonies that wretched men thought themselves caught up above the world, and all earthly thoughts being laid aside, they dozed so as to receive the oracles, and at the same time had the head covered to avoid everything which might call them off and distract them, and to be wholly intent on spiritual meditations.

As to his saying, *upon all arms,* and *upon the head of every stature.* I doubt not that the Prophet teaches by these words that these women exercised a promiscuous trade, making no distinctions, but gratifying all without choice, so long as they brought their money in their hands, as we shall by and bye see. Hence this mark of universality ought to be noticed emphatically, because these women did not attend to the disposition with which persons came, but only grasped at their reward, and thus the gate was as open to all as that of the market-place. For shops are open to all, since all are expected to promote profit and make bargains, and merchants by their allurements entice as many as they can to purchase their goods. So also veils were provided for all heads and cushions for all arms, for there was no difference except in reference to profit from these profane and base transactions. With regard to the word "stature," the opinion of those who think it used, because the women ordered those who consulted the oracles to stand, appears to me forced, and not in accordance with the Prophet's intention. I have no doubt that the Prophet uses the word for "age," or person, as others correctly interpret it; as if he had said, that they made no difference between

[1] "Lib. I. ch. xxxii. See also chap. xxxvi., '*statua Atti capite velato,* referring to '*Attus Navius, inclitus ea tempestate augur.*'"

old and young, tall and short, but prostituted their answers to all from whom they looked for gain.

It afterwards follows, *Is it not to hunt souls?* Here God reproves one crime, but he will shortly add another, namely, the profanation of his sacred name. But he here speaks only of the death of souls, as if he said that the women laid those snares to deceive wretched souls. And because Ezekiel was commanded to prophesy against them, he here addresses them more vehemently—*Will ye hunt the souls of my people?* It is literally the souls which belong to my people; but it will be more simple to receive it thus—*will ye hunt the souls of my people, and will ye give life to your own souls,* unless any one wishes to interpret it so as to make the Prophet repeat the same thing twice. For the souls of the people were also their own. For as we shall afterwards see, no one is deceived by the devil unless he offers himself of his own accord, and entangles himself in his snares on purpose. Since then it is always true that wretched men who catch at vain oracles devote themselves to the devil and his ministers, hence the passage may be explained in this way. But the sense which I have proposed is more simple, namely, that these women must not be yielded to *because they have hunted the souls of the people;* as if the Prophet had said, the people is precious to God, who has undertaken the care of them. Thus then he reasons; such is your audacity, nay, even fury, that ye doubt not to seize upon God's people: since therefore your impiety is so licentious and bold, will God suffer you to rage with impunity against the souls of which he is the guardian? Lastly, he signifies that punishment is prepared for the women who ensnare God's people, because although those who are deceived are worthy of death, yet God will still exact punishment of Satan's ministers who have endeavoured to despoil him of his rights. It follows—

19. And will ye pollute me among my people for handfuls of barley, and for pieces of bread, to slay the souls

19. Et profanastis me erga populum meum in pugillis hordeorum[1] propter frusta[2] panis: ut oc-

---

[1] Literally, "in handfuls of barley, or on account of them."—*Calvin.*
[2] Or, "fragments."—*Calvin.*

that should not die, and to save the souls alive that should not live, by your lying to my people that hear *your* lies?	cidatis animas quæ non moriebantur, et ad vivificandum animas quæ non vivebant, decipiendo populum meum audientes mendacium.[1]

Here God accuses these women of a double crime; one crime was that which I have mentioned, cruelly to destroy the souls which were sacred to God, and hence were destined to be saved; but he added a more atrocious crime—that of sacrilege, because they had abused the name of God to deceive. Nothing is less tolerable than when God's truth is turned into a lie, because this is like reducing him to nothing. God is truth; if, therefore, that is abolished, what else will remain behind? God will be, as it were, a dead spectre. Hence the Prophet, in God's name, complains of both: *ye have profaned me,* says he, *before my people.* For as the gift of prophecy was a rare and remarkable pledge of God's love and paternal anxiety towards the Israelites, so when that gift was corrupted, the name of God was at the same time polluted. For God was never willing to be disjoined from his word, because he is himself invisible, and never appears otherwise than in a mirror. Hence God's glory, and sanctity, and justice, and goodness, and power, ought to shine in the gift of prophecy; but when that gift is contaminated, we see how such a disgrace becomes a reproach against God. In this way his holiness is defiled, his justice, virtue, and fidelity, are corrupted, and his very existence called in question. So it is not without cause that God pronounces *his own name to be polluted.* Then he adds, *among the people.* And this circumstance increases the crime, since God's name was profaned where he wished it to be peculiarly worshipped; for it was also profaned among the Gentiles: but since God had never made himself known there, their profanation was the less detestable. But, because God erected his throne among the people of Israel, and wished his glory to shine there, we see how sacrilege increases, while his name is profaned in that sanctuary which he had chosen. This is one crime.

But he also adds, *on account of handfuls of barley and pieces of bread.* Here God shows how much and how basely

---

[1] That is, "those who hearken to a lie."—*Calvin.*

he was despised by those females, who sold their prophecies for a piece of bread or a few grains of barley which any one could hold in his hand. If they had demanded a great reward, their insatiable avarice would not have extenuated their crime; but their impiety is the rather discovered, when on account of a small reward they so prostituted themselves and the name of God. They boasted themselves to be the organs of the Holy Spirit: but when by this mask they deceived the people, injustice was done to the Holy Spirit, since for so paltry a reward they vainly boasted in their prophecies. They prostituted even God himself: and in fine, this was just as if, being corrupted by a small bribe of no value, they did not treat God's name with sufficient respect to be withheld from the crime by the slightness of the recompense. A comparison will make the matter clearer. If a person is tempted by a moderate reward to the perpetration of any crime and refuses, and then when he is offered a far more valuable reward, and thus yields to the temptation, this shows that his will was upright, though not sufficiently firm. But if any one, for a single farthing, undertakes to do what he is ordered, and refuses no crime, this shows his readiness to all sorts of wickedness. If a girl rejects bribes when she knows her modesty to be assailed, but yet yields for a large reward, here, as I have said, virtue struggles with vice; but if she prostitutes herself for a morsel of bread, here she manifests that depravity which all abominate. This, then, is God's intention, when he says that these women traded in their lies *for handfuls of barley and pieces of bread.* If any one objects that prophecies were anciently saleable, since it was customary with the people to offer the prophets rewards, I answer, that the women are not condemned merely for receiving either the handful of barley or the piece of bread, but because they did not hesitate to corrupt God's truth for a trifling gain, and then to turn it into a lie. The Prophet afterwards points out the nature of their deceit, for it would not have been sufficient to blame these women generally, unless Ezekiel had pointed with his finger at their pestiferous impostures.

Now, therefore, he says, *that they slew the souls which were not dying, and kept alive the souls which were not living.* We have said before, that by this mark the true and righteous servants of God were distinguished from impostors. For the servants of God, who faithfully discharge the duty enjoined upon them, kill and make alive: for God's word is life, and brings health to lost mankind; but is a savour of death unto death in those who perish, as Paul says. (2 Cor. ii. 15, 16.) Hence it is true that prophets who faithfully and properly discharge their duty both kill and make alive: but they give life to the souls which are to be freed from death, and slay the souls which are devoted to destruction; for they denounce eternal death to all unbelievers unless they repent; and whatever they bind on earth is also bound in heaven. (Matt. xviii. 18.) Their teaching, therefore, is effective for destruction, as also Paul elsewhere teaches. We have at hand, says he, vengeance against every high thing which exalts itself against Christ. (2 Cor. x. 5, 6.) Hence honest teachers are armed by God's vengeance against all unbelievers who remain obstinate: but they convey life to those who repent, since they are messengers of reconciliation; nay, they reconcile men to God when they offer Christ to them as our peace, and by whom the Father is propitious to us. (Eph. ii. 16.) When false prophets desire to rival God's servants, they omit the principal part, namely, faith and repentance; hence it happens that they proclaim life to souls already adjudged to destruction; for they give life to the reprobate who are hardened in contempt of God by their flatteries; for they do not require of men either faith or penitence, but only a reward. Hence also it happens that they slay the souls which ought not to die, namely, because nothing is prouder or more cruel than these false prophets. For they fulminate according to their pleasure, and sink even to the lowest hell the whole world when no hope of profit appears.

Here then we see the vices of these women of whom Ezekiel treats so pointedly out, that no one need be any longer deceived by them except through his own fault. Hence also we gather a perpetual rule in examining doctrine, lest the deceits of Satan should surprise us for the word of God.

Let us learn, then, that the prophetic word is life-giving to us, if we are dissatisfied with our sins, and fly to God's pity with true and serious penitence; for all souls are slain who do not receive this kind of life; and whoever compares the papacy with that corruption which Ezekiel describes to us, will see that, although Satan has many methods of deceiving men, yet he will always be discovered like himself. Ezekiel spoke of veils and cushions. We see many rites exhibited in the papacy, so that the incredulous, being snatched as it were out of the world, are not only delirious, but suffer themselves to be drawn in any direction like cattle by the grossest impostures. But in their teaching we perceive what Ezekiel condemns, namely, that they give life to souls devoted to death, and slay souls which ought to be kept alive. For what is the meaning of their immense heap of laws, except to bury wretched consciences? For any one who wishes to satisfy the laws of the papacy from his heart, must cut himself to pieces, so to speak, through his whole life. We now perceive with what intent our Prophet will elsewhere say that legislators of this kind are implacable, since they remit nothing, and exact all their conditions with the utmost rigour. Hence it happens that these miserable souls perish, because despair oppresses them and overwhelms them in the deep. Meanwhile we see how they give life to souls subject to death, since pardon is prepared for adulterers, robbers, manslayers, and all criminals, if they only buy themselves off, as popish priests and monks pretend that God is appeased by satisfactions and prayers. Hence they thrust expiations of no value upon God; and, to speak more correctly, trifles and follies, which do not deceive even children, they call expiations, as if God could change his nature. Hence we must diligently remark this passage, that we may know how to distinguish between true and false prophets, and may not despise the test which the Prophet puts before us.

He says, *in deceiving my people by listening to a lie.* He accuses some of lying, and others of willingly embracing lies. For the noun כָּזָב, *kezeb*, which is repeated, is derived from the same root. Here, again, God undertakes the cause of his people; for though they were all worthy of being drawn into exile by Satan, yet when God took care of them, it was like snatching them out of Satan's hand, and claiming them as his own peculiar people. This is one point. But meantime these wretches are deprived of all excuse for seeking false oracles. For the Prophet pronounces them deceived *because they listened to vanity*, that is, because they wished to be deceived, since it was entirely their own fault, and they could not in any way throw it off. It is true they were deceived under false pretences through the abuse of the prophetic name, and hence their vision was obscured by a darkened cloud; but still they ought to have gone to the fountain, for no opening would have been found for Satan if they had been properly fortified: for God had surrounded them with ramparts by giving them a law to protect them from all fallacies. Since, then, they thus exposed themselves of their own accord, it is not surprising if God allowed them to be deceived.

20. Wherefore thus saith the Lord God, Behold, I *am* against your pillows, wherewith ye there hunt the souls to make *them* fly, and I will tear them from your arms, and will let the souls go, *even* the souls that ye hunt to make *them* fly.

20. Propterea sic dicit Dominator Iehovah, Ecce, ego ad vestros pulvillos quibus vos venamini illic animas ad volandum; et lacerabo eos desuper brachiis vestris, et eruam animas quas vos venamini, animas ad volandum.

Here Ezekiel begins to threaten those women with what would shortly happen, namely, that God would not only render them contemptible, but also ridiculous, before the whole people, that their delusions and impostures might sufficiently appear. This is the Prophet's intention, as we shall afterwards see; but the Prophet is verbose in this denunciation. God therefore says, *that he is an enemy to those cushions*, that is, to those false ceremonies which were like cloaks to deceive miserable men: hence he says, that those souls were a prey. He uses the comparison from hunting: *ye have hunted*, says he, *the souls of my people*. And this is the meaning of the word used immediately afterwards *for flying*. This word פרח, *pherech*, signifies also "to flourish;" but I here willingly subscribe to the opinion of all who interpret it to fly: unless the paraphrast is right in translating it " to perish ;" for he thought the Prophet was speaking metaphorically, as if he meant that those souls were ensnared, and so vanished away. But I do not think this quite suitable, since it is more probable that the Prophet is speaking of their lofty speculations. For we know that false prophets boasted in this artifice, when they either raise, or pretend they raise, men's minds aloft, and curious men desire this only; and hence it happens that the doctrines of the Law and the Gospel are insipid to them, because subtleties alone delight them. And we see at this day how many embrace the follies of Dionysius[1] about the celestial hierarchy, who treat all the prophets, and even Christ himself, as of no value. Hence the Prophet says, *that these women hunted the souls of the people*, because they had snares prepared in which they entangled all who were subject to their impostures and fallacies. Yet, in my opinion, he also alludes to birds. When, therefore, he has said that all impostures were Satan's method of hunting souls, he now adds obliquely another simile, that all false prophecies are so many allurements to catch birds. The sense of the passage now appears clear. *Behold*, therefore, says he, *God will arise against your cushions, by which ye have hunted birds to make them fly;* that is, when ye promised wonderful revelations those wretched dupes whom their own curiosity urged on were deceived by such enticements. Afterwards he adds, *I will free them from your arms*, and *I will let go the souls which ye have hunted to make them fly*, says he. He repeats again what we have already said about deep speculations, by the sweetness of which false prophets are accustomed to entice all fools who cannot be content with true doctrine, nor be wise with sobriety. Meanwhile it is by no means doubtful that God here speaks peculiarly of his elect, who were left among the people. For although they were but few, God was unwilling

---

[1] Dionysius was a Carthusian, a philosopher imbued with the mystic doctrines of Plato, on whose writings he wrote an elaborate comment. Calvin refers to his attempt to combine the scholastic theology of his day with the mystical fancies of Platonism. He was commonly called *a Ryckel*, and wrote A.D. 1471. See *Gieseler's* Eccl. Hist., edited in English by Francis Cuningham, vol. iii. p. 279, n. 7.

for them to perish : and for this reason he announces that he would be their avenger, and undeceive them, whether they had been already entrapped, or were just surrounded by these allurements. Since, then, he uses the same word, we gather from this that the phrase cannot be used indiscriminately. For God suffers many to perish, as he says by the Prophet Zechariah, "Let what perishes perish," (xi. 9) ; but meanwhile he rescued a small number as the remnant of his choice, as Paul says. (Rom. xi. 5.)

PRAYER.

Grant, Almighty God, since thou showest us that our salvation is so precious in thy sight, that through our ingratitude we may not cast away this testimony of thy favour, but be anxious to listen to thy instructions : Grant also, that being gifted by thee with the spirit of discretion, we may not be exposed to capture as a prey; but may we be so ruled by the light of thy word that we may hold on in the right way, till after our allotted time is finished we may arrive at that happy repose which is laid up for us in heaven through Christ our Lord.—Amen.

Lecture Thirty-Seventh.

21. Your kerchiefs also will I tear, and deliver my people out of your hand, and they shall be no more in your hand to be hunted ; and ye shall know that I am the Lord.

21. Et conscindam pepla vestra,[1] et eruam populum meum e manibus vestris: et non erunt amplius in manibus vestris in prædam: et cognoscetis quod ego Iehovah.

WHAT the Prophet had said concerning the pillows he now pronounces of the veils, by which they were accustomed to cover either their own heads, or those of the persons who consulted them. The conclusion is, that God would put an end to such follies. For the people were so fascinated by these silly things, that it became necessary to strip away these masks, since these women were always ready to deceive. He adds also, that he would do that for the benefit of his own people. We have said that this ought not to be extended generally to all the sons of Abraham according to the flesh. For God suffered almost all to perish, as he had said by Isaiah : " Even if thy people had been as the sand

[1] Or, " I will tear."—*Calvin.*

of the sea-shore, a remnant only shall be saved," (Isaiah x. 22.) When, therefore, God speaks here concerning his own people, this sentence ought to be restricted to the elect: as when it is said in the psalm, How soft and kind is God to his people Israel; and then he adds by way of correction, to those who are upright in heart, (Ps. lxxiii. 1,) Since many boasted themselves to be Israelites who are very unlike their father, and through being degenerate deprived themselves of that honour: hence the Prophet restricts God's goodness peculiarly to the elect who are upright in heart, after he had spoken of the whole people. Although Ezekiel did not distinctly express what we have cited from the psalm, yet the sense is the same; and this is easily gathered from the eleventh chapter of the Epistle to the Romans (verses 5, 6), where God sets before us the remnant preserved according to God's gratuitous election. For the same sense it is added, *that they should no longer be for a prey.* We have said how these women hunted these wretched souls, not only for purposes of gain, but also because Satan abused their fallacies. So, therefore, it happened that these souls were enticed to their destruction. For this reason God pronounces that they should no longer be their prey. And he repeats what he had already said, *ye shall know that I am Jehovah.* Here God brings before us his power, because we know how safely hypocrites illude his sacred name; and this easily appears in the boldness and licentiousness of these women. Hence God here threatens them: he says that they should feel at length who had spoken, since they ridiculed Ezekiel and his other servants. There is, then, a silent antithesis between God and the prophets; not that God separates himself from his servants; for the truth, of which they are ministers and heralds, is an indissoluble bond of union between them; but the language is adapted to the senses of those with whom the Prophet treats. Now, since these women were so wanton, he says that he was not despised by them, but God himself. It follows—

22. Because with lies ye have made the heart of the righteous sad, whom

22. Quia contristastis cor justi mendacio,[1] et ego non contrista-

---

[1] Or, " fallaciously."—*Calvin.*

I have not made sad; and strengthened the hands of the wicked, that he should not return from his wicked way, by promising him life;

23. Therefore ye shall see no more vanity, nor divine divinations: for I will deliver my people out of your hand; and ye shall know that I *am* the Lord.

veram ipsum;[1] et roborastis manus impii, ut non converteretur à via sua mala, vivificando ipsum.

23. Propterea mendacium non videbitis, et divinationem non divinabitis amplius: et eruam populum meum è manu vestra: et scietis quod ego Iehovah.

He explains in other words what we saw yesterday: but the repetition adds to the weight of the matter. The Prophet therefore shows that he had a just cause of complaint, because the women so deceived the people. He says now *that they made the heart of the righteous sad, and strengthened the hands of the wicked:* the sentiment is the same, though the words are changed. He had previously said that they gave life to those devoted to death, and slew those destined to life; but now he shows more clearly the meaning of killing the soul that should not, or ought not to die, when the heart of the righteous is made sorrowful. By the righteous he means those whom the false prophets inspired with causeless terror. But why, it is asked, does he say that the righteous are grieved, since we have formerly taught that no others were deceived unless those who spontaneously throw themselves into the snares and traps of Satan? I answer, that the false prophets thundered so, and their lies were so spread about here and there as to involve the simple: for they scatter their threats so as to reach all men. Hence they wound weak consciences; as at this day when the lies of Satan fly about by which true religion is corrupted, many simple ones are frightened, for they are destitute of judgment, and do not distinguish whether God threatens, or man vaunts himself rashly.

We see, then, how false prophets cause the righteous sorrow, when they suggest scruples, and, under the penalty of mortal sin, denounce first one thing and then another: then they deprive them of confidence in God's favour, and strike them with various terrors, as we discern clearly in the papacy of this very day. Let us take that one point

[1] The word is different, but only in one letter, and signifies to be sad and to be grieved.— *Calvin.*

which is with them without controversy, that our confidence springs from our works, and hence that we cannot determine whether God is propitious to us or not, and thus they overthrow all assurance of faith. They retain, indeed, the name of faith, but meantime they wish wretched consciences to vacillate and be turned about with disquiet, since no one can know whether he can invoke God as a father.[1] That confidence which Paul says is common to all Christians, they call presumption and rashness. (Eph. iii. 12.) We see, then, how that point not only grieves the righteous, but disturbs innocent consciences: for a series of traditions is afterwards added, and the penalty of eternal death is always annexed: hence it happens that those who wish to worship God in any other way, when they are thus rendered spiritless, know not which way to turn: hence also they lose all fear of God, since no one can seriously reverence God unless he who feels him to be easily entreated, as we learn from Psalm cxxx. 6.

We now understand what the Holy Spirit means when he reproves the women *because they made the heart of the righteous sad.* It is added, *but I was unwilling to grieve them.* For God's faithful servants often inspire terror, but only when necessary. For they cannot otherwise subdue those who exult in their lusts, and they cannot bring them to obedience unless they overcome them with fear. Hence even true prophets and evangelists cause pain, as Paul says: If I have caused you sorrow, I do not repent of it: for so I ought to do: for there is salutary grief. (2 Cor. vii. 8.) Besides, true prophets do not afflict men for nothing; they only cause anxiety in the minds of those whom God wishes to grieve: hence they do not fabricate the material for sorrow and pain in their own brain, but receive it from God's mouth and the spirit of revelation. Hence the word *righteous* is used, and *falsely* is added, by which particle the severity which true prophets are often compelled to use is distinguished from the roughness, or rather savage rudeness,

---

[1] The modern state of this controversy is fully explained in Ward's "Ideal of the Christian Church." He utterly rejects Calvin's theory, and then very consistently joins the Church of Rome.

of false prophets. For as I have said, they frighten wretched consciences. But by what right? by transferring God's power to themselves; just as at the present day the Pope with swelling cheeks thunders forth that himself and his throne are apostolic, and therefore infallible. Since, therefore, false prophets thus contend by fallacies, the simple are overcome by fear.

It is now added, *that they strengthened the hands of the impious* (literally, of the impious man in the singular). When the Prophet spoke of the righteous, he used the word *heart:* he now uses the word *hand,* and not without reason. For the false terrors in which the false prophets indulged, penetrate even to the intimate affections, and as each is affected by the fear of God, so he becomes afraid of those threats which he hears uttered in God's name. We see, then, that it was said with very good reason that the mind of the righteous was sadly grieved; and now when he says *that he had strengthened the hands of the impious,* he means that audacity was added, so that not only the wicked always remain obstinate against God, but they break out in unbridled license, and hesitate not openly to violate God's law: for strengthening the hands is more than grieving the mind. For it may and it does happen, that a man may swell with pride and contempt of God, and yet modesty may hinder him from basely contaminating himself with many crimes. But when the hands themselves are engaged in licentiousness, all evils are heaped together. Now, therefore, we understand the reason of this difference. In fine, Ezekiel means that the impious had been hardened by the blandishments of these women, so as not only to despise God in their minds, but to bear witness through their whole life, that they were openly and confessedly erecting the standard of war against God. In this sense, then, he says, that *they had strengthened the hands of the impious.*

He adds, *that he should not be converted.* Here he more clearly defines how those souls which were devoted to death[1] were kept alive, since such confidence was set before them

---

[1] The Latin edition of 1565 has "motu:" the true reading is "morte." The French version is correct in rendering it by "perdition."

as to lull and stupify their consciences. He does not say, then, *that the hands of the impious were strengthened*, as in a conspiracy of the wicked one often assists another, as if they mutually bound their hands together. But the Prophet now speaks in another sense, namely, that these women so hardened the wicked that they went on securely in their wickedness, and made a laughing-stock of God and his law. *Ye have strengthened the hands that they should not be converted:* but how? *by affording them life.* Hence we gather that men cannot be humbled otherwise than by placing death before them, because all willingly indulge themselves, and hypocrisy is so ingrained in us by natural corruption, that every one readily persuades himself that all things will turn out well. Unless, therefore, death is presented before our eyes, and God himself appears as a judge to destroy us, we remain like ourselves, and proceed to still greater audacity. The Prophet signifies this when he says, *that by giving life to the impious the false prophets strengthened their hands,* and opposed their repentance altogether. How so? When the sinner thinks God propitious to him, he is not anxious about reconciliation, but abuses God's forbearance, and is daily rendered bolder, until at last he puts off all sense of fear. Hence this is the true preparation for conversion, when the sinner is slain; that is, acknowledges himself liable to the judgment of God, and takes a formidable view of his wrath. When, therefore, he sees himself lost, then he begins to think of conversion; but when men sleep over their sins, as I have said, they persist till they arrive at constant apathy, as Paul says when he remarks that they have no longer any sense of sorrow. (Eph. iv. 19.)

It follows, *ye shall not see a lie any more.* He has hitherto explained the reason why God grew so warm against these women, because they destroyed miserable souls either by their cruelty or their flatteries, and thus were like false prophets: now he adds, *ye shall not see a lie any more.* This ought not to be understood as if God promised these women a sound mind, so that they should cease to hurt the people by their lies: but he confirms the sentiment previously expressed, namely, that they should be subject to the taunts of all men, as boys themselves acknowledge that what they boasted to be oracles were mere imposture. It is just as if he had said—I will make you ashamed, so that hereafter ye may be deprived of the use of the prophetic name, as ye have hitherto used it. Although these women persisted in their madness, yet they saw vanity no more, since it became openly apparent that those wretched ones who trusted in them were deceived. Lastly, this ought to be adapted not to any change of feeling in these women, but rather to a failure in the effect. It is just as if any one were to say to a foolish fellow boasting himself to be a lawyer or a physician,—I will take care that you profit no more as either a lawyer or a physician; and yet that foolish person should not be able to put away the opinion which he had ever formed of his own skill. But this is said, because the mere vanity of his boasting should be evident to all. So also God now speaks. This addition has the same meaning: *ye shall not divine divination any more.* And yet there is no doubt that they desired by all means to invent new prophecies, and to boast in new revelations: but they were despised, because God had detected their lies when Jerusalem was taken, and the people dragged into exile: then because they promised the people a speedy return, when the same God refuted them by prolonging their exile. When, therefore, any one suffers the just penalty of his impiety, then the vanity of those women was detected: in this way they ceased to divine. He repeats—*I will free my people from your hand: and ye shall know that I am Jehovah.* Since I have lately explained this phrase I now pass it by. It follows—

CHAPTER XIV.

1. Then came certain of the elders of Israel unto me, and sat before me.

2. And the word of the Lord came unto me, saying,

3. Son of man, these men have

1. Et venerunt ad me viri ex senioribus Israel, et sederunt coram facie mea.[1]

2. Et fuit sermo Iehovæ ad me, dicendo,

3. Fili hominis, viri isti ascendere

---

[1] "At my face."—*Calvin.*

set up their idols in their heart, and put the stumblingblock of their iniquity before their face: should I be enquired of at all by them?	fecerunt idola sua super cor suum, et offendiculum iniquitatis suæ posuerunt coram facie sua. An quærendo quærar ipsis?[1]

Here Ezekiel relates an event worthy of notice. For this was not a mere vision, but a real transaction, since some of the elders of Israel came to him for the sake of consultation. He says *that he sat*, as men who are perplexed and astonished by evils are accustomed to do, when they see no remedy. The gesture then which the Prophet describes was a sign of anxiety and despair. A person wishing for an answer is said to sit before another; but since it is probable that they disputed among themselves about beginning, and did not immediately discover how they should commence, hence they became anxious to consult the Prophet. Ezekiel, indeed, might be touched and softened by pity when he saw them seeking God in this way. For this was a sign of repentance when they turned to the true and faithful servant of God. But since they had no sincerity, the Prophet is warned in time against supposing them to come with cordiality. Hence God instructs his servant not to give way with too much facility when he sees old men coming to be disciples. But he shows their hypocrisy, because superstition still reigned in their hearts: nay, they desired openly to violate God's law, and they did not disguise this feeling whenever occasion offered. First, he says they *have set up idols in their hearts;* by which words he means that they were addicted to superstition, so that idols obtained a high rank in their hearts; as Paul exhorts the faithful, that the peace of God which passes all understanding may obtain the rule in their hearts (Phil. iv. 7; Col. iii. 15); so on the other hand the Prophet says that these men had given supreme sway to idols. And again an implied comparison must be remarked between God and idols. For God has erected the seat of his empire in our hearts: but when we set up idols, we necessarily endeavour to overthrow God's throne, and to reduce his power to nothing. Hence the most heinous crime of sacrilege is here shown in those old men *who caused idols*

---

[1] Or, "by them."—*Calvin.*

to rise above their hearts. For hence it follows that all their senses were drowned in their superstitions.

He adds, *they placed the stumblingblock of their iniquity before his face.* By this second clause he signifies their hardness and perverseness; as if he had said, although the doctrine of the law was put before their eyes, yet they had no regard for piety, and despised even God's threats, as if he were not going to be their judge. When, therefore, the sinner is not moved by any admonitions, and is more than convicted of his impiety, and is compelled, whether he will or not, to suffer God's anger, and yet afterwards despises it, he is said *to put the stumblingblock of his iniquity before his face.* For many slide away by error and thoughtlessness, because they do not think they can attempt anything against God. But here Ezekiel expresses that there was a gross contempt of God in these old men, and even a professed rebellion against him. Now he asks, *Shall I by enquiring be enquired of by them?* Some translate, Shall I, when consulted or asked, answer them? But this comment seems to me too remote from the mind of the Prophet; and it is probable that they thought this to be the sense, because they could not understand what else the Prophet meant. But God shows that this was like a wonder, since these old men dared to break forth, and to pretend to have some desire to inquire the truth. Hence their impudence is shown here, because they did not hesitate to place themselves before God's servant, and to pretend a regard for piety when they had none. God says, therefore, can it be done? For this question expresses the absurdity of the thing, and that for the above mentioned purpose, that their wickedness may be the more apparent in their daring to insult the face of God. For what else is it than openly to reproach God when impure men approach him, and wish to become partakers of his counsel? Meanwhile they show by their whole life that they are most inveterate enemies of the whole heavenly doctrine. Afterwards it follows—

4. Therefore speak unto them, and say unto them, Thus saith the	4. Propterea loquere ad ipsos, et dic illis: sic Dominator Iehovah,

Lord God, Every man of the house of Israel that setteth up his idols in his heart, and putteth the stumbling-block of his iniquity before his face, and cometh to the prophet, I the Lord will answer him that cometh according to the multitude of his idols.

vir vir è domo Israel,[1] ascendere fecerit idola sua super cor suum, et offendiculum iniquitatis suæ posuerit coram facie sua : et venerit ad prophetam : ego Iehovah respondebo huic[2] secundum multitudinem idolorum ejus.[3]

Here God seems to treat those hypocrites too indulgently who pretend to ask his advice and yet despise his counsel. But God here rather threatens what would be destructive to the wicked than promises anything which they ought to expect. It is indeed a singular testimony of God's grace when he answers us : for prophecy is an image of God's paternal anxiety towards us and our salvation. But sometimes prophecy only ends in destruction ; and this is but an accident. Although, therefore, God's word by itself is naturally to be greatly desired, yet when God answers as a judge, and takes away all hope of pardon and pity, no taste of his favour can then be perceived. Thus this passage must be understood. God pronounces that he would answer, but whom ? The reprobate, and those who tauntingly inquired of the Prophet what they should do. When he answers them, he only shows himself the avenger of their perfidy ; and thus his answer contains nothing else but the fearful judgment which hangs over all the reprobate. For God does not here impose a perpetual law on himself; for he does not always act in the same way towards all the reprobate, but says that those impious ones should feel that they shall not profit by their cunning and artifices, since they

[1] That is, " any one of the house of Israel."—*Calvin*.
[2] " It is another word : ענה, *gneneh*, is properly to answer—I will answer him in his enquiry."—*Calvin*.
[3] " Some think the letter ה to have been substituted for א, and translate it—I will answer him, *because* he comes in the multitude of his idols. But I follow the simpler sense, because I fear their explanation to be too forced, namely, that God would reply to the impious when they consulted him, but according to the multitude of their idols, that is, as they deserved."—*Calvin*.

The Hebrew word to which Calvin here refers is בה, *beh*, which is so entirely Syriac, that Eichhorn says the Masoretes wished to corrupt it to בא, *ba*. It is wanting in two MSS. Newcombe quotes the authority of Kennicott for reading בא, *ba*, though Houbigant treats it as a barbarism. The Chaldee interpretation is perhaps preferable. Rosenmüller discusses the point fully. See also Cappell. Crit. Sac., vol. i. p. 294. Edit. Hal.

shall find the difference between God and Satan: for they were accustomed to lies, and had itching ears; hence they wished to have some pleasing and flattering answer from the servant of God, since the false prophets gratified their inclinations. What then does God say? *I will answer them, but far otherwise than they either wish or desire: for I will answer them according to the multitude of their idols:* for they bring with them the material for their own condemnation: hence they shall take back nothing from me but the seal of that condemnation which is already placed upon their hearts, and appears on their hands. In fine, God here laughs at the foolish confidence of those who inquire about future events of his prophets; but meanwhile they have their heart bound up with superstitions, so as openly to show their gross impiety: hence he says, *that he would answer them*, not as they thought, but as they deserved.

5. That I may take the house of Israel in their own heart, because they are all estranged from me through their idols.

5. Ut deprehendam domum Israel in corde ipsorum, quia alienarunt se[1] a me in suis idolis omnes.

He shows God's object in being unwilling to dismiss without an answer the hypocrites who still impiously trifled with him. He says, *that I may seize the house of Israel in their heart.* It is yet asked how the impious are seized, when God answers them neither according to the opinion of their mind nor their expectation, but pronounces what they dislike and fear most grievously. I reply, that the impious are answered when they are driven to madness, and God thus extracts from them what was formerly hidden in their own hearts. He says, therefore, *that their impiety may be manifest to all, I will answer them.* For as long as God spares the impious, they endeavour to soothe him by a kind of flattery; but when they see that they take nothing by their false blandishments, then they roar, nay, bellow furiously against God: thus *they are caught in their own hearts:* that is, all their former dissembling is made bare, so that all may easily perceive that there never was a spark of piety in their hearts. God, therefore, bears witness that his answers

[1] Or, as others translate, " separate themselves."— *Calvin.*

would be of this kind, *that he may take the house of Israel in their hearts;* that is, that his severity may draw out into the light what was formerly hidden; for the word of God is a two-edged sword, and examines all the sentiments of men. (Heb. iv. 12.) Some are so slain by this sword that they grow wise again; but others are stung with fury when they see that they must engage with the power of God; therefore they are seized in their own hearts when God twists from them what they would willingly have kept always hidden. *Since they have estranged themselves from me,* literally, *in their idols.* This passage is explained in two ways, as we have said. Some say, because they separated themselves; but I approve of the other version, *because they have alienated themselves,* and we shall understand the point more clearly afterwards when the subject leads us to it. *They alienated themselves,* then, *from God;* that is, when they had utterly declined from God's law; yet, as long as this was concealed, they still wore their masks. The separation of which the Prophet here speaks seems to be referred to this pretence. Since, then, *they so alienated themselves from me by their idols;* that is, he says they are deceived in thinking that they cannot be discovered, and that their abominations, however foul they are, will remain secret. And this agrees with the last clause, namely, that he would seize the hypocrites in their own heart.

PRAYER.

Grant, Almighty God, since we are so inclined to all kinds of vices, that we may be restrained by the power of thy Spirit: then that we may be attentive to the teaching which sounds continually in our ears, so that we may persevere in the pure worship of thy name; and thus being strengthened against the cunning of the wicked, may we be upheld in our weakness, and preserved from all error, until we finish our course, and arrive at the goal which is proposed to us in Christ Jesus our Lord.—Amen.

Lecture Thirty-Eighth.

6. Therefore say unto the house of Israel, Thus saith the Lord God, Repent, and turn *yourselves* from your idols; and turn away your faces from all your abominations.	6. Propterea dic ad domum Israel, Sic dicit Dominator Iehovah, revertimini et redire facite ab idolis vestris, et à cunctis abominationibus vestris redire facite[1] facies vestras.

Now God shows why he had threatened the false prophets and the whole people so severely, namely, that they should repent; for the object of God's rigour is, that when terrified by his judgments, we should return into the way. Now, therefore, he exhorts them to repentance. Hence we gather the useful lesson, that whenever God inspires us with fear, he has no other intention than to humble us, and thus to provide for our salvation, when he reproves and threatens us so strongly by his prophets, and in truth is verbally angry with us, that he may really spare us. But the exhortation is short, *that they may be converted and turned away from their idols, and may turn their faces from all their abominations.* When he uses the word השיבו, *heshibev*, in the second clause, some understand "wives;" but this is frigid: others think the verb transitive, but yet impersonal, thus make yourselves return: this also is harsh.[2] I have no doubt that the Prophet here exhorts the Israelites that each should desire to reconcile himself to God, and at the same time bring others with him. As many were mutually the authors of evils to each other, he now orders them to do their utmost to bring back others with them: and surely this is a true proof of our repentance, when we are not only converted to God one by one, but when we stretch forth our hand to our brethren, and recall them from error; especially if they have wandered away through our fault, we must take care to make up for the injury by at least equal diligence. The sense therefore of the Prophet is, first, that the Israelites should repent; next, that one should assist another to re-

---

[1] Or, "turn away."—*Calvin.*

[2] Calvin has not explained the difficulty which he raises. The verb "return" is in Hiphil, and ought to have a case following it. Houbigant reads it in Hophal, and Newcombe prefers to understand "yourselves." Rosenmüller, as usual, is very explanatory.

pentance, or that they should mutually unite in the pursuit of piety, just as each was previously corrupted by his companion and brother. This seems to be the full meaning. Besides, this series must be remarked: because many show zeal in seizing others, and stretching out the hand to free them from error; but they themselves never think of repenting. But the Holy Spirit here shows us the true method of proceeding, when he commands us to repent, and then extends our desires to our brethren who have need of our exhortations. At length he adds, *withdraw your faces*, or turn away *from all your abominations*. A part is here put by the Prophet for the whole, since turning away the face means the same as withdrawing all the senses. Since, therefore, they had been almost affixed to their own abominations to which they had cast their eyes, and were completely intent upon them, he orders them *to turn away their faces*, so as to bid them farewell. It follows—

7. For every one of the house of Israel, or of the stranger that sojourneth in Israel, which separateth himself from me, and setteth up his idols in his heart, and putteth the stumblingblock of his iniquity before his face, and cometh to a prophet to enquire of him concerning me; I the Lord will answer him by myself.

7. Nam quisquis è domo Israel, et è peregrino qui peregrinatur apud Israelem, et separatus fuerit[1] de post me (*ad verbum*), et ascendere fecerit idola sua super cor suum, et offendiculum iniquitatis suæ posuerit coram facie sua, et venerit ad Prophetam ad inquirendum ipsum ex me,[2] ego Iehovah respondebo ei in me (*vel per me*).

Ezekiel again returns to threats, because exhortation was not sufficiently effectual with such hardened ones; for we have seen that they were obdurate in their vices and almost like untamed beasts. For unless God's judgment had been often set before them, there had been but small fruit of teaching and exhortation. This then is the reason why God here sets before them his vengeance: *a man, a man*, says he, *or even a stranger who sojourns among Israel.* When he adds strangers, he doubtless speaks of the circumcised who professed to be worshippers of the true God, and so submitted

[1] "It cannot be otherwise translated here: the word is נזר, *nezer*, which we yesterday saw might be derived from זור, *zor*, to be estranged. There is no doubt about the sense, ' he who has been separated.' "—*Calvin.*

[2] That is, "through me, or to inquire of him in or by me, or through my name."—*Calvin.*

to the law as to refrain from all impieties. For there were two kinds of strangers, those who transacted business there, but were profane men, continuing uncircumcised. But there were others who were not sprung from the sacred race, and were not indigenous to the soil, but yet they had been circumcised, and as far as religion was concerned, had become members of the Church; and God wishes them to be esteemed in the same class and rank as the sons of Abraham. The law shall be the same for the stranger and the home-born, wherever the promise is concerned, (Num. xv. 15, 16,) and the same sentiment is repeated in many places. Thus the word foreigners is now to be explained. But this circumstance exaggerates the crime of the chosen people. For if any one settled in the land of Canaan and embraced God's law, this was an accidental event: but the Israelites were by nature heirs of eternal life, for the adoption was continued through successive ages. Since then they were born sons of God, it was the more disgraceful to depart from his worship. And so when Ezekiel here gravely rebukes the strangers, he shows how much more atrocious the crime was in the case of those who were bound by a more sacred bond to the worship of God. He says, *and he was separated from after me.* The Prophet yesterday said מֵעָלַי, *megneli,* from near or from towards me: here he more clearly expresses declension, when men reject the teaching of the law, and openly show that they pay no obedience to God. For he is said to follow God or to walk after him, who proposes to himself God as a guide, and is devoted to his precepts, and holds on in the way pointed out by him. Thus by the obedience of faith we follow God or walk after him: so we recede from him when we reject his law, and are openly unwilling to bear his yoke any longer. Hence he shows of what kind the separation of the people or of individuals from God is, namely, when they refuse to follow his law. The Israelites indeed wished God always to remain united to them, but they made the divorce, although they denied it: hence the Prophet cuts away from them beforehand this prop of backsliding, when he says that *they separated from God* by not following him.

At length he repeats what we saw yesterday, *he who caused his idols to ascend unto his heart, he who placed the stumblingblock of his iniquity before his face,* that is, was drowned in his own superstitions, so that his idols bore sway in his heart: lastly, he who is so forward in audacity that he did not conceal his wish to oppose the Almighty: *if any one,* says he, *came to a prophet to enquire of him in me,* or my name, *I will answer him.* He confirms what we saw yesterday, that he could no longer bear the hypocrites who deluded themselves so proudly. And certainly when they openly worshipped idols, and were filled with many superstitions, what audacity and pride it was to consult true prophets? It is much the same as if a person should wantonly insult and rail at a physician, and not only load him with reproaches, but even spit in his face: and should afterwards go and ask his advice, saying, "What do you advise me to do? How must I be cured of this disease?" Such pride could not be borne between man and man. How then will God permit such reproaches to go unpunished? For this reason he says *that he would answer*, but after his own manner, as if he had said—they seek flatteries, but I *will answer in myself:* that is, in my natural character. I will not change it according to their pleasure, for they change my character by their fictions, but they are deceived: they profit nothing when they expect me to answer according to their views: *I will answer,* says he, *in myself;* that is, they shall feel that the answer proceeds from me, and they shall have no reason for thinking that my servants will be submissive to them, as they are accustomed to abuse the false prophets whom they buy for reward, because they are venal. For when any one is venal he is compelled to flatter like a slave. For there is no freedom but in a good and upright conscience. Hence God here separates his servants from impostors who make a trade of their flatteries. Now it follows—

8. And I will set my face against that man, and will make him a sign

8. Et ponam faciem meam in viro illo,[1] et ponam illum[2] in sig-

---

[1] Or, "upon that man."—*Calvin.*

[2] Some translate, "I will destroy him," changing the point from left to right; but the reading, "I will place him," is better.—*Calvin.* Cal-

| and a proverb, and I will cut him off from the midst of my people; and ye shall know that I *am* the Lord. | num et proverbia et excidem eum è medio populi mei: et cognoscetis quod ego Iehovah. |

Here God adds, that the execution of his wrath would be ready when the prophets had denounced it. For profane men always fabricate for themselves empty treaties, and when God threatens they say that it is only thunder without lightning. Since the prophetic threats moved the reprobate either nothing or but little, so God now shows that he would not only answer what they did not wish to hear, but they should perceive by its effect how truly he had spoken. And this ought to be understood from the last sentence; for when God answers by himself, he neither lies nor strikes the air with threatening words, but denounces what he determined to fulfil and accomplish in his own time. For God never answers in himself without joining the effect with the prophecy. But hypocrites are too stupid to acknowledge this, unless a clearer explanation was afforded. This then is the reason why the Prophet brings a message respecting the effect. He says, *I will put my face upon that man:* when God speaks openly against us, this is sufficient for our destruction; but he wished to express more in this case, namely, that prophets were the heralds of his wrath, and that hypocrites should be admonished about the penalties which await them, and even now hang over them, since his hand is stretched out against them. He is said to place his face against another who rises against him, or descends to a contest and engages hand to hand. So also God pronounces that he would be an adversary to all the reprobate who thus endeavoured to elude him.

He says, *I will place him for a sign and a proverb.* He marks the heaviness of the punishment by these words: for God sometimes chastises the faults of men, but after a common and accustomed manner. But when punishment excites the wonder of all and is like a portent, then God puts forth the sign of his wrath in no common fashion, as they say.

vin's meaning is, that by altering the point over the Hebrew letter שׁ the meaning of the word is changed: in this and in the previous verses, Calvin prefers the reading of our authorized version.

The Prophet then means this, and hence at the same time admonishes us how detestable a crime it is to decline from the pure worship of God. For God chastises thefts and lewdness, drunkenness, deceits, and rapines: but not always so rigorously that the punishment is remarkable, and turns the minds of all towards itself. Hence from the greatness of the punishment the atrocity of the crime is made known. He now adds, *for proverbs*. This phrase is taken from the law, as the prophets who are the interpreters of Moses make use of words from it. (Deut. xxviii. 37.) When any remarkable slaughter occurs it is said to be *for a proverb*, as all persons usually boast when speaking of any slaughter, that none is equal to it or more horrible. But משל, *meshel*, is also used for a disgrace: as if he had said, it should not only be material for remark among the whole people, but their name should be subject to reproach and contempt. At length he adds, *I will cut him off from my people*. This is most severe of all, for even the hope of pity is taken away. A person may be a wonder for a time: then his calamity may be the subject of vulgar taunts and proverbs: and yet God is still exorable, and may not cut him off from his people. But when any one is cut off from God's people, his safety is already beyond hope. It is not in vain that this sentence is so often repeated, *ye shall know that I am Jehovah*, says he, since we even formerly saw hypocrites always put a veil before them, since they think they have only to do with the prophets, and thus they despise mortals with security. Hence God here inscribes his name on his word, that they may know that he has spoken, and may experience the effect of his words by his hand. It follows—

9. And if the prophet be deceived when he hath spoken a thing, I the Lord have deceived that prophet; and I will stretch out my hand upon him, and will destroy him from the midst of my people Israel.	9. Et Propheta cum deceptus fuerit, et locutus fuerit sermonem: ego Iehovah decepi prophetam eum: et extendam manum meam super ipsum, et delebo illum è medio populi mei Israel.

Here God meets that foolish thought in which many minds are wrapt up. When they had their own impostors at hand, they thought that all God's threats could be repelled as it were by a shield. Jeremiah and Ezekiel threaten us, say they, but we have others to cheer us with good hope: they promise that all things shall be joyful and prosperous to us: since, therefore, only two or three deprive us of the hope of safety, and others, and those, too, far more numerous, promise us security, we have no need to despair. Since they thus oppose their impostors to the true prophets, and imagine a kind of conflict, in which imposture prevails and God's truth is vanquished, he says there is no reason why the flatteries of the false prophets should deceive you. For if you say that they bear also the prophetic name and office, I reply, that they err through your fault; for I deceive them because your impiety deserves it. This may as yet be obscure, but I will endeavour to explain it by a familiar example. At this time we see that many through sloth withdraw themselves from all fear, and promise themselves freedom from punishment, while they reject all care for God. O, say they, what have I to do with religion? for this only occasions me trouble; whoever wishes to give himself up seriously to God amidst these dissensions and divisions will enter a labyrinth. Since, therefore, many think themselves free from fault, even if they reject God, this doctrine may be turned against them. There are, indeed, at this day dissensions in religion which disturb many; but do you think that this happens rashly? Oh! we know not which party to follow: inquire; for God has not so given the rein to Satan and his ministers, that the Church is disturbed, and men are mutually opposed by chance. But when this happens by the just judgment of God, it is certain that no one can be deceived unless of his own accord. For the Prophet takes that principle from Moses, whenever false prophets come forth, that this is a proof of faithfulness and of sincere piety. Thy God tries thee, says Moses, whether thou lovest him. (Deut. viii. 3.) Since, therefore, no false prophet arises without the just judgment of God, and since God wishes to distinguish between sincere worshippers and hypocrites, it follows that no one can be excused on this pretext, of differing opinions which arise by wise ordination. For since God wishes to make an experiment, as I have said, concerning his servants and sons, and since false prophets so mingle all things, and involve the clear daylight in darkness, no one who truly and heartily seeks God shall be entangled among their snares.

But Ezekiel will proceed still further, as I have previously hinted, namely, that all impostures and errors do not spring up rashly, but proceed from the ingratitude of the people itself. For if they had not so willingly given themselves up to the false prophets, God would doubtless have spared them. But since false prophets abounded on every side, and were so plentiful everywhere, hence it may be understood that the people were worthy of such impostures. Now then we perceive the meaning of the Holy Spirit when God pronounces that he is the author of all the error which the false prophets were thus scattering abroad. For it is not sufficient to observe merely the sound of the words, and then to illicit the substance of the prophetic teaching; but we must attend to the Spirit's purpose. I have already explained why the Prophet says this, namely, that the Israelites should cease to turn their backs according to their custom, saying, that if they remained in doubt amidst various opinions, this ought not to be imputed to them as a crime. For he answers, that the false prophets only took this license, because the people deserved to be blinded: and in fine, he says that Satan's lies multiplied not at random or at the will of men, but because God repays a graceless and perfidious people with a just recompense. So Paul says that error has a divine efficacy, when men prefer embracing a lie to the truth (2 Thess. ii. 11, 12), and do not submit themselves to God, but rather shake off his yoke. Now, therefore, whoever wishes to excuse himself under the pretext of simplicity for not acquiescing in God's word, this answer is at hand—that all things are thus mingled by God's just decree. Since, therefore, Satan eclipses the light whenever clouds are scattered to disturb the weak, we here find God to be the author of it, since man's impiety deserves it. For the Prophet does not here discourse profanely about God's absolute power, as they say; but when he brings forward God's name, he takes it for granted that God is not delighted with such disturbance, when false prophets seize upon his name. It is certain, then, that God does not delight in such deception; but the cause must be sought, as we shall soon see: the cause is not always manifest; but without controversy this is fixed, that God punishes men justly, when true religion is so rent asunder by divisions, and truth is obscured by falsehood.

We must hold, then, that God does not rage like a tyrant, but exercises just judgment. Besides, this passage teaches us that neither impostures nor deceptions arise without God's permission. This seems at first sight absurd, for God seems to contend with himself when he gives license to Satan to pervert sound doctrine: and if this happens by God's authority, it seems perfectly contradictory to itself. But let us always remember this, that God's judgments are not without reason called a profound abyss (Ps. xxxvi. 6), that when we see rebellious men acting as they do in these times, we should not wish to comprehend what far surpasses even the sense of angels. Soberly, therefore, and reverendly must we judge of God's works, and especially of his secret counsels. But with the aid of reverence and modesty, it will be easy to reconcile these two things—that God begets, and cherishes, and defends his Church, and confirms the teaching of his prophets, all the while that he permits it to be torn and distracted by intestine broils. Why so? He acts thus that he may punish the wickedness of men as often as he pleases when he sees them abuse his goodness and indulgence. When God lights up the flame of his doctrine, this is the sign of his inestimable pity; when he suffers the Church to be disturbed, and men to be in some degree dissipated, this is to be imputed to the wickedness of men. Whatever be the explanation, he pronounces *that he deceived the false prophets,* because Satan could not utter a single word unless he were permitted, and not only so, but even ordered; while God exercises his wrath against the wicked.

In another sense Jeremiah says that he was deceived (chap. xx. 7). I am deceived, but thou Jehovah hast deceived me: for there he speaks ironically. For when ungodly men boasted that so many of his prophecies were delusive, and derided him as a foolish and misguided man, he says, If I am deceived, thou, O Lord, hast deceived me. We see, then, that by false irony he reproves the petulance of those who despised his prophecies; and finally, he shows that God was the author of his teaching. But in this place God pronounces without a figure that he deceived the false prophets. If any one now objects, that nothing is more remote from God's nature than to deceive, the answer is at hand. Although the metaphor is rather rough, yet we know that God transfers to himself by a figure of speech what properly does not belong to him. He is said to laugh at the impious; but we know that it is not agreeable to his nature to ridicule, to laugh, to see, and to sleep. (Ps. ii. 4; xxxvii. 13.) And so in this place, I confess, there is an improper form of speaking; but the sense is not doubtful—that all impostures are scattered abroad by God—since Satan, as I have said, can never utter the slightest word unless commanded by God. But the kind of deceit which will solve this difficulty for us is described in the sacred history. For when Ahab had a great crowd of false prophets, Micaiah alone stood firm, and faithfully discharged his duty to God: when brought before king Ahab, he immediately blows away their boastings— Behold! all my prophets predict victory: he answers—I saw God sitting on his throne; and when all the armies of heaven were collected before him, God inquired, Who shall deceive Ahab? And a spirit offered himself, namely, a devil, and said, I will deceive him, because I will be a lying spirit in the mouth of all his prophets. God answers, Depart, and thus it shall be. (1 Kings xxii.; 2 Chron. xviii.) Afterwards it follows, Therefore the Lord put a lie in the mouth of all those prophets. Here he distinctly shows us the manner in which God maddens the false prophets, and deceives them, namely, since he sends forth Satan to fill them with his lies. Since, then, they are impelled by Satan, the father of lies, what can they do but lie and deceive? The whole of this, then, depends on the just judgments of God, as this place teaches. God, therefore, does not deceive, so to speak, without an agency, but uses Satan and impostors as organs of his vengeance. If any one flies to that subtle distinction between ordering and permitting, he is easily refuted by the context. For that cannot be called mere permission when God willingly seeks for some one to deceive Ahab, and then he himself orders Satan to go forth and do so. But the last clause which I have quoted takes away all doubt, since God put a lie in the mouth of the prophets, that is, suggested a lie to all the false prophets. If God suggests, we shall see that Satan flies forth not only by his permission to scatter his impostures; but since God wished to use his aid, so he afforded it on this condition and to this end. But we shall leave the rest for the next lecture.

PRAYER.

Grant, Almighty God, since we are so prone to error, that thy truth may always shine upon us amidst the darkness of this world: Grant, also, that we may gaze upon it with open eyes, and subject ourselves to thee with true docility, so that being governed by both thy Word and thy Spirit, we may fulfil our course, and at length arrive at that happy rest, which thine only begotten Son has prepared for us.—Amen.

Lecture Thirty-Ninth.

WE saw in the last lecture with what intention God permits so much license to the false prophets to deceive the people. For men would desire to throw the fault of their errors on God, if he did not meet their rashness. But God has pronounced in this place, that his judgment is just, since the exiles as well as the Jews remaining in the city were equally blind. Hence we must understand that there was no cause for excuse when God's hand was against an impious and wicked people. He now adds, that he would be an avenger in destroying the false prophets from the midst of the people. This seems at first sight not to be in accordance with justice, that God should impel and precipitate men into error, and then exact punishment of them: and as I have said, men think themselves free from blame, if God blinds them, casts them into a reprobate state of mind, and even hurries them into impious desires. But I have already remarked that those act erroneously who estimate God's judgment by their own notions. For how small is the measure of our intelligence: for God's judgments are a profound abyss. (Ps. xxxvi. 6.) Nothing therefore remains, except waiting for that day in which we shall see face to face the things which we now behold darkly and obscurely, as Paul says. (1 Cor. xiii. 12.) Whatever may be the sense, God does rightly in deceiving the false prophets by way of punishing an impious people; and when he summons the false prophets to judgment, that also is free from blame. But if men are restive through their own rashness and audacity, God will free himself from all their calumnies. Wherefore let us diligently mark this passage where God pronounces that he is the deceiver; because however Satan may plot by his lies to abolish the truth, yet he can accomplish nothing unless God permit him, as we have already explained at full length. But when false prophets are dragged to punishment, they have no cause of expostulation with God: and they profit nothing by their complaints, since their own consciences condemn them. They cannot object that they were compelled or drawn violently aside by God, since of their own accord and by their own efforts they endeavoured to deliver wretched men to destruction by their lies. Since this is the case, God justly extends his hands to punish them, as he now says. But let us proceed to the next verse.

10. And they shall bear the punishment of their iniquity: the punishment of the prophet shall be even as the punishment of him that seeketh *unto him*.	10. Et ferent iniquitatem suam, sicut iniquitas sciscitantis sic iniquitas Prophetæ erit.

Here what Ezekiel had partially touched upon is more clearly taught. For he had said, that at length false prophets should meet with punishment, but he now joins the whole people with them, and at the same time repels the empty pretences by which men are always willing to conceal their fault. For when he mentions their iniquity by name, it is the same as forbidding them to turn their back any more. In this way, then, God removes all the cavils to which men usually resort, since they never pursue these tortuous paths without being conscious of their iniquity. For when God says that he is a searcher of hearts, he brings openly before us the secret feelings of mankind. As long as hypocrites have to deal with men, they easily delude them: and then they put on various disguises, by which they throw off the blame from themselves. But when God addresses them, his language necessarily penetrates to their hidden thoughts. Now therefore we understand the force of the words which God uses, *they shall bear their iniquity.*

He now adds, *the iniquity of the enquirer shall be like that of the prophet.* We have said that the sacred name of prophet is improperly transferred to impostors: but God often speaks thus by concession, and in this way a stumblingblock occurs by which the weak are disturbed. For when they hear that deceivers, who not only obscure God's word but pervert it, proudly boast in their title, they are moved, and not without reason. For divine things ought seriously to move us to reverence, since prophets are organs of the Holy Spirit. Hence that man is worthy of such honour that no man ought to despise one who is reckoned a prophet. But because God tries his own people and blinds the reprobate, as we have said, when he sends them false prophets, in order that the faith of the pious should not faint when they hear that sacred name profaned, he says by concession—well, they shall be called prophets—but he does not mean that those shall be truly and really esteemed such who falsely claim to themselves that glory. Now let us come to the next clause, *the iniquity of the enquirer shall be like that of the prophet.* We have already spoken of the iniquity of those who, being led captive by the lies of Satan, endeavour to pervert both the worship and the pure doctrine of God. Since therefore they propose to contend with God, their iniquity is by no means excusable. But another question may arise concerning the people, which, although we have solved it before, yet it may be expedient to repeat it. He says, then, that those who had been deceived by the false prophets would be subject to punishment, that they may sustain the same penalty. This seems hard, as I have said: but the Prophet had previously taught that the people would be justly involved in the same punishment with the impostors, because they erred knowingly and willingly. For if they had cordially devoted themselves to God, and had suffered themselves to be ruled by his Spirit, and by the teaching of the law, they had doubtless been freed from all error. For God takes care of his own people, though he does not defend them from the insults of the ungodly, yet he fortifies them by the foresight and fortitude of his Spirit. Those who are deceived, receive the just reward of either their sloth or pride or ingratitude. For many scarcely deigned to inquire what the will of God was: others looked down as from an eminence on whatever was uttered in God's name: for through self-confidence they receive with difficulty any instruction but their own. Since then they were so unteachable, they are worthy of the reward which I have mentioned. Others again are ungrateful to God: for they stifle his instructions and the knowledge of heavenly things, and contaminate and pollute what is sacred; so that God justly joins the disciples with their masters when he revenges sacrilege as we see, since all sacred teaching is overthrown.

But Ezekiel expresses more when he says, *that the people had enquired.* For they had counsellors, who thereby gave a direct approbation to their employment. If they had been teachable they would not have betaken themselves so eagerly to the false prophets: hence the greater their diligence in this direction, the more their crime was apparent, since they purposely rejected God and his servants, by transferring themselves to the false prophets. We now understand the meaning of this sentence. It only remains that each of us should apply what is here said to his own profit. The Papists think themselves to be twice or thrice absolved if they have been deceived in any quarter. But, on the other hand, Christ exclaims—If the blind lead the blind, it is not surprising if both fall into the ditch. (Matt. xv. 14.) The reason is here expressed, because however those who are deceived show their simplicity, it is by no means doubtful that they flee from the light and desire the darkness by a crooked and perverse craving. Hence it happens *that the iniquity of the enquirer is like that of the prophet.*

11. That the house of Israel may go no more astray from me, neither

11. Ut non errent amplius domus Israel à me,[1] et non polluantur am-

[1] Verbally, " from after me."—*Calvin.*

be polluted any more with all their transgressions; but that they may be my people, and I may be their God, saith the Lord God.	plius in cunctis sceleribus suis: ut sint mihi in populum, et ego sim illis in Deum, dicit Dominator Iehovah.

Here God shows that there was no other remedy, if he would recall to safety those who had almost perished, and at the same time he teaches that it is useful to the Church to chastise those who had so impiously declined from himself. Meanwhile it happens that God thunders, and exercises his judgments even to the extreme of rigour: meanwhile men do not repent but remain obstinate: nay, the punishment which God inflicts upon the reprobate sinks them into deeper destruction. How so? Those who harden themselves against the hand of God heap upon themselves severer punishments, since the reprobate do not submit to the yoke when God wishes to correct their hardness and obstinacy. But here God announces that he will not be so severe as not to consult for their safety. But this contradiction might disturb many, since God destined the people as well as the false prophets to destruction, for this seems to render his covenant vain. But he prevents this question, and says, since he should exact such severe penalties from the despisers of his word and from apostates, that rigour would be useful to the Church. Now we understand the meaning of the saying, *the house of Israel shall not err any more:* since otherwise their obstinacy was incurable: and unless God had seriously roused them up, they had never been brought back into the way of their own accord. Here therefore God obliquely rebukes the hardness of his people, because they could not be instructed except by punishment. For incorrigible indeed are those sons who, while their father cherishes and indulges them, despise him, and become worse by the indulgence. Of this then God now complains, that the children of Israel were so untractable that they could not bear instruction, unless he descended to the utmost rigour. For it was a very sad spectacle, that God's truth should be corrupted and adulterated by lies, and that the people, with those who imposed upon them, should utterly perish. But we now hear that there was but one remedy since the children of Israel were untameable, unless they were completely broken down. He now adds, *from me:* a phrase worthy of notice, for we here gather, that as soon as we bend ever so little from following God, we wander after errors: for we shall never hold on in the right way unless we follow God, that is, unless we are intent upon the end which he sets before us: and then unless our eyes are turned in the direction that he points out, lest we bend to either the right hand or the left. Thus we shall be beyond any danger of wandering if we follow God: on the other hand, if our minds turn to either this side or that, and we are not retained in obedience to God alone, the Prophet teaches that we wander in error, and that this will at length turn out unhappily for us. When he speaks of the house of Israel, he does not embrace without exception those who spring from Jacob; for both the false prophets and those who consulted them were of Jacob's line, and had a name in that family. But we have already seen what was decreed concerning them, namely, that God would destroy them and blot them out from the midst of his people. We see then that they are not comprehended under the offspring of Abraham or the house of Israel; but this is restricted to the remnant of the people whom God wished to spare. For we know that there was always some seed left, that the covenant which had been made with Abraham might be firm and sacred. This sentence then properly refers to the elect, who are called by Paul the remnant of grace. (Rom. xi. 5.) But God says that the example would be useful to the survivors, since the punishment of others would instruct them: and when they should see the false prophets perish, and should acknowledge God's remarkable judgment in their destruction, then they would profit by it. Now we understand what the Prophet means by the destruction of the false prophets and of those hypocrites who despised the true prophets, and prostituted themselves to be deceived by impostors: when God makes them an example of his wrath, the Prophet says that the house of Israel should receive advantage from their perishing, and profit by their utter ruin.

Now he adds, *And that they should not be polluted any more in all their wickedness.* Here he purposely enlarges on their crime, that he may the more magnify the mercy of God; for if they had been only moderately guilty, his pardoning them had not been so remarkable. But the Prophet here pronounces them abandoned in sin, and does not condemn them for one sin but for many: he says *they were polluted* and *contaminated in their crimes:* and when God's mercy is extended to such as these, we discover with certainty how inestimable it is. Finally, let us learn from this passage, that God not only pardons men who transgress but lightly through want of thought and error, but that he is also merciful to the abandoned who are convicted of many iniquities. He says, *that they may be my people and I may be their God.* God had already adopted the whole seed of Abraham, and all were circumcised to a man: and thus they bore personally the testimony and covenant of God's paternal favour. Since, therefore, they were already God's people, and were considered as members of the Church, what can it mean *that they shall be my people?* For God seems here to promise them something new. But by this form of speech the Prophet marks their declension and manifests their deserts. For although God had thought them worthy of such honour as to reckon them among his elect people, yet they had cast themselves out by their own depravity. For since all religion among them was corrupt, God's worship was profaned, his whole law almost buried, and they were separated as far as possible from God, as we shall afterwards see. On the part of God the adoption remained firm: but here Ezekiel regards their condition if they would really look at it themselves, namely, as one of estrangement, since their own wickedness had cut them off: hence he speaks as of a new benefit when he says, *they should be for a people* when they repented.

The second chapter of Hosea will help us to understand this more clearly, when it is said, " I will call them my people who are not my people, and her beloved who is not beloved." (Ver. 23.) For the Prophet was commanded to go into an improper house and to take an impure female and to beget sons: he says that a son was born to whom God gave the name לאעמי, *la-gnemi,* it shall not be my people: and then when a daughter was born, she was unworthy of love. There Hosea signifies that the Jews were cut off from the sacred root, and he speaks not of one or two, but of the whole race; for they were neither God's people nor a beloved daughter. Afterwards when reconciled, they begin again to be God's people and a beloved daughter. Paul does not accommodate that sentence to the calling of the Gentiles rashly, (Rom. ix. 25,) namely, that there was no difference between Jews and Gentiles, since the former were rejected. Whatever it is, we see that those who had a place and a name among God's people, and whom he had chosen for himself, were cast off and had become strangers through their own fault. Thus they begin to be God's people afresh when they repent and God receives them to favour. The conclusion is, I will restore them afresh, that my covenant may be renewed in some way, *that they may be my people* as they formerly were; *and I may be to them a God*, since by their own backsliding they deserved to be treated as entire strangers. Besides, it is well to remember what we said elsewhere, that under these words is contained whatever belongs to solid happiness. For if God acknowledges us as his people, we are certain of our salvation, as when he pronounces that he will be our God while we call upon him as a father. But whoever shall call upon the name of the Lord shall be saved. (Joel ii. 32; Acts ii. 21; Rom. x. 13.) Then we must remember that celebrated sentence of the Prophet Habakkuk, Thou art our God: we shall not die. (Chap. i. 12.) Lastly, we have nothing else to wish for towards the fulness of all good things and confidence in eternal life, than that God should reckon us among his people, so that there may be open to us a free access to him in prayer. It follows—

| 12. The word of the Lord came again to me, saying, | 12. Et fuit sermo Iehovæ ad me, dicendo. |
| 13. Son of man, when the land sinneth against me by trespassing grievously, then will I stretch out mine hand upon it, and will break the staff of the bread thereof, and will send famine upon it, and will cut off man and beast from it: | 13. Fili hominis terra cum scelerate egerit erga me,[1] et extendero manum meam super eam, et confregero in ipsa baculum panis, et immisero in ipsam famem, et excidero ex ipsa hominem et jumentum. |

[1] " By prevaricating prevarication," according to some, מעל, *megnel*, properly signifies perfidy, hence the version just given.—*Calvin*.

The next verse ought to be joined: for some interpreters altogether pervert the Prophet's sense by finishing the sentence there, as if he had said, I will extend my hand over it, &c. But the sentence is dependent, as we shall see—

14. Though these three men, Noah, Daniel, and Job, were in it, they should deliver *but* their own souls by their righteousness, saith the Lord God.

14. Et fuerint tres viri isti in medio ejus, Noe, Daniel, et Job, ipsi in justitia sua eripient[1] animas suas, dicit Dominator Iehovah.

Here again God threatens the people of Israel with final destruction: but the words seem opposed, that God would be merciful and propitious to his people, and yet that no hope of pardon would be left. But we must remember the principle, that the prophets sometimes directed their discourse to the body of the people which was utterly devoted to destruction, since its wickedness was desperate; yet afterwards they moderated that rigour, when they turned to the remainder, which is the seed of the Church in the world, that God's covenant should not be extinguished, as we have already said. Hence, when we meet with this kind of contradiction, we know that God affords no hope to the reprobate, since he has decreed their destruction: so that language ought to be transferred to the body of the people which was already alienated, and like a putrid carcase. But when God mingles and intersperses any testimony of his favour, we may know that the Church is intended, and that he wishes a seed to remain, lest the whole Church should perish, and his covenant be abolished at the same time. The Prophet, therefore, as before, so also now, sets before himself the people desperate in wickedness, and says that they had no right to hope that God would act mercifully as usual, since necessity compelled him to put his hand for the last time to the destruction of the impious. This is the full meaning. We had a similar passage in Jeremiah (xv. 1), where he said, If Moses and Samuel had stood before me, my mind is not towards this people; that is, it never could be that I should return to favour them, even if Moses and Samuel should intercede for them, and endeavour to obtain pardon by their own intercession. The papists foolishly distort this passage

[1] Or, "shall free."—*Calvin.*

to prove that the dead intercede for us, for Moses and Samuel had been dead some time; but God says, Even if they should pray for the people, their prayers would be in vain. But this passage refutes that gross ignorance: for God is not here making a difference between the living and the dead; but it is a kind of personification, and of bringing back Moses and Samuel from the grave; as if he had said, Were they living at this time, and entreating for these wicked ones, I would never listen to them: for Ezekiel here mentions three, Noah, Job, and Daniel. But Daniel was then alive: he had been dragged into exile, and lived to a mature old age, as is well known. Then he expresses his meaning more clearly, by saying, *if they had been in the midst of the city they had escaped in safety themselves*, but they would not have prevailed for others. The whole meaning is, that God cuts off all hope of mercy from the abandoned people.

We must remark the form of speech which is used: he relates four kinds of punishments by which men's crimes are usually avenged, and enumerates them distinctly. *If I shall break the staff of bread*, says he, *because the land has revolted from me, and I shall send famine upon it, Daniel, Job, and Noah, shall preserve their own souls, but shall not profit others* by their holiness: then he adds, *if I shall send a sword*, that is, if I shall follow up the impious by wars, *even Daniel, and Job, and Noah, shall save their own souls, but they shall not intercede for others.* He pronounces the same of pestilence and wild beasts. At length he reasons from less to greater. When I shall have punished any nation, says he, with famine, pestilence, and the sword, and wild beasts, how much less shall Daniel, Job, and Noah, prevail with me by their intercession? But God had condemned the house of Israel to all punishments, just as if he had poured all his curses like a deluge to destroy them. Hence he concludes that there is no reason for cherishing any hope of escape from these imminent dangers. Now then we comprehend the Prophet's meaning.

Now let us come to the first kind of punishment. *If the land*, says he, *acts wickedly against me*, or conducts itself wickedly, חטא, *cheta,* to act wickedly, *but by prevaricating with prevarication.* By these words the crime of perfidy is distinguished from error, because men often fall away and depart far from God through ignorance of the way which they ought to pursue. But here the Prophet condemns the people's defection through perfidy, as if he had said that they purposely, and by deliberate malice, were estranged from God, since they had been correctly taught how God ought to be worshipped. Although the Prophet speaks generally, yet he wished to shew God's wrath to be of no ordinary kind: for God will often chastise men's sins by either pestilence, or sword, or famine, and yet will not be implacable. But he here speaks of a desperate people, and one already addicted to eternal destruction. He says, therefore, *by prevaricating with prevarication;* that is, by deceiving my confidence by open and gross perfidy.

Again, *and I will stretch forth my hand upon it, and will break the staff of bread, and will send famine upon it, and will cut off from it man and beast.* Here, as I have mentioned, he touches upon only one kind of punishment; for God is accustomed to take vengeance on men in four ways; and the prophets, as you have often heard, usually adopt the form of speech used by Moses. These four curses of God are everywhere related in the law,—war, famine, pestilence, and the assault and savageness of wild beasts. Now the Prophet begins with hunger; but he points out the kind of hunger—*if God has broken the staff of bread.* For sometimes, when he does not reduce men to poverty, yet he puffs up the bread, so that those who think to use it as nourishment do not gather any vigour from it. But the Prophet properly means it in this second sense, as we see in chapters iv. and v. The metaphor is in accordance with the word staff: for as the lame cannot walk unless they lean on a staff—and tremulous old men need a similar support—so by degrees men's strength vanishes, unless new vigour is replaced by meat and drink. Bread is, therefore, like a staff which restores our strength when want has weakened it.

We now come to the word *breaking.* How does God break the staff of bread? By withdrawing the nourishment which he had infused into it; for the virtue which we perceive in bread is not intrinsic: I mean this—that bread is not naturally endued with the virtue of continuing and inspiring life within men; and why? Bread has no life in it: how then can any one derive life from it? But the teaching of the law has been marked: that man lives not by bread only, but by every word proceeding from God's mouth. (Deut. viii. 3.) Here Moses intends, that even if God has inserted the virtue of nourishment in bread, yet this is not to be so attributed to it as if it were inherent in it. What follows then? That as God breathes a secret virtue into the bread, it sustains and refreshes us, and becomes our aliment. On the other hand, God says that he breaks the virtue of the bread when he withdraws from it that virtue: because, as I have already said, when we taste bread, our minds ought to rise immediately to God, since men, if they cram themselves a thousand times, yet will not feel their life to be deposited in the bread. Therefore, unless God breathes into bread the virtue of nourishment, the bread is useless; it may fill us up, but without any profit. Now, then, we understand the meaning of this sentence, about which we shall have something more to say.

PRAYER.

Grant, Almighty God, since thou shinest so clearly upon us with the teaching of thy Gospel, in which thy Son reveals himself familiarly to us,—Grant that we may not shut our eyes to this light, or turn them hither and thither by depraved curiosity, but may remain in simple obedience, until at length having passed through the course of this life, we may arrive at the fulness of light, when thou wilt transform us into thy glory by the same— thine only-begotten Son.—Amen.

Lecture Fortieth.

I HAVE already partially explained the Prophet's design, when he says, *if God has sent famine upon a land, and Job, Noah, and Daniel were in it,* that they indeed should be safe, but that the land should perish, since he had determined to destroy it. Moreover, he described the kind of famine, when he said, *when I shall have broken the staff of bread;*

because, though wheat should be plentiful, and men be prevented from starving, yet they would not be refreshed, since the bread would only burden them. On the whole, God means that famine, even if it arise from natural causes, proceeds from his judgments: for by continual rains the seed rots in the ground, and drought consumes all its juice and substance. Then, if hail devastates the sown fields, the causes of the ensuing famine are manifest. But it is necessary to look higher, because, as we are nourished by God's bounty, so we never suffer poverty unless when he withdraws his hand.

Let us now come to the next verse. *If these three men, the most just of all, had been in the land, they should only free their own souls.* The exclusive particle is not expressed, but it is easy to gather the Prophet's sense from the context; as if he had said that God's decree was fixed when he had determined to afflict the land grievously. It is sometimes asked why Noah, Daniel, and Job are named, rather than Abraham, Jacob, or David, or any others. Those who wish to be precise guess various comments; namely, because Noah could not preserve the old world from the deluge, but only his sons and their wives. But this example does not suit: and as to the others, they say that Job did not preserve his own sons, since they were all consumed by the lightning. But the same thing happened to others. Thus Abraham was the common father of the people, and even he could not snatch his posterity from the wrath of God: nay, Jeremiah describes Rachel, though dead, weeping for her children, and refusing consolation because none of them survived. (ch. xxxi. 15.) We see, then, that this is cold. Others say that these three men had experienced three different kinds of life; that Noah, living before the deluge, had seen the horrible devastation of the whole earth, and yet the renovation of the world had followed: they say, also, that Job had flourished in prosperity, and then was deprived of all his goods and his children, and was so defiled by disease and filth as to be rather a carcase than a living man, and yet was restored like a captive from the enemy's hand. Daniel, again, had lived at Jerusalem, had been taken captive, and had lived there in exile ; that he at length saw the beginning of the restoration of the people when that sudden change happened, and the Babylonian monarchy passed to the Persians. These things, at the first glance, seem to be clever ; but whatever is affected is always cold and tame. Ezekiel here mentions these three men, simply because they first occurred to him. For we must remember that passage of Jeremiah which I quoted yesterday, (ch. xv. 1,) where it is said, If Moses and Samuel had stood before me, I should not have listened to them for the safety of the people. A question may arise, why Jeremiah names Moses and Samuel rather than any others ? What will these clever speculators say ? We see, therefore, that each of these things must not be so scrupulously beaten out, since it is enough to understand the general intention of the Holy Spirit. Three men, then, are placed here, whose holiness was celebrated. Daniel was then living : the others had been dead many ages ago ; but the integrity of them all was universally manifest. It is then as if he had said, even if those should come who either are or have been most perfect among men, yet they would avail nothing in interceding for a land already devoted to destruction.

But the Prophet's saying, *they should be saved on account of their own righteousness,* seems absurd : for no one can be found whose righteousness can stand before God's tribunal: for if God was to reason with men, every one must be found guilty, as the Scripture also often teaches, and experience most fully convinces us. Here the Prophet seems to extol too much the merit of works, when he attributes the person's freedom to his righteousness. But the solution is easy ; namely, this righteousness of which mention is made ought not to be separated from gratuitous pardon, which reconciles men to God, so that their sins are not imputed to them : for as to some saying that they were justified by faith, this does not forward the inquiry ; and besides that, it is forced. By their own righteousness shall they free their own souls, that is, say they, by their faith. But when God addresses Noah himself, (Gen. vii. 1,) and says that he was found just through his piety, he does not mean that he was endued with faith; this would be nugatory. There is no doubt, then, that he commends sanctity and integrity in his servant; so also in this passage, under the word *righteousness* or justice, he implies the fear of God, in which all virtues are founded, and chastity and temperance, and whatever belongs to the rule of living holily and justly. But meanwhile this derogates nothing from the righteousness of faith; for the faithful are reckoned just before God, and their works are also reckoned just—not by any inherent merit—not because they bring any perfection of that kind before God which may conciliate his favour, and in which they can stand; but because God pardons them indulgently through his own paternal clemency, and so approves their righteousness, which otherwise might be deservedly rejected. For example, Phinehas was thought just when he avenged the reproach of the sanctuary. (Numbers xxv. 7, 8.) When inflamed with zeal, Phinehas brought out of the midst the courtezan with her paramour; for this cause, as is said in the psalm, (cvi. 31,) he was reckoned just. But that could not suffice for a man's righteousness, since one special act could not render a man just. Phinehas, then, could not be reckoned just on that ground; but while his work was pleasing to God, for that reason it was just. But, on a serious inquiry, that work was also condemned as being infected with some fault, and so was not just in itself. But because God pardons his sons, as we have said, hence he accepts their works: so he acknowledges them also as just, and they do not obtain this by either their own worthiness or peculiar merits. For the beginning of the righteousness about which we are now speaking is a gratuitous reconciliation by which all the faults of the faithful are buried: whence it happens also that their integrity, although not perfect, is still pleasing to God. We see, therefore, that these things are easily reconciled; that men are freed by their righteousness, and yet that their temporal safety depends only on the mere pity of God: for when God's gratuitous favour has gone before, hence he seems to acknowledge as true righteousness what was in itself mutilated and but half complete. Now it follows—

15. If I cause noisome beasts to pass through the land, and they spoil it, so that it be desolate, that no man may pass through because of the beasts:

16. *Though* these three men *were* in it, *as* I live, saith the Lord God, they shall deliver neither sons nor daughters; they only shall be delivered, but the land shall be desolate.

15. Si bestiam malam transire fecero per terram, et orbaverit eam, et fuerit vastitas ut nemo transeat propter bestiam.[1]

16. Tres viri isti in medio ejus, vivo ego, dicit Dominator Iehovah, si filios et filias liberabunt: ipsi soli liberabuntur, et terra erit in vastitatem.

Now he mentions the second kind of punishment. For we said that God's four scourges were here brought before us, which are more familiarly known to men through frequent use. They are hunger and wild beasts, war and pestilence. The Prophet has spoken of famine; he now comes down to wild beasts. This kind of scourge is rarely used in Scripture; for God more frequently mentions the sword, pestilence, and famine; but when he distinctly treats, of his scourges, he adds also savage beasts. Now therefore he says, *if he had sent wild beasts to lay waste the land, and Noah, Job, and Daniel, had been in that land, they would be free from the common slaughter, but that their righteousness would not profit others.* He expresses a little more clearly what he had spoken briefly and obscurely when he treated of the famine. *If*, says he, *I shall cause an evil beast to pass through and injure the land, so as to lay it waste, that no one may pass through on account of the wild beasts, as I live*, says he, *if these three men shall free their sons and their daughters.* This passage teaches what I lately touched upon about the famine, namely, that the beasts did not break in by chance to attack and rage against men, but that they are sent by God. Thus God follows out his judgments no less by means of lions, and bears, and tigers, than by rain and drought, the sword and the pestilence: and surely this may be understood, if we reflect upon the great savageness of these beasts; first, when hunger arouses them they are carried along by a ravenous impulse; and then, without the compulsion of necessity, they are hostile to the human race, and without doubt they would urge themselves on to tear to pieces all whom they met with, unless restrained by God's secret instinct. If, therefore, God restrains the

---

[1] That is. "beasts." for there is a change of number.—*Calvin.*

wild beasts, thus also he sends them forth as often as it pleases him, to exercise their ferocity against mankind, and in this way to become his scourges. But here an oath is interposed that God may inspire confidence in his sentence; so God swears by his own life. This is the meaning of the phrase *as I live;* that is, I swear by my life. This is indeed spoken improperly, but elsewhere we have seen that God swears by his life; that is, just as if he swore by himself, because he has no greater by whom he can swear, as the Apostle says (Heb. vi. 13); and as often as we swear by the name of God we attribute the supreme power to him, and thus we profess our life to be in his hand, and he to be our only Judge. When, therefore, he swears by himself, he admonishes us at the same time that his name is profaned if we swear by any others: then he shows how much religion is to be exhibited in oaths. Let us follow, therefore, God's example, when our speech needs confirmation, by calling in a witness and judge: next, that we should not use his name rashly and falsely, but that our oath should be truly a testimony to our piety. But here in truth a question arises,— How God can say that the land should perish which has been once subjected to wild beasts? For sometimes wild beasts have infected many regions, and God has immediately restrained them, and so their cruelty has passed away like a storm.

Again, we know that the prayer of the saints are not superfluous when they pray for others; but God seems here to deny what is clearly manifest. But the solution is easy. For since he does not inflict his judgments equably but variably, and at one time hastens punishments and at another suspends them : at one time punishes men's sins and at another delays doing so, he fixes for himself no sure law by which he is always bound, but he speaks of the land which he has destined to destruction. God therefore will strike one region with famine, another with war, a third with pestilence, a fourth with wild beasts, and yet he can mitigate his own rigour, and when men begin to be terrified, he can withdraw his hand. But if it has been once decreed that any land must perish, all the saints would run together in vain, because no one would be a fit intercessor to abolish that inviolable decree. We now understand the Prophet's intention, for he does not speak generally of any lands whatever, but he points out the very land which was devoted to final destruction. It follows—

17. Or *if* I bring a sword upon that land, and say, Sword, go through the land; so that I cut off man and beast from it:	17. Vel gladium transire fecero super terram illam, et dixero gladio, Transi per terram, ut excidatur ex ea homo et jumentum.
18. Though these three men *were* in it, *as* I live, saith the Lord God, they shall deliver neither sons nor daughters, but they only shall be delivered themselves.	18. Et tres viri isti in medio ejus, vivo ego, dicit Dominator Iehovah, non liberabunt filios et filias, quia ipsi soli liberabuntur.

The Prophet now descends to the third kind of punishment. Hence God says, *if he send a sword upon a land, he cannot be entreated so as not to consume it utterly*, neither will he admit any man's intercession, although the most holy dwell there, namely, Job, Noah, and Daniel. But the phrase used must be marked: *if I shall say to the sword, pass through to exterminate and blot out the whole land,* or cut off from it, *both man and beast*, because we here gather the great power of God's secret government. For we think that wars are stirred up at random: and as men are in agitation, so also we imagine war to be nothing but confusion and turbulence. But God governs even wars by his inestimable wisdom, and also men and their swords: men are enraged, their swords fly about in their hands, and they seem to go hither and thither at random by blind impulse. But God here announces that he permits swords to pass through a land, and to destroy both men and cattle. If he had said, after the language used in many places, that he would arm men, it would not have been very wonderful: for everywhere throughout the Prophets he calls the Chaldeans and Assyrians executors of his judgment. Hence that sentence of Jeremiah, Cursed is he who has done God's work negligently. (Jer. xlviii. 10.) But that work of God was the slaughter at Jerusalem. So also Nebuchadnezzar is called God's servant and minister when he laid waste Egypt, and God promises him the reward of his labour. (Ezek. xxix. 20.) So here Ezekiel proceeds further, not only that the hands of men are directed as God wishes, but also that their swords listen to his secret command, so that they neither pass by nor strike any man or animal except as far as God pleases. But if God so commands the swords, let us know that whenever men rise up against us, that our patience is exercised and our sins chastised in this way: and that the impious are God's agents: and let us determine that we shall never profit by noise and resistance, since there is but one remedy, to humble ourselves under God's strong hand. Now the fourth kind of punishment follows—

19. Or *if* I send a pestilence into that land, and pour out my fury upon it in blood, to cut off from it man and beast:

20. Though Noah, Daniel, and Job, *were* in it, *as* I live, saith the Lord God, they shall deliver neither son nor daughter; they shall *but* deliver their own souls by their righteousness.

19. Vel pestem immisero in terram illam, et effudero iracundiam meam super ipsam in sanguine ad perdendum[1] ex ea hominem et jumentum.

20. Et Noe, Daniel, et Job in medio ejus, vivo ego, dicit Dominator Iehovah, si filium et filiam liberaverint: ipsi in justitia sua liberabunt animam suam.

He now affirms of the fourth kind of punishment, what he has hitherto pronounced of the rest. He says, then, If I shall have sent a pestilence, and have devoted a land to devastation, that Job, Daniel, and Noah, should be safe if they dwelt there: but that their righteousness should not profit even their sons and their daughters. Nay, he seems to speak with greater restriction, since he has substituted the singular number for the plural: for he had just said, they shall not free either sons or daughters: he now says, *not even a son or a daughter*, that is, they shall not prevail with me by their intercession so much as to save from death even a single son or daughter. We must also remember what I have said, that God does not always act in the way related here: for he has manifold and various methods of carrying out his judgments. Hence it would not be just to impose a law not to liberate any one, and according to his own will either to hear or reject their prayers. But here he only means, that when he has determined to destroy a land, there is no hope of pardon, since even the most holy will not per-

---

[1] Or, " to cut off."—*Calvin.*

suade him to desist from his wrath and vengeance. But now the conclusion follows—

21. For thus saith the Lord God, How much more when I send my four sore judgments upon Jerusalem, the sword, and the famine, and the noisome beast, and the pestilence, to cut off from it man and beast?

22. Yet, behold, therein shall be left a remnant that shall be brought forth, *both* sons and daughters; behold, they shall come forth unto you, and ye shall see their way and their doings: and ye shall be comforted concerning the evil that I have brought upon Jerusalem, *even* concerning all that I have brought upon it.

21. Quoniam sic dicit Dominator Iehovah, Quanto magis cum quatuor judicia mea mala, gladium, et famem, et bestiam malam, et pestem immisero contra Hierusalem ad excidendum ex ea hominem et animal?

22. Et ecce evasio in ea residua,[1] evasio egredientium, *inquit* nempe filii et filiæ: ipsi egredientur ad vos: et videbitis vias ipsorum, et opera ipsorum: et consolationem sumetis super malo quod venire fecero super Hierusalem, super omni quod venire fecero super eam.

He now reasons, as we said in the beginning, from the less to the greater. Hitherto he has said, If I shall have sent forth only one weapon to take vengeance upon men, no one will oppose my following out my decree: then he enumerated four weapons, one after another. Now he adds, What then, when I shall have heaped together all punishments, and not only shall have sent pestilence or sword or famine, but as it were when I have four armies prepared and drawn up, and shall command them to attack and destroy mankind, how shall even one person escape? If Job, Daniel, and Noah, cannot snatch away even their sons and daughters from a single scourge, how shall they snatch them from four at once! We see, then, that God here cuts away the false and specious hopes by which the false prophets deluded the miserable exiles when they promised them a return to their country, and daily proclaimed how impossible it was that the sacred city, the earthly dwelling-place of God, could be taken by the enemy, and the religion which God had promised should be eternal could perish. Since, therefore, the false prophets so deceived these miserable exiles, here God shows how greatly they erred while they cherished any hope in their minds; because he had

[1] That is, "some remnant which shall escape shall remain in it."— *Calvin.*

not only held one kind of scourge over Jerusalem, but approached it with a whole heap of them to destroy and cut off both man and beast. This then is the full meaning.

Now he says, *If I shall have sent my four evil judgments.* Here God calls *his judgments* evils, in the sense in which he says in Isaiah, that he creates good and evil, (chap. xlv. 7,) since immediately afterwards he expresses his meaning by saying life and death. Hence what is against us is here called evil, and so this epithet ought to be referred to our perceptions. For our natural common sense dictates that whatever is desirable and useful to us is good: food and life and peace are good, and whatever is conducive to life, and what we naturally wish for, we call good. So also, on the other hand, death and famine are evils: so are nakedness, want, and shame: why so? since we dread whatever is not useful to us; and because we fly from evils as soon as reason dawns. In fine, evil here is not opposed to justice and right, but, as I have said, to men's opinion and our natural senses. He now confirms what we before said, namely, that these are God's judgments when enemies rage against us, pestilence attacks us, poverty assails us, and wild beasts break in upon us. When therefore we suffer under these afflictions, let us learn immediately to descend into ourselves and to discover the cause why God is so angry with us. For if we turn our attention towards the sword, and pestilence, and famine, we are like dogs which gnaw and bite what is thrown at them, and do not regard the hand which threw it, but only vent their rage upon the stone. For such is our stupidity when we complain of famine being injurious to us, wild beasts troublesome, and war horrible. Hence this passage should always be borne in mind that these are *God's evil judgments,* that is, scourges by which he chastises our sins, and thus shows himself hostile and opposed to us.

He now adds, *there shall be a remnant in that escape.* They explain this verse parenthetically, as if God by way of correction engaged to act more mercifully towards that city, than if he struck any land with only one scourge. They explain it thus: although these four scourges should meet together, yet I will mitigate the rigour of my vengeance, since some shall go out safely, and reach even to you. Almost all agree in this sense; but when I weigh the Prophet's intention more accurately, I cannot subscribe to it: because God seems to me to confirm what he had said before, that he would be a just avenger of wickedness while he treats the Jews so harshly. To discover the most suitable sense, we must consider the condition of the exiles: it was surely worse than if they had been destroyed by a single death: for they were dying daily; and at length, when cast out of the sacred land, they were like the dead. Hence that exile was more sorrowful than death, since it was better to be buried in the holy land than among the profane. Since, then, they had been mixed with dogs, it was no life to them to protract a wretched existence amidst constant languor; and if the hope of restoration had been taken away, concerning which we are not now treating, and to which not a single syllable applies, exile was by itself like death. Since, then, the Prophet here says, *that some should be left to escape*, he does not mean that they should be safe: hence this is not a mitigation of their punishment. For as we saw before, and especially in Jeremiah, those who died quickly were less to be deplored. (Chap. xxii. 10.) Finally, when the Prophet here says that some should come to Babylon, he does not promise them pardon, as if God was propitious to them, or noticed them favourably; no such thing: for he speaks of the reprobate, and of those who bore on their forehead the manifest sign of their impiety, and show by their whole life that they are abandoned, and most worthy of final destruction.

For he says, *a departure of those who go forth shall come: sons as well as daughters shall come to you*, says he, *and ye shall see their ways and their work*: that is, ye shall see that the men are so wicked, that their ungodliness shall compel you to confess the city to be worthy of perishing, and the people deserving destruction. For the word *consoling*, which the Prophet uses immediately afterwards, refers here to the acknowledgment of their wickedness appeasing the minds of those who formerly roared and murmured against God. Neither does he mean that consolation which, according to the common proverb, has many friends; but only the calm acknowledgment of God's just vengeance, in which the ten tribes acquiesced. For before they saw the state in which the inhabitants of Jerusalem were, they thought that God was too severe, and hence their outcry and complaint against God. The Prophet, therefore, now says, that the sight of your wickedness will bring you consolation; for ye shall see that it could not be otherwise, and that ye deserved such punishment: hence, when ye have acknowledged your abandoned wickedness, ye will regard my justice with peaceful and tranquil minds; and ye will so finish and cease your complaints which now agitate your minds in different directions. The rest to-morrow.

PRAYER.

Grant, Almighty God, since thou daily exercisest thy judgments in all parts of the world, and since many regions are harassed by pestilence and war, that so long as thou sparest us we may profit by the evils and slaughters of others: Grant, also, if thy scourges reach also unto us, that we may not be obstinate, but may submit ourselves to thy judgment, and being truly humble, may we seek pardon by the serious pursuit of piety, so that we may truly acknowledge thee; and may feel thee to be a propitious Father to us, until at length we enjoy thy love in thy heavenly kingdom, through Christ our Lord.—Amen.

Lecture Forty-First.

WE said in yesterday's lecture, when the Lord pronounces that he would have some remnants when destroying Jerusalem, that this is no act of clemency, as if he had relaxed the rigour of his justice. For exile was not preferable to death, as we may collect from the context, since God does not use these words of his elect. For there is no mention of repentance, so that the cause of his vengeance would be conspicuous in their crimes. *Ye shall see,* therefore, *and shall take comfort:* because the exiles who were then in Chaldæa could not subscribe to the judgment of God. But when they saw their brethren of such abandoned morals, the review of their sins availed to their comfort, that is, to appease their minds. He repeats the same in the last verse of the chapter.

23. And they shall comfort you, when ye see their ways and their doings: and ye shall know that I have not done without cause all that I have done in it, saith the Lord God.	23. Et consolabuntur vos, quia videbitis vias ipsorum et opera ipsorum: et scietis quod non frustra fecerim quæcunque feci in ea, dicit Dominator Iehovah.

He now puts the verb for comforting in the third person, but in the same sense, because after the Jews shall have been led captive, they will bear sure and special marks of God's justice against their sins. This, then, is the consolation, as I explained it yesterday, while the exiles acknowledge that cruelty cannot be ascribed to God, as if he had exceeded moderation in exacting punishment; for the desperate wickedness of the people demanded it. But this passage contains a useful doctrine, since we collect from it that we are never tranquil in our minds unless when the greatest equity and justice appears in God's judgments, and become present to our minds. As long, therefore, as we do not acknowledge God to be severe in just cases, our minds must necessarily be disturbed and disarranged: hence the word "consolation" is opposed to those turbulent thoughts. But since nothing is more miserable than to be distracted and drawn hither and thither, and to be anxiously disturbed, let us learn that those profit most who acquiesce in God's judgments, although they do not perceive the reason of them, yet modestly adore them. But when God shows why he treats either us or others so severely, this is a special favour, since he offers us material for joy and tranquillity. Let us proceed.

CHAPTER XV.

1. And the word of the Lord came unto me, saying,	1. Et fuit sermo Iehovæ ad me dicendo,
2. Son of man, What is the vine-tree more than any tree, or *than* a branch which is among the trees of the forest?	2. Fili hominis, quid erit[1] lignum vitis præ omni arbore rami[2] quæ est inter arbores sylvæ?

[1] Or, "what is these."—*Calvin*.	[2] Or, "branching."—*Calvin*.

3. Shall wood be taken thereof to do any work? or will *men* take a pin of it to hang any vessel thereon?

4. Behold, it is cast into the fire for fuel; the fire devoureth both the ends of it, and the midst of it is burned. Is it meet for *any* work?

5. Behold, when it was whole, it was meet for no work: how much less shall it be meet yet for *any* work, when the fire hath devoured it, and it is burned?

3. An sumetur ex eo[1] lignum ad formandum, ut sit opus, vel an sument,[2] ex eo paxillum, ut suspendatur in eo omne vas?[3]

4. Ecce in ignem traditur[4] ad consumptionem, duas extremitates ejus consumpsit ignis, et medium ejus exustum est,[5] an utile erit ad opus?

5. Ecce, cum esset integrum non factum fuit[6] ut esset opus: quanto magis postquam ignis consumpsit ipsum et exaruit[7] formabitur adhuc ut sit opus?

The Prophet's intention is to humble the foolish confidence of the people, who boasted of the gratuitous kindness of God, as if they were naturally excellent: hence, also, their obstinacy against his threats was so great. For when the prophets reproved them sharply, they boasted against them the remarkable gifts by which they were divinely adorned: as if they had been so armed by God's benefits to resist his power, for we know that they were so blinded. Since, then, that disease had attacked the people, it is not surprising that the prophets in many places refute such folly. But the Prophet here uses a simile to show the Jews that they were not intrinsically but only accidentally excellent, since God had treated them as worthy of remarkable benefits. Since it is so, their arrogance is easily refuted, when they oppose their superiority to God, as if it were peculiar to them, and not God's special gift. But we must understand the simile which Ezekiel uses: *what is the vine more than other trees of the woods?* It is certain that the vine produces very good fruit, and therefore is preferred to other trees: the very flower of the vine has a most delicious scent; but the fruit which it produces proves its excellence. For the wood of the vine is without elegance and shapeless: it does not attain to any thickness; it is slender, pliable, and twisted. In looking at a vine, it seems scarcely worth

---

[1] " Namely, wood."—*Calvin.*
[2] Verbally, in taking, that is, if they take.—*Calvin.*
[3] Whatever vessel.—*Calvin.*   [4] Or, "is cast."—*Calvin.*
[5] That is, "after the fire had consumed it."—*Calvin.*
[6] That is, "was not formed or fitted."—*Calvin.*
[7] Or, "was burnt as before."—*Calvin.*

numbering among shrubs: if compared with trees, it clearly has no value; but in the excellency of trees something is easily acknowledged which surpasses all vines. For when we cast our eyes upon a branching tree, we are struck with admiration, while the vine lies at our feet. If, therefore, a tree is compared with the wood of the vine, it will be praised for its beauty, while the vine will be despised as a low and insignificant wood. Hence God collects that the Jews were in no respect more excellent than others, unless because they are planted by himself, as he says in many places in Isaiah, O my vine, I have planted thee. (Chap. v.) Then in the 80th Psalm: He brought his vine out of Egypt, and planted and propagated it even to the sea, (v. 9-12; Jer. ii. 21.)

Now we understand the Prophet's meaning, namely, that the Jews excelled, indeed, in privileges, but not in nature, nor yet by themselves, but by the gratuitous kindness of God: and if other nations were compared with them, they had greater dignity than the Jews. And we know that other nations flourished in arts and wealth, in population, in warlike valour, and in other respects: the profane nations were like lofty trees which grow up and attract all eyes to themselves. But the Jews were like a vine which, being planted by God's hand, deserved more praise than the trees of the wood which were fruitless. Ezekiel now carries on the comparison at greater length: *if the vine is torn up, can its wood*, says he, *be fitted to any use?* it will not make beams or tables, or any vessels; it will not make a peg or a hook on which to hang a hat or cloak, or anything of the kind. Since, then, the wood of the vine is useless when torn from the soil, and is of no use but for burning, hence the Jews are made acquainted with their condition since their excellence and worthiness depend on the mere good pleasure of God: since, as he planted them, he can pluck them up in a moment; and when they have been torn up, they will be altogether useless, and will be cast into the fire, while trees are of some use. But the Prophet proceeds another step: if a bundle of twigs were cast into the fire, and the two extreme parts were burnt up, and the middle made dry, that scorched part would be much less useful. For since fire penetrates to the very marrow, wood, which is half consumed, is reduced to powder by the touch alone. He afterwards accommodates what he had said about the vine to the city of Jerusalem ; therefore let us go on to the rest of the context.

6. Therefore thus saith the Lord God, As the vine-tree among the trees of the forest, which I have given to the fire for fuel, so will I give the inhabitants of Jerusalem.

6. Propterea sic dicit Dominator Iehovah, Quemadmodum lignum vitis in ligno sylvæ, quod posui[1] in ignem ad consumptionem, sic dedi habitatores Hierusalem.

Here the Prophet shows that the citizens of Jerusalem were cast into a fire, by which they suffered various kinds of death : for although they were not immediately and entirely consumed, yet the extremities were burnt off. For the whole region was laid waste all around, and the kingdom of Israel was entirely cut off : Jerusalem remained like the middle portion of the bundle. But the inhabitants of Jerusalem were so worn down by adversity, that they were like a stick burnt at both ends. Since this was so, we here perceive their great stupidity in persisting in contumacy, although God had humbled them so in various ways. Now, therefore, we understand the meaning of this point. But the words of the Prophet must be explained, *what shall be,* or what is *the wood of the vine compared with other wood ?* Some translate, with the palm branch ; others, with the wild vine ; but both of these are foreign to the mind of the Prophet : especially the wild vine cannot have any place here. As far as the palm is concerned, what reference is there to the palm branch in the midst of a wood ? for palms are not planted in woods amidst lofty trees. But since the wood, זמורה, *zemoreh,* signifies boughs as well as palms, it agrees best with the sense to speak of every tree as branching. *What, therefore, is the vine in comparison with every branching tree which is among the trees of the forest ?* Here the Prophet brings before us fruitless trees, but yet those which attract our notice by their beauty : and so he implies, if the Jews wish to compare themselves with the profane nations, they are not superior in any worthiness or elegance

[1] " I have lost."—*Calvin.*

which they have naturally and of themselves. This must be diligently noticed; although God sometimes adopts those who excel in ability and learning, in warlike prowess, in riches, and in power, yet he gathers his Church as much as possible from lowly-born men, in whom no great splendour is refulgent, that they may be objects of wonder to the world. For what end, then, does God do this? for he could fashion his own elect, that they may be completely perfect in every way. But since we are too inclined to pride, it is necessary that our infirmity should always be set before our eyes to teach us modesty. For if nothing in us reminded us of our weakness, our worthiness would blind us, or turn away our eyes from ourselves, or intoxicate us with false glory. Hence God wishes us to be inferior to the profane, that we may learn always to acknowledge as received from him whatever he has gratuitously conferred upon us, and not to arrogate anything to ourselves when our humility is so plainly set before our eyes. But as far as concerns the Jews, they were, as we have said, like a vine, because their excellence was not natural, but external. God had fashioned them, as it were, from nothing: and although they were adorned with many remarkable gifts, yet they could claim nothing from themselves.

Shall there be taken, says he, *any wood from it to fashion it for any work?* God here shows that the Jews were deservedly preferred to others, because he had planted them with his hand; for if they had been pulled out of the earth, he shows that the wood would be useless, since it could not be used for any purpose. And Christ uses the same simile (John xv. 1-7), when he shows that we have no root in us by nature, nor yet sap or moisture or vigour, since we are a vine planted by our heavenly Father. But if he roots us up, nothing remains for us but to be cast into the fire and utterly burnt. Lastly, God shows that the Jews should be viler than the nations, if he took away from them whatever he gave them; and he admonishes them that their state has no firmness unless through his goodwill towards them. For if the Prophet had only said, that whatever the Jews had they owed to God, and for this reason were bound to his liberality, yet they might still exalt themselves. But it is added in the second place, that they remained safe day by day, as far as God spares them, cherishes, defends, and sustains them. Therefore the Prophet means this when he says, *Shall it be taken to form any work from it, or will they take it for a peg to hang any vessels upon it. Behold,* says he, *it was given for consumption, and its two ends were burnt up.* Here, as I said, he points out various calamities by which the Jews were almost struck down, though not subdued. For they were hardened in their obstinacy; and although they were like burnt and rotten wood, yet they boasted themselves to be perfect through their adoption, and through the covenant which God had made with Abraham: they boasted themselves to be a holy race, and a royal priesthood. Yet God reproves their sloth when he says theirs was like burnt wood, when a bundle of twigs has been cast into the fire, and there is some remnant so injured by the smoke as to be deprived of its strength.

Behold, says he, *when it was whole could it be formed into any work! how much less after the fire has consumed it.* Here he pursues the same sentiment. If any one should take any part of the bundle after the fire had dried it, could he fit it for any work? If he should take the twig when whole, it would not be fit to receive any shaping: how much less could the burnt wood be used for a peg, or anything else. If, then, not even a peg can be found in the entire bundle, when the stem is like an ember through being parched by fire, how can it be turned to any use? Now follows the application: *as I have given the wood of the vine among woods,* says he: verbally, in the wood of the forest. Hence gather we what I formerly said about the branch, that it agrees with trees, and is not put for the wild vine or the palm branch: for he now says, simply, *amidst all the wood of the forest.* But he says that *the wood of the vine was among the wood of the forest*—not because vines are merely planted there, but this comparison is used: that is, among woods, or even among all the woods of the forest, because these trees are felled, and destined for buildings, or vessels are made from them, and all kinds of wooden furniture, as well as the materials of houses, are taken from trees. He says, therefore, *that the wood of the vine is given among the wood of the forest*, that is, among the woods of the forest, since the twigs are burnt, as they cannot be rendered useful to men: *so have I given*, says he, *the citizens of Jerusalem*.

Now after we understand the Prophet's meaning, let us learn that the Holy Spirit so addressed the Jews formerly, that this discourse might profit us in these days. We must perceive, in the first place, that we are superior to the whole world, through God's gratuitous pity: but naturally we have nothing of our own in which to boast. But if we carry ourselves haughtily, through reliance on God's gifts, this arrogance would be sacrilege: for we snatch away from God his own praise, and clothe ourselves, as it were, in his spoils. But Paul, when he speaks of the Jews, shortly, but clearly, defines both sides: Do we excel? says he—(for he there makes himself one with the people)—Do we excel the Gentiles? says he, (Rom. iii. 1); by no means: for Scripture denounces us all to be sinners—all to be accursed. Since, therefore, we are children of wrath, he says, there is nothing which we can claim to ourselves over the profane Gentiles. After he has so prostrated all the pride of his own nation, he repeats again—What? Are we not superior to others? Yea, we excel in every way. For the adoption, and the worship, and the law of God, and the covenant, confer upon us remarkable superiority, and such as we find nothing like it in the whole world. How do these things agree? That the Jews excel, and are to be preferred to others, and yet that they excel in nothing! namely, since they have nothing in themselves to cause them to despise the Gentiles, or boast themselves superior; hence their excellence is not in themselves but in God. And so Paul here does not commend their virtues, but says that they excel by gratuitous adoption, because God made his covenant with Abraham, and they were to arise from the holy nations, because he instituted a fixed line of piety among them, in promising himself to be a Father to them; nay, he determined that Christ should spring from them, who is the life and light of the world. We see, then, the former privileges of the Jews:

ours is the same in these days. As often as we are favoured with God's gifts, by which we approach near him and overcome the world, we ought also to remember what we were before God took us up. Then our origin will prostrate all arrogance, and prevent us from being ungrateful to God. But that is not yet sufficient; but we must come to the second clause, that not only has God's free grace raised us to such a height, but also sustains us; so that our standing is not founded in ourselves, but depends only on his will. Hence not only the remembrance of our origin ought to humble us, but the sense of our infirmity. Whence we gather that we have no perseverance in ourselves unless God daily, nay, momentarily strengthen us, and follow us up with his favour. This is the second point: the third is, if God afflicts or chastises us with his rods, we should know that the foolish confidence by which we deceive ourselves is by this means beaten out of us. Here we ought diligently to weigh the meaning of the phrase—*the wood of the vine is useless when it is torn up,* and especially when dry. For although the profane nations perish, yet it is not surprising if God's judgments are more severe towards the reprobate, who had obtained a place in his Church, and who had been enriched with his spiritual gifts. This ingratitude requires us to become an example to others, so that the whole world may be astonished at beholding in us such dreadful signs of God's anger. Hence the Jews were for a hissing and an abhorrence, an astonishment and a curse to the profane nations. Why so? They had more grievously exasperated God who had acted so liberally towards them, and were not only ungrateful and perfidious, but had purposely provoked him. Thus also it happens to other reprobates. So this clause is to be diligently noticed, when the Prophet says *that the wood of the vine is cast into the fire,* although trees, when cut down, are still useful either for building or for furniture. Now it follows—

7. And I will set my face against them; they shall go out from *one* fire, and *another* fire shall devour

7. Et ponam faciem meam in ipsos: ex igni egredientur, et ignis vorabit[1] eos: et scietis quod ego

---

[1] Or, " shall consume."—*Calvin.*

them: and ye shall know that I *am* the Lord, when I set my face against them.	Iehovah, cum posuero faciem meam in ipsis.[1]
8. And I will make the land desolate, because they have committed a trespass, saith the Lord God.	8. Et ponam terram in vastitatem, quia transgressi sunt transgressione[2] dicit Dominator Iehovah.

He confirms what had been said in the last verse, and at the same time explains it: as if the citizens of Jerusalem retained some form, because they were not reduced to dust; but the fire had burnt all round them, as if the flame was licking a bundle of twigs. While the royal seat remained to them, the name of a people remained, and hence an opportunity for their obstinacy. For they were not to be subdued, since they were not entirely consumed: and now another madness is added; for as soon as they had escaped from any misfortune, they thought themselves quite safe,— "O now we shall rest," said they; if the enemy had departed from the city, or if new forces had not arrived against them, or if provisions failed the enemy's troops, they immediately regained their courage, and not only breathed again, but proudly laughed at God and his prophets, as if they were beyond all danger. For this reason he now says, *I have set my face against them.* To set, or, if any one prefers it, to establish one's face, is to persist constantly, so as not only to do anything on passing, but to remain there until we have accomplished our intention; so that those are not bad expounders of the Prophet who say, "I have set my face firmly:" they do not translate verbally, but according to God's meaning. For he often chastises a whole nation or city, and yet he does not set his face, that is, he does not stay there, but chastises them lightly, and but for a short time, as if passing in another direction. But he means something else here—*that he would set his face;* that is, never desist until the people's name, as well as their city, was utterly abolished. For we have said that the prophets speak of the present state of the people when they threaten such destruction.

[1] Or, "against them."—*Calvin.*
[2] Or, "they have prevaricated with prevarication," as some translate; that is, have acted perfidiously, or have been shamefully perfidious.—*Calvin.*

I will set my face, therefore, *against them: they shall escape from one fire, and another shall devour them.* Here the Prophet strikes down that foolish opinion by which the Jews deceived themselves. For if they escaped from one danger, they thought it the last, and hence their security, and even obstinacy. But the Prophet says here, after they had escaped from one fire, that a new fire to consume them was lighted up: he means, that there were different means in God's hand by which he destroys and extinguishes a people: as he had previously said, that he was armed with pestilence and the sword, and famine and wild beasts; so now under the name of fire he comprehends various scourges. If, therefore, men have escaped the sword, a new attack shall meet them, since God will press them with famine, or urge them with pestilence, or in other ways: *and then they shall know,* says he, *that I am Jehovah, when I shall set my face against it.* By these words he signifies that his glory could not otherwise remain safe, since impunity blinded the Jews—nay, hardened them till they became like the brutes. If, therefore, God had spared them, his glory would have been as it were buried, and through so long a connivance he had been no longer acknowledged as God. There was a real necessity for so much rigour: since he would never show himself to be God otherwise than by destroying the impious who were so stupified by their sins as long as he bore with them. At length he adds, *I will lay the land waste since they have prevaricated by prevarication.* Here, also, God expresses how terrible, yet just, was that judgment, because the Jews were no trifling offenders, but perfidiously departed from his worship, and from the whole teaching of the law, and were obstinate in their ingratitude. Since they were so abandoned, we gather that God was not too severe when he put forth his hand to destroy them utterly.

PRAYER.

Grant, Almighty God, since thou hast not only deigned to separate us from the common herd of men, but also to renew thine image in us: and whilst thy favours towards us are conspicuous, thou exhortest us at the same time to glorify thy name : Grant that being mindful of our calling we may study to devote ourselves wholly to thee, and so to extol thee by peculiar and true and rightful praises, that we may be at length partakers of the glory to which thou invitest us, and which has been acquired for us by the blood of thine only begotten Son.—Amen.

Lecture Forty-Second.

CHAPTER XVI.

1. Again the word of the Lord came unto me, saying,	1. Et fuit sermo Iehovæ ad me, dicendo,
2. Son of man, cause Jerusalem to know her abominations,	2. Fili hominis, indica[1] Hierosolymæ suas abominationes,
3. And say, Thus saith the Lord God unto Jerusalem, Thy birth and thy nativity *is* of the land of Canaan; thy father *was* an Amorite, and thy mother an Hittite.	3. Sic dices, Sic dicit Dominator Iehovah Hierosolymæ, habitationes tuæ, et natales tui è terra Chanaan : pater tuus Amorrhæus, mater tua Hithæa, *et quæ sequuntur.*

THIS chapter contains very severe reproaches against the people of Judea who were left at Jerusalem. For although Ezekiel had been a leader to the Israelites and the Jewish exiles, yet God wished his assistance in profiting others. Hence the office which God had imposed upon his Prophet is now extended to the citizens of Jerusalem, whose abominations he is ordered to make manifest. The manner is afterwards expressed, when God shows the condition of that nation before he embraced it with his favour. But after recounting the benefits by which he had adorned the people, he reproves their ingratitude, and shows in many words, and by different figures, how detestable was their perfidy in revolting so far from God after he had treated them so liberally. These things will now be treated in their own order. As to Ezekiel's being ordered *to lay bare to the Jews their abominations,* we gather from this that men are often so blinded by their vices that they do not perceive what is sufficiently evident to every one else. And we know that the people was quite drunken with pride, for they voluntarily blinded themselves by their own flatteries.

[1] Or, " make evident."—*Calvin.*

It is not surprising, then, that God orders them to bring their abominations into the midst, so that they may at length feel themselves to be sinners. And this passage is worthy of notice, since we think those admonitions superfluous until God drags us into the light, and places our sins before our eyes. There is no one, indeed, whose conscience does not reprove him, since God's law is written on the hearts of all, and so we naturally distinguish between good and evil; but if we think how great our stupidity is concealing our faults, we shall not wonder that the prophets uttered this command, to lay open our abominations to ourselves. For not only is that self-knowledge of which I have spoken cold, but also involved in much darkness, so that he who is but partially conscious grows willingly hardened while he indulges himself. Again, we must remember that the Jews were to be argued with in this way, because they pleased themselves with their own superstitions. For the Prophet shows that their chief wickedness consisted in deserting God's law, in prostituting themselves to idols, and in setting up adulterous worship like houses of ill fame; but in this they pleased themselves, as we daily see in the papacy, that under this pretext the foulest idolatries are disguised, since they think themselves to be thereby worshipping God.

It is not surprising, then, if God here obliquely blames the stupidity and sloth of the Jews when he *commands their abominations to be laid open*, which are already sufficiently known to all. Afterwards, that God may begin to show how improperly the people were behaving, he recalls them to the first origin or fountain of their race. But we must notice that God speaks differently of the origin of the people. For sometimes he reminds them of Abraham's condition before he had stretched forth his hand and dragged them, as it were, from the lowest regions into life, as it is said in the last chapter of Joshua, (ver. 2, 3,) Thy father Abraham was worshipping idols when God adopted him. But sometimes the beginning is made from the covenant of God, when he chose Abraham with his posterity for himself. But in this passage God takes the time from the period of the small band of men emerging by wonderful increase into a nation, although they had been so wretchedly oppressed in Egypt; for the redemption of the people which immediately followed is called sometimes their nativity. So here God says that the Jews were there born when they increased so incredibly, though when oppressed by the Egyptian tyranny they had scarcely any place among living men. And what he says of Jews applies equally to all the posterity of Abraham: for the condition of the ten tribes was the same as that of Judah. But since the Prophet speaks to a people still surviving, he is silent about what he would have said, if he had been commanded to utter this mandate to the exiles and captives, as well as to the citizens of Jerusalem. Whatever its meaning, God here pronounces *that the Jews sprang from the land of Canaan, from an Amorite father, and from a Hittite mother.*

A question arises here—When God had adopted Abraham two hundred years previously, why was not that covenant taken into account? for he here seems not to magnify his own faithfulness and the constancy of his promise when he rejects the Jews as sprung from the Canaanites or Amorites; but this only shows what they were in themselves: for although he never departed from his purpose, and his election was never in vain, yet we must hold, as far as the people were concerned, that they are looked upon as profane Gentiles. For we know how they corrupted themselves in Egypt. Since, then, they were so degenerate and so utterly unlike their fathers, it is not surprising if God says that they *were sprung from Canaanites and Amorites.* For by Hosea he says, that they were all born of a harlot, and that the place of their birth was a house of ill fame. (Chap. ii. 4.) This must be understood metaphorically: since here God does not chide the women who had been false to their husbands, and had borne an adulterous offspring; but he simply means that the Jews were unworthy of being called or reputed Abraham's seed. Why so? for although God remained firm in his covenant, yet if we consider the character of the Jews, they had entirely cut themselves off by their faithlessness. Since, then, they did not differ from the profane Gentiles, they are deservedly rejected with reproach, and are called an offspring of Canaan, as in other places. Now, therefore, we understand the intention of the Prophet, or rather of the Holy Spirit. For if God had only said that he would pity that race when reduced to extreme misery, it would not have been subjected to such severe and heavy reproof, as we shall see. Hence God not only relates his kindness towards them, but at the same time shows from what state he had taken the Jews when he first aided them, and what was their condition when he deigned to draw them out of such great misery. Moreover, since he was at hand to take them up, their redemption was founded upon covenant, and so they were led forth, because God had promised Abraham four centuries ago that he would be the liberator of the people. That they should not be ignorant of the favour by which God had bound himself to Abraham, the Prophet meets them, and pronounces them a seed of Canaan, having nothing in common with Abraham, because, as far as they were concerned, according to common usage, God's promise was extinct, and their adoption dead and buried. Since they had acted so perfidiously, they could no longer boast themselves to be Abraham's children. Hence he says, *thy habitations*, that is, the place of their origin. Jerome translates it "root;" but the word "nativity" suits better, or native soil, or condition of birth *in the land of Canaan: and thy father an Amorite and thy mother a Hittite.* There were other tribes of Canaan, but two or three kinds are put here for the whole. Now it follows—

4. And *as for* thy nativity, in the day thou wast born thy navel was not cut, neither wast thou washed in water to supple *thee:* thou wast not salted at all, nor swaddled at all.

5. None eye pitied thee, to do any of these unto thee, to have compassion upon thee; but thou wast cast out in the open field, to the loathing of

4. Et nativitates tuæ in die qua nata es tu[1] non præcisus fuit umbilicus tuus, aquis non fuisti lota, ad mollitiem[2] sale non fuisti salita, et non fuisti involuta fasciis.[3]

5. Non misertus est super te oculus faciendum tibi unum ex his ad considerandum super te: et projecta fuisti in superficie agri, in

---

[1] That is, "of thine origin or nativity."—*Calvin*.
[2] Or, "to soften thy flesh:" we shall speak of this afterwards.—*Calvin*.
[3] Verbally, "wrapped in wrappings."—*Calvin*.

| thy person, in the day that thou wast born. | probrum animæ tuæ quo die nata es. |

Here the Prophet metaphorically describes that most miserable state in which God found the Jews. For we know that scarcely any nation was ever so cruelly and disgracefully oppressed. For when they were all driven to servile labour without reward, the edict went forth that their males should be cut off. (Exod. i. 16, 22.) No species of disgrace was omitted, and their life was worse than a hundred deaths. This, then, is the reason why God says that the Jews were so *cast forth on the face of the earth* without any supply of the common necessaries of life. He takes these figures from customary usage; for it is usual to cut the navel-string of infants: for the navel affords them nourishment in their mothers' womb, and mother and child would both perish unless a separation took place; and if the navel-string were not tied the child would perish; for all the blood flows through that organ, as the child received its sustenance through it: and this is the midwife's chief care as soon as the child is born, to cut away what must afterwards be restored to its place, and to bind up the part, and to do it, as I have said, with the greatest care, as the infant's life depends upon it.

But God says, *that the navel-string of the Jews was not cut off.* Why so? *because they were cast*, says he, *on the surface of the earth;* that is, they were deserted and exposed,— using but a single word. He now adds, *they were not washed with water:* for we know how young infants require ablution; and unless it be performed immediately, they will perish. Hence he says, *they were not washed with water.* He adds, to soften or refresh, or " fettle" them, as the common phrase is; for water softens and smooths the skin, though others translate it in the sense of causing it to shine: but we understand the Prophet's meaning sufficiently. He afterwards adds, *they were not rubbed with salt;* for salt is sprinkled on the body of an infant to harden the flesh, while care must be taken not to render it too hard; and this moderate hardness is effected by the sprinkling of salt. The full meaning is, that the Jews at their birth were cast out with such contempt, that they were destitute of the necessary care which life requires. He adds, *No eye pitied thee, so as to discharge any of these duties, and to shew thee pity:* and this is sufficiently evident, since the Israelites would have been destroyed had no one taken compassion on them; for they were in some sense buried in the land of Egypt; for we know how cruel was the conspiracy of the whole land against them. No wonder, then, if God here relates that they were cast upon the surface of the land, so that no eye looked upon them and showed them pity. He adds, *they were cast to the loathing of their life.* He simply means, that they were so despicable that they had no standing among men; for loathing of life means the same as rejection. It now follows—

6. And when I passed by thee, and saw thee polluted in thine own blood, I said unto thee, *when thou wast* in thy blood, Live; yea, I said unto thee, *when thou wast* in thy blood, Live.	6. Et transivi juxta te, et vidi te fœdatam[1] in sanguinibus tuis: et dixi tibi, in sanguinibus tuis, Vive: et dixi tibi, in sanguinibus tuis, Vive.

I have already explained the time to which the Prophet alludes, when the seed of Abraham began to be tyrannically oppressed by the Egyptians. For God here assumes the character of a traveller when he says *that he passed by.* For he had said that the Jews and all the Israelites were like a girl cast forth and deserted. Now, therefore, he adds, that this spectacle met him as he passed by: as those who travel cast their eyes on either side, and if anything unusual occurs they attend and consider it; meanwhile God declares that he was taking care of his people. And truly the matter is sufficiently evident, since he seemed to have neglected those wretched ones, while he had wonderfully assisted them. For they might have perished a hundred times a-day, and if he had not taken notice of them, they had not dragged out their life to the end. That celebrated sentence is well known—I have seen, I have seen, the affliction of my people. When he sent for Moses and commanded him to liberate the people, he prefaces it in this way, I have seen,

---

[1] Or, "contaminated:" some translate "trodden down," I know not why.—*Calvin.*

I have seen. (Exod. iii. 7.) Hence he had long ago seen, though he seemed to despise them by shutting his eyes. There is no doubt that the doubling of the word here means that God always watched for the safety of this desperate people, although he did not assist them directly: he now means the same thing when he says, *that he passed by: I passed by*, then, *near thee, and saw thee defiled with blood.* That spectacle could not turn away God's eyes; for whatever is contrary to nature excites horror. God therefore here shows how compassionate he was towards the people, because he was not horrified by that disgraceful foulness, when he saw the infant so immersed in its own gore without any shape. As to the following phrase, *I said to thee*, he does not mean that he spoke openly so that the people heard his voice, but he announces what he had determined concerning the people. The expression, *live in thy blood*, may indeed be taken contemptuously, as if God had grudged moving his hand, lest the very touch should prove contagious; for we do not willingly touch any putrid gore. The words, *live in thy blood*, may be thus explained, since at first God did not deign to take care of the people. But it is evident from the context, that God here expresses the secret virtue by which the people was preserved contrary to the common feelings. For if we consider what has been previously said, the people surely had not lived a single day, unless it had received vigour from this voice of God. For if a new-born child is cast out, how can it bear the cold of the night? surely it will instantly expire: and I have already said that death is prepared for infants, unless their navel-string be cut. Since therefore a hundred deaths encompassed the people, they could never have continued alive, had not the secret voice of God sustained them.

God therefore in commanding them to live, already shows that he was willingly and wonderfully preserving them amidst various kinds of death. As it is said in the 68th psalm, (ver. 20,) " In his hands are the issues of death," so that death is converted into life: since he is the sovereign and lord of both. But this phrase is doubled, since the people were afflicted in Egypt for no short period. But if that tyranny had endured only a few years, they must have been consumed. But their slavery was protracted to many years: whence that remarkable wonder occurred, that their remembrance and their name were not often cut off. We see then that God has reason enough to speak that sentence in which the safety of the people was included, *live in thy bloods, live in thy bloods.* The fact itself shows the people to have been preserved, since it pleased God. The history which Moses relates in the book of Exodus is a glass in which we may behold the living image of that life of which we have made mention as drawing its whole vigour from the secret good pleasure of God. Now the reason is asked why God did not openly and directly take up his people, and treat them as kindly as he did during their youth? The reason is sufficiently manifest, since if the people had been freed at the very first, the memory of the benefit would have by and bye vanished away, and God's power would have been more obscure. For we know that men, unless thoroughly convinced of their own misery, never acknowledge that they have obtained safety through God's pity. The people then ought so to live, as always to have death before their eyes—nay, as if they were bound by the chains of death. *It lived,* then, *in bloods,* that is, in the tomb, like a carcase remaining in its own putridness, and its life in the meantime lying hid: so it happened to the sons of Abraham. Now then we understand God's intention why he did not raise up the children of Abraham with grandeur from the beginning, but suffered them to drag out a miserable life, and to be steeped in the very pollution of death. It now follows—

7. I have caused thee to multiply as the bud of the field, and thou hast increased and waxen great, and thou art come to excellent ornaments: *thy* breasts are fashioned, and thine hair is grown, whereas thou *wast* naked and bare.	7. Et magnum te feci quasi germen agri:[1] et crevisti, et adolevisti,[2] et venisti in ornamentum ornamentorum:[3] ubera tua aptata sunt,[4] et pilus tuus germinavit: tu autem nuda et discooperta eras.

[1] Others translate, " ten thousand," and רבבה, *rebbeh*, means this, but the other sense is simpler : I made thee fruitful as the bud of the field.—*Calvin.*   [2] " Thou becamest great."—*Calvin.*
[3] Or rather, " to beauty of beauties; that is, the greatest beauty."—*Calvin.*   [4] Others translate, " swelled or were prominent."—*Calvin.*

Here what I lately touched upon is now clearly expressed, that the people in their extreme distress were not only safe, but increased by God's singular favour. For if the infant after exposure retains its life, it will still be a weak abortion. Hence God here by this circumstance magnifies his favour, since the people increased as if it had been properly and attentively cared for, and as if no kind office had been omitted. This is the meaning of the words *they were increased;* for though he looks to the propagation of Abraham's family, yet the simile is to be observed, for the people is compared to a girl exposed in a field from its birth, and their growth took place when God increased them so incredibly, as we know. And surely God's blessing was great when they entered Egypt, 75 in number, and were many thousands when they left it. (Acts vii. 14 ; Exod. xii. 37.) For within 250 years, the family of Abraham was so multiplied, that they amounted to 800,000 when God freed them. But since the Prophet speaks metaphorically, when he says *the people were increased,* and, under the image of a tender girl, *until they grew up to a proper age;* meanwhile he shows that this was done only by the wonderful counsel and power of God. *I placed thee,* says he. God claims to himself the praise for this great multiplication, and then strengthens what I have said, namely, that the people's safety was included in that phrase *live in bloods:* then he says, *she came into ornament of ornaments.* Here עדי, *gnedi,* cannot mean any occasional ornament, since it is added directly, *thou wast naked and bare.* It follows then that it refers to personal comeliness. It means not only that the girl grew in loftiness of stature but in beauty of person. Hence elegance and loveliness are here marked, as the context shows us. *Thou camest* then *to excellent* or exquisite *beauty,* for we know this to be the meaning of the genitive, signifying excellence. He adds at the same time, *thy breasts were made ready,* for כון, *kon,* means to prepare, to strengthen : but as he is speaking of breasts, I have no doubt that he means them to have swelled as they ought to do. *Thy breasts then were fashioned,* that is, of the right size, as in marriageable girls. *Thy hair also grew long.* Finally, the Prophet expresses thus grossly what he could have said more concisely, in consequence of the people's rudeness. *Thy hair grew long, whilst thou wast naked and bare;* that is, as yet thou hadst no outward ornament, thou wast like a marriageable girl—thou hadst great beauty of person, a noble stature, and all parts of thy body mutually accordant, but thou hadst cause to be ashamed of thy nakedness. And such was the condition of the people since the Egyptians devised everything against them, and conspired by all means for their destruction: we see then how God stretched forth his hand not only for the people's defence, but to carry them forth against the tyranny of Pharaoh and of all Egypt. He points out the time of their redemption as near, because the people had increased and multiplied, just like a girl who had reached her twentieth year. Now it follows—

8. Now when I passed by thee, and looked upon thee, behold, thy time *was* the time of love; and I spread my skirt over thee, and covered thy nakedness: yea, I sware unto thee, and entered into a covenant with thee, saith the Lord God, and thou becamest mine.	8. Et transivi juxta te, et vidi te; et ecce tempus tuum tempus amorum: et extendi alam meam[1] super te, et texi nuditatem tuam,[2] et juravi tibi, et veni in fœdus tecum, dicit Dominator Iehovah: et fuisti mea.

God now reproaches the Jews with his kindness towards them, since he had clothed them in splendid ornaments, and yet they afterwards cast themselves into the vilest lusts, as we shall see. But we must remember that the Prophet is now speaking of the time of their liberation. But God says *that he passed by again* and *saw the state of the people,* —not that he had ever forgotten it. For we know that even when he dissembles and seems to shut his eyes and turn them from us or even to sleep, yet he is always anxious for our safety. And we have already said that there was need of his present power, that the people might prolong their lives, since if he had not breathed life into them, a hundred deaths would have immediately prevailed. But it is sufficiently common and customary to mark an open declaration of help by God's aspect. When God appears so openly to deliver us that it may be comprehended by our senses, then he

---

[1] That is, "the skirt of my garments."—*Calvin.*
[2] Or, "shame."—*Calvin.*

is said to look down upon us, to rise up, and to turn himself towards us. *He passed by*, then, *near the people*, namely, when he called Moses out of the desert and appointed him the minister of his favour, (Exod. iii.,) he then saw his people, and proved by their trial that he had not utterly cast them away. *I looked*, then, and *behold thy time, thy time of years*. Here God speaks grossly, yet according to the people's comprehension. For he personates a man struck with the beauty of a girl and offering her marriage. But God is not affected as men are, as we well know, so that it is not according to his nature to love as young men do. But such was the people's stupidity, that they could not be usefully taught, unless the Prophet accommodated himself to their grossness. Add also that the people had been by no means lovely, unless God had embraced them by his kindness, so that his love depended on his good pleasure towards them. So by *the time of loves*, we ought to understand the complete time of their redemption, for God had determined to bring the people out of Egypt when he pleased, and that had been promised to Abraham: after four hundred years I will be their avenger. (Gen. xv. 13, 14; Acts vii. 6, 7.) We see, then, that the years were previously fixed in which God would redeem the people. He now compares that union to a marriage. Hence if God would bind his people to himself by a marriage, so also he would pledge himself to conjugal fidelity. But I cannot proceed further—I must leave the rest till to-morrow.

PRAYER.

Grant, Almighty God, since from our first origin we have been entirely accursed, so that we were entirely foul and polluted in thy sight, that we may be mindful of our condition, and acknowledge thine inestimable pity towards us, since thou hast deigned to draw us from the lowest estate, and to adopt us among thy children: and may we so desire to spend our whole life in obedience to thee, that we may at length enjoy that blessed glory to which thou hast called us, and which thou hast prepared for us in thine only-begotten Son.—Amen.

Lecture Forty-Third.

WE began yesterday to explain another point of which the Prophet treats, namely, the liberation of the people. For then was the fitting time in which God espoused them to himself. He now adds, *that he spread out the skirt of his garment to cover the foulness and disgrace of the people.* This spreading comprehends all the virtues which God exercised in freeing his people. For he then delivered them from all reproaches by which they were shamefully and disgracefully treated in Egypt. Some think that it was a nuptial rite for a spouse or husband to cover the bride with his garment, but this is only a conjecture. Hence I simply interpret it, *the border of the garment was spread out,* when God vindicated his people from the reproaches by which they had been deformed. He afterwards adds, *and I have sworn to thee, and come into covenant with thee.* There is no doubt that this ought to be referred to the promulgation of the law. For although God had long ago made a covenant with Abraham, and the adoption of the people was founded upon it, yet that favour on the people's part had almost vanished away, as I yesterday said; hence God pronounces that he had, as it were, adopted the people afresh. It was like the renewal of the covenant, when God bound the people to himself by a fixed law, and prescribed a fixed method of worship. These, then, were the accustomed marriage rites. But God deservedly announces *that he had come into covenant,* because he then coupled the people to himself; whence also that elogy of Moses—What nation is so illustrious under heaven, which has God so near them, as thy God approaches unto thee? Ye shall be to me a kingdom of priests; ye shall be my inheritance. (Deut. iv. 7; Exod. xix. 6.) We should remark the word *swear* as emphatic, for God increases his indulgence when he says *that he swore.* If we think of the majesty of God, and of what his people was, this is surely incredible, that God should deign to descend so far as to swear like men accustomed to pledge their faith, and to sanction it by an oath. Now, therefore, we see the singular benefit expressed here with which God adorned his people, when, at the giving of the law, he chose them as his own, and appointed them to be a kingdom of priests. It now follows—

9. Then washed I thee with water; yea, I throughly washed away thy blood from thee, and I anointed thee with oil.

9. Et lavi te aquis, et mundavi[1] sanguines tuos abs te[2] et unxi te oleo.

Here God more clearly explains what had been formerly touched upon, namely, that he then married the people, as a young man marries his bride. But he here states that he endowed her; for they would not have been sufficiently adopted by God unless they had been adorned with superior presents; since if they had been left in that miserable slavery by which they were oppressed, God's favour would have been very obscure. Now, therefore, God means, that by his law he had entered into a new covenant with his people, so that he did not leave them naked and bare, but clothed with remarkable gifts. First of all, he says, *I washed thee with water.* Although he had just said that the people were like a beautiful damsel, and had praised their beauty, yet the filth of which the Prophet had spoken yet remained: it ought, therefore, to be cleansed from those stains: *I have cleansed thee with water,* says he, *and washed off thy bloods,* namely, the corrupt blood which the damsel whom Ezekiel mentions had retained from her birth. Lastly, Ezekiel says that God performed those offices which the nurse discharges for the child. Afterwards he adds—

10. I clothed thee also with broidered work, and shod thee with badgers' skin, and I girded thee about with fine linen, and I covered thee with silk.

10. Et vestivi te Phrygionica veste,[3] et calceavi te taxo,[4] et cinxi te bysso, et operui te serico.

11. I decked thee also with ornaments, and I put bracelets upon thy hands, and a chain on thy neck.

11. Et ornavi te ornatu, et posui armillas in manibus tuis, et torquem in collo tuo.

12. And I put a jewel on thy forehead, and earrings in thine ears, and a beautiful crown upon thine head.

12. Et posui circulum super faciem tuam,[5] et inaures super aures tuas, et coronam decoris in capite tuo.[6]

[1] Or, "I wiped."—*Calvin.*
[2] Or, "down from thee."—*Calvin.*
[3] Or, "variegated."—*Calvin.*
[4] Or, "purple."—*Calvin.*
[5] Or, "thy nose or nostrils."—*Calvin.*
[6] "These are all to be united together."—*Calvin.*

13. Thus wast thou decked with gold and silver; and thy raiment *was of* fine linen, and silk, and broidered work; thou didst eat fine flour, and honey, and oil; and thou wast exceeding beautiful, and thou didst prosper into a kingdom.	13. Et ornata fuisti auro et argento, et vestitus tuus byssus, et sericum[1] et variegatus:[2] similam, et mel, et oleum comedisti, et pulchra fuisti in valde valde,[3] et prospere[4] progressa es usque ad regnum.

Here the Prophet, in a metaphor, relates other benefits of God by which he liberally adorned his people; for we know that nothing has been omitted in God's pouring forth the riches of his goodness on the people. And as to the explanations which some give of these female ornaments allegorically, I do not approve of it, as they fruitlessly conjecture many trifles which are at variance with each other. First of all, their conjectures may be refuted by the Prophet's words: then, if we suffer the Prophet's words to be turned and twisted, what these allegorical interpreters chatter with each other is entirely contrary in their meaning. Let us, therefore, be content with the genuine sense, that God was so generous towards the Israelites that he poured forth all his blessings in enriching them. Now, if one asks how the people were adorned? I answer, in two ways—first, God embraced them with his favour, and promised to be their God, and this was their chief honour; as Moses says they were naked, and their shame was discovered when they set up an idol in the place of God. He now adds a second kind of blessing, when God took care of them in the desert: he appeared by day in a cloud, and by night in a pillar of fire: the water flowed for them from the rock; daily food was given them from heaven, as if God with his own hands had placed it within their mouths: then in his strength they conquered their enemies, and entered the promised land; while he slew the nations for them, and gave them quiet possession and dominion there: then he blessed the land, so that it nourished them abundantly, and made it testify that it was no vain promise that the land should flow with milk and honey. (Exod. iii. 17; xiii. 21, 22; xvi. 15, 16; xvii. 6; xxii. 25; Num. xx. 11.) Ezekiel includes all these things under *necklaces, bracelets, gold, silver, linen garments, broid-*

---

[1] Or, "silk cloth."—*Calvin.*   [2] Or, "many-coloured."—*Calvin.*
[3] That is, "beyond measure."—*Calvin.*   [4] Or, "happily."—*Calvin.*

ered work, &c. As to the particular words I will not accurately insist, unless I shortly touch on a point or two which may occasion doubt.

When he says that *he clothed them*, רקמה, *rekmeh*, this is in accordance with eastern customs: for they were accustomed to use clothing of different colours ; as Benjamin wore a dress of this kind when he was a boy ; and this was no royal splendour on his father's part, who was a shepherd, but simply the usual custom. At this day, indeed, if any one among us wore a party-coloured garment, it would not be manly : nay, women who desire such variety in colours show themselves to have cast off all modesty. But among the Orientals, as I have said, this was the usual kind of dress. He afterwards adds, *I shod thee with badgers' skin.* I know not why Jerome translates it violet-coloured, and others hyacinth : it is sufficiently clear that it was a precious kind of skin. The word is often used by Moses when treating of the tabernacle ; for the coverings were of violet-coloured skin, and the whole tabernacle was covered with them. The badger was an animal unknown to us : but since he is here treating of shoes, there is no doubt that the skin was more elegant, and more highly esteemed by God. (Exod. xxxv. 23 ; xxxvi. 19.) Afterwards he adds, *I bound thee with fine linen.* We know that linen garments were in more frequent use among that people than in Greece or in Italy, or in these parts : for linen was rarely used by the Romans even in their greatest luxury ; but in the East they wore linen, as that region is very warm. But we know that linen is very fine, and that they were accustomed to weave transparent veils. Now this clothing was commonly worn by men in the East, though it is by no means manly : nay, in women it is scarcely tolerable. But the priests afterwards adopted the custom, and clothed themselves in linen while performing sacred rites. The Papal priests too—apes in all things— have imitated the custom ; and although they do not wear fine linen, yet use linen robes, which they call surplices.

He now adds, *and I covered thee with silk*, or silken garments, or silk cloth. He adds, *that he placed bracelets upon the hands :* barbarians call them armlets. This luxury was spread abroad almost everywhere; but the circular ornament which the Prophet adds to it was rejected by other nations. He puts *a chain round the neck:* chains were in common use as they are this day: nay, to necklaces were added looser chains—double, threefold, and fourfold; for this fault was too common. And what he afterwards adds of the ring was left to the Orientals, for they had jewels hanging from their nostrils: and I wonder why interpreters put earrings here, and then instead of earrings put nose-rings. But the Prophet here means a ring, whence a jewel was hung from the nose; and this with us is ridiculous and deforming: but in those barbarous regions both men and women have gems hanging from both their noses and ears. He adds, *a crown on thy head.* He does not mean a diadem or crown as a sign of royalty, but an ornament sufficiently common.

If any one makes any inquiry about these various kinds of dresses, whether it was lawful for women to use so many ornaments, the answer is easy, that the Prophet here does not approve of what he relates, but uses a common image. We said that his only intention was to show that God could not have treated his people more freely; since in every way he had unfolded the incomparable treasures of his beneficence in adorning the Israelites. He now describes this in a metaphor, and under figures taken from the common practice everywhere received. It does not follow, therefore, that women ought to adorn themselves in this way. For we know that superfluous ornaments are temptations; and we know also the vanity of women, and their ambition to show themselves off, as the saying is: and we see how sharply this eager desire of women is blamed, especially by Isaiah. (Chap. iii.) But it is sufficient to elicit what God wished to teach by these figures, namely, that he had not omitted any kind of liberality. Whence it follows, that the people's ingratitude was the less excusable, as Ezekiel will immediately add. But before we proceed further, we must turn this instruction to our use. What has hitherto been said of the Israelites does not suit us, I confess, in all things: but yet there is some likeness between us and them. If we reflect upon our origin, we are all born children of wrath, all cursed, all Satan's bondsmen, (Eph. ii. 3 ;) and although many have been well brought up, yet as to our spiritual state we are like infant children or the new-born babe, exposed and immersed in its own filth and corruption. For what can be found in man before his renewal but the curse of God? Hence we are such slaves of Satan, that God hates us, as it is said in Genesis, (chap. vi. 7,) I repent of having formed man; where he does not acknowledge his image in us, which is not only defiled by original sin, but is all but extinct, surely this is the height of deformity: and though we do not perceive what is said by our senses, yet we are sufficiently detestable before God and the angels. We have no cause, then, to please ourselves; nay, if we open our eyes, the foulness which I have mentioned will be sufficiently clear to us. Meanwhile, God so aided us, that he truly fulfilled what Ezekiel relates. For although we were not freed from any external tyranny, yet God espoused us: then he adopted us into his Church: this was our greatest honour; this was more than royal dignity. We see, then, that this instruction is useful for us also at this time, if we only consider in what we are like the ancient people. I had almost omitted one point—the nourishment. God here not only reminds them that he had adorned the people with various kinds of clothing, and necklaces, and gems, and silver; but he adds also, *thou didst eat fine flour*, or fine meal, *and honey and oil*, and *thou wast very beautiful*, and *proceeded prosperously, even to a kingdom*. Here God again commends and extols his beneficence, because he not only clothed sumptuously his spouse of whom he speaks, but also fed her plentifully with the best, and sweetest, and most delicate food. He puts only three species: he makes no mention of wine or flesh; but by fine flour he means that they lacked no delicacy: the oil and honey mean the same thing. This clause points out an accumulation of grace when he says *that they progressed happily even to a kingdom:* all God's benefits could not be recounted: he says that his bride was not only magnificently clothed and delicately brought up, but *that she proceeded even to the royal dignity.* In the next verse he still reminds them of his benefits.

14. And thy renown went forth among the heathen for thy beauty: for it *was* perfect through my comeliness, which I had put upon thee, saith the Lord God.

14. Et egressum tibi fuit nomen in gentibus in pulchritudine tua:[1] quia perfecta fuisti in decore quem posueram super te, dicit Dominator Iehovah.

Here the Prophet still continues to recite those blessings of God by which he had bound the people to himself. As to his saying, *that its name had gone forth*, it cannot be restricted to a short period; but it embraces a continued series of God's favours until the people reached the highest point of happiness; and this happened under David. There is no doubt that God here means that he was so continually liberal towards the people that their fame became celebrated, for the name of the Israelites were spread far and wide; and God deservedly recounts their nobility or celebrity of fame among his benefits: hence he adds, *on account of the beauty* or elegance *which I have placed upon thee*, says he; *because thou wast perfect through the ornament which I had placed upon thee*. Here, therefore, God signifies that the people had not earned their fame by their own virtue, nor were they noble through their own native excellence, so to speak; but rather by ornament bestowed upon them. *Thou, therefore, wast of great name among the nations*, said he. But wherein was that nobility and excellence? Certainly from my gifts. For nothing was accomplished by thyself so to arrive at a name and dignity more than royal. *Through that ornament thy fame was spread abroad among the nations*. But this enlargement must be noticed, since the people had not only experienced God's goodness in that corner of Judea, but, when they ought to be content with their lot, were held in admiration and repute among foreigners. Now follows the reproof—

15. But thou didst trust in thine own beauty, and playedst the harlot because of thy renown, and pouredst out thy fornications on every one that passed by: his it was.

15. Et confisa es in pulchritudine tua, et fornicata es pro nomine tuo,[2] et effudisti fornicationes tuas ad omnem transeuntem;[3] illius fuit.

Here God begins to expostulate with his people; and with this view relates all the benefits which for a long time

---
[1] Or, "on account of thy beauty."—*Calvin.*
[2] Or, "according to thy name."—*Calvin.*
[3] That is, "to whomsoever she met."—*Calvin.*

he had bestowed upon the Israelites, and especially upon the tribe of Judah. The Prophet now addresses them. Nothing was more unworthy or preposterous than for the Jews to be proud through the pretext of God's gifts. But this vice has always been rife in the world, as it is now too prevalent, and especially among handsome women; for, though beauty is God's gift, nine women out of ten who possess it are proud, and fond of men, and unite lust with elegance of form. This is quite unworthy of them; but it was customary in all ages, as it is this day: for we recognise the same in men; for as each excels in anything, so he arrogates to himself more than he ought, when he exults against God, and is reproachful towards others. If any one abounds in riches, he immediately gives himself to luxury and empty pomp; and others abuse them to various perverse, and even corrupt uses. If any one is endowed with ability, he turns his acuteness to cunning and fraud; then he plans many devices, as if he wished to mingle earth and heaven. Thus almost all men profane God's gifts. But here the Prophet shows the fountain of this pride, when he says that the Jews *trusted in their own beauty:* for if modesty flourished in us, it would certainly suffice for restraining all insolence; but when that restraint has been once thrown off, there is no moderation before either God or man. This passage, then, is worthy of observation, where God reproves his ancient people for *trusting in their beauty:* because the figure signifies that they drew their material for pride from the gifts which ought rather to lead them to piety; for the gifts which we receive from God's hand ought to be invitations to gratitude: but we are puffed up by pride and luxury, so that we profane God's gifts, in which his glory ought to shine forth. We must also observe that God has thus far recited his benefits, that the people's ingratitude may appear more detestable: for God gives all things abundantly, and upbraids not, as James says, (chap. i. 5;) that is, if we acknowledge that we owe all things to him, and thus devote and consecrate ourselves in obedience to his glory, with the blessings which he has bestowed upon us. But when God sees us impiously burying and profaning his gifts, and, through trusting in them, growing insolent, it is not surprising if he reproves us beyond what is customary. Hence we see that God assumes as it were another character, when he expostulates with us concerning our ingratitude; because he willingly acknowledges his gifts in us, and receives them as if they were our own; as we call that bread ours by which he nourishes us, although it is compelled to change its nature as far as we are concerned. It always remains the same in itself; but I speak of external form. God therefore, as it were, transfigures himself, so as to reprove his own gifts, conferred for the purpose of our glorying only in him. (Matt. vii. 11; Luke xi. 13.)

God afterwards says, *that the people had played the harlot according to their renown.* I have no doubt that the Prophet alludes to famous harlots who excel in beauty, and interpreters have not observed this sufficiently; for they do not explain anything by saying, thou hast committed fornication in thy name: for as many lovers flow from all sides in troops towards a famous harlot, so the Prophet says the Jews were like her; and since they were universally noted, they were exposed to promiscuous lust, and attracted lovers to themselves. Here the Prophet condemns two kinds of fornication in the Jews; one consisting in superstitions and in the multiplication of idols,—the other in perverse and unlawful treaties: and we know this to be the worst kind of fornication, when God's worship is vitiated; for this is our spiritual chastity, if we worship God purely according to the prescription of his teaching, if we do not bend to either the right or the left from his commands: so on the other hand, as soon as we pass the goal fixed by him, we wander like impure harlots, and all our superstitions are so many acts of defilement. The Prophet begins with the former kind, when he says *that the Jews had committed fornication,* namely, with their idols. But before he comes to that, he shows that their lust had been unsatiable, since they had so eagerly and ardently approached their various idols, just as a harlot burns with unsatisfied desire, and is carried hither and thither, and must have a number of men; so the Prophet here says that the Jews committed fornication, not with one or two only, but with whomsoever they met; and this was occasioned by that favour of which we formerly spoke. It now follows—

16. And of thy garments thou didst take, and deckedst thy high places with divers colours, and playedst the harlot thereupon: *the like things* shall not come, neither shall it be *so*.

16. Et sumpsisti e vestibus tuis, et fecisti tibi excelsa conspersa maculis,[1] et scortata es cum illis: non venientes:[2] deinde et non erit.

He says that the Jews erected houses of ill fame for themselves; and the language is mixed, because the Prophet expresses simply the kind of harlotry of which he is speaking, and yet in the meantime mingles another figure; for he says *that they took garments and made themselves altars.* No doubt he compares the high places to tents, just as if a harlot wished to attract a number of eyes to herself, and, through desire of a crowd, should place her standard on a lofty place. So also the Prophet says that the Jews, when they gave themselves up to fornication, *made high places for themselves.* When he says *high places with different colours,* some refer this to ornaments; yet it may be taken in a bad sense, since those high places were stained, so that they could be distinguished from chaste and modest dwellings; as if he had said, If thou hadst been a modest woman, thou hadst remained in retirement at home, as honest matrons do, and thou wouldst not have done anything to attract men to thee; but thou hast erected thy high places, like conspicuous houses of ill fame, as if a female, forgetful of modesty and delicacy, should set up a sign, and show her house to be open to all, and especially to her own adulterers. It seems to me that the Prophet intends this; for when he adds, *that they committed fornication with them,* he means doubtless with their lovers and all besides; but this is not the sense of the words במות טלאות, *bemoth telaoth.*

Now, at the end of the verse, where he says, *they do not come, and it shall not be,* some explain this part as if the Prophet had said that there was no instance like it in former ages, and there should be none such hereafter. In this way they understand that the insane lust of the people is con-

---

[1] Or, "tinged with divers colours," as some translate.—*Calvin.*
[2] But it is in the feminine gender.—*Calvin.*

demned, as if it were a prodigy, such as was never seen, nor yet to be expected. Others say, that such was the multitude of high places, that nothing was ever like it; because, although the Gentiles built idols, and temples, and altars everywhere, yet the Prophet says that the madness and fury of the people surpassed the intemperance of the Gentiles:—this is indeed to the purpose. Meanwhile, as to the general scope, it is not of much consequence; as in the former verse, where he said *it shall be theirs*, some understand appetite or desire. But I interpret it more simply— that she was exposed to every passer-by, and that it was in his power to engage her. The sense does not seem to me doubtful, because the Jews were so cast out, that no liberty remained to them, as when a woman becomes abandoned, she is the slave of all, and all use her disgracefully after that, since she is no longer her own mistress. Ezekiel now reproves the Jews for the same vice.

PRAYER.

Grant, Almighty God, that we may diligently consider in how many ways we are bound to thee, and may deservedly magnify thy fatherly indulgence towards us, so that in return we may desire to devote ourselves to thee: Grant also, that as thou hast adorned us with thy glory, we may endeavour to glorify thy name, until at length we arrive at the enjoyment of that eternal glory which thou hast prepared for us in heaven by Christ our Lord.—Amen.

Lecture Forty-Fourth.

17. Thou hast also taken thy fair jewels of my gold and of my silver, which I had given thee, and madest to thyself images of men, and didst commit whoredom with them.

17. Et sumpsisti vasa pulchritudinis tuæ ex auro meo et ex argento meo quæ dederam tibi: et fecisti tibi imagines masculi,[1] et scortata es cum illis.

THE Prophet reproves them because they used silver and gold in making idols for themselves. He not only condemns idolatry, but ingratitude, since they turned to God's dishonour the gifts which he had bestowed. First, the profanation of his gifts was base; besides this, they had rashly

[1] That is, "masculine."—*Calvin.*

and purposely abused his liberality to his dishonour, and that was not to be endured. He reproves at the same time their blind intemperance, since they willingly gave themselves up to licentiousness, and buried themselves in their superstitions. But he does not say that they simply took gold and silver, but *vessels of elegance or beauty of gold and silver.* Whence it appears that they were blinded by furious lusts, as we have seen. He still pursues the simile of fornication, when he calls these manufactured deities *images of males;* and it seems obliquely to mark the excess of lust in having to do with shadows; by which he means that they were hurried away about nothing by their unbridled appetites, just as a woman feeds her passion by the mere picture of her paramour. It now follows—

18. And tookest thy broidered garments, and coveredst them: and thou hast set mine oil and mine incense before them.

19. My meat also which I gave thee, fine flour, and oil, and honey, *wherewith* I fed thee, thou hast even set it before them for a sweet savour: and *thus* it was, saith the Lord God.

18. Et tulisti[1] vestes tuas discolores,[2] et operuisti eos[3] et oleum meum, et suffitum meum dedisti coram ipsis.[4]

19. Et panem meum quem dederam tibi, similam, et oleum, et mel quibus te cibaveram[5] etiam dedisti coram ipsis in odorem quietis: et ita fuit, dicit Dominator Iehovah.

Here God complains that the Jews turned their abundance of all things to perverse worship: for, as a husband who indulges his wife freely supplies all her wants, so a woman who is immodest wastes what she has received from her husband, and bestows it on adulterers; so also the Jews were prodigal in the worship of idols, and wasted upon them the blessings which God had bestowed upon them. Ezekiel, therefore, now follows up this sentiment. He says *that they took those variegated garments,* of which we spoke yesterday, and *covered their idols;* just as if an adulteress were to clothe her paramours in the very garments which she had received from her husband's liberality: *thou hast covered them,* he says. He afterwards adds, *thou hast offered my oil and incense.* Here he speaks more clearly, although he does not depart far from the figure, for they were accustomed to

---
[1] Or, " has taken."—*Calvin.*
[2] Or, " variated."—*Calvin.*
[3] Namely, " the false gods or lovers."—*Calvin.*
[4] That is, " has offered to them."—*Calvin.*
[5] Or, " had nourished."—*Calvin.*

use oil in sacrifices; and incense was used by all nations when they wished to propitiate their deities. There is no doubt that the unbelievers imitated the holy fathers, but sinfully, because they did not consider the right end. We know that the fathers used oil in their sacrifices, (Lev. ii. 1, and often elsewhere;) we know that incense was prescribed by God's law, and it was used promiscuously by all the nations, but without reason and judgment. So now God complains that they made incense of his herbs, and an offering of the oil which he had bestowed upon the Jews. He then adds the same of bread, and *fine flour, oil, and honey*. We said yesterday that by these words ample and delicate food was intended; for by the figure, a part for the whole, fine flour comprehends the best and sweetest bread, as well as other viands. *Oil and honey* are added. It is then just as if the Prophet had said that the Jews overflowed with all luxuries, yet consumed them badly. But this was a mockery not to be borne, when the Jews, after being enriched by God's beneficence, rashly threw it all away, and not only so, but adorned their false gods to the dishonour of God himself, when they ought to have offered to him what they wasted upon idols. For this reason he calls it *his own bread*, and explains the passage in this sense, that the Jews could neither ascribe to themselves the abundance of their possessions, nor boast in the fruitfulness of the soil; for all these things flowed from the mere benevolence of God. This ingratitude, then, was too foul—to bestow upon idols what God had given for a far different purpose. *I*, says he, *have fed thee*. He shows the legitimate use of such manifold abundance. Since they abounded in wheat, whence they obtained fine flour, and were stuffed full of other delicacies, they ought to be elevated towards God, and to exercise themselves in the duties of gratitude; but they abused that abundance in adorning false deities.

Thou hast offered it to them, therefore, *for a savour of peace*. Rest no doubt signifies appeasing here, as frequently with Moses, though others translate "for an odour of sweetness;" but they do not sufficiently express the meaning of Moses; for he means that when God is appeased there is peace between himself and men. (Lev. iii. 9, 13, 17, and often.) There is no doubt that "the odour of quiet" signifies a just expiation, by which God is appeased, so that he receives men into favour. This is everywhere said of the sacrifices of the law, since there was no other means by which men could be reconciled to God, unless by offering sacrifices according to his command. Now the Prophet transfers this ironically to their impious worship, when he says that they offered to idols all the delicacies by which God nourishes his people. To what purpose? *for a sweet savour;* that is, that they may be propitious to you. But it was ridiculous to wish to appease gods of stone and wood and silver. We see then how Ezekiel reproves the people's folly, when he says, *that they offered both fine flour and other things* to their idols to reconcile themselves to them. Now the crime is increased since the Jews did not recognise that singular blessing of being so reconciled to God, that he no longer imputed their sins to them. Woe indeed to us if we are destitute of this remedy! because we constantly commit various faults, and are thus subject to God's judgments. Unless, then, God receives us into favour, we see that nothing can be more miserable for us. But he has prescribed a fixed and easy rule by which he will be appeased, namely, by sacrifices—I am speaking of the fathers who lived under the law: for we know that we of this day must flee to the only sacrifice of Christ, which the sacrifices of the law shadowed forth. Since, therefore, the Jews could return to God's favour, and bury all their sins, and redeem themselves from the curse, how great was their madness in willingly depriving themselves of so inestimable a boon! Hence the Prophet now rebukes this folly, when he says that they propitiated their idols that they might appease them. He concludes at length, *and it was so, saith the Lord Jehovah.* Here God takes away all occasion for their turning aside, when he says *it was so :* for we know that men always have various pretences by which they lay the blame on some other parties, or soften it off, or cover it with some disguise. But God here says that there is no occasion for dispute, since the matter is perfectly plain. We see, then, that this word is used emphatically, when he says *I am the Lord;* for, if Ezekiel had announced it, they would not have listened to him; but God himself comes before them, and cuts off all excuses from the Jews. It follows—

20. Moreover, thou hast taken thy sons and thy daughters, whom thou hast born unto me, and these hast thou sacrificed unto them to be devoured. *Is this* of thy whoredoms a small matter?	20. Et sumpsisti filios tuos, et filias tuas quos genueras mihi: et jugulasti eos[1] ad comedendum:[2] an parum a scortationibus tuis?

Here God blames them for another crime, that of sacrificing their offspring to idols. This was a very blind superstition, by which parents put off the sense of humanity. It is indeed a detestable prodigy when a father rejects his children, and has no regard or respect for them. Even philosophers place among the principles of nature those affections which they call natural affections.[3] When, therefore, the affection of a father towards his children ceases, which is naturally implanted in all our hearts, then a man becomes a monster indeed. But not only did an inconsiderate fury seize upon the Jews, but, by slaying their own offspring, they thought that they obeyed God, as at this day the Papists are content with the name of good intentions, and do not think that any offering can be rejected if it be only daubed over with the title of either good intention or zeal for good. Such also was the confidence of the Jews; but, as I have said, we see that they were seized with a diabolic fury when they slew their sons and daughters. Abraham prepared to offer his son to God, but he had a clear command. (Gen. xxii. 9, 10, and Heb. xi. 19.)

Then we know that his obedience was founded on faith, because he was certainly persuaded, as the Apostle says, that a new offspring could spring up from the ashes of his son. Since, therefore, he extols the power of God as equal to this effect, he did not hesitate to slay his son. But since these wretches slew their sons without a command, they must be deservedly condemned for prodigious madness. The Prophet therefore now brings this crime before us: *that they*

---

[1] Or, " hast slain them."—*Calvin.*
[2] Or rather, " to consume them."—*Calvin.*
[3] Calvin uses here the appropriate Greek word στέργη.

had taken their sons and their daughters, and slew them to idols. He now adds, *to consume them,* since it is probable, and may be collected from various passages, that the sons were not always slain, but there were two kinds of offerings.[1] Sometimes they either slew their sons or cast them alive into the fire and burnt them as victims. Sometimes they carried them round and passed them through the fire, so that they received them safe again. But God here shows that he treats of that barbarous and cruel offering, since they did not spare their sons.

In this sense he adds, *that they slew their sons to eat them up,* or consume them. But another exaggeration of their crime is mentioned, when God expostulates concerning the insult offered: *thou,* says he, *hast slain thy sons and daughters,* but they are mine also, for thou barest them to me. Here God places himself in the position of a parent, because he had adopted the people as his own: the body of the people was as it were his spouse or wife. All their offspring were his sons, since, if God's treaty with the people was a marriage, all who sprung from the people ought to be esteemed his children. God therefore calls those his sons who were thus slain, just as if a husband should reproach his wife with depriving him of their common children. God therefore not only blames their cruelty and superstition, but adds also that he was deprived of his children. But this, as is well known, is a most atrocious kind of injury. For who does not prefer his own blood to either fields, or merchandize, or money? As children are more precious than all goods, so a father is more grievously injured if children are taken away, as God here pronounces that he had done: *thou hadst born them unto me,* says he. Hence sacrilege was added to idolatry when thou didst deprive me of them. He will soon call them again his own in the same sense. A question arises here, how God reckons among his sons those who were complete strangers to him? He had

---

[1] A passage in Dionysius Halicarnassus illustrates this idolatrous practice:—" And after this, having ordered that fires should be made before the tents, he brings out the people to leap over the flames, for the purifying of their pollutions."—Antiq. Rom. Bk. I., sect. 88, p. 72, and marg. 75. Edit. Hudson.

said in the beginning of the chapter (verse 3) that the people derived their origin from the Amorites and Hittites, since they had declined from the piety of Abraham and the other fathers. Since then the Jews were cast off while they were in Egypt, and after that had been such breakers of the covenant as the Prophet had thus far shown, were they not aliens? Yes; but God here regards his covenant, which was inviolable and could not be rendered void by man's perfidy. The Jews, then, of whom the Prophet now speaks, could no longer bear children to God: for he said that the body of the people was like a foul harlot, who walks about and turns round and seeks vague and promiscuous meetings. Since it was so, the children whom such idolaters bore were spurious, instead of being worthy of such honour that God should call them his sons: this is true with respect to them, but as concerns the covenant, they are called sons of God. And this is worthy of observation, because in the Papacy such declension has grown up through many ages, that they have altogether denied God. Hence they have no connection with him, because they have corrupted his whole worship by their sacrilege, and their religion is vitiated in so many ways, that it differs in nothing from the corruptions of the heathen. And yet it is certain that a portion of God's covenant remains among them, because although they have cut themselves off from God and altogether abandoned him by their perfidy, yet God remains faithful. (Rom. iii. 3, 4.) Paul, when he speaks of the Jews, shows that God's covenant with them is not abolished, although the greater part of the people had utterly abandoned God. So also it must be said of the papists, since it was not in their power to blot out God's covenant entirely, although with regard to themselves, as I have said, they are without it; and show by their obstinacy that they are the sworn enemies of God. Hence it arises, that our baptism does not need renewal, because although the Devil has long reigned in the papacy, yet he could not altogether extinguish God's grace: nay, a Church is among them; for otherwise Paul's prophecy would have been false, when he says that Antichrist was seated in the temple of God. (2 Thess. ii. 4.) If in the papacy there had been only Satan's dunghill or brothel, and no form of a Church had remained in it, this had been a proof that Antichrist did not sit in the temple of God. But this, as I have said, exaggerates their crime, and is very far from enabling them to erect their crests as they do. For when they thunder out with full cheeks—" We are the Church of God," or, " The seat of the Church is with us,"—the solution is easy; the Church is indeed among them, that is, God has his Church there, but hidden and wonderfully preserved : but it does not follow that they are worthy of any honour ; nay, they are more detestable, because they ought to bear sons and daughters to God : but they bear them for the Devil and for idols, as this passage teaches. It follows—

21. That thou hast slain my children, and delivered them to cause them to pass through *the fire* for them?

21. Et mactasti filios meos, et posuisti eos ut transirent illis.[1]

He strengthens the same sentence, and more clearly explains that they offered their sons and daughters by cruelly sacrificing them when they passed them through the fire. This was a kind of purifying, as we have seen elsewhere. When, therefore, they passed their children through the fire, it was a rite of lustration and expiation ; and they brought them to the fire, as I have lately explained, in two different ways. Here the Prophet speaks especially of that cruel and brutal offering. We have already mentioned the sense in which God claims a right in the sons of his people, not as members of the Church properly speaking, but as adopted by God. And here again we must hold what Paul says, that all the progeny of Abraham were not lawful sons, since a difference must be made between sons of the flesh and sons of promise. (Rom. ix. 7, 8.) This is as yet partially obscure, but it may be shortly explained. We may remark that there was a twofold election of God : since speaking generally, he chose the whole family of Abraham. For circumcision was common to all, being the symbol and seal of adoption : since when God wished all the sons of Abraham to be circumcised from the least to the greatest, he at the same time chose them as his sons: this was one kind of

[1] Verbally, for passing them over to them, that is, to idols.—*Calvin.*

adoption or election. But the other was secret, because God took to himself out of that multitude those whom he wished: and these are sons of promise, these are remnants of gratuitous favour, as Paul says. (Rom. xi. 8.) This distinction, therefore, now takes away all doubt, since the Prophet speaks of the unbelievers and the profane who had departed from the worship of God. For this their unbelief was a complete abdication. It is true, then, that as far as themselves were concerned, they were strangers, and so God's secret election did not flourish in them, but yet they were God's people, as far as relates to external profession.

If any one objects that this circumcision was useless, and hence their election without the slightest effect, the answer is at hand: God by his singular kindness honoured those miserable ones by opening a way of approach for them to the hope of life and salvation by the outward testimonies of adoption. Then as to their being at the same time strangers, that happened through their own fault. Hence we may shortly hold, that the Jews were naturally accursed through being Adam's seed: but by supernatural and singular privilege, they were exempt and free from the curse: since circumcision was a testimony of the adoption by which God had consecrated them to himself: hence they were holy; and as to their being impure, it could not, as we have said, abolish God's covenant. The same thing ought at this time to prevail in the Papacy. For we are all born under the curse: and yet God acknowledges supernaturally as his sons all who spring from the faithful, not only in the first or second degree, but even to a thousand generations. And so Paul says that the children of the faithful are holy, since baptism does not lose its efficacy, and the adoption of God remains fixed, (1 Cor. vii. 14,) yet the greater part is without the covenant through their own unbelief. God meanwhile has preserved to himself a remnant in all ages, and at this day he chooses whom he will out of the promiscuous multitude.

Now let us go on. I had omitted at the end of the last verse the phrase, *Are thy fornications a small matter?* By this question God wishes to press the Jews home, since they had not only violated their conjugal fidelity by prostituting themselves to idols, but had added the cruelty which we have seen in slaying their sons. Lastly, he shows that their impiety was desperate.

> 22. And in all thine abominations and thy whoredoms thou hast not remembered the days of thy youth, when thou wast naked and bare, *and* wast polluted in thy blood.

> 22. Et in omnibus abominationibus tuis et scortationibus tuis non recordata es dierum adolescentiæ tuæ, cum tu esses nuda et discooperta, et fœdata in sanguinibus tuis esses.

Here God accommodates to his own ends what he has hitherto related, namely, the extreme wickedness and baseness of the people's ingratitude in thus prostituting themselves to idols. Hence he recalls to mind their condition when he espoused them. For if the wretched slavery from which they had been delivered had been present to their mind, they had not been so blinded with perverse confidence, nor had they exulted in their lasciviousness. But since they had forgotten all God's benefits, they became lascivious, and prostrated themselves to foul idolatries, and provoked God in every way. Now the Prophet proves this when he says, *behold, through these abominations the people did not remember their youth.* Whence happens it that impure and lustful women thus despise their husbands, unless through being blinded by their own beauty? And since they do not recognise their own disgrace, they please themselves in foul loves, as saith the Prophet Hosea, (chap. ii. 5.) Such then was the self-confidence of the Jews, that they pleased themselves by their beauty and ornaments: though God's glory and brightness shone forth in them, yet they did not perceive the source of their dignity; and hence the addition of ingratitude to pride. *Thou hast not remembered,* says he, *the days of thy youth, when thou wast naked, and bare, and defiled in thy blood.* It follows—

> 23. And it came to pass, after all thy wickedness, (woe, woe unto thee! saith the Lord God,)
> 24. *That* thou hast also built unto thee an eminent place, and hast made thee an high place in every street.
> 25. Thou hast built thy high place

> 23. Et fuit post omnem malitiam tuam, Væ væ tibi, dicit Dominator Iehovah.
> 24. Et ædificasti tibi excelsum, et fecisti tibi excelsum in omni platea.[1]
> 25. Ad omne caput[2] viæ ædificasti

---

[1] "In every street."—*Calvin.*

[2] Or, "beginning."—*Calvin.*

at every head of the way, and hast made thy beauty to be abhorred, and hast opened thy feet to every one that passed by, and multiplied thy whoredoms.

excelsum tuum : et abominabilem fecisti tuam pulchritudinem: et divaricasti[1] pedes tuos omni transeunti, et multiplicasti tuas scortationes.

The first verse is variously explained. Some read the clause separately, ויהי אחרי כל רעתך, *vihi achri kel regnethek*—*it was after all thy wickedness:* and they think that God threatens the Jews here as he did in Hosea, (chap. ii. 9, 10.) For after God had there complained that his wool and his flax had been taken away, and offered as gifts to idols, he afterwards adds, I will demand all things back again, and then all thy beauty shall be taken from thee, and thy nakedness shall be laid bare, so that thou shalt be deservedly ashamed. Thus then they explain these words, that the condition of the Jews should be as it formerly was; as if he had said in one word, I will so avenge myself, that whether you will or not, you shall be compelled to feel the disgrace of your nakedness, since I will manifest it again. But this sense seems forced; therefore I unite it with the remainder of the verse which follows it. Thus then the language of the Prophet flows on : *and it was after all thy wickedness that thou buildest a high place for thyself—thou madest for thyself a lofty place in every street:* there are two different words, but the sense is the same : *thou didst set up thy high places in all the principal ways, and so,* says he, *thy beauty became abominable.* But this is inserted by way of parenthesis, *Alas! alas for thee!* This exclamation is abruptly interposed. But, at the same time, I have no doubt that these things all adhere together, since the Jews added sin to sin, and never made an end of sinning. He says, therefore, after they had been perfidious and ungrateful to God, after they had basely devoted all they had to perverse worship, then this new crime was added, *that they had erected high places in every street and in every path.*

If any one objects that this was not a greater crime than others, the answer is easy, that God does not speak of one high place only, or of one altar, but he comprehends all the

---

[1] " Thou hast poured forth, or opened; but we may use the proper word, thou hast spread."—*Calvin.*

signs of idolatry by which they had infected the land; for it was the height of impudence to erect everywhere the standard of their superstitions. For every high place and every altar was a testimony of their backsliding; just as if they had openly boasted that they would not magnify the worship of the law, and intended purposely to overthrow whatever God had prescribed. God therefore, not without cause, burns with wrath *because the Jews had erected high places and altars everywhere.* Now, then, we understand the Holy Spirit's meaning as far as these words are concerned. *It is added, after all thy wickedness,* says he; that is, in addition to all thy crimes, this sin and impudence is added, that thou hast built not only one, but innumerable high places *in every street, nay, in every pathway of importance,* that is, in the most celebrated places. For the heads of the pathways are the most conspicuous places, and whatever is done there is more exposed to the eyes of all.

We must now notice the exclamation which is interposed. *Alas! alas! for thee, saith the Lord Jehovah.* Since the Jews, through their sloth, were not at all attentive to the reproofs of the prophets, that God might waken them up, he here pronounces his curse twice. It is clear that they were not moved by it: but this vehemence tended to their severer condemnation, since though they were drowned and sunk in deep sleep, yet they might be raised by this formidable voice. There is no doubt that they applauded themselves for their own superstitions; but it is on that account profitable to estimate the weight of these words of God. For we gather from hence, that when idolaters indulge in their own fictions, and think themselves entirely free from blame, the word of God is sufficient, by which he thunders against them, saying, *alas! alas! for thee.* Hence men cease to judge according to their own notions, and are rather attentive to the sentence of God, and acknowledge his curse passing on them when they think that they are rightly discharging the duty of piety in worshipping idols.

He now adds, *that he made their beauty to be abhorred.* I have no doubt that the Prophet alludes to the filthiness of abandoned women; and even the Latins called them " worn out," whose foulness arises from their utterly giving themselves up to every wickedness. The Prophet then says that the people were not only like an abandoned woman who engages in impure amours, but that their conduct was gross in the extreme; for though many gratify improper desires through intemperate lust, yet they fastidiously reject those foul and shameless females who are notorious for profligacy. The Prophet means, then, that the people had come to such a pitch of abomination, just as the most abandoned of the sex. He now adds, *thou hast spread thy feet to every passer-by, and hast multiplied thy fornications.* This is taken also from the conduct of harlots, and confirms what we have already explained, that the Jews indulged not only in one kind of idolatry, but were prone to all abominations, like females who beset the paths, and address all they meet, and not only so, but shamelessly *spread their feet* everywhere to entice admirers.

PRAYER.

Grant, Almighty God, since thou deignest to receive us not only into confidence and dependence, but to the condition of sons, that we may worship thee with sacred love, and revere thee through our whole life as a Father; and may we so submit ourselves to thee as to feel thy covenant firm and sacred towards us; and may we experience that thou never callest men to thee in vain, so long as they obey thee and respond to thy promises; until at length we enjoy that blessedness which is laid up for us in heaven, through Christ our Lord.—Amen.

Lecture Forty-Fifth.

26. Thou hast also committed fornication with the Egyptians thy neighbours, great of flesh; and hast increased thy whoredoms, to provoke me to anger.

26. Et scortata es cum filiis Ægypti vicinis tuis magnis carne: et multiplicasti scortationes tuas ad irritandum me.

I MENTIONED at the beginning of the chapter, that the Prophet blames the Jews not for one single kind of fornication, but for two different kinds. Interpreters do not observe this, but think that the Prophet is always discoursing of idols and superstitions. But if we prudently weigh all

.cumstances, what I have said will not appear doubtful, ..iely, that the Jews were condemned not only for vitiating the worship of God by their perverse fictions, but for flying, now to the Egyptians, now to the Assyrians, and thus involving themselves in unlawful covenants. It is a very common method with the Prophets to call such covenants fornications: for as a wife ought to lie under the shadow of her husband, so God wished the Jews to be content under his protection. But as soon as any danger frightened them, they fled tremblingly to either Egypt, or Assyria, or Chaldæa. We see, then, that they had in some sense renounced God's help, since they could not rest under his protection, but were hurried hither and thither by vague impulse. After the Prophet had inveighed against their superstitions, he now approaches another crime, namely, the Jews implicating themselves in forbidden treaties. He begins with Egypt. God had clearly forbidden the elect people to have any dealings with Egypt. Even if God had not made known the reason, yet they ought to have obeyed his command. But I have already explained the reason why God was unwilling that the Israelites should enter into any covenant with the Egyptians, because he wished to try their faith and patience, and if they would fly to his help when any danger pressed upon them, as the saying is, like a sacred anchor. There was also another reason, because from the time when God drew his people out from thence, he wished them separated from that nation which had raged so cruelly against their miserable guests. As far as the Chaldæans and Assyrians are concerned, the former reason prevailed thus far, that it was not lawful for them to distrust God's aid in their dangers.

Now, therefore, we understand the Prophet's meaning when he says, *that the Jews had committed fornication with the sons of Egypt.* He adds, *they were gross in flesh.* He means that they were foul and immodest, and were inflamed with disgraceful lust.[1] He uses a grosser simile by and bye,

[1] Calvin's Latin adds, " ut inhiarent longis et crassis mentulis." The Reformer dwells so minutely on the language of the Prophet, that the refined taste of modern days will not bear a literal translation of some clauses.

the circumstances, what I have said will not appear doubtful, namely, that the Jews were condemned not only for vitiating the worship of God by their perverse fictions, but for flying, now to the Egyptians, now to the Assyrians, and thus involving themselves in ·unlawful covenants. It is a very common method with the Prophets to call such covenants fornications: for as a wife ought to lie under the shadow of her husband, so God wished the Jews to be content under his protection. But as soon as any danger frightened them, they fled tremblingly to either Egypt, or Assyria, or Chaldæa. We see, then, that they had in some sense renounced God's help, since they could not rest under his protection, but were hurried hither and thither by vague impulse. After the Prophet had inveighed against their superstitions, he now approaches another crime, namely, the Jews implicating themselves in forbidden treaties. He begins with Egypt. God had clearly forbidden the elect people to have any dealings with Egypt. Even if God had not made known the reason, yet they ought to have obeyed his command. But I have already explained the reason why God was unwilling that the Israelites should enter into any covenant with the Egyptians, because he wished to try their faith and patience, and if they would fly to his help when any danger pressed upon them, as the saying is, like a sacred anchor. There was also another reason, because from the time when God drew his people out from thence, he wished them separated from that nation which had raged so cruelly against their miserable guests. As far as the Chaldæans and Assyrians are concerned, the former reason prevailed thus far, that it was not lawful for them to distrust God's aid in their dangers.

Now, therefore, we understand the Prophet's meaning when he says, *that the Jews had committed fornication with the sons of Egypt.* He adds, *they were gross in flesh.* He means that they were foul and immodest, and were inflamed with disgraceful lust.[1] He uses a grosser simile by and bye,

---

[1] Calvin's Latin adds, " ut inhiarent longis et crassis mentulis." The Reformer dwells so minutely on the language of the Prophet, that the refined taste of modern days will not bear a literal translation of some clauses.

coured his nephew. But if we seek the principle and the cause which induced Abraham to enter into a treaty with his neighbours, we shall find his intention to be nothing else but to dwell at home in peace, and to be safe from all injury. He was solitary, as Isaiah calls him : he had, indeed, a numerous family, but no offspring ; and hence he could not escape making treaties with his neighbours. But when the Lord placed the people in the land of Canaan on the condition of defending them there, of protecting them on all sides, and of opposing all their foes, we see them enclosed, as it were, by his protection, so as to render all treaties useless ; since they could not treat with either the Egyptians or the Assyrians without at the same time withdrawing themselves from God's aid.

As far as we are concerned, I have said that we have more freedom, if we are only careful that the lusts of the flesh do not entice us to seek alliances which may entangle us in the sins of others ; for it is difficult to retain the favour of those with whom we associate, unless we entirely agree with them. If they are impious, they will draw us into contempt of God and adulterous rites, and so it will happen that one evil will spring from another. Nothing, therefore, is better than to reef our sails, and to look to God alone, and to have our minds fixed on him, and not to allow any kind of alliance, unless necessity compels us. And though we must prudently take care that no condition be mingled with it which may draw us off from the pure and sincere worship of God, since the devil is always cleverly plotting against the sons of God, and draws them into hidden snares. When, therefore, we are about to contract an alliance, we should always take care lest our liberty be in any degree abridged, and lest we be drawn aside by stealthy and concealed arts from the simple worship of God. It now follows—

27. Behold, therefore I have stretched out my hand over thee, and have diminished thine ordinary *food*, and delivered thee unto the will of them that hate thee, the daughters of the Philistines, which are ashamed of thy lewd way.

27. Et ecce, extendi manum meam super te, et diminui demensum tuum, et tradidi te desiderio[1] earum quæ te oderant filiarum Philistim, quæ pudefactæ sunt a viis tuis sceleris.[2]

[1] Or, " lust."—*Calvin.*   [2] That is, " which were wicked."—*Calvin.*

Here God reproves the hardness of the Jews because admonition did not render them wise. The common proverb aptly says, " fools grow wise only by the rod ;" and when their obstinacy is such that the rod does no good, their faults are indeed desperate. Hence God complains, when he had chastised the Jews, that even this did not profit them, for they were so perverse that they did not apply their minds to reflect upon their sins. For God's blows ought to rouse us up, so that our faults previously hidden ought to be brought to light and knowledge ; but when we champ the bit, and are not affected by the blows, then our abandoned disposition is made manifest. Now the Prophet condemns this obstinacy in the Jews : *I have extended,* says he, *my hand over thee.* He now enumerates two kinds of chastisement, first, when God deprived the Jews of the abundance of the possessions by which they were enriched ; and then because he had subjected them to the lust of their enemies. Those who translate justification as Jerome does, depart from the sense of the Prophet : חק, *chek,* signifies, indeed, a statute and edict, and he explains it of the law. But how will this agree with the Prophet's retaining the simile already used ? for he compares God to a husband. God now pronounces *that he had taken away their appointed portion,* when he saw himself a laughingstock through his impure wife ; that is, what he had intended for both food and clothing : for husbands spend a fixed sum on their wives in food, clothing, and ornament. And God previously recounted, among other things, that what he had conferred upon the Jews they had spent in superstitions. Hence, for this reason, he now says, *I have taken away their allotted portion,* that is, what I had assigned to them. This was one part of the chastisement : for he compares the fruitfulness of the land and other advantages to the portion which the husband assigns to the wife.

Now the other chastisement follows—their being harassed by their enemies ; for not only did the Jews find themselves encompassed by the Philistines, but they were delivered up and bound to slavery, as Moses says, (Deut. xxxii. 30,) How, then, could one vanquish ten, and ten chase a thousand, unless we had been shut up in his hand? He shows, therefore, that our enemies are never our superiors unless God enslaves us to them. But those who do not calmly subject themselves to God's command, but are refractory, are delivered into the enemy's hand, that their contumacy may be subdued by severe tyranny. Now we understand what the Prophet means by this verse: he enlarges upon the people's wickedness in not turning to God, though they felt by clear experience that they were under a curse. They ought to examine their lives, to groan before God, to acknowledge their fault, and to beg for pardon: since no feeling was awakened, the Prophet gathers that their obstinacy was desperate. This passage is worthy of our notice, that we may be attentive to God's chastisements. Whenever God even raises his finger and threatens us, let us know that he is anxious for our safety: hence in our turn let us rouse ourselves and implore his pity, and especially let us repent of our sins by which we see his anger to have been enflamed. (Jer. ii. 30.) But if we remain slothful, we see that no excuse for us remains, since God elsewhere complains that he is trifled with, when he has chastised his children in vain. Here נפש, *nephesh*, the soul is used for lust or desire, as I have explained it. It follows—

28. Thou hast played the whore also with the Assyrians, because thou wast unsatiable; yea, thou hast played the harlot with them, and yet couldest not be satisfied.

28. Et scortata es cum filiis Assur,[1] quia à non esse satietatem tibi,[2] scortata es *inquam* cum illis, et ne sic quidem fuisti satiata.

I interpret this verse also of the covenant by which the Jews had entangled themselves, when they willingly joined themselves to the Assyrians; for this was a sure sign of distrust, when they so desired foreign aid, as if they had been deprived of God's protection. And it would be absurd to explain this verse of idolatries, since the prophets were not accustomed to speak in this way, that the people committed fornication with the Assyrians, because they imitated their superstitions and perverse worship. As, therefore, we formerly saw that the Jews had defiled themselves with

[1] " Of Assyria."—*Calvin.*
[2] Verbally, " because there was no satisfying thee."—*Calvin.*

idols, and prostituted themselves to impious ceremonies, forgetful of God's law ; so now the Prophet accuses them of a different kind of pollution, since they eagerly sought for aid from all quarters, as if God had not sufficient strength for their protection. For otherwise there was no religious reason for their not making peace with the Assyrians ; but when they saw themselves oppressed by the kings of Israel and Syria, then they thought of sending for the Assyrians ; and this was like thrusting God from his place. (2 Kings xvi. 7-9.) For God was willing to defend the land with extended wings, and to cherish the Jews as a hen does her brood, as Moses says, (Deut. xxxii. 11.) Now, in thinking themselves exposed to any danger, they really throw off the help of God. It is not surprising, then, that the Prophet says, *that they had polluted themselves with the Assyrians, because they were not satisfied.* He pursues the simile on which we have dwelt sufficiently ; for he blames the Jews for their insatiable lust, just as when a woman is not content with a single follower, and attracting a crowd obtrudes herself without modesty or delicacy, and sells herself to wickedness. Such was the licentiousness of the Jews, that they united many acts of pollution together. They had already departed from the true faith in making a treaty with the Egyptians, and they added another imagination, that it was useful to have the Assyrians in alliance with them: hence that unbridled lust which the Prophet metaphorically rebukes. It follows—

29. Thou hast moreover multiplied thy fornication in the land of Canaan unto Chaldea; and yet thou wast not satisfied herewith.

29. Et multiplicasti[1] scortationes tuas super terram Chanaan in Chaldæa, et ne in hoc quidem fuisti satiata.

Here the Prophet teaches that the Jews were immoderate in their desires, just as if a woman was not satisfied with two or three followers, should wantonly crave after many lovers: such, says the Prophet, was the Jews' licentiousness. As to his saying, *over the land of Canaan in Chaldæa,* some think it means, that they heaped up the impure rites of all the nations, and not only defiled themselves with the ancient

---

[1] Or, " thou hast increased."— *Calvin.*

idolatries of the nations of Canaan, but imitated the Chaldæans in their impiety. Others say in Chaldæa, which is next to the land of Canaan; but this comment, like the last, is too forced: others take אל, *al,* comparatively, for "through" the land of Canaan. But I only understand it as a particle expressing likeness, thus, *thou hast multiplied thy pollutions in Chaldæa just as in the land of Canaan.* It is not surprising if they defiled themselves with their neighbours, as the Prophet had formerly said they did with the Egyptians, but when they ran about to a remote region of the world, this indeed was most remarkable. This then seems the real sense, and it reads best, *that they increased their defilements in Chaldæa as in the land of Canaan.* For if a female meets with a stranger she may act sinfully without so much disgrace, but when she runs about to a distance to seek followers, this proves her most abandoned. I have no doubt that the Prophet here exaggerates the people's crimes by comparison, since they penetrated even to the Chaldæans to pollute themselves among them. He says *that the Jews were not satisfied even with this,* using the same expression as when treating of the Assyrians. The sum of the whole is, that the Jews were seized with such a furious impulse that they manifested no moderation in their wickedness. For they had not revolted from God once only, or in one direction, but wherever occasion offered, they were accustomed to seize it too eagerly, so that they showed in this way that not even a drop of piety remained in their minds. Let us learn then from this passage to put the bridle on our lusts in time: for when the fire is lighted up, it is not easily extinguished, and the devil is always supplying wood or adding oil to the furnace, as the phrase is. Let us then prevent the evil which is here condemned in the Jews, and let us restrain ourselves, lest the devil seize upon us with insane fury. It follows—

30. How weak is thine heart, saith the Lord God, seeing thou doest all these *things,* the work of an imperious whorish woman.

30. Quam molle[1] est cor tuum! dicit Dominator Iehovah, cum facis hoc totum opus mulieris meretricis robustæ.[2]

The Prophet seems at variance with himself when he compares the Jews to a robust or very strong woman, and

[1] Or, " dissolute."—*Calvin.*   [2] Or, " ruling."—*Calvin.*

yet says that their heart was dissolute. For those who translate an obstinate heart are without a reason for it, for this seems to imply some kind of resistance, as they were strong and bold, and yet of a soft or weak or infirm heart. But in the despisers of God both evils are to be blamed when they flow away like water and yet are hard as rocks. They flow away, then, when there is no strength or constancy in them; for they are drawn aside this way and that, as some explain it, by a distracted heart, but we must always come to the idea of softness. All who revolt from God are borne along by their own levity, so that the minds of the impious are changeable and moveable: for the heart is here taken for the seat of the intellect, as in many other places. Hence the Prophet accuses the Jews of sloth, but under the name of a dissolute heart: as in French we say *un cœur lasche*, and the Prophet's sense is best explained by that French word—faint-hearted. But it is sufficient to understand the Prophet's meaning, that the Jews were unstable, and agitated and distracted hither and thither, since there was nothing in them either firm or solid. Meanwhile he compares them to a strong and abandoned woman, since we know the boldness of the despisers of God in sinning against him. Since then they are dissolute, because they have no power of attention, and nothing is stable in their minds: yet they are like rocks, and carry themselves audaciously, and do not hesitate to strive with God. Although therefore these two states of mind appear contrary in their nature, yet we may always see them in the reprobate, though in different ways. Thus he properly calls the Jews not only *a robust* or abandoned woman, but "a high and mighty dame," as it may best be rendered in French, *une maitresse putain ou paillarde*.[1] It is forced to explain the word "lofty," as taking license for her desires. I do not hesitate to interpret it of the people being like dissolute women, who throw aside all modesty, and seek lovers from all quarters, and entertain them all. This is the Prophet's sense. It now follows—

[1] The readers of Shakspeare will readily translate this into idiomatic English.

31. In that thou buildest thine eminent place in the head of every way, and makest thine high place in every street; and hast not been as an harlot, in that thou scornest hire.	31. Cum extulisti sublime tuum in capite omnis viæ, et excelsum tuum fecisti in omni celebri loco: et non fuisti tanquam meretrix ad spernendum munus.

Here the Prophet again reproves the superstitions to which the Jews had devoted themselves: but yet he speaks figuratively, because by high places he does not simply mean altars, but tents by which the Jews had attempted to entice their neighbours: just as if an immodest female should choose a high place, and build her couch there conspicuously to attract her followers. Although therefore he inveighs against superstitions, the language is not simple, but retains the same simile as had been previously used. He says that the Jews were so prone to lust, that they were ostentatious and sought followers from a distance, and erected their tents or couches in high places. Since this has been treated before, I now pass it over slightly. But we may remark that a thing which seems of slight importance is here seriously condemned by the Prophet, whence we may learn that the worship of God is not to be estimated by our natural perception. For who would think it so great a crime to build an altar on a high place to God's honour? but we see that the Prophet abhors that superstition. Since therefore God wishes nothing to be changed in his worship, as the principal part of his worship is obedience, which he prefers to all sacrifices, (1 Sam. xv. 22,) let us learn that things which we might tolerate ought to be detested by us, because God condemns them so severely.

Since therefore thou hast erected and made for thyself a high place at the head of all streets and paths, that is in every celebrated place. Here we see how ardently they were enflamed by idolatry so as to provoke the anger of God, and this seemed unworthy of them, as the papists at this day, who are bent upon idol worship, and under the title of "devotion," think that any vice both can and ought to be excused before God. But, on the other side, the Holy Spirit says that idolaters sin the more grievously in being so eager for those impure rites. He says, *thou wast not like a harlot in despising hire.* Some explain this coldly, that harlots mentally despise the folly of those who reward them, but this comment is incorrect: the other view is more probable, namely, that the Jews were not like a harlot who despises the bribe by which she is deceived: for by this craftiness they gain most influence when they contemptuously despise what is offered them, and scarcely deign to touch it: they do this that the wretched lover may not think himself sufficiently liberal, and so may double his gift and squander away all his goods. This passage then may mean that the people were not like a harlot who despises her reward that the wretched lover may feel ashamed and increase his offer. But the Prophet's sense seems to me different, though I do not altogether reject this. I interpret it thus: the Jews were not like a harlot, since they despised any reward for their sin, and harlots do not: they make a gain of their lusts, whence the name they bear. Since then such persons sell themselves for reward, the Prophet says that the Jews were not like them: how so? because they despised reward, and through the mere desire of gratifying their appetites, they neither asked nor expected any reward. Afterwards it follows—

32. *But as* a wife that committeth adultery, *which* taketh strangers instead of her husband!

32. Mulier adultera loco viri sui sumit extraneos.

Some translate it an adulteress under her husband's roof, and תחת, *thecheth*, signifies "instead of:" and they explain it thus, that adulteresses do not divorce themselves from their husbands when they violate the marriage bond, but always remain at home for the purpose of admitting strangers; and they think the people's crime increased by this comparison, that they not only acted deceitfully towards God, but openly revolted from him, and left his home; for many shameless women remain at home, and hide their crimes as far as they can; but when a woman deserts her husband and children, then her case is most deplorable: they think, therefore, that the Prophet is here exaggerating the divorce or revolt of the people from God; but the sense seems better simply to compare them to an adulteress who admits strangers in her husband's stead: *thou art*, says he, *an adulteress who hath sent for strange lovers instead of thy husband:* for a woman married to a liberal husband is treated by him honourably; and if she seeks lovers from all sides, she is induced by neither avarice nor covetousness, but by her own lusts. In fine, as the Prophet lately said that they despised all gain through being blinded by their appetites, so he now says they were like an adulteress who rejects her husband; and not only so, but throws herself into the protection of others, while she has an honourable and happy home.

PRAYER.

Grant, Almighty God, since thou hast thought us worthy of such honour, that we should be bound to thee in thine only-begotten Son by the bond of a spiritual marriage,—that we may remain in that fidelity which we promised to thee, since we have found thee faithful to us by so many proofs on thy part, until, having passed through this present life, we arrive at the enjoyment of that blessedness which is the fruit of our faithful chastity, through Jesus Christ our Lord.—Amen.

Lecture Forty-Sixth.

33. They give gifts to all whores; but thou givest thy gifts to all thy lovers, and hirest them, that they may come unto thee on every side for thy whoredom.

33. Cunctis meretricibus dant munus,[1] tu autem dedisti munera tua cunctis amatoribus tuis: et conduxisti eos ut ingrederentur ad te undique[2] in scortationibus tuis.

HERE the Prophet shows the great folly of the Jews in shamelessly squandering their goods; for gain impels harlots to their occupation: they feel the disgrace of it, but want urges them on. But the Prophet says, that when the Jews committed sin they did it with extravagance, since they spared no expense in attracting their lovers. He pursues the simile which we have had before; for he compares the nation to a perfidious woman who leaves her husband and offers herself to adulterers. We now understand the Prophet's meaning. It is clear that the Jews did not act thus on purpose, for they thought they would profit by their treaties with the Egyptians and Assyrians: they were un-

---

[1] That is, "presents are accustomed to be given."—*Calvin.*
[2] "From all around."—*Calvin.*

willing to serve their idols for nothing, since they hoped for most ample rewards from this their adulterous worship. But the Holy Spirit does not regard either what they wished or hoped for, but speaks of the matter as it was. It is clear, then, that the Jews were very prodigal in their superstitions, and we see this even now in the papacy. Those who grudge even a farthing for the relief of the poor will throw away guineas when they wish to compound for their sins; and there is no end to their extravagance under this madness. The very same rage prevailed among the Jews for which Ezekiel now reproves them. He says, then, *that they offered gifts to their lovers;* for, as I have said, they were so prodigal in the worship of false gods, that when they desired a treaty with either the Egyptians or Assyrians, they were necessarily loaded with valuable presents; and history bears witness that they entirely exhausted themselves. Lastly, the Prophet here shows that the Jews were so blind, that in leaving God, and devoting themselves to idols, they failed to obtain any advantage. Then, when they implicated themselves in perverse and wicked treaties, he shows that they were so utterly deranged as to deprive themselves of all their goods, and yet to receive nothing but disgrace in return for their extravagance: *presents are given to all harlots, but thou bestowest thine.* Jerome takes the pronoun passively, meaning the blessings which God had bestowed upon the people: and this passage is like that in Hosea, (chap. ii. 5-8,) where God complains that the Jews had profaned the blessings which he had conferred upon them, just as if a wife should bestow on adulterers what she had received from her husband. Foul indeed is this! for a husband thought these would be pledges of chastity when he adorned his wife with precious garments, or enriched her with other presents and ornaments; but when a wife, forgetful of modesty and propriety, throws her husband's gifts at the feet of adulterers, this is indeed outrageous. Hence this sense does not displease me, although it would be more simple to understand it that the Jews had wasted away all their goods. He says, *that they had hired their lovers to come in from every side for wickedness.* He repeats again what we saw before, that the Jews were abandoned sinners, for some, though impure, are content with a single lover. But as he had before said that the Jews spread their feet widely, so he now adds, *that they hired lovers from all sides.* Shameful indeed is such conduct in any woman: yet Ezekiel reproves the Jews for this indelicacy, and we saw the reason in yesterday's lecture. It follows—

34. And the contrary is in thee from *other* women in thy whoredoms, whereas none followeth thee to commit whoredoms: and in that thou givest a reward, and no reward is given unto thee, therefore thou art contrary.

34. Et fuit in te inversio a mulieribus, in scortationibus tuis, et post tua postrema[1] non erit scortatio:[2] quia dedisti munus, et munus tibi non fuit datum: ita fuisti in contrarium.[3]

But the Prophet only confirms his former teaching, that the Jews were seized with such lust, and in so unaccustomed a manner, that they could only satisfy their desires with severe loss; but this comparison only magnifies their crime, since they were worse than any harlots; for although they basely sell themselves, yet the hope of gain is a kind of pretext and excuse, and a starving woman may be led into great excess; but far fouler and less excusable is her conduct who purchases her lovers. It now follows—

35. Wherefore, O harlot, hear the word of the Lord:
36. Thus saith the Lord God, Because thy filthiness was poured out, and thy nakedness discovered through thy whoredoms with thy lovers, and with all the idols of thy abominations, and by the blood of thy children, which thou didst give unto them;
37. Behold, therefore I will gather all thy lovers, with whom thou hast taken pleasure, and all *them* that thou hast loved, with all *them* that thou hast hated; I will even gather them round about against thee, and will discover thy nakedness unto them, that they may see all thy nakedness.

35. Propterea, meretrix, audi sermonem Iehovæ.
36. Sic dicit Dominator Iehovah, quia effusum fuit infimum tuum,[4] et detecta fuit turpitudo tua[5] in scortationibus tuis erga amatores tuos, et erga omnia idola abominationum tuarum, et in sanguinibus filiorum tuorum quos dedisti illis.
37. Propterea ecce congregabo cunctos amatores tuos, quibus te oblectasti erga eos, et omnes quos dilexisti, et quos odisti: congregabo inquam, eos contra te à circuitu, et retegam[6] pudenda tua[7] coram ipsis, et videbunt totam turpitudinem tuam.

---

[1] That is, " following thee."—*Calvin.*
[2] " Understand like thine."—*Calvin.*
[3] The meaning is the same, the verb הפך, *hephek*, means to overthrow; hence the noun signifies " inversion," or " the contrary."—*Calvin.*
[4] Properly " thy money;" but it is taken metaphorically for " thy lower parts."—*Calvin.* [5] Or, " nakedness."—*Calvin.*
[6] Or, " I will discover."—*Calvin.* [7] Or, " thy disgrace."—*Calvin.*

After God has inveighed against the people's sins, and treated the whole nation as guilty, he now pronounces judgment on their wickedness. He repeats shortly what he had said, as a judge explains the reason of his sentence. *Since,* says he, *the lower parts of thy body and thy disgrace has been uncovered before thy lovers.* This is the reason of the judgment, whence it is collected that God is induced to treat his people harshly for just and necessary causes. It now follows: *therefore,* says he, *I will assemble all thy lovers, with those also whom thou hatest, I will assemble them, and uncover thy shame before them.* We may now see what the Jews are threatened with, namely, a disgraceful destruction, so that they become a common laughingstock without any one to succour them; for the diction is metaphorical when he speaks of lovers and of parts of the body; for by lovers he here means the Egyptians, Assyrians, and Chaldæans. Whence their opinion is refuted who think that the Prophet treats only of superstitions. Nor can this language be transferred to idols, since we know that false·gods were not spectators of the punishment which the Prophet denounces against the Jews. Whence it follows that this language will only suit those persons to whose protection the Jews trusted, so as to treat God's help as useless. Since, then, such is the metaphorical sense of the passage, we understand that shame means spoliation and slaughter; nay, the destruction of both the kingdom and city, and even of the temple. Thus the nation was a common laughingstock, and in this way like a foul and aged harlot. Now we understand the Prophet's intention. As to Jerome's translating "wealth," it is altogether adverse to the Prophet's meaning; there is no doubt that he means the lower part of the body, and it follows in the same sense, *thy shame was uncovered.* But at the same time God expresses why it was done, *namely, for fornication,* as if an abandoned woman were to act so disgracefully. He now says it was done,*towards thy lovers, towards the idols of thine abominations:* על, *gnel,* is here taken for towards or against. He distinguishes between lovers and idols. Those who think that the Prophet treats only of superstitions think the copula superfluous; but there is no doubt that the Prophet means, on one side, the Assyrians, and Egyptians, and Chaldæans; and on the other, false gods.

And in bloods, says he. He here adds another crime, namely, that of barbarous cruelty, because they did not spare their own sons, as we saw before: many offered up their children, and some were found so excited as to cast them into the fire: it was indeed a monstrous crime when they hesitated not to rage against their own offspring: but they were so carried away by insane zeal that they burnt up their children when others only drew them through the fire. Hence the Prophet again accuses them of cruelty for offering their children to idols, and so pouring forth innocent blood. Now follows the punishment. *Behold,* says he, *I collect all thy lovers.* We said that this ought to be understood of the Egyptians, Assyrians, and Chaldæans, all of whom looked upon the slaughter of that perverse and perfidious nation, but none of them helped her. God therefore pronounces the destruction of the people just like that of a harlot abandoned by her lovers, and perishing through hunger, want, and other miseries: for it very often happens that a person under the impulse of love prefers a harlot to his own life; for he will throw off all regard for his wife; he will be disrespectful to both his father and mother, and will break through every restraint to enjoy her company: but when such persons are grown old, and their hair becomes white, which represents the winter of life, and when wrinkles deform the face, then they are despised, and especially if they suffer through disease. So also the Prophet now says that the Jews would be despised by all, so that their lovers should be compelled to behold that example; and meanwhile they scarcely deign to look at the foul appearance which had formerly sweetly delighted them.

Then he proceeds further, namely, *that their enemies should behold their ignominy:* we know that the Jews were surrounded on all sides by enemies, and that all their neighbours were hostile to them. The Prophet now says *that the nation's disgrace should be exposed before their lovers,* that is, the Egyptians, the Assyrians, Chaldæans, Philistines,

Edomites, and other nations. This passage teaches us, that although the reason for God's judgments does not always clearly appear, yet they are never too severe; and when he condescends to afford us a reason, he grants us a gratuitous indulgence. But when he silently executes his judgments, let us learn to acquiesce in his justice, and not to cry out if he exceeds moderation; because when he has once explained that his severity is only justice, hence we must gather the general rule, that whenever he seems to treat his people too severely and harshly, yet he has just reasons for it. Let us learn, also, that the Jews only suffered a just recompence when God so cursed all their counsels. They thought themselves very provident and circumspect when they engaged in alliances with Egyptians and Assyrians. But all their plans turned out unhappily for them, since they consulted their own will contrary to that of God. Let us learn, then, if we wish to promote our own salvation, and to obtain a prosperous result, to do nothing without God's permission, and not to undertake any deliberations except those which God has dictated and suggested by his word and Spirit. For here every future event is shown to us as in a glass when we wish to be wiser than they ought, and than God permits them. It now follows—

38. And I will judge thee, as women that break wedlock and shed blood are judged; and I will give thee blood in fury and jealousy.

38. Et judicabo te judiciis adulterarum, et fundentium sanguinem · et ponam te sanguinem excandescentiæ[1] et zeli.[2]

This verse is only added for the sake of explanation. Already God had explained shortly and clearly every event which should happen to the Jews, yet they should perish in the greatest disgrace and be destitute of all help, since through distrust in God they sought the favour of men, like a woman eager for lovers. But he confirms the same teaching, that they should suffer double punishment, since they not only polluted themselves thus shamefully, but also by impious slaughters, since they burnt their children in honour of false gods. This sentence may be explained generally, *I will judge you with the judgments of women pouring out blood,*

[1] Or, "of emulation."—*Calvin.*   [2] Or, "of envy."—*Calvin.*

as we know that not only idolatry was rampant at Jerusalem, but rapine, and all kinds of cruelty ; for since they had departed from God and his worship, they boldly violated his law. By the second word we may understand all the crimes by which they had provoked God's anger on account of their cruelty. But since he has lately spoken of sons, I willingly retain that sense, *that they should suffer as an adulteress and a parricide who has put her children to death.* But they thought that they obeyed God : but he not only rejects, but abominates such foolish thoughts ; for nothing is more disgraceful than, under the pretence of piety, to slay and to burn one's own children : this, I say, was a profanation of God's name scarcely tolerable. No wonder, then, that he denounces double vengeance, since, when the Jews pleaded their zeal, God branded upon them the mark of wickedness, though they thought him bound to their interests. It afterwards follows—

39. And I will also give thee into their hand, and they shall throw down thine eminent place, and shall break down thy high places : they shall strip thee also of thy clothes, and shall take thy fair jewels, and leave thee naked and bare.

39. Et dabo te in manum eorum : et sublime tuum diruent,[1] et disrumpent[2] excelsa tua ; et spoliabunt te vestibus tuis, et sument vasa gloriæ tuæ,[3] et dimittent te nudam et discoopertam.

Here Ezekiel enlarges upon God's judgment, when he teaches that the Jews would not only be exposed to every disgrace, as if they were brought forward into a noble and conspicuous theatre, but they would suffer spoliation and rapine from those in whom they formerly trusted. *I will give thee,* says he, *into their hands.* He speaks of lovers and enemies : in truth, he says all shall meet together—thine ancient allies and friends as well as thine enemies : and we know that they were spoiled at one time or another by the Egyptians, Assyrians, and Chaldæans. For at the time when Jerusalem was taken and cut off, the Assyrians were reduced under the monarchy of the Chaldees. Babylon had oppressed Nineveh, as is well known, but the strength of both people were joined together. Thus the Jews were spoiled by them when they thought that they had provided

---

[1] Or, " overthrow."—*Calvin.*   [2] Or, " break down."—*Calvin.*
[3] Or, " of beauty ;" that is, " thy precious furniture."—*Calvin.*

for themselves very successfully by an alliance with the Assyrians against the kings of Israel and Syria: and afterwards, when they had formed an alliance with the Chaldæans, they thought themselves beyond the reach of all danger. But now the Prophet derides that foolish confidence, and says that they should be spoiled by all their friends: so also he says that their altars should be thrown down. Those who translate it "a house of sin" do not sufficiently consider what I yesterday observed, that the Prophet uses the figure so as to mark a thing simply from any part of it. The Prophet's language is moderate or mixed, because he speaks partially of lofty and profane altars, and at the same time follows out his own simile. There is no doubt, therefore, that by *a high place* and *lofty things* he means altars themselves: although he does allude to these sinful houses, because he said in yesterday's lecture that the Jews stood at the top of the streets so as to entice any casual and unknown strangers to them. As also the Chaldæans did not spare the temple, so there is no doubt that they destroyed all the altars promiscuously: and yet the Jews had wished to gratify them by destroying a part of them. But God shows how foolishly men imagine they shall succeed while they purposely fight against him: and experience teaches that the same thing happens to all unbelievers. For when any one has embraced his own superstitions, and despises what others think sacred and holy, then the conquerors destroy temples and images, and deform the region which they wish to be ruined and desolate. So also it is now said, *they shall destroy thine altars and high places.* He now adds, *and they shall spoil thee of thy garments, and take away the vessels of thy beauty.* The Prophet comprehends in these words whatever benefits God had conferred on the Jews; for we know how liberally he had adorned them with his gifts, and especially in rendering the earth wonderfully fruitful by his blessing. He signifies in a word, that the Jews, when deprived of all their ornaments, would be disgraced; as it follows, and *they shall send thee away naked and bare;* that is, they shall cast thee off, just as a lover when satisfied rejects the companion of his iniquity.

40. They shall also bring up a company against thee, and they shall stone thee with stones, and thrust thee through with their swords.

40. Et ascendere facient contra te coetum,¹ et lapidabunt te lapidibus,² et perfodient te gladiis suis.

Since what Ezekiel has hitherto brought forward was incredible, he now explains the manner of its accomplishment—that the Chaldæans and Assyrians should bring a large army *and bury the whole of Judæa with stones, and pierce it through with swords.* By these figures he simply means that there should be such slaughter that the whole region should be made desolate, just as if the enemy should slay all that they met with stones and swords. Some think that he alludes to stones which were thrown by engines of war; but I doubt whether the Prophet thought of this. What I have stated is more simple, that the Jews had no cause to think themselves free from that final slaughter of which the Prophet spoke, since *numerous and powerful armies should come and overwhelm them with stones, and pierce them through with swords.* It follows—

41. And they shall burn thine houses with fire, and execute judgments upon thee in the sight of many women: and I will cause thee to cease from playing the harlot, and thou also shalt give no hire any more.

41. Et exurent domos tuas igni,³ et facient in te⁴ judicia in oculis mulierum multarum, et cessare faciam te à scortando: atque etiam munus non offeres amplius.

After he had spoken of the slaughter of men, he adds the burning of their dwellings. This was sad indeed, that the whole land should be deprived of inhabitants: but the deformity of this last slaughter was heaped upon them when the houses were burnt up; for the country was laid waste for the future, and for a length of time. For when men are slain others may succeed, if they find houses prepared, and fields not uncultivated. But when all these things are consumed by fire, and by other means of ruin, all hope for the future is taken away. The Prophet now means this when he says, *that the houses were burnt up.* He adds, *they shall execute judgment against thee in the sight of many women.* As he had used the simile of a harlot for the Jewish people, that

¹ Or, "army."—*Calvin.*
² But the noun is superfluous, since רגם, *regem,* signifies to stone to death.—*Calvin.*   ³ The noun "fire" is redundant.—*Calvin.*
⁴ Or, "they shall execute."—*Calvin.*

the clauses of the sentence may correspond, he understands the neighbouring people under the name of women. He confirms what we formerly saw, that the penalty which should be exacted of the Jews should be joined with the greatest disgrace. But this is very bitter, when not only we must perish, but the cruelty of enemies must be satiated while many behold us; and doubtless it was much more severe for the Jews to sustain the ridicule of their foes than to perish at once. If they had perished at once, death had not been such a torture to them as those mockeries by which they were harassed by their enemies. For we said that they were hated by almost all; and in the 137th Psalm (verse 7) it is shown that the Edomites, and others like them, said, by way of congratulation, Hail! hail! when Jerusalem was destroyed: Remember, O Lord, the sons of Edom, who said in the day of Jerusalem, Down with it, down with it, even to the ground. The Prophet, therefore, announces this, that the punishment which he formerly mentioned should be an example to all nations. He speaks improperly of the Chaldæans, when he says that they should be the executors of God's judgments, for there was not a duty assigned to them; but God often transfers to man as the instrument of his wrath what peculiarly belongs to himself alone. And in this way he wounds the Jews more severely when he makes the Chaldæans their judges. God, properly speaking, was the sole judge who avenged the people's wickedness; but meanwhile he substitutes the Chaldæans for himself, that the punishment might be the more disgraceful. He adds, *and I will make thee cease from fornication, nor shalt thou offer gifts any more.* God does not mean that the Jews would be better when in exile, but simply reminds them that the opportunity for their sinning would be wanting, as when an immodest person is ashamed through being despised by every one, not through any improvement in her disposition, since her licentious feelings are the same as before. So also the Jews were always obstinate in their wickedness, though deprived of the opportunity of sinning. It follows—

42. So will I make my fury toward thee to rest, and my jealousy shall de-

42. Et quiescere faciam excandescentiam meam in te, et recedet

part from thee, and I will be quiet, and will be no more angry.	æmulatio mea abs te: et quiescam, et non irascar amplius.

Although God seems here to promise some mitigation of his wrath, there is no doubt that he expresses what we formerly saw, namely, that such should be the destruction of the nation that there would be no need to return again to punish them. When, therefore, he says, *I will make my indignation rest upon thee*, it means that he would satiate himself with vengeance for all their crimes: so that the consumption of the people is here called the rest of God's indignation, as if he had said, When I have utterly reduced you to nothing, then my indignation against thee shall rest. In the same way he afterwards adds, *and my indignation shall depart from thee.* But I cannot finish to-day.

PRAYER.

Grant, Almighty God, since thou hast hitherto sustained us, and since we are worthy of being utterly destroyed a hundred times,— Grant, I say, that we may repent of ourselves, and prevent that horrible judgment of which thou settest before us a specimen in thine ancient people: and may we so devote ourselves to thee in the true chastity of faith, that we may experience the course of thy goodness until we enjoy the eternal inheritance which thine only-begotten Son has acquired for us by his blood.—Amen.

Lecture Forty-Seventh.

WE stopped yesterday at the passage where God pronounces *that his rivalry should depart from the Jews.* Some interpret this of jealousy, and this sense does not displease me; for we know that God has hitherto spoken in the character of a husband. But when a husband avenges the injury which he has suffered, he is enflamed with jealousy. Hence he has no moderation in his wrath; but when he begins to despise his wife because she is defiled, and to think her unworthy of further notice, then his anger and indignation is allayed. So, therefore, some understand it, My jealousy shalt depart from thee, that is, Thou shalt be no longer esteemed as my wife, but I shall despise thee as if thou wert altogether strange and unknown to me. But the word *jealousy* or rivalry may be taken otherwise; as he said yesterday, I will put upon thee the blood of indignation and jealousy, that is, I will treat thee in no milder way than those do who burn with wrath, and breathe out nothing but slaughters; as when any one is enflamed against his enemies, he slays all he meets. As, therefore, God put aside, in the last lecture, the blood of jealousy and anger, so in this place the word may be taken to mean simple rivalry; *for God's* קנאה, *kenah, zeal,* or ardour in vengeance, *shall depart from the Jews,* because material shall be deficient, as we explained it yesterday, *I shall be at rest,* says he, *and shall not be angry any more.* By these words he confirms the same thing, that such should be the destruction of Jerusalem that God shall cease his wrath, as if he were satiated. He does not here promise any mitigation, as some think, but expresses its formidable nature, since it should consume and abolish the whole people, so that God's anger ceases, just like a fire is extinguished of its own accord when no fuel is left. This is the full sense. It follows—

| 43. Because thou hast not remembered the days of thy youth, but hast fretted me in all these *things;* behold, therefore I also will recompense thy way upon *thine* head, saith the Lord God: and thou shalt not commit this lewdness above all thine abominations. | 43. Quia[1] non es recordata dierum adolescentiæ tuæ, et irritasti me in hoc toto[2] etiam ego viam tuam in caput reddam,[3] dicit Dominator Iehovah: et non fecisti cogitationem super cunctis abominationibus tuis.[4] |

He first blames the Jews for not reflecting on the liberality of their treatment. But that ingratitude was too shameful, since God had not omitted any kind of beneficence for their ornament. But since they thought themselves not adorned with sufficient splendour by God, and that he was less munificent than he ought to be, it may here be gathered that they were unworthy of such great and remarkable benefits. Finally, God here shows that how severely soever

---

[1] " Because."—*Calvin.*

[2] Or, "thou hast been tumultuous against me."—*Calvin.*

[3] " I will put."—*Calvin.*

[4] Others translate, " that thou mayest not execute thy thought in all thine abominations." Jerome reads it in the first person, and translates it thus: " I have not fulfilled my thought according to thine abominations," as if God would praise his own clemency here in being so moderate in his wrath; but this is altogether foreign to the subject.—*Calvin.*

he punished the Jews, yet they deserved it for their ingratitude in not thinking him sufficiently liberal towards them: for their spirits were utterly broken. If a wife leave her husband, she is either compelled to do so by his perverse conduct, or else she betrays an illiberal disposition if she has been treated honourably. But since the Jews were bound to God so strongly in so many ways, their perfidy and revolt was so much the more detestable ; for God does not suffer his blessings to be despised by us : since we must always mark the reason of his omitting nothing which may testify his paternal love towards us, namely, that we may celebrate his goodness. But when we turn his benefits to the profanation of his name, that is like mingling heaven and earth. Hence this passage against ingratitude must be remarked.

He now adds, *thou hast been tumultuous against me*, or hast moved or irritated me. רגן, *regen*, sometimes signifies to frighten, but it means here to quarrel with, contend, or be in a rage with : for the word may, in my opinion, be taken either actively or passively, and also as a neuter. If we take it in the neuter sense, it will mean that the Jews were tumultuous against God, as if they were seized by a turbulent spirit, so as to neglect and despise him, and to indulge themselves in wickedness. If you prefer the active sense, it means thou hast irritated me. He adds again, *I also will recompense thy way upon thy head,*[1] by which words God again affirms that he was not induced to punish the Jews by any rash or inconsiderate zeal, since if any one considered their crimes, he will acknowledge that they had received a just recompense. In fine, the mouth of the Jews is here stopped, lest they should suppose God to act unfairly when they were only reaping the fruit of their deeds. He next adds, *and thou hast not made consideration*. I have already given two expositions in the note, but neither of them pleases me, for it seems altogether adverse to the Prophet's context to receive it as if God were the speaker : besides, it is not necessary to change the tense of the verb, and take the past for the future, when the sense tends in another direction. It agrees far better that the Jews did

[1] We must understand the pronoun " thy" before " head."—*Calvin.*

not recall to mind their own abominations so as to be displeased with them. *To make consideration*, means to reflect upon. זָמָה, *zemeh*, is mostly taken in a good sense, and signifies consideration simply ; and as this is the word's proper meaning, we see that the Prophet here accuses the Jews of stupidity, because they did not turn their attention to reconsider their abominations. Those who take it for lewdness distort the sense. The whole meaning is, that the Jews were worthy of the horrible destruction which hung over them, because they were not only obstinate in their ingratitude, but altogether stupid : for their abominations were so foul before the nations, as we have formerly seen, that the daughters of the Philistines were ashamed of the wickedness of the nation, but they did not apply their minds to the consideration of these things. Since, therefore, their abominations were so gross, it was a mark of the greatest indolence not to turn their attention to review them. It now follows—

44. Behold, every one that useth proverbs shall use *this* proverb against thee, saying, As *is* the mother, *so is* her daughter.

45. Thou *art* thy mother's daughter, that loatheth her husband and her children ; and thou *art* the sister of thy sisters, which loathed their husbands and their children : your mother *was* an Hittite, and your father an Amorite.

46. And thine elder sister *is* Samaria, she and her daughters that dwell at thy left hand : and thy younger sister, that dwelleth at thy right hand, *is* Sodom and her daughters.

44. Ecce quisquis proverbiat[1] super te proverbiabit dicendo, Sicut mater filia ejus.

45. Filia matris tuæ es quæ abjecit[2] maritum suum et filios suos: et soror sororis tuæ[3] quæ repudiarunt maritos suos, et filios suos. Mater vestra Chitæa, et pater vester Amorrhæus.

46. Et soror tua major Samaria est, et filiæ ejus, quæ habitant ad sinistram tuam : et soror tua minor præ te, quæ habitat a dextris tuis, Sodoma et filiæ ejus.

Here the Prophet uses another form of speech ; for he says that the Jews deserved to be subject to the taunting proverbs of those who delight in wickedness. The sense is,

---

[1] " Verbally."—*Calvin*.   [2] Or, " repudiated, abominated."—*Calvin*.

[3] I rather think the place corrupt, and that אֲחוֹתֵךְ, *achothek*, is put for אֲחוֹתִיךְ, *achothik*, for it follows—" who have turned away from their husbands;" and this does not agree with a single sister : then shortly after the Prophet will say, that the Jews had two sisters, Sodom and Samaria ; and surely what follows cannot be understood of one woman ; for it says, " they have despised their husbands."—*Calvin*. Newcome agrees with this emendation of Calvin's; so also does Maldonatus, the Jesuit, *Comment. in Ezekiel*, &c. p. 413.

that they were worthy of extreme infamy, so that their disgrace was bandied about in vulgar sayings. This is one point: he now adds, that proverbs of this kind were the Jews' desert—*the daughter is like her mother and sisters.* Then he says, *their mother was a Hittite, and their sisters Samaria and Sodom.* We must briefly treat these clauses in order. When the Prophet speaks of proverbs, he doubtless means what I have touched on, namely, that the crimes of the nation deserved that their infamy should fly abroad on the tongues of all; for there are many sins which are hidden, through either their being spared, or their not seeming to be much noticed. If any one surpass all others in cruelty, avarice, lust, and other vices, his disgrace will be notorious, and he will be pointed at by vulgar proverbs. Hence Ezekiel dwells on the people's wickedness, since they supply material for all men to laugh at their expense; for he alludes to buffoons and wits, and such as are ingenious in fabricating vulgar sayings.

The maker of proverbs shall utter this proverb against thee: like mother like daughter. There is no doubt that they used this saying at that period, and it often happens that daughters' faults are like their mothers'. Daughters indeed often degenerate from the best mothers, and matrons will be found who excel in the virtues of modesty, chastity, sobriety, and watchfulness, while their daughters are rash and proud, luxurious, lustful, and intemperate; but it usually happens that a mother has wicked daughters like herself: this happens less by nature than by education; for a woman of a perverse inclination will think that a stigma attaches to herself if her daughter is better than she is, and so she will wish to form her after her own morals; hence it happens that few daughters are found modest whose mothers are immodest: few sober who have been brought up by drunkards. Since therefore experience always taught the similarity between mothers and daughters, hence this proverb was in the mouth of every one. Proverbs, however, are not always true, but only on the whole; but God sometimes extends his pity so far that the daughter of a wicked woman is honourable and well conducted. But this is very rare: hence this proverbial saying cannot be rejected,—*like mother like daughter.* It now follows: *Thou art the daughter of thy mother;* that is, altogether like her: and this phrase is equally common among us, " *Thou art thy father's son,*" namely, thou art like him in thy sins. Thus the Prophet means that the nation was like their mother, since it differed in nothing from the Canaanites and the Hittites. He adds also, *sisters and their daughters,* as if he would collect the whole family. He says *that Samaria is their elder sister,* and *Sodom their younger.* I know not whether those who think that Samaria is called older than Jerusalem, through its revolting first from the worship of God, have sufficient grounds for their interpretation: for as we go on we shall see that Samaria is compared with Sodom, and since Sodom is the worst, it is very naturally compared with it. For Jerusalem will afterwards be placed in the highest rank, because it had surpassed them all in enormity. *Samaria therefore is one of the sisters,* and *so is Sodom:* these towns are called *daughters,* for we know that Sodom was not the only one destroyed by fire from heaven, since there were five cities. (Gen. x. 19, and xix. 25.) We see, then, why those smaller cities near at hand were called daughters of Sodom, and as far as Samaria is concerned, it was the head of the kingdom of Israel: hence all the cities of the ten tribes were called its daughters.

With relation to the father, the Prophet says here more than he had ventured before. He says, *their father was an Amorite,* as if the Jews had sprung from profane nations, and did not draw their origin from a holy parent; and the Prophet very often makes this objection, not that they were spurious or descended according to the flesh from the uncircumcised Gentiles, but because they were unworthy of their father Abraham, through being degenerate. In fine, God here signifies that the parents of the Jews were not only profane nations but utterly reprobate, and those whom God for very just reasons had ordered to be destroyed, since they had contaminated the earth with their crimes far too long. He says that the Jews were like a daughter sprung from most abandoned parents. As to his saying, *that the mother as well as sisters had despised their husbands,* this may seem absurd. But we know that in proverbs, parables, examples, and comparisons, all things ought not to be exacted with the utmost nicety. When Christ's coming is said to be stealthy, (Matt. xxiv. 43, 44,) if any one here desires to be cunning and inquires how Christ is like a thief, that will be absurd. And also in this place when it is said, *thy mother has abandoned her husband and her sons, and thy sisters have done the same.* God simply means that both the mother and sisters of Jerusalem were impure and perfidious women; and cruel also, since they not only had violated the marriage pledge and had thus broken through all chastity, but were like ferocious beasts against their own sons. (Luke xii. 39, 40; 1 Thess. v. 2.) He reproves the crime which we yesterday exposed, that of the Jews burning their own sons. In fine, he means to compare the Jews with the Canaanites, the Samaritans, and the Sodomites, in both perfidy and cruelty. Hence they are first condemned for throwing away all modesty and conjugal fidelity, and next for forgetting all humanity. It now follows—

47. Yet hast thou not walked after their ways, nor done after their abominations; but, as *if that were* a very little *thing*, thou wast corrupted more than they in all thy ways.	47. Et non in viis ipsarum ambulasti, et non secundum abominationes earum fecisti quasi parum[1] et exiguum: et corrupta es præ illis in cunctis viis tuis.

Now the Prophet, not content with the simile which he had used, says that the Jews were far worse than either their mothers or sisters. Yet he is not inconsistent, for God wished by degrees to drag the wicked to trial. If at the very first word he had said that they were worse than the Sodomites, they would have been less attentive to this accusation. But when he proposed a thing incredible, namely, that they were the daughters of the nations of Canaan, and the sisters of Samaria and Sodom, and afterwards proceeded further, and pronounced that they surpassed both their mother and sisters, this, as I have said, would stir up their minds more vehemently. This difference then contains no inconsistency, but rather tends to magnify their crimes. *Thou,* says he, *hast not walked according to their ways.* He does not here exempt the Jews from participating in sins as

[1] " A small matter."—*Calvin.*

if they were faultless through not imitating the Hittites, or Sodomites, or Israelites: but the word *walking* ought to be restricted to the sense of equality, as if he said, ye are not equal. But it is a kind of correction when God says that the Jews were not equal to the Hittites or Sodomites, meaning that their impiety was more detestable, since they rushed forward to all kinds of wickedness with greater license. We now understand the Prophet's meaning when he says that the Jews *had not walked in the ways* of either Sodom or Samaria or the nations of Canaan, since they had gone before them, and even with greater ardour of pursuit; for if they had simply imitated the three people of whom mention has been made, *they had walked in their ways.* But when they were so hurried on in their intemperance as to run before them, they did not walk in their ways only through leaving them behind. And this comparison will sufficiently explain the Prophet's mind, that the Jews did not follow either the Sodomites, Israelites, or Canaanites, but through their haste and headlong violence left them far behind. And he says, *as if it were only a small matter,* that is, as if it were of little moment to thee to be like thy mother and sisters. But *thou hast been corrupt,* says he, *before them.* He now explains the case more clearly, since they had not walked in their ways through precipitating themselves with greater license, as we have already said. It follows—

48. *As* I live, saith the Lord God, Sodom thy sister hath not done, she nor her daughters, as thou hast done, thou and thy daughters.	48. Vivo ego, dicit Dominator Iehovah, si fecerit Sodoma soror tua ipsa et filiæ ejus quemadmodum fecisti tu, et filiæ tuæ.

Since what we have lately seen was difficult to be believed, hence God interposes an oath. Nor is it surprising that shame was so despised and cast far away by the Jews, since they were inured to it; and we know how they were swollen with pride, for they always boasted in their adoption and gloried in the name of God. Besides, we know that at this day, if any one accuses a wicked nation, yet it is not so detestable as Sodom, and if he uses this phrase, he inflames all against himself, and causes them to reject his language with indignation. For who will suffer either one city or nation to be compared with Sodom? As far as concerned the Jews, we have said that it was intolerable in them to be fastidious and proud. There was also another reason why they should be indignant at being pronounced worse than the Sodomites: since God had not chosen them as his peculiar treasure in vain and marked them with magnificent titles: ye shall be a nation of priests unto me, ye shall be my inheritance, and besides, my son—my first-born Israel. (Exod. xix. 6, and iv. 22.) We now see how necessary the interposition by oath was to sanction what the Prophet had said. God therefore here swears by himself, because we call him in as a witness and judge when we swear. But he swears by himself or by his life, because, as the Apostle teaches, he has no greater by whom to swear. (Heb. vi. 13.) Whatever it be, he here prostrates all foolish boasting, by which the Jews were puffed up when he swears by himself, *that they were worse than Sodom and her daughters.* And here also he calls in like manner the smaller cities *daughters of Jerusalem.* This was very hard upon the Jews, when the Prophet says and often repeats, *thy sister Sodom.* But he wounds their feelings far more bitterly, *that Sodom was just in preference to Jerusalem:* this was indeed intolerable, and yet we see that the Holy Spirit by no means indulges them here. Hence we must not regard what the reprobate are able to bear, but they must be treated according to their own disposition, and since they rise fiercely against God, so also are they to be subdued, and, according to the common proverb, "a hard wedge must be formed for a hard knot." It now follows—

49. Behold, this was the iniquity of thy sister Sodom, pride, fulness of bread, and abundance of idleness was in her and in her daughters, neither did she strengthen the hand of the poor and needy.	49. Ecce hæc fuit iniquitas Sodomæ sororis tuæ, superbia, satietas panis, et securitas otii[1] fuit illi et filiabus ejus: et manum egeni et inopis non apprehendit.

Here God begins to show the reason why he extenuated the wickedness of Sodom in comparison with that of his own people: for if he had spoken generally, without explaining the counsel of God, his language would have been incredible, and so would have been ineffectual. But now God shows that he did not pronounce rashly what we heard before,

---

[1] Or, "quiet peace;" others, "abundance of ease."—*Calvin.*

namely, that the Jews were worse than the Sodomites. How so? for *this was the iniquity of Sodom thy sister*, says he, first *pride*, then *fulness of bread*, and luxury in which they were in the habit of indulging, and of drowning themselves in ease to enjoy a long peace; afterwards, *they did not seize the hand of the poor*. Now he adds—

50. And they were haughty, and committed abomination before me: therefore I took them away as I saw *good*.

50. Et superbe se extulit, et fecit abominationem coram me, et abstuli ipsos quemadmodum vidi.[1]

We must diligently attend to this passage; for God does not here excuse the wickedness of Sodom; but, abominable as that people was, he says that the Jews were yet more abandoned. We know why God inflicted his vengeance in a terrible manner against the Sodomites and their neighbours, for that was a fearful example; and Jude says that it was a kind of mirror of the wrath of God which awaits all the impious, (verse 7;) and Scripture often recalls us to that proof of God's judgment: but we must see how Sodom rushed forward to that degree of licentiousness so as to be horrified by no enormity. God says that they began by pride, and surely pride is the mother of all contempt of God and of all cruelty. Let us learn, then, that we cannot be restrained by the fear of God, unless moderation and humility reign within us. Pride, we know, has two horns, so to speak; one is, when men forget their own condition, and claim to themselves not only more than is right, but what God alone calls his own. This, then, is one horn of pride, when men, trusting in their dignity, excellence, plenty, and wealth, are intoxicated by false imaginations, so as to think themselves equal to God. Now, another horn of pride is, when they do not acknowledge their vices, and despise others in comparison with themselves, and please themselves in enormities, just as if they were free from any future account. Since, therefore, pride is contained in these two clauses, when men arrogate too much to themselves, and thus are blind to their own vices, each of these is doubtless condemned in the Sodomites, since they first *raised themselves by a rash confidence*, and then refused to subject them-

[1] That is, "as I pleased."—*Calvin*.

selves to God, and rebelled against him as if they could shake off his yoke.

He afterwards adds *fulness of bread*. But the Prophet seems to condemn in the Sodomites what was not blameable in itself: for when God feeds us bountifully, fulness is not to be considered a crime; but he takes it here for immoderate gluttony; for those who have abundance are often luxurious, and nothing is more rare than self-restraint when materials for luxury are supplied to us. Hence *fulness of bread* is here taken for intemperance, since the Sodomites were so addicted to gluttony and drunkenness, that they gratified their appetites worse than the brutes, who do retain some moderation, for they are content with their own food: but men's covetousness is altogether insatiable. Let us observe, then, that by *fulness of bread* we are to understand that intemperance in which profane men indulge when God supplies them bountifully with the means of living; for they do not consider why they abound in wine, and corn, and abundance of all things, but they drown themselves in luxuries with a blind and brutal impulse. Hence such greediness, so inflaming to the spirits of the Sodomites, is added to pride, that they arrogate to themselves more than is just. He afterwards adds, *and rest;* שלות, *sheloth:* some translate it abundance, but almost everywhere it means peace; the noun שקט, *sheket*, which is added next, means properly rest; so that it will be the peace of rest or ease, and this seems without blame: for why shall we not be permitted to enjoy ease, if no one molests or troubles us? nay, it is reckoned among God's blessings: thou shalt sleep, and no one shall frighten thee. (Lev. xxvi. 6.) Since God, therefore, wishes this to be considered among his blessings, that the faithful should sleep soundly, without any anxiety or trouble, why is Sodom condemned for thus enjoying ease and peace? But here its excess is pointed out, not its true use, since the use of peace is to render our minds tranquil, that we may return thanks to God, and dwell calmly under his sway. But how do the reprobate act? They grow brutish, so to speak, in their own peacefulness. Hence sloth is in this passage meant by the peacefulness of ease, and God means that the Sodomites were intoxicated by their luxuries when they enjoyed peace. We must put off the remainder.

PRAYER.

Grant, Almighty God, since thou hast deigned to graft us once into the body of thine only-begotten Son, that we may be mindful of our origin, since from our very birth we were lost and cursed; and grant that we may be mindful of that grace by which thou hast honoured us, so that we may worship thee as a father, and preserve our trust in thee inviolate: and may we be so obedient to thee that thy image may be renewed in us more and more in all righteousness and holiness, until thy glory may perfectly shine forth in us in thy heavenly kingdom by the same Jesus Christ our Lord.—Amen.

Lecture Forty-Eighth.

WE began in the last lecture to treat that passage where God pronounces that the Jews surpassed in all kinds of wickedness both the Sodomites and the ten tribes of Israel. When he wished to prove this he said that the iniquity of Sodom was *pride, fulness of bread,* and then *ease, with sloth and cruelty:* afterwards he put another kind of pride, since the people were intoxicated with confidence, and indulged in unbridled and brutal license, as he afterwards says. For he adds, that the cities were overthrown and destroyed since they had perpetrated foul abominations. With regard to excess, we said that good living simply is not here condemned when any one uses the affluence granted to him for God's glory; but luxury and intemperance. For the rich boast as much as possible, and are not only eager for delicacies, and stuff themselves to the full, but they triumph and luxuriate in what is sure to destroy them. The Prophet then blames this in the Sodomites. We said also of quiet and rest, that it denoted that sloth by which the profane madden themselves; but that is more clearly expressed shortly by *vain-boasting.* The Prophet now adds, *that they had not seized the hand of the poor and needy.* We must notice this, since pride is almost always cruel; and truly no one heartily succours his poor brethren who is not affected by their necessities. But those who are intoxicated by false confidence, and claim everything for themselves, despise their brethren, and thus carelessly permit them to be utterly oppressed by poverty and want. The Prophet here pronounces nothing concerning Sodom but what we too often perceive by daily experience. He now adds—

| 50. And they were haughty, and committed abomination before me: therefore I took them away as I saw *good*. | 50. Et extulit se,[1] et fecerunt abominationem coram facie mea, et abstuli eas quemadmodum volui.[2] |

Here God shows that Sodom had not at first fallen into those foul and gross crimes which were the cause of its final destruction. We must diligently mark this: for when Satan begins to entice us, we think that we shall be free to retract our steps whenever we please; but we are ensnared, some in one way and some in another. But when we are entangled by Satan's deceits, it is not in our power to escape from them; nay, we feel that we are involved in a complete labyrinth. Since, then, men proceed gradually in provoking God's wrath, we must observe this passage, in which God informs us that the Sodomites were not given up at once to enormous lust, but they began with smaller sins, and then became luxurious through their abundance, and were stupified by ease and quiet; meanwhile they despised the poor and needy, and did not stretch forth their hands to them. For to *seize the hand* means the same as to stretch forth the hand, when we set up again those who have fallen, or prop up those who are slipping. Hence God shows that the Sodomites were afterwards so corrupted by luxuries, that he at length adds, *that they raised themselves up,* that is, that they purposely, and of their own accord, exempted themselves from all fear of punishment: for this is the meaning of the word raised up; that is, they buoyed themselves up, since they promised themselves freedom from punishment; and in that fallacious hope *they dared to perpetrate abomination before my face.* Hence we must always fear lest

[1] " And they raised themselves up," for he comprehends the daughters of Sodom, that is, the neighbouring cities.—*Calvin.*
[2] That is, " as I pleased and desired."—*Calvin.* He repeats ver. 50.

Satan should entangle us by his enticements, and at length so fascinate and stupify our senses that we can no longer distinguish between good and evil, as the Sodomites exceeded the brutes in their abominations, which were the cause of their ruin.

When God announces *that he removed those cities as he pleased,* he wishes to inspire the Jews with terror, lest they should suppose that they would profit by turning their backs; because, whether they wished it or not, he would at length drag them before his tribunal. God, therefore, here passes the final sentence, that the Jews may feel that they must render an account to him. Now, if any one should ask whether these crimes which Ezekiel relates are worse than those of the Jews, the answer is at hand, that the Sodomites were not under the law; and hence it is no wonder if they wandered and stumbled in darkness: but when the right course of life was pointed out to the Jews, they professedly sought their own destruction, they knowingly and wilfully rejected God's yoke, and haughtily despised all the prophets who daily desired to recall them into the path of duty. Other circumstances are also to be noticed, that the Jews not only abused the goods which God plentifully bestowed upon them, but, as we have seen, squandered them upon adulterous worship, and then they fetched from thence all kinds of superstition, and became worse than the beasts, as we have seen elsewhere. While we know that the imitation of the people of Sodom was very common in Judæa, when they were tainted with many corruptions through forgetfulness of the law. If, therefore, we weigh these points together, it will not be surprising that God pronounces the Jews to have sinned more grievously than the Sodomites. It now follows—

| 51. Neither hath Samaria committed half of thy sins: but thou hast multiplied thine abominations more than they, and hast justified thy sisters in all thine abominations which thou hast done. | 51. Et Samaria secundum dimidium scelerum tuorum non scelerate egit: et multiplicasti abominationes tuas præ illis, et justificasti sorores tuas in omnibus abominationibus tuis quas patrasti. |

God now pronounces the same thing concerning Samaria, whom he had formerly called the younger sister. By Samaria, as we said, he means the Israelites, because that city was the head of the kingdom of Israel: the ten tribes had been already driven into exile; and he says they were not half so wicked when compared with the Jews. This, at the first glance, may seem absurd; for we know that God's worship was continued at Jerusalem when the Israelites rejected the law, and basely and openly turned aside to idolatry. Since, therefore, some sound piety flourished at Jerusalem when the Israelites wickedly revolted from God's law, what can it mean by the Jews being censured as worse than they were? We must always come to the fountain which I have pointed out; for ingratitude has great influence in exaggerating men's crimes. But another reason must also be remarked. The Jews had seen how severely God had avenged the superstitions of the kingdom of Israel: they were so far from repenting that they rather courted their alliance, as if for the very purpose of provoking God afresh. If we reflect upon these two points, the question will be solved as far as relates to the present passage. God says what is incredible to us, that the Jews were worse than the Israelites: but he asserts this, because ingratitude had rendered them less excusable; for God had retained them under his own charge when that wretched dispersion happened, and the ten tribes were all but absorbed. God's candle was always shining at Jerusalem, as it is said. (Exod. xxvii. 20.) When, therefore, God had preserved for himself that small band as the very flower of the people, safe and sound, the revolt of this people was far more criminal than that of the ten tribes: for these tribes were drawn away from the worship of God by little and little, as is well known. For Jeroboam always set before himself one definite object—the worship of God as the liberator of the people, (1 Kings xii.:) for the Israelites did not look on themselves as apostates, although they had degenerated from their fathers. But the Jews addicted themselves to gross superstitions, of which the Israelites at first were ashamed; and then they were warned by many penalties not to imitate their kinsmen: still, as we saw before, the temple was defiled by many pollutions; for Ezekiel, in the eighth chapter, says that he saw there many defilements. Since then the Jews profited so badly, though God set his vengeance before their eyes, it is not surprising that they are said to have sinned grievously.

In conclusion, he adds, *thou hast multiplied thine abominations beyond them; and thou hast justified thy sisters in all the abominations which thou hast perpetrated.* Here the word "justified" is to be received at first comparatively: it does not signify that the fault of others is extenuated by the wickedness of the Jews; but if the people wished to offer excuses, they might easily be convinced that both Sodom and the kingdom of Israel were just in comparison with the Jews. To justify is usually received for to absolve; and we must observe this when we treat of justification, since the papists always seize upon the quality, as if to be justified was in reality to be just. Hence they are unable to comprehend a doctrine sufficiently familiar to Scripture, and plain enough —that we are justified by faith: for they examine man, that they may find justice there, and do not ascend any higher: but to be justified by faith signifies nothing but to be absolved, though we are not just in ourselves; hence a justification by faith without us must be sought for, and hence we gather that it is not a quality. Hence *Jerusalem justified her sisters*, although Sodom and Samaria were found worse than herself. It follows—

| 52. Thou also, which hast judged thy sisters, bear thine own shame, for thy sins that thou hast committed more abominable than they: they are more righteous than thou; yea, be thou confounded also, and bear thy shame, in that thou hast justified thy sisters. | 52. Etiam tu porta probrum tuum quæ judicasti sororem tuam in sceleribus tuis quibus impie egisti [1] præ illis: justificatæ sunt præ te. Atque etiam tu [2] pudefias, et porta probrum tuum, quod justificaveris sorores tuas. |

Here at length God announces that he would punish the Jews according to their deserts. Hitherto he has recounted their crimes, as judges are accustomed, when they condemn criminals, to state the reasons which induce them to pass sentence: thus God shortly shows how wicked the Jews were. He now adds, that he would avenge them according to the magnitude of their crimes. For they would easily have swallowed all reproaches if the fear of punishment had not been infused into them. This second head, then, was

---

[1] Or, "thou wast abominable."—*Calvin.*   [2] "Even thou."—*Calvin.*

necessary, lest they should get off with impunity, since they had surpassed both Sodom and Samaria. *Do thou also bear thy disgrace who hast judged thy sisters.* Here Ezekiel seems to be at variance with himself, for he said just now and will repeat again shortly, that Jerusalem had justified her sisters; and this is contrary to judging. But he says that Samaria was condemned by the Jews; and the solution of this discrepancy is easy: for the Jews justified both the Israelites and the Sodomites, not by absolving them in any sentence passed on them, but because they were worthy of double condemnation; as Christ says, In the last day it shall be more tolerable for Sodom and Gomorrah than for the Jews. (Matt. xi. 24.) But what is here said of condemnation has another meaning—that the Jews insulted over their brethren when they saw their kingdom destroyed, and the Israelites driven away from their land. Since they spoke so proudly of the slaughter of the ten tribes, as if innocent themselves, the Prophet here reproves them as if they judged them. And this is too common with all hypocrites, to inveigh hardly against all others, and to grow hot against them, as if in this way they covered their own crimes. And Paul reproves this vice in them, since they were supercilious censors of others, and at the same time committed every sin. Thinkest thou, O man, says he, when thou judgest others, that God will not condemn thee; for who art thou, O mortal man? Dost thou claim the office of a judge? (Rom. ii. 1-3.) Meanwhile will God be deprived of his rights, so as not to call thee to account for thy sins? Now, therefore, we understand the Prophet's intention: for he exaggerates the crimes of the Jews when he pronounces sentence from on high against the ten tribes. Truly God blotted out this kingdom deservedly: for they were apostates; they had revolted from the family of David, and had violated that sacred unity by which God had bound to himself the whole family of Abraham. They had indeed just cause for speaking thus in condemning the Israelites; but when they were worse than them, what arrogance it was to harass their brethren, and to be blind to their own vices, nay, to grow utterly callous to them!

Thou, therefore, *hast judged thy sister*, that is, thou hast taken God's office upon thee, and yet thou wast worse than thy sister. Some explain it otherwise, that the Jews judged the ten tribes as long as they remained in a moderate degree worshippers of God: but they do not attend to the context. There is no doubt that the Prophet here rebukes the pride with which the Jews were puffed up, while they judged others severely and themselves leniently. *They were justified in comparison with thee*, says he: *thou, therefore*, he repeats, *blush and bear thy disgrace*. This repetition is not superfluous, although in the former words there was nothing obscure, for it was difficult to persuade the Jews that they should suffer punishment, since God had borne with them so long. God's goodness, then, which invited them to repentance, had rather hardened them, and had occasioned so much torpor that they thought themselves free from all danger. Hence this is the reason why the Prophet confirms his former teaching concerning the nearness of God's vengeance against them. He says, *when thou hast justified them.* He here repeats the cause, and does so to restrain all pretences by which the Jews could in any way protect themselves. For by one word he shows that they must perish, since they had justified those who had been treated so strictly. For it is by no means likely, that God should cease for his office of judge in one direction, since he had been so severe against the Sodomites, who were in some way excusable for their errors. This then is the reason why the Prophet affirms again *that Sodom and Samaria were justified by the Jews.* It follows—

53. When I shall bring again their captivity, the captivity of Sodom and her daughters, and the captivity of Samaria and her daughters, then *will I bring again* the captivity of thy captives in the midst of them.

53. Et convertam captivitatem earum, captivitatem Sodomæ et filiarum ejus, et captivitatem Samariæ et filiarum ejus, et captivitatem captivitatum tuarum in medio ipsarum.

He here confirms again what we lately saw, that the Jews were doomed and devoted to final destruction, nor was it possible for them to escape any more than for Sodom to rise again and Samaria to be restored to her original dignity. The Jews foolishly corrupt this passage, since they think that restoration is promised to Israel and Sodom. But by Sodomites they mean the Moabites and Ammonites, the descendants of Lot who dwell at Sodom: but a child may see that this is trifling. There is no doubt that the Prophet here deprives the Jews of all hope of safety by reasoning upon an impossibility: as if he had said, thou shalt be safe when Sodom and Samaria are. We now understand the Prophet's meaning. But the inquiry arises—how can he pronounce none of the Israelites safe, when their return home is so often promised? But we must bear in mind, what we saw elsewhere, and what it is often necessary to repeat, since many passages in the prophets would otherwise give rise to scruples. Therefore we have sometimes said, that the prophets speak of the people in two ways; for they sometimes regard the whole body of the nation promiscuously: but the Israelites were already alienated from God; afterwards the Jews also cut themselves off from him. Since therefore each people, considering them in a body and in the mass, to speak roughly, was outcast, it is not surprising if the prophets use this language—that no hope of mercy remained—since they had excluded themselves from God's mercy. But afterwards they change their discourse to the remnant: for God always preserves a hidden seed, that the Church should not be utterly extinguished: for there must always be a Church in the world, but sometimes it is preserved miserably as it were in a sepulchre, since it is nowhere apparent. God, therefore, when he denounces final vengeance on the Jews, regards the body of the people, but then he promises that there shall be a small seed which he wishes to remain safe. Hence it is said in Isaiah, (chap. viii. 16,) seal my law, bind up my testimony among my disciples; that is, address my disciples as if you were reading in a hidden corner any writing which you did not wish to be made public. Do thou therefore collect my disciples together, that thou mayest deliver to them my law and my testimony like a sealed letter. But now God cites to his tribunal those degenerate Jews who had nothing in common with Abraham, since they had made void and utterly abolished his covenant: Now, therefore, we see how the Jews perished together with Sodom and Samaria, and were never restored, that is, as far as relates to that filth and dregs which were utterly unworthy of the honour of which they boasted. *I will restore*, therefore, *their captivities; namely, the captivity of Sodom and of its cities, and the captivity of Samaria and its cities, and the captivity of thy captivities*, that is, and the captivity of all thy land: I will restore you, says he, altogether; but he speaks ironically, and, as I have said, he shows that God's taking pity upon the Jews was impossible. It follows—

54. That thou mayest bear thine own shame, and mayest be confounded in all that thou hast done, in that thou art a comfort unto them.	54. Ut portes probrum tuum, et pudefias ab omnibus quæ fecisti, consolando ipsas.

Hence we gather from the last verse, that God gave the Jews no hope of safety, but rather confirms their utter destruction, so that no future safety was to be hoped for. For he says, *that thou mayest bear thy reproach and become ashamed*, namely, because they had sinned grievously, as I have said before, and had not repented of their wickedness. He adds, *in consoling them*. He speaks after the ordinary manner of men, since the miserable feel some consolation in seeing themselves perish among a great multitude. This then is the consolation of which the Prophet speaks, not that the sorrow of Sodom and Samaria was mitigated when they saw the Jews joined to themselves, but, as I have said, God adopts the common language of men. It follows—

55. When thy sisters, Sodom and her daughters, shall return to their former estate, and Samaria and her daughters shall return to their former estate, then thou and thy daughters shall return to your former estate.	55. Et sorores tuæ Sodoma, et filiæ ejus revertentur ad pristina sua,[1] et Samaria et filiæ ejus revertentur ad antiquitatem suam,[2] et tu et filiæ tuæ revertimini ad pristinum statum.

A clearer explanation of the former doctrine now follows, that the Jews should thus feel God merciful when his mercy reached Samaria and Sodom; but that never could be done, and hence the Jews were reduced to despair; for, as

---

[1] " To their ancient state."—*Calvin.*
[2] That is, " to their former state."—*Calvin.*

I have said, the Prophet argues from what is impossible and almost absurd. Just as Virgil writes—

> " The inhabitants of seas and skies shall change,
> And fish on shore, and stags in air shall range:"
> *Virgil, Dryden, Eclogue I.* v. 60—

which can never take place: so that it implies the complete denial of what might seem doubtful. This way of speaking is proverbial, when Ezekiel says that *the Sodomites and Israelites should return to their ancient state* or their former dignity; and that could never be hoped for, as I have said: hence it follows, that the Jews could not be safe when God draws them into the same punishment. Besides, the Prophet speaks as if the city should be cut off and temple overthrown, since the Jews had often been threatened with this, and he had shown them the wrath of God present before their eyes. But although they had always hoped well, yet he despises their pride by which they were blinded, and utters his prophecies openly as if God had executed whatever he had threatened. For this reason he says, *the captivity of thy captivities shall be in the midst of them.* But they might object, that they enjoyed their country, that they still cultivated their fields, and had sufficient food for their support although besieged by their enemies. But the Prophet looked down upon it all, because before God the city was as it were taken and all were exiles, since God had not threatened them in vain. Weakness here compels me to break off.

PRAYER.

Grant, Almighty God, since in thine inestimable mercy thou hast deigned to separate us from the profane nations, and to adopt us into thy family, that we may so conduct ourselves that thou mayest not treat us as strangers: but whilst thou acknowledgest us as thy sons, may thy Spirit govern us until the end, so that thy name may be glorified in us, and at length we may be made partakers of that glory which has been acquired for us through Jesus Christ our Lord.—Amen.

Lecture Forty-Ninth.

56. For thy sister Sodom was not mentioned by thy mouth in the day of thy pride,	56. Et non fuit Sodoma soror tua in sermonem in ore tuo in die superbiarum tuarum,[1]
57. Before thy wickedness was discovered, as at the time of *thy* reproach of the daughters of Syria, and all *that are* round about her, the daughters of the Philistines, which despise thee round about.	57. Priusquam detegeretur malitia, tua secundum tempus probri filiarum Syriæ, et omnium quæ in circuitu ejus sunt filiarum Philistim, quæ spreverunt[2] te à circuitu.

GOD here blames the Jews because they did not attend to that remarkable judgment which he had executed against the Sodomites: for they had always before their eyes what ought to retain them in the fear of God; for that was a formidable spectacle, as it is this day. They knew that region to have been like the paradise of God, as it is called by Moses. (Gen. xiii. 10.) Since, then, the fertility and pleasantness of the place was so great, to see there the lake of sulphur and bitumen was sufficient material for instructing them, unless they had been utterly sluggish. But the Prophet says, that there was no mention of Sodom while the Jews lived happily; and we know that it was a great crime not to consider God's judgments, as we read in Isaiah. (Chap. v. 12.) Among other things he says, that the Jews and Israelites were so corrupt that they did not regard God's works: hence as it is a useful exercise to consider God's judgments, yea, this is the chief prudence of the faithful; so, on the other hand, those who shut their eyes to the manifest judgments of God are like the brutes. And yet this is a very common fault, especially when the circumstance here expressed is added, that profane men do not attend to God's operations through being intoxicated by prosperity; for in this passage we have two ways of explaining the word גאוניך, *gaonik*, which the Prophet uses for pride or loftiness. Sometimes the word גאון, *gaon*, is taken in a bad sense, as well as for sublimity or any high degree of honour. Besides, the Prophet's meaning is clear, while things proceeded according to the Jews' desires they were not anxious about rendering an account before God; nay, they passed by with

---

[1] Or, "loftiness."—*Calvin.*   [2] Or, "have seized."—*Calvin.*

their eyes shut that memorable example which God designed for them in Sodom and the neighbouring cities. Therefore we should learn from this passage, when God indulges us, and treats us softly and delicately, that we must always recall his judgments to mind, that we may be restrained from all licentiousness, lest prosperity should incite us to self-indulgence; for such remembrance is most needful. For we know that nothing is more dangerous than to exult like ferocious horses when God feeds us in abundance. Hence the remedy must be taken in time that we may receive instruction from the examples of punishment which we read in Scripture, or in other histories, or such as we witness with our own eyes. He adds, *before thy wickedness was discovered.* Here Ezekiel says that their wickedness was discovered, when it appeared that God was hostile to their sins; because even then, when their sins could be pointed out with the finger as notorious throughout Jerusalem, yet the people gloried in them; just as if an immodest woman, who is the town's talk, is saluted honourably by all because she has many admirers to worship and adore her, and so sets herself above every chaste matron: but if they all reject her, and she is reduced to want, and to foul and disgraceful ulcers, then all her enormities are made evident. This is the effect of which the Prophet speaks: *before,* says he, *thy enormities were discovered.* How so? God, indeed, constantly proclaimed them by his prophets, and the wickedness of the people was open enough; but then they also remained as if buried: for they proudly rejected all the prophetic warnings, and were even restive against God himself: thus they lay hid under their own hiding-places. But when they became a laughingstock they were spoiled by their neighbours, and suffered the extremity of reproach, and then it was apparent that God had rejected them; for their crimes were detected by punishments, since neither reproofs nor threats profited them in any way.

Besides, interpreters explain this of the slaughter which the Jews suffered in the time of Ahaz. (2 Kings xvi.) For then the King of Syria laid waste almost the whole region, and the citizens of Jerusalem were grievously fined. The

Philistines took advantage of this occasion and made an irruption: they think, therefore, that the time is pointed out when the King of Syria made war upon the Israelites, and violently assaulted Judæa. But I know not whether the Prophet looks to the future, as I said yesterday; for he speaks of punishment at hand, just as if God was fulfilling what he had already determined. I am inclined to think that the beginning and the end ought to be united. Hence God begins to disclose the wickedness of the people from the time when the burning consumed their neighbours till it reached themselves; for the slaughter of the tribes of Israel brought upon them many losses, as we know well enough. But God seems to embrace their ultimate destruction, which was now at hand. Hence he says, that they had been, and would be, a laughingstock to the daughters of Syria, and the nations all around, and also to the daughters of the Philistines. But because they were spoiled by the Philistines, who took their cities, as the sacred narrative informs us, it is very suitable thus to explain the word שׁאט, *shat*, to despise, in this passage. But because it signifies to despise, and the Prophet spoke of reproach, he may repeat the same thing of the Philistines which he had a little before said of the Syrians. It follows—

58. Thou hast borne thy lewdness and thine abominations, saith the Lord.   58. Pravas cogitationes tuas,[1] et abominationes tuas, tu portasti ea, dicit Iehovah.

Here God repeats what we saw before, that the Jews were deprived of all excuse. We know how bold they were in their expostulations, and how they always cried out when God treated them severely. Because, therefore, complaints were always flying about from this proud people, here, as before, God pronounces that they deserved their sufferings: *thou bearest*, says he, not any immoderate rigour of which you falsely accuse me, but *thine abominations* and crimes. זמה, *zemeh*, signifies simply purpose, but also abomination, so that it is better to translate it wickedness or baseness. Now, therefore, we understand the Prophet's intention, that the Jews, indeed, suffered the just reward of their wicked-

[1] Or, "thine enormities."—*Calvin.*

ness; and the penalties which awaited them could not be imputed to God as too severe, since, if they weighed their enormities, they would be found heavier than God's treatment of them. Besides, this verse also embraces the final destruction of the city and temple; although God at the same time adds the punishment by which he wished to recall them into the way of life. It follows—

| 59. For thus saith the Lord God, I will even deal with thee as thou hast done, which hast despised the oath in breaking the covenant. | 59. Quia sic dicit Dominator Iehovah, et faciam tibi quemadmodum fecisti, quæ[1] sprevisti jusjurandum ad dissipandum[2] fœdus. |

Here, also, God meets the false objection by which the Jews might strive with him; for whatever they were, yet God had entered into covenant with them. They might, therefore, fly to this refuge, that God had bound himself in covenant with them, since he had adopted Abraham with his seed. Although they had provoked God's anger a thousand times, yet this exception remained, that God ought to stand to his agreement, and not to look at what they had deserved by their ingratitude, but rather to be consistent with his promises. Now, therefore, he returns to this cavil, and says that he is free to break the covenant since they have done so first. *I will do,* says he, *to thee as thou hast done.* We see, therefore, that the calumny is here repelled by which the Jews could obliquely defame God, as they were accustomed to do, as if he had rendered his covenant void. He says, then, that in agreement it is customary for a person, when deceived, no longer to be necessarily bound to a perfidious breaker of agreements; for covenanting requires mutual faith: but the Jews had violated their agreement, and reduced it to nothing. Hence, through their perfidy and wickedness, God had acquired the liberty of rejecting them, and of no longer reckoning them among his people. Hence, as in the last verse, he said that the Jews paid a just penalty; so now, he adds specially, that he could not be condemned for bad faith in departing from his agreement, because he had to deal with traitors and covenant-breakers who had rendered void their agreement: for there

[1] Or, "because."—*Calvin.*
[2] Or, "that thou shouldst render vain."—*Calvin.*

is no covenant when either party declines it. *I will do, therefore, to thee as thou hast done,* namely, *because thou hast despised an oath, so as to render the covenant void.* Here God enlarges upon the crime of revolt, because the Jews had not only dissipated the covenant, but had despised an oath. אלה, *aleh,* signifies both an oath and a curse; (Deut. xxvii.;) hence some think that the Prophet here looks to the curses by which the law was sanctioned, which I willingly adopt. But we must remark what I have already said, that their criminality is increased, because the Jews had not only acted falsely, but had also set at nought that solemn oath by which they had bound themselves. For as God promised that he would be their God, so Moses stipulated in his name that the people should remain obedient to him, and they all answered, Amen; (Levit. xxvi.) A punishment was announced, and such as ought to have terrified them. For the Jews then to neglect this covenant as a mere trifle, was the act of brutal stupidity. Whence we see that their crime was doubled, when the Prophet accuses them of not only being truce-breakers, but also of wantonly deriding God, and of treating their own solemn oath, by which they had bound themselves, as a childish action. It follows—

60. Nevertheless, I will remember my covenant with thee in the days of thy youth, and I will establish unto thee an everlasting covenant.	60. Et memor ero[1] fœderis mei tecum diebus adolescentiæ tuæ: et stabiliam tibi fœdus perpetuum.

Because God here promises that he would be propitious to the Jews, some translate the former verse as if it had been said, "Shall I do with thee as thou hast done?" or, I would do as thou hast done, unless I had been mindful; but that is too forced in my opinion. I have no doubt that the Prophet restrains himself, so to speak, and directs his discourse peculiarly to the elect, of whom we spoke yesterday. Hitherto he had regarded the whole body of the people which was abandoned, and hence he put before them nothing but despair. But he now turns himself to the election of grace, of which Paul speaks, (Rom. xi. 5;) and

[1] Or, "I shall yet be mindful," for the copula ought to be resolved into the adversative particle.—*Calvin.*

for this reason promises them that God would be mindful of his covenant, though he would not restore the whole people promiscuously. For the body on the whole must perish; a small band only was reserved. We know, therefore, that this promise was not common to all the sons of Abraham who were his offspring according to the flesh, but it was peculiar to the elect alone. God therefore pronounces, *that he would be mindful of his covenant which he had made with that people in their youth,* by which words he signifies, that his pity should not go forth except from the covenant. For God always recalls the faithful, as it were, to the fountain, lest they should claim anything as their right, or imagine this or that to be the cause of God's being reconciled to them. He shows, therefore, that this pity has no other foundation than the covenant; and this is the reason why he says, *that he would be mindful of his covenant.* He now adds, *and I will establish a perpetual covenant with thee.* Here God promises, without obscurity, a better and more excellent covenant than that ancient one already abolished through the people's fault. This passage, then, cannot be understood except of the new covenant which God has established by the hand of Christ. But these two clauses are so mutually united that they ought to be carefully weighed, namely, that God here gives the hope of a new covenant, and yet teaches us that it originates in the old one already abolished through the people's fault. Thus we see that the New Testament flows from that covenant which God made with Abraham, and afterwards sanctioned by the hand of Moses. That which is promulgated for us in the Gospel is called the New Covenant, not because it had no beginning previously, but because it was renewed, and better conditions added; for we know that the Law was abrogated by the New Covenant. Whether it be so or not, the excellence of the New Testament is not injured, because it has its source and occasion in the Old Covenant, and is founded on it. It follows—

61. Then thou shalt remember thy ways, and be ashamed, when thou shalt receive thy sisters, thine

61. Et recordaberis viarum tuarum, et pudefies cum tu assumes sorores tuas majores præ te, et cum

elder and thy younger: and I will give them unto thee for daughters, but not by thy covenant.

minoribus præ te: et dabo ipsas tibi in filias: et non a fœdere tuo.

As God, then, shows that he would not be merciful to the Jews for any other reason than through being mindful of his covenant, so now, in return, he informs us what he requires from them, namely, that they should begin to acknowledge how basely they had abjured their pledged fidelity—how unworthily they had despised his law—how impiously obstinate they had been against all his prophets in deriding their threats, and in being stupid under manifest penalties. But this passage is worthy of notice, since we gather that none are capable of obtaining God's mercy except those who are dissatisfied with themselves, and, being ashamed and confounded, betake themselves to his mercy. In fine, we see that God's grace does not profit the obstinate at all: it is offered to all in common; but none receive it except those who condemn themselves, and bear in mind their crimes, so that they are forgotten before God. If, therefore, we wish our sins to be buried before God, we must remember them ourselves; if we wish our iniquities to be blotted out before God and the angels, we must disgrace ourselves; that is, we must blush and be ashamed of our baseness whenever we transgress and provoke God's wrath. Hence we here see that the whole contents of the Gospel are shortly summed up; for the Gospel contains nothing else but repentance and faith, as is well known. Concerning faith, Ezekiel has proclaimed that God, mindful of his covenant, will become reconciled to the lost; but he now adds an exhortation that they should acknowledge their faults: but we know that the shame of which the Prophet speaks is the fruit or part of repentance, as is evident from Paul's description of penitence in the seventh chapter of his second epistle to the Corinthians, (ver. 9-11.) But we shall have yet to speak on this subject, so that I now hasten forwards, because what I have hitherto taught cannot be understood until we come to the end of the verse.

He says, *when thou shalt receive thy sisters, as well the elder as the younger;* for he does not speak here of Sodom and Samaria alone, but of all nations; for all the nations may properly be called sisters, for all the world was corrupt. Since, therefore, they were all alike in vices, their union was like that of relationship. For this reason he says, that when the Jews shall return to favour, they shall then have a great multitude with them, *who shall receive their own sisters;* that is, shall collect from all sides an immense multitude, so that all shall be assembled in obedience to God, and shall be partakers of the same covenant. If any one object that this has never been fulfilled, the answer is at hand, that the prophets speak of the calling of the Gentiles in two ways. They sometimes proclaim it so as to declare that the Jews and Israelites are the leaders of all the others, so as to confer upon them the favour and patronage of God. In that day seven men shall lay hold of the skirt of a single Jew, and shall say, Lead us to your God, (Zech. viii. 23 ;) and this was the legitimate order, that the Jews, as firstborn, should join others in alliance to themselves, and thus unite all into one body and one Church: but because the Jews were cut off through their ingratitude, the prophets make mention of another calling, that the Gentiles should succeed in the place of the ungrateful people, as Paul says that the natural branches were cut off, and that we were graffed in who belonged to the unfruitful tree. (Rom. xi. 16-19.) The Prophet adds this former reason, *that the Jews should receive their sisters, both elder and younger*, since they should collect God's Church from all nations ; and this has been partly fulfilled. For whence came the Gospel except from this fountain ? as it had been foretold, A law shall go out from Zion, and God's word from Jerusalem. (Isaiah ii. 3 ; Micah iv. 2.) Again, in the 110th Psalm, (ver. 1,) Thy sceptre shall go forth from Zion ; that is, the kingdom of Christ shall be propagated throughout the whole world: because, therefore, salvation flowed from the Jews, and the Gospel emanated from thence, what is here promised was partly fulfilled, namely, that other people were received by the Jews.

He now subjoins, *I will give them to thee for daughters:* for if the Jews had not, by their ingratitude, rejected the honour of which God had reckoned them worthy, they had always been the first-born in the Church. Then the Gentiles would have been, as it were, under a mother, since they were "the primitive Church," (according to the language of the day,) and thus they would have obtained the degree of mother among all nations. Therefore God here deservedly pronounces *that he would give them all nations for daughters*, to be added to the Jews, when the Gentiles were grafted into the same body of the Church by faith in the Gospel. But he adds, *not from thy covenant.* Some refer this to ceremonies, since, when the Gentiles were adopted, they still remained free from the ceremonies of the law; but that is cold. Others compare this passage with Jeremiah: I will establish a new covenant with you, not such as I established with your fathers, which they rendered vain; but this is the covenant which I will make with you, &c. (Chap. xxxi. 31-33.) Since, then, it is here said, *the covenant shall not be according to the covenant of the people*, this is said with truth, because it will be a New Testament. But such expounders are partly right, but not wholly so; for a contrast must be understood between the people's covenant and God's. He had said just before, I will be mindful of my covenant: he now says, *not of thine.* Hence he reconciles what seemed opposites, namely, that he would be mindful of his own agreement, and yet it had been dissipated, broken, and abolished. He shows that it was fixed on his own side, as they say, but vain on the people's side. *I will be reconciled, then, but not through thy covenant;* for there was now no covenant, as Hosea says—Not my people, not beloved. (Chap. i. 9.) All the progeny of Abraham were not God's people, nor all their daughters beloved: but although the covenant was vain through the people's perfidy, yet God overcame their malice, and so he again erected his own covenant towards them. And when he says, *I will establish a covenant*, we may explain it, I will set it up again, or restore it afresh: for we said that the New Testament was so distinguished from the Old, that it was founded upon it. For what is proposed to us in Christ, unless what God had promised in the law? and therefore Christ is called the end of the law, and elsewhere its spirit: for if the law be separated from Christ, it is like a dead letter: Christ alone gives it life. Since, therefore, God at this day exhibits to us nothing in his only-begotten Son but what he had formerly promised in the law, it follows that his covenant is set up again, and so perpetually established; and yet this is not man's part. Wherefore? For men had so revolted from the faith, that God was free; nay, the covenant itself had no force, and lost its effect through their perfidy: for it is easy to collect the points in which the New and Old Testaments are alike, and those in which they differ. They have this similarity, that God at this day confirms to us what he had formerly promised to Abraham, and in no other sense could Abraham be called the Father of the Faithful.

Since, therefore, Abraham is at this time the father of all the faithful, it follows that our safety is not to be sought otherwise than in that covenant which God established with Abraham; but afterwards the same covenant was ratified by the hand of Moses. A difference must now be briefly remarked from a passage in Jeremiah, (chap. xxxi. 32,) namely, because the ancient covenant was abolished through the fault of man, there was need of a better remedy, which is there shown to be twofold, namely, that God should bury men's sins, and inscribe his law on their hearts: that also was done in Abraham's time. Abraham believed in God: faith was always the gift of the Holy Spirit; therefore God inscribed his covenant in Abraham's heart. (Gen. xv. 6; Rom. iv. 3; Eph. ii. 8.) He inscribed his law on the heart of Moses and on the rest of the faithful. This is true: but at first that inner grace was more obscure under the law, and then it was an additional benefit. It could not therefore be ascribed to the law that God regenerated his own elect, because the spirit of regeneration was from Christ, and therefore from the Gospel and the new covenant. But yet we must remember what I have said, that the faithful under the ancient covenant were gifted and endowed with a spirit of regeneration. As far as relates to the remission of sins, it was still more obscure: for cattle were sacrificed, which could not acquire salvation for miserable men, nor blot out their sins. Therefore, if the law is regarded in itself, the promise in the new covenant will not be found in it: I will not remember thy sins: yet to this day God is propitious to us, because he promised to Abraham that all nations should be blest in his seed. (Jer. xxxi. 34 ; Gen. xii. 3, and xviii. 18.) We see then that the difference which Jeremiah points out was really true ; and yet the new covenant so flowed from the old, that it was almost the same in substance, while distinguished in form.

PRAYER.

Grant, Almighty God, since thine only-begotten Son has appeared for us, who filled up all the measure of thy grace, that we may not be ungrateful in despising so inestimable a boon ; but may we embrace with true and sincere faith what thou offerest us, namely, the mercy which we always need, and also the spirit of regeneration ; that we may so devote ourselves to thee through a whole life of obedience, that at length we may arrive at that glory which at this day shines upon us as in a mirror, until its fruition shall appear in heaven, by the same Christ our Lord.—Amen.

Lecture Fiftieth.

62. And I will establish my covenant with thee ; and thou shalt know that I am the Lord.

62. Et stabiliam ego fœdus meum tecum, et cognosces quod ego Iehovah.

THE Prophet here confirms his former teaching, namely, that although the Jews rendered God's covenant vain as far as they possibly could, yet it should be firm and fixed. But we must hold what I have mentioned, that this discourse is specially limited to the elect, because the safety of the whole people was already desperate. Hence God shows that the covenant which he had made with Abraham could not be abolished by the perfidy of man. And this is what Paul says in the third chapter of the Epistle to the Romans, (verse 4,) Even if the whole world were liars, yet God must always remain true. But we see that the covenant of which we are now teaching was new, and yet had its origin from the old, because we are so reconciled to God by Christ that we ought to be grafted into the body of the ancient Church, and be made sons of Abraham, since, as we saw before, he is not called the father of the faithful in vain. God says, therefore, *that his own covenant should be firm with the people,* not with that people which had been already deserted through its perfidy, but with the true and genuine children of Abraham, who followed their father in faith and piety, as it is said in the 102d Psalm, (verse 18,) A people shall be created to the praise of God. For the Prophet now shows that God's covenant could not be otherwise constituted afresh unless a new Church were formed, and God was to create a new world: for this is the meaning of the words, A people when created shall praise God. The Spirit, therefore, obliquely reproves the Israelites, as if he had said that the praises of God were abolished among them: but when the new people shall come forth, then God should be glorified. He adds, *and thou shalt know that I am Jehovah.* This phrase is often repeated, but in a different sense. For when a prophet threatened the people, he always added this particle, and thus a contrast must be understood between the people's stupidity and good sense; for all their prophecies were neglected by the people. God's servants indeed uttered their voice, and severely blamed the impious and wicked, but without any effect. Since, therefore, they so wantonly played with reproaches and threats, it was often said to them, Ye shall begin to feel me to be God when I shall cease to speak to you, and shall instruct you by scourges. But now the Prophet, as we see, preaches concerning the gratuitous reconciliation of the people with God. Hence they really felt him to be God, because he stood firm to his promises, although, through the fault of man, his covenant had fallen to pieces and become invalid. The Prophet here announces that they should feel God to be unlike themselves, that is, not to change his counsels, or to vary with the levity and inconstancy of men: as also it is said in Isaiah, My thoughts are not as your thoughts: as far as the heavens are distant from the earth, so are my thoughts distant from yours, and my ways from your ways. (Isa. lv. 8, 9.) God here means that the Jews acted wrong in estimating his pity by their own common sense: for he says that he differed very much from them, since his pity was unfathomable, and his truth incomprehensible.

Now, therefore, we understand what the Prophet means in this verse. In the first clause he pronounces, that the covenant which God would make with his new and elect people should be firm: then he adds, that the Jews should know that they were dealing with God, because they could not take away what God was then promising. Now we can understand the reason why God's covenant in Christ was perpetual: because, as we read in Jeremiah, he inscribed his law on the hearts of the righteous, and remitted their iniquities. (Chap. xxxi. 33.) This, then, was the cause of its perpetuity. Besides, although the Prophet magnifies God's grace in the second clause, yet at the same time he recalls the Jews from every perverse imagination which might entirely shake their confidence. For when they thought themselves plunged in an abyss, they were ready to collect that there was no further remedy. But if God wished to preserve them, why did he not send them help in time? But when he suffered them to be led into exile, and to be plunged into the lowest depths, there was no hope of restoration. For this cause Ezekiel announces that the faithful ought not to persist in their own thoughts, but rather to raise their minds to heaven, and to expect what seemed altogether out of place, since they ought to judge according to the nature of God, and to measure the effects of his promises by the immensity of his power rather than by their own perceptions.

63. That thou mayest remember, and be confounded, and never open thy mouth any more because of thy shame, when I am pacified toward thee for all that thou hast done, saith the Lord God.

63. Ut recorderis, et pudefias, et non sit tibi amplius apertio oris propter probrum tuum cum propitius fuero tibi in omnibus quæ fecisti, dicit Dominator Iehovah.

Ezekiel again exhorts the faithful to repentance and constant meditation. We have said that these members cannot be divided, namely, the testimony of grace with the doctrine of repentance: we have said, also, that this is the substance of the gospel, that God wishes those to repent whom he reconciles by gratuitous pardon. For he is appeased by us only when he makes us new creatures in Christ, and regenerates us by his Spirit; as it is said in Isaiah, God will be propitious to the people who shall have returned from their iniquity. (Chap. lix. 20.) That promise is restricted to those who do not indulge and revel in sin, but humble themselves before God, and decide their own salvation to be impossible without their being severe judges to their own condemnation. Therefore Ezekiel follows up this point when he says *that thou mayest remember and be ashamed.* I have said that penitence is not only to be commended here, but the continual desire for it. And this must be remarked, because it is troublesome to us to be often shaking off our sins; and hence we escape as far as we can from the perception of them: for we desire our own enjoyment, and every one willingly puts his sins out of sight. Surely if we do look upon them, they first compel us to be ashamed, and then we are wounded with serious grief; conscience summons us to God's tribunal: we then acknowledge the formidable vengeance which slays even the boldest, unless they are upheld by the assurance of pardon. Since, then, the acknowledgment of sins brings us both shame and sorrow, we endeavour to put it far away from us by all means. But no other way of access to embracing God's favour is open to us, except that of repentance of sins. This, then, is the reason why God insists so much on this point: we do not follow him directly; hence it is not sufficient to show us what ought to be done, unless God pricks us sharply, and violently draws us to himself. This passage, then, must be remarked where the Prophet commands the faithful, after they have obtained pardon, to remember their sins, for hypocrites are here distinguished from the true sons of God. Hypocrites boast with swelling words, that they rely on the mercy of God, and speak mightily of the grace of Christ, but meanwhile they wish the memory of their sins to remain buried. On the other hand, we cannot be otherwise truly humble before God, unless we judge ourselves, as I have said. If we desire, therefore, our sins to be blotted out before God, and to be buried in the depths of the sea, as another Prophet says, (Micah vii. 19,) we must recall them often and constantly to our remembrance: for when they are kept before our eyes we then flee seriously to God for mercy, and are properly prepared by humility and fear.

The Prophet adds also, *that thou mayest be ashamed:* for

it is not sufficient simply to remember, unless we add the shame of which the Prophet speaks. For we see that many remember their faults and confess their sins, but they do it lightly, and as a matter of duty; nay, they acknowledge them so as to remain in their integrity, and, as they say, to preserve their credit. But the recognition here required is accompanied by shame, as Paul, when addressing the faithful, puts before them their past life thus: "What fruit could you gather from that course of life?" (Rom. vi. 19-21.) Ye blush now in truth when so many crimes are heaped upon you: ye were then blind, and wandered in darkness: but when God shone upon you by the gospel, ye acknowledge your baseness and foulness, from which shame is produced. He now adds, *neither mayest thou open thy mouth any more.* It is not surprising if the Prophet uses many words in explaining one thing which is not obscure in itself. But I have already shown why he does so, because we are with the greatest difficulty led on to that shame which the Prophet mentions. We condemn ourselves indeed verbally at once; but scarcely one in a hundred can be found so to cast himself down as to sustain willingly the reproach which he deserves. Since then voluntary submission is not found in man, it is necessary that we should be impelled more hardly and sharply, as the Prophet does here. When he says, *there shall be no opening of the mouth,* he means, that no partial confession of sins shall be exacted by which men bear witness, and acknowledge themselves liable to God's judgment; but a full and entire confession, so that they may be held convicted on all sides. And this must be diligently noticed. For we see that the world is always endeavouring to escape God's sentence by turning away from it; and since it cannot do this completely, it invents subterfuges, so as to retain some portion of its innocence.

Hence the fiction among the papists of partial justification: hence also their satisfactions; for they are compelled, whether they wish it or not, to confess themselves worthy of death: but afterwards they use the exception, that they have merited something before from God through their good works, and are not altogether worthy of condemnation: then they descend to compensations, and wish to treat with God, as if they could appease him by what they call works of supererogation. Whatever be the sense, men can scarcely be found who sincerely and honestly acknowledge that there exists in themselves nothing but material for condemnation. We confess, as I have said, that we are guilty before God, but only for one or two faults. What then does the Holy Spirit here prescribe ? *that there should be no opening of the mouth ;* as also Paul says, adopting his form of speech from this and similar passages. It is often said in the Prophets, Let all flesh be silent before God, (Zech. ii. 13 ;) but here the Prophet speaks specially of the shame by which God's children lie so confused, that they are altogether silent. Paul also says, that every mouth may be shut, and all flesh humbled before God. (Rom. iii. 19.) He afterwards shows that Jews as well as Gentiles were involved in the same condemnation, and that there was no hope of safety left except through God's mercy: he then adds, that God's justice truly shines forth when our mouth is stopped, that is, when we do not turn aside and offer any excuses, as hypocrites divide the merit between God and themselves. I indeed confess that I have sinned ; but why may not my good works come into the account ? why should I be condemned for one fault only ? as if those who violate law do not depart from righteousness. We see, then, that we are properly humbled when we are silent and do not reproach God, when we do not quibble or allege first one thing and then another to extenuate or excuse our fault. God indeed wishes our mouth to be open ; as Peter says, that we are called out of darkness into marvellous light, to show forth his praises who delivered us. (1 Pet. ii. 9.) For this purpose, then, God was merciful to us, that we might be heralds of his grace. And in this sense, also, David says, O Lord, open thou my lips, and my mouth shall declare thy praise ; that is, by giving me material for a song, as he elsewhere says, He has put a new song into my mouth. (Ps. li. 15 ; xl. 3.) God, therefore, opens the mouths or lips of the faithful whenever he is liberal or beneficent towards them. But he is here treating of the exceptions of those who would willingly transact business with God, as if they were not wholly worthy of condemnation. In fine, Ezekiel signifies that this is the true fruit of penitence when we do not defend ourselves, but silently confess ourselves convicted. A passage of Paul's may possibly be objected as apparently contrary to this of our Prophet, in which he reckons defence among the effects or fruits of penitence, (2 Cor. vii. 11 ;) but defence is not here used in our customary sense : for any one who asserts that he has acted rightly, and so without fault is said to defend himself. But a defence in Paul's sense is nothing else but a prayer against punishment when a sinner comes forward, and after confessing his fault, begs of God to pardon it, and, as it were, covers himself with mercy, so that his condemnation is nowhere apparent. We see, then, that the language of Paul is not in opposition to that of the Prophet.

He now adds, *from thy disgrace*, verbally from the face of thy disgrace, *when I shall be propitious to thee*. We again see that these things agree well together, that God buries our sins and we recall them to memory. For we turn aside his judgment when we willingly accuse and condemn ourselves. For when conscience is asleep, it nourishes a hidden fire, which at length emerges into a flame and lights up God's wrath. If, therefore, we desire the fire of God's wrath to be extinguished, there is no other remedy than to shake off our sins and to set before our eyes the disgrace which we deserve, and God's mercy induces us to this. For we must remark the connection, *when I shall be propitious to thee, thou shalt be silent in thy disgrace*. And surely the more any one has tasted of the grace of God, the more ready he is to condemn himself, and as unbelief is proud, so the more any one proceeds in the faith of God's grace, he is thus humbled more and more before him. And that is best expressed in the words of the Prophet, since he teaches that silence is the effect of grace or of gratuitous reconciliation. When therefore he says, *I shall have been propitious to thee, then thou shalt blush that thou mayest be mute*, namely, *on account of thy disgrace*. And we see that the people were so taught by legal ceremonies to apprehend the mercy of God, and to be touched at the same time with the serious affection of penitence; for without a victim, God was never appeased under the law. And now although animals are not sacrificed, yet when we consider that no other price was sufficient to satisfy God, except his only-begotten Son poured forth his blood in expiation, there matter is set before us for embracing the grace of God, and at the same time we are touched, as the saying is, with the true affection of penitence. Besides, God amplifies the magnitude of his grace when he says לכל אשר עשׂית, *lekel asher gnesith, on account of all things which thou hast done.* For the people ought not only to feel God merciful, but to examine their faults, and then to feel how manifold and remarkable was God's mercy towards them. For if the people had only been guilty of one kind of sin, they would have valued God's grace the less: but when they had been convicted of so many crimes, as we have seen, hence the magnitude of his grace became more apparent.[1] Let us now go on.

CHAPTER XVII.

1. And the word of the Lord came unto me, saying,	1. Et fuit sermo Iehovæ ad me, dicendo,
2. Son of man, put forth a riddle, and speak a parable unto the house of Israel.	2. Fili hominis, ænigmatisa ænigma, et proverbia proverbium[2] ad domum Israel.

In this chapter the Prophet shows that the Jews were utterly foolish in thinking themselves safe, since they had God as their adversary. At the end of the chapter he promises indeed the restoration of the Church, and heralds the

---

[1] In commenting on this chapter, Calvin takes occasion to explain the gospel doctrines of justification, faith, and repentance, and refers to the adverse fictions of the papacy. This interesting subject is fully treated by Bishop Davenant in his *Disputatio de justitiâ habituali et actuali*, delivered when professor of divinity at the University of Cambridge (1631). The English translation by the Rev. Josiah Allport, 1844, is a most valuable work, and treats largely on this and all collateral subjects. His "Determinationes," edit. 1634 and 1639, may also be consulted: with Penrose on the Atonement, 1843; and St. Bernard's Sermon on Isaiah, chap. vi. 1, 2. Œcolampadius, on the 55th verse of this chapter, is copious, spiritual, and practical; and Maldonatus gives the sense of the Hebrew remarkably well and with great consistency, though he adds no practical comments. Theodoret and Jerome are both very explanatory, especially on verse 45. See Dissertations at the end of this volume.

[2] That is, "bring forward a remarkable sentence."—*Calvin.*

kingdom of Christ: but the principal part of the chapter is consumed with this teaching, that the Jews were utterly foolish in promising themselves safety for the city, the temple, and their kingdom: for, as it now appeared, they had violated the covenant of God and he had rejected them. When deprived of God's help, what could they do? This was egregious folly to hope for a prosperous state of their kingdom when their power was diminished and cut off, and they were reduced almost to the very last straits. But since the Prophet's discourse cannot be understood without a knowledge of the history, I shall therefore make a beginning: When Nebuchadnezzar appointed Zedekiah king, he also made him tributary to himself. He was made king at the will or rather by the lust of the king of Babylon, when Jeconiah was led captive. (2 Kings xxiv. 15-17; 2 Chron. xxxvi. 10; Jer. xxxvii. 1.) Jeconiah had not sinned greatly, but when he saw himself unable to resist, he surrendered himself with his mother and children; he was carried away to Babylon, and there was treated humanely and even splendidly, although not royally. Nebuchadnezzar, foreseeing much trouble if he set any of his satraps over Judæa, and fearing daily tumults, appointed Mattaniah king, to whom he gave the name Zedekiah; this was the last king: already, as I have said, the royal dignity was greatly diminished: it was tributary to Nebuchadnezzar, and Zedekiah's sway was but precarious. His position depended on the will of his conqueror, and he who placed him on the throne could remove him as often as he pleased. A little while afterwards, when he saw that Nebuchadnezzar was at a distance, he made an agreement with the king of Egypt, and thought he should have sufficient help if Nebuchadnezzar were to return again with an army. And the Egyptians, as we have elsewhere said, were sufficiently desirous of this treaty. For they saw the Babylonian monarchy gradually increasing, and it was probable that, when the Jews were utterly subdued, Nebuchadnezzar would not be content with those boundaries, but would attack Egypt in like manner, and absorb that kingdom, as he had done others. Hence a reason for their entering into the treaty was at hand, since the king of Egypt thought that Judea would be a defence if Nebuchadnezzar should come down with his army: and certainly the Jews must receive the assault first. Whatever be the meaning, Zedekiah, through despising his oath, as we shall see, revolted to the Egyptians, and when Nebuchadnezzar afterwards demanded tribute, Zedekiah refused, through reliance on that covenant which he had made with the Egyptians. We now see how foolish the Jews were in sleeping carelessly in that miserable state to which they had been reduced. For when their power was unbroken they could not sustain the attack of the king of Babylon: their king was then a mere dead image, and nothing but a shadow: yet they indulged in pride not only against Nebuchadnezzar but also against the Prophets and God himself, just as if they were flourishing in wealth and power and complete prosperity. Hence Ezekiel now refutes and rebukes this arrogance. He shows how easy it was for the Babylonians to overthrow them again, since when they attacked them before they were subdued, they easily compelled them to surrender.

But I come to the words *Son of man, set forth an enigma:* the noun and the verb mutually answer to each other, hence any one may if he please render the Prophet's words, by saying enigmatize an enigma: for the Prophet here speaks of allegorical language, חידה, *chideh*, signifies the same as "allegory," where the words are different from the sense, that is, where the sense is wrapt up in obscure involutions: but we know that God sometimes spoke enigmatically when unwilling to be understood by the impious and disbelieving. But here the obscurity of the sentence has another meaning, namely, that the Jews should be waked up, and this prophecy should penetrate their minds: we know their extreme hardness, and hence if the Prophet had spoken simply and in his accustomed language, they had not been so attentive. This therefore is the reason why God orders him to speak enigmatically. He now adds, ומשל משל, *vemeshel meshel.* We know that *meshel* is a remarkable sentence, and is the word used by Solomon as the title of his proverbs: משל, *meshel*, then, means the same as apothegm: but it is sometimes taken for likeness: and in this place

God so denounces destruction upon the Israelites in an allegory, as to illustrate his language by a comparison, since otherwise it would have been obscure. Be this as it may, God so prefaced his address, that the Jews might acknowledge the message to be no common one, but that it ought to affect them seriously. The usual reason for speaking enigmatically does not hold good here, namely, that the Jews were unworthy of the doctrine of salvation, since the Prophet will very shortly explain what he had hitherto uttered in figure and allegory. It is indeed true, that Christ spoke in parables to the people, because the disciples alone were capable of familiar and pure teaching. Of unbelievers, also, Isaiah says, Prophecy shall be to you a sealed book. Hence I will speak with this people in a strange and barbarous tongue, and they shall not proceed beyond the rudiments. (Matt. xiii.; Mark iv.; Luke viii.; Isaiah xxix. 11, 12.) But, as I have said, the obscurity of this teaching was only a preparation, that the people should strictly attend to the subject here set before them.

3. And say, Thus saith the Lord God, A great eagle with great wings, long winged, full of feathers, which had divers colours, came unto Lebanon, and took the highest branch of the cedar:

4. He cropped off the top of his young twigs, and carried it into a land of traffic; he set it in a city of merchants.

3. Et dic, Sit dicit Dominator Iehovah, aquila magna, magna alis, longa penna[1] plena[2] plumis quæ illis variæ[3] erant venit ad montem Libanum, et accepit summitatem cedri.

4. Caput[4] surculorum ejus avellit, et transtulit in terram mercatoris,[5] in urbe mercatorum posuit eam.[6]

Here the Prophet reasons from the greater to the less: for if Nebuchadnezzar was able to subdue the whole kingdom with ease, when as yet the Jews were untouched, how much more readily would he overthrow them when wretched and all but ruined: for nothing remained which was not threatened with ruin; and this is the meaning of the Prophet. But he compares King Nebuchadnezzar to an eagle,

---

[1] Or, "wings"—there is a change of number.—*Calvin.*

[2] Or, "thick with," "plentiful in."—*Calvin.*

[3] The number, though singular, is taken for plural, that is, "of divers colours."—*Calvin.*   [4] Or, "the top."—*Calvin.*

[5] The word כנען, *cengnen*, (or, *chnaan*,) is not a proper name, but is taken appellatively.—*Calvin.*   [6] Or, "that top."—*Calvin.*

whom he says was great, and then with *large* or extended *wings.* There is no doubt that by *wings, feathers, and plumes,* he means the regions and peoples over which Nebuchadnezzar presided; for we know that the Chaldæans possessed the monarchy of the East. Since, therefore, so many regions and people obeyed Nebuchadnezzar's sway, it is not surprising that the Prophet calls him *a great eagle, with ample wings, and with numerous feathers* or plumes; for where he now says, מְלֵא הַנּוֹצָה, *mela henotzeh,* full of feathers, he will shortly say, רֹב נוֹצָה, *reb notzeh,* many feathers, when speaking of the king of Egypt. He says, *the wings were of divers colours;* it is the same noun which the Prophet used in the last chapter, when he said that the people were clad in precious garments; for thus the Hebrews speak of Phrygian texture: hence he compares the wings of the king of Babylon to a woven garment, resplendent with various colours; for although Nebuchadnezzar held his throne at only one place, yet he had seized and subdued many tributaries on all sides. This, therefore, is the reason for this variety;—but I cannot proceed further at present.

PRAYER.

Grant, Almighty God, since thou hast treated us so liberally by opening the immense and inestimable treasures of thy grace, that being mindful of our condition we may always bewail it, and remember what we were when thou deignest to adopt us as sons, and how often and how variously we have provoked thee, and rendered thy covenant vain: Grant, also, that we may glorify thee in our shame, and perpetually magnify thy name by our humility, until we become partakers of that glory which thine only-begotten Son has procured for us through his own blood.— Amen.

Lecture Fifty-First.

WE began yesterday to explain the saying of the Prophet, *that an eagle came to mount Lebanon, and there cropped off the top of a cedar,* that is, the highest bough. Some interpreters seem to me to labour in vain about the word Lebanon. They think it means Jerusalem, and cite the passage in Zechariah where it is said, Open thy gates, O Lebanon. (Chap. xi. 1.) But Zechariah does not speak of the city here, but of the temple, because it was built of a great mass of cedar. But here Ezekiel means the land, and names Lebanon rather than other places, not only because that mountain was the remarkable ornament of the region on account of its lofty cedars, and balsam and aromatic trees, but because this was needful to complete his allegory. If he had said that an eagle had come to a city, it would have been absurd. Hence we see that the word Lebanon is taken for that part of Judæa in which the most beautiful trees spring up and flourish. But he says, *that it plucked off a bough from the top of the cedars*, because Nebuchadnezzar, who is intended by the eagle, took away King Jeconiah, as we said yesterday. Hence King Jeconiah is compared *to a very lofty bough of a cedar*, because at that time all thought that the kingdom was superior to every danger; for the Jews boasted that they were under God's protection, and that the city was impregnable: hence that occurrence was incredible. Now the Prophet adds, *that the eagle plucked off the head* or summit of the boughs, as the Hebrews call the tender shoots; and here the word means the tender branches: and it means, as we shall afterwards see, the elders who were dragged away into exile. *It took away the head into the land of the merchant.* We said that this was a mere appellative here, *chnaan*, because it follows a little afterwards in the plural number: בעיר רכלים שמו, *begnir-reklim shemo*, in the city of merchants he set it: he says, then, *that the boughs were placed in a city of merchants*. This name was given to Babylon, not only because it was a celebrated mart of trade, but because it was a firm and strong place of custody through the multitude of inhabitants, so that it was not easy to draw captives from it. For any one could easily be rescued from a solitude without resistance; but in a great concourse it is not so easy to plan or attempt anything. I do not doubt, therefore, that the Prophet means that the higher classes of the kingdom, together with Jeconiah, were shut up in firm custody that they should not escape. It follows—

5. He took also of the seed of the land, and planted it in a fruitful field; he placed it by great waters, and set it as a willow-tree:

6. And it grew, and became a spreading vine of low stature, whose branches turned toward him, and the roots thereof were under him: so it became a vine, and brought forth branches, and shot forth sprigs.

5. Et sustulit[1] è semine terræ, et posuit illud in agro seminis,[2] sumpsit super aquas multas, tanquam salicem posuit illud.

6. Et germinavit, et fuit in vitem luxuriantem, humilem statura, ut respicerent palmites ejus ad ipsam,[3] et radices ejus sub ea essent: et fuit in vitem, et produxit palmites[4] et emisit propagines.

After Ezekiel has narrated that Jehoiachin was carried away with his counsellors and the flower of the whole people, and was so deprived of his native country as to be without hope of return, he now says, *that the eagle took up the seed in Judæa, and placed it in a fertile land;* for he calls it *a land of seed*, since it was cultivated and produced fruit abundantly. He says, that the seed was afterwards hidden in the soil, that it grew immediately, and became a luxuriant vine. He says also, *that its roots were irrigated, like a willow planted by a river's bank.* The Prophet afterwards explains himself: hence it is sufficient to state briefly what he means. The seed, then, which he here means is Zedekiah, the last king. It is said *to have been planted beside the waters;* for his condition was tolerable, since the royal name and dignity and wealth was left to him. For although he was tributary, the kindness with which he was treated by Nebuchadnezzar was not to be despised, since, by the right of war, he was able to lead him captive, together with his nephew; for Zedekiah was the uncle of Jeconiah or Jehoiachin. But he said, *that this vine*, which sprang from a seed or germ, *grew so that it was of low stature;* the Prophet means by these words, as we shall afterwards see, that Zedekiah was not a king, that he was restrained by a bridle from daring to rebel against the king of Babylon; and hence it is added, *that its branches turned towards the eagle, and its roots were under him;* but in the next clause Ezekiel announces, *that it became a vine which sent forth branches, and shot forth boughs,* which he repeats again, that Zedekiah's ingratitude may appear the greater, who, not content with his moderate confinement, perfidiously revolted from the king of Babylon,

[1] " He took."—*Calvin.*
[2] That is, " a fertile or rich field."—*Calvin.*
[3] " The eagle."—*Calvin.*
[4] Or, " twigs."—*Calvin.*

through reliance on the new treaty, on which we touched yesterday. It now follows—

7. There was also another great eagle with great wings and many feathers; and, behold, this vine did bend her roots toward him, and shot forth her branches toward him, that he might water it by the furrows of her plantation.	7. Et fuit aquila una[1] magna, magnis alis, et copiosa plumis: et ecce vitis ista collegit radices suas ad eam,[2] et palmites suos emisit ad eam, ut irrigaret ipsam alveis[3] plantationis suæ.[4]

He now detects, under a figure, the perfidy of Zedekiah, since he very soon applied himself to the king of Egypt, and bent his roots and branches towards him, that they might be irrigated. I do not disagree with the opinion of those who think that the Prophet alludes to an Egyptian custom; for we know that they dug furrows through which water flowed through the whole region: hence the fruitfulness of the soil; and thus Egypt is elsewhere compared to a garden. (Deut. xi. 10.) Whatever the meaning is, the Prophet shows that Zedekiah was deceived by a foolish confidence when he thought himself safe under the protection of the king of Egypt; for he had said that the seed was so planted that the vine did not rise to a great height, but spread itself under the wings of the eagle. But Zedekiah despised the king of Babylon, thinking that he should improve his condition by entering into a treaty with the king of Egypt. It now follows—

8. It was planted in a good soil by great waters, that it might bring forth branches, and that it might bear fruit, that it might be a goodly vine.	8. Super agrum bonum[5] juxta aquas multas[6] ipsa plantata erat, ut produceret folia, et proferret fructum ut esset in vitem magnificam.[7]

He exaggerates the ingratitude of Zedekiah, because, as we have said, he had been treated humanely by the king of Babylon; for he had been but a private man till that time: he was elevated to a throne and to a sway over the people beyond his expectation, and he had an avenger if any one

---

[1] That is, "another eagle."—*Calvin.*

[2] That is, "applied."—*Calvin.*

[3] Or, "beds, or rows or furrows," ערגות, *gnergoth*, signifies properly "furrows."—*Calvin.*

[4] Or, "in its plantation," to make the sense clearer.—*Calvin.*

[5] That is, "in a good soil."—*Calvin.*   [6] Or, "copious."—*Calvin.*

[7] Or it is usually rendered, "others have a beautiful vine:" אדר, *ader*, signifies properly to strengthen: hence it may be translated a strong vine; but here it means beautiful, elegant, or superb.—*Calvin.*

despised him. For when he was tributary to the king of Babylon, he would doubtless have been assisted by him in adversity : hence his revolt was less excusable, since he had been treated liberally beyond all anticipation. For this reason it is said, *the vine was planted in a good soil, and near many waters, that it might put forth branches and bear fruit, so that it might be a goodly vine.* It follows—

9. Say thou, Thus saith the Lord God, Shall it prosper? shall he not pull up the roots thereof, and cut off the fruit thereof, that it wither? it shall wither in all the leaves of her spring, even without great power, or many people to pluck it up by the roots thereof.	9. Dic, Sic dicit Dominator Iehovah, An feliciter aget?[1] an non radices ejus evellet? et fructum ejus succidet? et siccabit omnes surculos germinis ipsius, ut arefiat[2] et non in brachio magno et populo multo ad tollendum[3] è radicibus suis.
10. Yea, behold, *being* planted, shall it prosper? shall it not utterly wither when the east wind toucheth it? it shall wither in the furrows where it grew.	10. Et ecce plantata : an prosperabitur?[4] an non cum attigerit[5] ipsam ventus orientalis arescendo arescet super areas[6] plantationis suæ arescet?

Here God announces that this vine could not flourish any longer and bring forth fruit ; for it had been planted to flourish under the shadow of an eagle, and it had removed itself away. Nothing therefore remains, than that the former eagle should avenge the injury committed against it. This is the meaning of the passage : hence he says, *Shall it prosper ? Shall not* the eagle *tear up its roots, and cut off its fruit ?* Ezekiel assumes this principle, *that the vine could not* be otherwise preserved than by the power and aid of the eagle which had planted it ; for when it passed away from that eagle to another, the Prophet says that the end of the ungrateful vine was at hand ; *all the leaves of its branching shall wither, and so be dried up, and that not in a mighty branch, nor in much people.* It is certain that Nebuchadnezzar was accompanied with a great army when

---

[1] Or, as they commonly say, " shall it prosper ?"—*Calvin.*

[2] Or, " grow dry."—*Calvin.*

[3] It is a noun put in the place of an infinitive, " for taking it away," or " for its being taken away."—*Calvin.*

[4] That is, " shall it do prosperously or happily ?" or, " shall it have good success ?" for *prosperari* is not a sufficiently classical word, unless derived from *prosperare*, used by Horace, and so is passive.—*Calvin.*

[5] Or, " shall have struck or touched," for it signifies either.—*Calvin.*

[6] Or, " furrows."—*Calvin.*

he came down upon Judæa. But the Prophet means, even if Nebuchadnezzar had only brought with him a small band, yet Zedekiah could not remain king, since destruction awaited him through perfidy and revolt, as will afterwards be said. The Prophet then speaks by concession, as if he had said that, by a single blast, Zedekiah and all the people would wither away, since he could not remain in safety unless he drew sap from his own root; but he had removed his root elsewhere, and so Ezekiel pronounces that he must immediately wither away. *It was not then in the power of much people to tear it from its own roots;* for Zedekiah had purposely cut off his own roots, when, through his own levity, he had transferred himself to the king of Egypt. *Behold,* says he, *he had been planted; but should he have good success?* as if he had said, it is vain for Zedekiah to hope for safety from him, whom his own perfidy prevented from befriending him; and therefore the comparison of an east wind is added: *since then the east wind has struck it, will it not wither and decay, even upon the furrows of its branching?* that is, although it has furrows whence it may expect perpetual moisture; for Egypt was, as we have said, artificially watered; and the Prophet describes Zedekiah's state just as if the king of Egypt were nourishing him by a stream of water: *upon his beds,* or furrows, *will he wither when the east wind shall strike it.* We know that the east wind destroys the fruits in that region, and so it is often mentioned in a bad sense. It now follows—

11. Moreover, the word of the Lord came unto me, saying,	11. Et fuit sermo Iehovæ ad me, dicendo,
12. Say now to the rebellious house, Know ye not what these *things mean?* tell *them,* Behold the king of Babylon is come to Jerusalem, and hath taken the king thereof, and the princes thereof, and led them with him to Babylon;	12. Dic quæso,[1] domui rebelli[2] an non cognoscitis quid hoc sit? dic, Ecce venit rex Babylonis Hierosolymam, et abstulit regem ejus, et proceres ejus, et adduxit eos ad se Babylonem.
13. And hath taken of the king's seed, and made a covenant with him, and hath taken an oath of him: he hath also taken the mighty of the land:	13. Et sumpsit e semine regio, et percussit cum eo fœdus, et descendere fecit[3] ad jusjurandum: et fortes terræ accepit,
14. That the kingdom might be base,	14. Ut esset regnum humile,

[1] " Say now."—*Calvin.*   [2] Or, " bitter."—*Calvin.*
[3] " Lead him to take."—*Calvin.*

that it might not lift itself up, *but* that by keeping of his covenant it might stand.

15. But he rebelled against him, in sending his ambassadors into Egypt, that they might give him horses and much people: shall he prosper? shall he escape that doeth such *things?* or shall he break the covenant, and be delivered?

16. *As* I live, saith the Lord God, surely in the place *where* the king *dwelleth* that made him king, whose oath he despised, and whose covenant he brake, *even* with him in the midst of Babylon he shall die.

15. Et rebellis fuit ei ad mittendum nuntios suos in Egyptum, ut darentur equites, et populus multus. An feliciter aget? an evadet qui hoc fecit? et qui irritum fecit fœdus an evadet?[1]

ac ne se afferret, ut servaret fœdus suum; ut staret in ipso.

16. Vivo ego, dicit Dominator Iehovah, si non in loco regis qui regnare fecit eum, cujus sprevit jusjurandum, et cujus irritum fecit fœdus cum ipso in medio Babylonis moriatur.

An explanation of the allegory is now added. The figure being dropped, God shows what he had hitherto set forth enigmatically. We said the object of the allegory was to induce the Jews to apply their minds more diligently to the Prophet's instruction; for if he had used common and ordinary language, we know how carelessly they were accustomed to despise all rebukes and threatenings; but a riddle, while it held them in suspense, at the same time roused them, and so they were prepared for receiving the instruction which now follows. God says, therefore, *that the king of Babylon came to Jerusalem.* This reason has induced some to think that Lebanon is metaphorically called Jerusalem, but falsely, as we have already said. As long as the Prophet spoke figuratively, the parts ought to be mutually fitted to each other, as a tree and its branches have some connection with an eagle. *The king of Babylon came to Jerusalem, and took the king away, and the elders, and led them off to Babylon.* Although the Jews ought to be sufficiently moved by simple narrative, yet God here reproves them, because he saw how sluggish they were. First, he calls them a *rebellious house;* then he asks, *Whether they know the meaning of all this?* This is a kind of reproach by which God reminds them of their stupidity; since that riddle was not so obscure as to prevent them from understanding what had happened, unless they had been destitute of reason and judgment. But the

[1] "The copula is here redundant, or is taken for a note of interrogation."—*Calvin.*

Prophet thrusts at them more pointedly, by calling them a *rebellious house*, although at the same time he obliquely reproves their stupidity in not immediately perceiving the meaning of the riddle. He now adds, *that the king of Babylon had taken from the royal seed.* We said that Zedekiah was the uncle of Jehoiakim: he was placed on the throne beyond all expectation; because, if Jehoiakim had begat sons when he was still secure, they would have been his successors: hence it was an extraordinary advantage to Zedekiah in being placed on the throne. But he says, *that he was so created king, that the king of Babylon made a covenant with him, and induced him to take an oath.* Here God shows that, humanly speaking, Zedekiah's revolt could not prosper; for even profane men are always persuaded that the perfidy of him who breaks his word will not go unpunished, especially in treaties, which are held sacred by common consent. Since, therefore, the sacredness of treaties was so great, that they could not be violated without weakening the bonds of society, hence the general persuasion that the falsehood of all truce-breakers will turn out unhappily. Now, therefore, God leaves his own cause, and takes up that of King Nebuchadnezzar: Behold, says he, thou wast made king by gratuitous liberality: a conqueror indeed imposed conditions upon thee, but still thy state was desirable—thou couldst rule thine own people splendidly and with moderate dignity: now, because thy covenant has been despised, and thine oath broken, thou hast been ungrateful to the king of Babylon, who had bound thee to himself by his munificence: how can this perfidy prosper? Now, therefore, we see the Prophet's meaning, when he says that *the king of Babylon made a treaty with King Zedekiah,* and *took an oath of him:* this is added for the sake of amplifying; for although men never enter into treaties without a mutual oath, yet Ezekiel seems to have doubled the crime of Zedekiah, when he expresses *that an oath intervened.* He says *that he took the strong of the land,* namely, as hostages. There is no doubt that Nebuchadnezzar assembled this troop around him that the Jews might be more quiet; for he knew the turbulent character of the nation, and that the maintenance of so many was expensive: but, as I have said, it was his plan to hold the whole country at peace in this way. But Zedekiah rendered his own brothers and relations liable to death, since Nebuchadnezzar might be induced, by just anger, to slay them all. Hence Zedekiah's revolt was the betrayal of his brothers: for this reason the Prophet adds, *that the strong ones of the people were led away to Babylon;* that is, those of the first rank, who were held in honour by the people.

He now adds, *that the kingdom might be humbled.* Zedekiah then could not pretend error, nor turn his back, as if he had been outwitted by the cunning and secret counsels of the king of Babylon: for Nebuchadnezzar dealt with him openly, and proscribed the conditions on which he wished him to reign. Since, then, the king of Babylon showed Zedekiah openly and sincerely what he wished him to do, that wretched man could not say that he was imposed upon, and not made sufficiently aware of the cunning of the king of Babylon: no such excuse was left to him. And therefore the Prophet clearly expresses that Nebuchadnezzar imposed conditions upon Zedekiah, that *his kingdom should be lowly, so as not to lift itself up,* but that it should keep the agreement. This was most equitable: for when he appointed a king, he might have imposed upon him very hard conditions, but he was content with moderation, which was surely tolerable even among the best friends. For he made a treaty with him, and then he wished the kingdom to be lowly for its preservation. For it is just as if the Prophet had said, that Nebuchadnezzar thought of nothing else than that Zedekiah might reign in peace; and since he saw it to be useful to the king and the whole people to be restrained within some bounds, he followed that plan. Since, then, Nebuchadnezzar consulted the public advantage by this method of action, Zedekiah was the more wicked in not allowing his own safety to be consulted, since nothing was better or more desirable than for him to remain humble, and not to raise himself up to his own destruction, as afterwards happened. It now follows, *that he rebelled by sending his messengers into Egypt, that they might give him horses and much people.* These points ought to be mutually compared;

that the contrast might correspond: Nebuchadnezzar regarded nothing else but the peace of the country, for he wished to prevent all fears and disturbances. What, then, was Zedekiah? *a rebel.* And why? *for sending messengers to Egypt to fetch many troops of both horse and foot* to succour Judæa against Nebuchadnezzar. After the conclusion of the war he had done nothing hostile, for it was a part of his paternal anxiety to give them a king of their own nation, and so to set the whole country at rest, that there should be no occasion for tumult. Why, then, should Zedekiah seek help from the Egyptians? Thus we see that the Prophet is removing from him all excuses for self-defence. He now adds, *shall he prosper? shall he who has acted thus escape?* The Prophet asks with emphasis; because, as I have said, this persuasion was engraven on the minds of all, that vengeance must overtake all the perfidious, especially if they had violated their oath in treaties. The Prophet, therefore, does not simply pronounce that Zedekiah should perish through violating the treaty, but he rises more confidently, and inquires, as of a thing settled and undoubted, *Shall he prosper? shall he who has planned such a crime escape?* He now adds, *shall he who has violated a treaty escape?* This repetition is not superfluous: he had formerly said, *shall he who has done this escape?* he immediately repeats, *shall he who has violated a treaty escape?* There was nothing obscure in the first clause: but the Prophet added this, not for the sake of perspicuity, but to give more weight to the sentence. The conclusion is, that it was not possible to escape God's vengeance for such perfidy, as we shall treat the point more at length to-morrow.

It now follows, *As I live, says the Lord Jehovah, in the dwelling of the king who placed him on a throne, shall he die.* Although the Prophet had sufficiently shown that Zedekiah could not escape the penalty of his revolt, yet God here again comes forward, and swears by himself, or by his life, that he would punish Zedekiah. Hence the great stupidity of the people appears, for God never acts falsely by his own name, or brings it forward in vain, but when necessity demands it, he swears by himself. And by his own example he prescribes to us, that we should not rush rashly upon an oath, but be sober in this respect. But God swears *that Zedekiah should die on the spot,* that is, *at the capital of the king who put him on the throne ;* that is Babylon, where he died : and yet he did not see Babylon, because his eyes were put out at Riblath, as we saw elsewhere. (Jer. xxxix. 7 ; lii. 11.) But the Prophet simply denounces the penalty, that he should die in exile, *and in the dwelling of the king who had placed him on his throne, and from whose covenant he had departed, and whose oath he had despised.*

PRAYER.

Grant, Almighty God, since thou showest thy regard for mutual fidelity between man and man, that we may so conduct ourselves in every way that we may not deceive our brethren, but assist each other with sincere affection : Grant, also, that with true consent we may afford thee that confidence which thou requirest, and which we are bound to pay thee ; since thou deignest not only to enter into covenant with us by means of thine only-begotten Son, but also to seal it with his blood, until we enjoy that inheritance which thou hast obtained for us by the sacrifice of his death.—Amen.

Lecture Fifty-Second.

17. Neither shall Pharaoh, with *his* mighty army and great company, make for him in the war, by casting up mounts, and building forts, to cut off many persons.

17. Et non in exercitu magno, et in multitudine multa faciet cum eo Pharao in prælio, fundendo aggerem, et extruendo turrem[1] ad excidendum animas multas.

As Ezekiel has before pronounced that there was no need of great forces when God wished to punish Zedekiah by means of the king of Babylon ; so he now teaches, on the other hand, how great and powerful an army Pharaoh would collect, and yet it would profit nothing, since Nebuchadnezzar would be victorious. Some interpreters explain the passage otherwise, namely, that Pharaoh would not perform his promise ; for kings are accustomed to boast of their supplies when they enter into treaties : they promise 50,000, but only supply 10,000. They think, therefore, that these vain pro-

[1] Or, " *turrim.*"—*Calvin.*

mises by which Zedekiah was deceived are here reproved, since Pharaoh boasted that he would come with very great forces, so as easily to repel the Babylonian army. But the sense which I propose is far more suitable, namely, that whatever Pharaoh should attempt, it would fail to assist him. Although he should come well attended, and oppose the Chaldæans by immense forces, *yet he should effect nothing in battle with him :* although this may be true equally of Zedekiah as of the king of Babylon. For Pharaoh did nothing with King Nebuchadnezzar, since he was quickly compelled to retreat into his own territories, and could scarcely defend his own kingdom, for he did not succeed against Nebuchadnezzar : and he did Zedekiah no good, since he did not assist him in his misfortunes, as he had promised. But as far as concerns the general sense, we see that the Prophet means that Zedekiah would be deceived although Pharaoh should faithfully perform his promises, since he was undertaking an expedition against the will of God, which must turn out disastrous. He adds, *when he shall throw up a mound and build a tower,* (towers are meant, for there is a change of number,) as is customary in besieging cities. This ought to be referred to Nebuchadnezzar, for he began to cast up mounds and build towers against Jerusalem when Pharaoh led away his army. Since Nebuchadnezzar could not contend with both the Egyptians and Jews together, he raised the siege and set out to meet Pharaoh, who, when conquered, retreated with trembling within his own boundaries. Nebuchadnezzar afterwards returned, and after preparing all things, he did not desist till he had stormed the city. Now Ezekiel means this, that Pharaoh would come to his help in vain, when Nebuchadnezzar began to cast up his mounds and build towers against the city. It follows—

18. Seeing he despised the oath by breaking the covenant, when, lo, he had given his hand, and hath done all these *things,* he shall not escape.

18. Sprevit jusjurandum ad abolendum fœdus, et ecce porrexit manum suam : et totum hoc fecit, non evadet.[1]

Ezekiel repeats again, that, even humanly speaking, Zedekiah could not succeed, since he violated the treaty : for we

[1] Or, " be liberated."—*Calvin.*

yesterday said that this persuasion is always fixed in men's minds, that treaties are sacred, and cannot be broken with impunity. Since, therefore, the sacredness of treaties was always prevalent among men, Ezekiel here pronounces that the issue would be disastrous, because Zedekiah *despised his oath when he broke the treaty after stretching out his hand.* He describes a gesture, as I think, customary among men— that of stretching forth the hand when they wish to witness a covenant. The alliance, then, between the Egyptians and the Jews is here described by an outward gesture, because Zedekiah stretched forth his hand, and yet had violated it in this way: but since he perfidiously revolted from King Nebuchadnezzar, to whom he had pledged his faith, *he has done all this,* says he, *therefore he shall not be liberated.* It follows—

19. Therefore thus saith the Lord God, *As* I live, surely mine oath that he hath despised, and my covenant that he hath broken, even it will I recompense upon his own head.	19. Propterea sic dicit Dominator Iehovah, Vivo ego, si non jusjurandum meum quod sprevit, et fœdus meum quod irritum fecit, rependam[1] in ejus caput.

The former sentence is confirmed. The Prophet had spoken after the usually received manner when he said that Zedekiah's perfidy would not be unrevenged; but he now brings forward God as the speaker, because, unless he appeared as an avenger of perfidy, mankind would scarcely ever be seriously persuaded that punishment was prepared for perjurers and truce-breakers. As I have said that this opinion was fixed in the hearts of all, so it must be understood that this opinion was received, and that men were fully persuaded of it: but persuasions which are called "common"[2] vanish away; there are common thoughts which are almost born with us, and follow nature, but they are not firm, because the profane do not hold the principal point, that God is the judge of the world: this sentence, therefore, is added of necessity. Now God swears that Zedekiah should suffer punishment, because *he had despised the oath and rendered the covenant void.* But we must notice the epithet; for God calls the oath and the covenant *his own: he has despised,* says he, not simply the oath, but *mine:* he

[1] Or, "I will throw it back."—*Calvin.*   [2] κοινας εννοιας.—*Calvin.*

has violated *my* treaty. The reason of this language is, that God wishes fidelity between man and man to be cultivated: and so he detests all perjury and all frauds. Now, since there is no more sacred method of contracting a treaty than by solemn rites, there also God shows his judgment in a peculiar manner. In fine, we may deservedly call him the guardian of treaties; for when heathens entered into treaties, they were accustomed to bring forward the name of Jupiter the supreme, because they thought he would inflict vengeance on all who violated their pledge. But God here comes forward, not like an imaginary Jupiter, but because he wished confidence to flourish in human society; since, unless men act sincerely to each other, all society would be broken up. This, then, is the reason why Ezekiel says that the treaty struck with King Nebuchadnezzar was divine, since God would be its vindicator. Meanwhile we must remark that this treaty was lawful and pleasing to God. (Jer. xxvii. 17.) And we see from chapters xxviii. and xxix., that God wished the Jews to suffer under this disgrace for a time. For King Zedekiah, if he had truly discharged his office, was an image of the Messiah, the first-born among the kings of the earth: hence it was unworthy of him to become tributary to a profane monarch and a cruel tyrant. But since God had so imposed slavery on his own people, Zedekiah ought to be under the yoke, as it is there said, Be ye servants to King Nebuchadnezzar and live; that is, there is no other method of obtaining safety, unless ye suffer the Chaldæans to rule over you, and ye bear their sway calmly, since Nebuchadnezzar is God's scourge. This covenant, as I have said, was approved by God, otherwise he could not have been its avenger. We know that there are three kinds of treaties. When there has been war between two kings, if the conqueror wishes to spare his enemy, he receives him into covenant, but imposes conditions at his own discretion. We know that the Romans followed that custom, since it was too difficult for them to hold in subjection all whom they had subdued, and especially at the beginning; and thus they entered into treaties with many tribes under many circumstances. Another sort of agreement is, that between either kings or people when at variance with each other; but before they actually engage they make a truce with each other, and so remove the occasion of the war—this is another kind. Lastly, those who never were enemies enter into an alliance; and such was the treaty between Zedekiah and the king of Egypt. For they wished to be cautious, and to anticipate the danger which he feared from the Chaldæans; and hence he entered into the agreement. Thus the Israelites were formerly joined with the Syrians, and afterwards with the Assyrians. So we saw that the Jews committed adultery when they ran about first to Egypt, then to Assyria, and then to Chaldæa. But this treaty, of which mention is now made, was necessary; for Zedekiah could not escape from embracing the conditions imposed on him by King Nebuchadnezzar. For this reason God pronounces himself the avenger of perfidy.

It is now asked, Whether we may never break our word when any one has been violently attacked, and promised what was otherwise unjust? The reply is at hand, that God's name is more precious than all human advantages. If any one, therefore, object that he was deceived, and oppressed by unjust conditions, still God's name must prevail. Hence we must always weigh what is due to the name of God; and hence we shall readily conclude that those can never be excused who violate their engagements on the pretext of being violently compelled, or induced by fraud, or not allowed the liberty of considering whether their promise was according to equity. For this reason, also, it is said in the 15th Psalm, (ver. 4,) that the sons of God swear and suffer loss, because when God's name has been interposed, no utility ought to be of such importance as to outweigh the oath that has been taken. And so not without reason God now pronounces that he would avenge the perjury which Zedekiah had committed, since, in truth, we cannot depart from promises which have been sanctioned by an oath in God's name, without seeming to slight the Almighty himself. Meanwhile, it is certain that there was another reason why God punished the Jews; but here, as I have previously shown, the Prophet mentions what was more familiar to men. The first cause of the destruction of the city and of the whole kingdom, was idolatry, as we saw before, and then the many crimes of the people were added. For from the period of the corruption of true religion, the pollution of many vices increased through the city and the whole land. Hence it happened that God destined his people to destruction; hence also King Zedekiah was deprived of sight. For, as the sacred history testifies, God wished to destroy the whole people: for this reason Zedekiah fell, and provoked the Chaldæans against him. We see, therefore, that there is a continued series of causes in the eternal providence of God, but not as the Stoics supposed; for they concocted their fate from complex windings or implicit causes, without any will of Deity in that confusion. But God, as I have said, has different reasons why he does one thing or another. Some causes are remote and incomprehensible to us, and others manifest to us: so the proximate cause of the destruction of the people was the revolt of Zedekiah from King Nebuchadnezzar; but there was another more important reason, namely, that the people deserved to perish. Hence Zedekiah was rendered blind by the just judgment of God, since he passed over perfidiously to the king of Egypt, and so armed himself against King Nebuchadnezzar. But we must hold that the reason universally manifest is here reviewed. It follows—

20. And I will spread my net upon him, and he shall be taken in my snare; and I will bring him to Babylon, and will plead with him there for his trespass that he hath trespassed against me.

20. Et extendam[1] super ipsum rete meum, et capietur in plagis meis,[2] et venire faciam ipsum Babylonem, et judicabo[3] cum eo illic de transgressione[4] qua prævaricatus est contra me.

Here he points out the kind of punishment which he was about to inflict on King Zedekiah. He had said generally that his perfidy should fall upon his own head, but he now proceeds further, namely, that Zedekiah should be a captive. For God might chastise him by other means, but the prophecy was thereby confirmed, since the Prophet had clearly

---
[1] Or, "I will spread."—*Calvin.*
[2] Some translate "drag-net," but erroneously, for the word is derived from hunting.—*Calvin.*
[3] Or, "plead in a trial."—*Calvin.*   [4] Or, "prevarication."—*Calvin.*

threatened Zedekiah as we see. But he speaks in the person of God that his language may have more weight. *I will spread my net,* says God, *and he shall be taken in my snares.* The passage is metaphorical, but it best explains what often occurs in Scripture, namely, that while the impious take first one course and then another, they are agents of God who governs them by his own secret virtue, and directs them wherever he wishes. As, therefore, men take up all things confusedly, and are, as we see, driven about hither and thither by their lusts, and disturb heaven and earth; yet God moderates their attacks by his secret providence. We gather this from the Prophet's words when he calls the army of the king of Babylon, and his plans, and the apparatus of war, *God's net and snares.* Although Nebuchadnezzar was impelled by his own ambition and avarice, and did not suppose himself under the divine sway, yet we see what the Spirit pronounces. And we must diligently observe this doctrine, because, if we repose on the paternal solicitude of God, although armies surround us on all sides, yet we may confide securely, and await the end with quiet and tranquil minds, since men can do nothing without God. But when we provoke God's wrath against us, we must bear in mind, that while men have their reasons for being hostile to us, yet God governs them, or that they are *his nets or snares,* as the Prophet here says.

I will bring him, says he, *to Babylon, and there will I dispute with him in judgment, according to the prevarication by which he has prevaricated.* Not only did God dispute with Zedekiah there, but he inflicted a heavy and formidable judgment upon him in Riblah, when he saw his own sons put to death first, and then his own eyes were put out, and then he was bound by chains. But he almost pined away in his captivity, and was treated shamefully even unto death; for this reason God says that he would judge him at Babylon: and yet there will be nothing out of place if we comprehend Riblah also. For although Zedekiah had been partially punished before he entered Babylon, yet God there inflicted his own sentence, after he was dragged from his country and led into exile. He was buried indeed not without honour, as we saw in Jeremiah, (chap. xxxiv. 5,) for they bewailed him at his burial—Alas, my brother! alas, O master! as the Prophet says: yet till his death he was like the vilest prisoner, for he pined away in his chains, and was meanly clothed, when the king treated Coniah nobly and splendidly: hence Zedekiah's captivity was the seal of this prophecy: for Ezekiel could not have pronounced this sentence, unless he had been the organ of the Holy Spirit. It follows—

21. And all his fugitives with all his bands shall fall by the sword, and they that remain shall be scattered toward all winds; and ye shall know that I the Lord have spoken *it*.

21. Et omnes profugi ejus in omnibus copiis ejus in gladio cadent: et qui residui erunt ad omnem ventum dispergentur: et cognoscetis quod ego Iehovah loquutus sim.

The Prophet now descends to the whole people, especially to the soldiers, whom Zedekiah himself thought would be fit guardians of the city. He says, then, *thus shall all his forces be dissipated, so that they shall be dispersed hither and thither and fall by the sword.* By these words he means the slaughter of the army, since as long as soldiers stand in their own ranks they sustain and repel a hostile attack; but when they are dispersed, every one is subject to the enemy, and hence a promiscuous slaughter arises. He says, therefore, that Zedekiah's soldiers *would be fugitives amidst all their bands:* that is, although he had a large army, yet all his forces should be dispersed, and while each should consult his own advantage, he should fall into the enemy's hands: thus, *all shall fall by the sword;* then *those who remain shall be dispersed towards every wind.* We saw the same thing before, for when the Prophet had declared that all the people should suffer by the sword, he added, at the same time, that all the survivors should be fugitives, just as if any one should throw out refuse or hair which the wind would blow hither and thither. Hence he repeats the same now, namely, that the whole people would be like a torn body, since if they escaped the sword, yet they would find no place of rest. Hence while a few would flee to Egypt, some to the Moabites, and others to the neighbouring nations, the whole body of the people would be dissipated. He adds, *and ye shall know that I Jehovah have spoken.* We have explained the meaning of this, and why the Prophet repeats it so often, namely, because the Jews were untractable and derided all God's threats: the Prophet teaches that they should really feel that he had spoken, and this is the wisdom of fools, as the common proverb expresses it. For because they do not obey any counsels, nor admit any admonitions, and receive no teaching, they are instructed only by the event itself. It follows—

22. Thus saith the Lord God, I will also take of the highest branch of the high cedar, and will set *it* ; I will crop off from the top of his young twigs a tender one, and will plant *it* upon an high mountain and eminent.	22. Sic dicit Dominator Iehovah, Et assumam[1] e summitate cedri excelsæ,[2] et ponam è capite propaginum ejus, tenerum evellam, et plantabo ego super montem excelsum et elevatum.

Here the Prophet begins to treat of the restoration of the nation and kingdom. Thus this prophecy without doubt refers to Christ, because though in some sense God had pity on the people when they enjoyed the liberty of returning under Cyrus and Darius, yet what is here written was never fully exhibited except under Christ. It is indeed true, as I have elsewhere expressed, that when the prophets promise restoration to the Church, that they do not restrict their discourse to the person of Christ, but begin with the return of the people: for that was the beginning of the full and solid liberty which was at length made manifest in Christ. And Christian writers have erred in urging so precisely that anything said about the restitution of the Church must be understood of the person of Christ, and thus they make themselves ridiculous to the Jews. But, as it has been said already, as often as the Prophets hold out the hope of liberty to the elect and the faithful, they embrace the whole of the time from the return of the people, or from the end of their exile to the end of the kingdom of Christ. When, therefore, the reign of Christ is treated, we must date its commencement from the period of the building of the temple after the people's return from their seventy years' captivity: and then we must take its boundary, not at the ascension of Christ, nor yet in the first or second centuries, but through the whole progress of his kingdom, until he shall appear at

[1] " The copula is redundant."—*Calvin.*   [2] Or, " of a tall."—*Calvin.*

the last day. Now let us come to the Prophet's words, *thus saith the Lord Jehovah, I will take from the top of the lofty* (or tall) *cedar.* God pursues the allegory which we saw: for as he said that the top was torn off, or that the highest branch was plucked from the cedar of Lebanon, so he now says, *that he would take from the top of the cedar, and after he had plucked* or wrenched off a bough, *and planted it,* such would be the increase, that all the trees would acknowledge that to be a wonderful work. Now this restoration is described to us variously, because after God had spoken of a lofty bough, he descends to a low and abject one; he then pronounces that such should be the beginning of the new kingdom, that he would make the dry tree to bud and humble the lofty one. These things at first sight seem to be opposite to each other, but they agree very well, because God took from the top of a lofty cedar when he planted a new king. For Christ, as respects God's eternal decree, was always more excellent than heaven and earth; at the same time God afterwards says that he was humble, as he certainly was. But let us follow up the words, *I will take,* says he, *from the top of a lofty cedar, and I will set it: from the top of its twigs I will pluck a tender one, and I will plant it upon a lofty and elevated mountain.* Here, as I have said, he speaks of a tall and lofty cedar, and then he speaks of a high branch, but he adds afterwards, *I will pluck a tender one from it,* by which he means that the twig which he should pluck and plant would be without strength. Here, therefore, is shown the contemptible beginning of the reign of Christ, as the Prophet afterwards more clearly explains himself.

23. In the mountain of the height of Israel will I plant it; and it shall bring forth boughs, and bear fruit, and be a goodly cedar: and under it shall dwell all fowl of every wing; in the shadow of the branches thereof shall they dwell.

23. In monte excelso Israel plantabo illud, et tollet ramum, et faciet fructum, et erit in cedrum elegantem:[1] et habitabit sub eo[2] omnis avis[3] omne pennatum[4] in umbra surculorum[5] ejus habitabit.

[1] Or, "magnificent;" it is the same word of which we spoke yesterday.—*Calvin.* [2] "Under that branch or cedar."—*Calvin.*
[3] That is, "birds of all kinds."—*Calvin.*
[4] Or, "flying thing."—*Calvin.* [5] Or, "boughs."—*Calvin.*

When God announces *that the twig which he will plant shall become a lofty cedar,* he shows by these words that the increase of Christ's kingdom shall be so wonderful, that it shall surpass the common rule of nature ; which indeed was shadowed forth in the person of Zerubbabel, who was chosen to bring back the people from their sad and disgraceful captivity. (Ezra ii. 2 ; Haggai i. 14.) For it does not naturally happen that a twig increases in a short time to a lofty cedar, for we know how slowly cedars grow, and hence we see the Spirit's intention in saying that a tree should spring from a very small twig. And this prophecy answers to one of Isaiah's, where he says, (chap. xi. 1,) A branch shall spring from the root of Jesse: for the house of Jesse was cut off, and he names the house of an obscure and private man as if the remembrance of David were utterly lost. The house of Jesse then was cut off like a tree : that twig, says he, shall spring from its root. Now the Prophet signifies the same thing, and almost under the same similitude. I leave the rest for the next lecture.

PRAYER.

Grant, Almighty God, since thou hast deigned to enter into a perpetual and inviolable covenant with us which thou hast sanctioned by the blood of thine only-begotten Son, that we may faithfully stand to it ; and may we be so obedient to thee unto the end, that we may experience thee a propitious Father to us, until we enjoy that eternal inheritance which thou hast prepared for us in heaven, through the same Christ our Lord.— Amen.

Lecture Fifty-Third.

IN the last lecture we began to explain that passage of the Prophet in which God promises that he would take from the boughs of the lofty cedar a tender branch, which should soon grow into a tall tree. We said that the restoration of the people was the foretaste of this grace, since God already showed that he cared for his people whom he seemed utterly to reject when he suffered them to be dragged into exile. We said also, that although Zerubbabel was a captive and an exile, yet that he was the twig plucked from the tall tree, as he was of the royal stock whence Christ would at length spring forth. But at the same time we added that this prophecy was not complete until the kingdom of Christ of which it was the beginning, when he was manifest in the flesh, and thence it made daily progress until the end of the world. Thus then we see that the twig was plucked from the cedar, *and from a tall or lofty one, and it was planted upon a mountain.* The mountain on which the branch was to be planted was called sublime and lofty, and there is no doubt that God meant Mount Zion: it is indeed a small hill, but Isaiah shows us the reason why it was called lofty, because it excelled in dignity and eminence all the heights of the world. (Chap. ii. 2, 3.) It is there said, I will make Mount Zion conspicuous above all lofty mountains: that eminence indeed was not perceptible by the eye, but the Prophet at the same time declares what he means, since a law should go forth from Zion and God's word from Jerusalem. We see, therefore, that Mount Zion, although low among hills, was eminent and conspicuous among the highest mountains, since God's glory shone forth from it, and it was rendered conspicuous to even the ends of the earth. Hence the Prophet repeats a second time, *On a lofty mountain of Israel will I plant it,* namely, the twig, and *it shall raise* or bear *a bough, and produce fruit, and it shall be a magnificent* or elegant *cedar,* as we said, *and every bird,* that is, all birds, *shall dwell under it, every winged thing,* or flying thing, *shall dwell under the shadow of its branches* or boughs. The repetition shows that something rare is here denoted, and what would scarcely be comprehended in an ordinary sense, when God speaks of a high and elevated mountain. So that it confirms what we said, that this place ought to be understood of Mount Zion, which was supernaturally elevated when Christ's sceptre went forth from it, by which he reduced the whole world under his yoke. He now adds, *that it should be a magnificent cedar, so that the birds of the air should nestle in it and rest under its shadow.* This simile is used by Daniel when treating of the sway of Nebuchadnezzar, (chap. iv. 8, 9, 17-19,) it is common to all kingdoms to protect men under their shadow, as birds find their dwelling-place only in trees, and repair and collect themselves there. But meanwhile the Prophet shortly states that the kingdom of which he is treating would be for the common safety and advantage of the whole people. For as kings usually think the human race created for their sakes, they are taken up with their own private reasonings, and do not consult the interests of the wretched people whom they are divinely appointed to cherish under their wings. The Prophet therefore shows that the kingdom which God had determined to set up in his chosen people would be useful to all, when he says, *under its shadow there would be safety for all birds.* It now follows—

24. And all the trees of the field shall know that I the Lord have brought down the high tree, have exalted the low tree, have dried up the green tree, and have made the dry tree to flourish: I the Lord have spoken, and have done *it.*	24. Et cognoscent omnes arbores agri, quod ego Iehovah, qui humilio arborem excelsam, et extollo in sublime arborem humilem: arefacio arborem viridem, et fructuosam reddo arborem aridam: ego Iehovah loquutus sum, et feci.[1]

In this verse the Prophet signifies that God's work would be memorable. For when he says that all trees should feel themselves in God's hand and power, to raise what was fallen, and to cast down and to prostrate what was elevated, he doubtless expresses no common action. By trees he means all the kings of the earth, and all possessed of any dignity. For he follows up his own metaphor: as he called the kingdom of Christ a tree or cedar which grew from a small twig, so he now speaks metaphorically of kings when he says, *that all should take notice; for they shall know that I Jehovah bring down the high tree.* Ezekiel may here seem to be inconsistent with himself, as I have already noticed, because God said that he would take from a lofty cedar a little twig, which he wished to plant: but he now says that God would raise what was low and abject. But we have dissipated this absurdity, because, from the beginning Christ was in the glory of his Father, and thus, as Micah says, his beginning was from eternity. (Chap. v. 2.) This excellency of Christ, therefore, is noticed, because, from the time when

---

[1] Or, "I will do it."—*Calvin.*

God erected David's throne, he at the same time gave a visible sign of the more excellent kingdom which was then secretly hoped for. For this reason Christ was taken from his lofty place, and since he not only put on the form of a slave, but emptied himself even unto death, (Phil. ii. 7,) it is not surprising that the Prophet should say, *like a tree cast down*. Although, as I have remarked, this sentence is not to be restricted to the person of Christ, but ought to be adapted to his kingdom; that is, to his manner and way of governing: since we know, and it has been lately stated, that the gospel is like a sceptre, by which Christ subdues all people, and rules them for himself. Now if we reflect on what the preaching of the gospel was, we shall see, as in a glass, the Prophet's meaning here, that the low tree was elevated, since no one would have thought, that from such slender beginnings the increase which God afterwards bestowed on it could arise. It follows, then, that the height was wonderful, since it could not be comprehended by the human senses.

Meanwhile he adds, *I am he who humble the lofty tree*, which is not only understood of the Jews, but, in my judgment, embraces all the empires and principalities of the world. God, therefore, humbles lofty trees, because, whatever opposes itself to Christ's kingdom, must necessarily fall; and this is described more at length in Daniel. (Chap. iv.) For although all the empires of the world are founded in Christ, and sustained by his virtue, yet, since earthly kings rise up and desire to lay Christ prostrate, their pride is the reason why Christ's empire causes their ruin. This contrast, then, must be noticed, that God sets up low trees, or takes them away, and casts down lofty ones, since we are here taught to hope better of the reign of Christ than we can estimate by our senses; since, if we cast our eyes round us, many things meet us which diminish and weaken our hope. For what is the outward appearance of Christ's kingdom? In truth we shall feel nothing but despair if we judge of Christ's kingdom by the present state of affairs. But when we see how the gospel creeps along the ground, this passage should come to our minds, that God will raise up the tree that is abject and contemptible. At the same time, let us learn, that the changes which happen and are perceived in the world are to be imputed to the pride of those who are blinded by their own boasting; for kings, as we have said, forget that they are men, and so rebel against God: hence they must of necessity fall. If this is not fulfilled immediately, let us learn patiently to await the effect of this prophecy. Whatever happens, God has so established the kingdom of Christ alone, that it shall last as long as the sun and moon, but the other empires of the world shall vanish away with their own splendour, and their loftiness shall fall although at present they overtop the clouds. *I, says Jehovah, have spoken, and I will do it.* God here recalls the minds of the faithful to his power, because, from the time the people were dispersed—I speak of the final overthrow of the city and temple—there was no hope of restoration. Since, then, it was difficult to persuade men of what God now pronounces, he brings pointedly forward his own prowess, in order that men, by holding in check their carnal senses, should raise themselves above the world, and wait for the inestimable prowess of God which does not yet appear to them. It now follows—

CHAPTER XVIII.

1. The word of the Lord came unto me again, saying,

2. What mean ye, that ye use this proverb concerning the land of Israel, saying, The fathers have eaten sour grapes, and the children's teeth are set on edge?

3. *As* I live, saith the Lord God, ye shall not have *occasion* any more to use this proverb in Israel.

4. Behold, all souls are mine; as the soul of the father, so also the

1. Et fuit sermo Iehovæ ad me, dicendo,

2. Quid vobis? vos proverbiantes proverbium[1] super terram Israel, dicendo, Patres comederunt omphacem,[2] et dentes filiorum obstupescunt.

3. Vivo ego, dicit Dominator Iehovah, Si erit vobis amplius[3] qui utatur hoc dicterio[4] in Israele.

4. Ecce omnes animæ mihi,[5] sicut anima patris sic anima filii mihi.[6]

---

[1] That is, "that ye use this saying or apothegm."—*Calvin.*

[2] Sour grape—I know not why some translate it "the wild vine," for it does not suit.—*Calvin.*

[3] Or, "hereafter."—*Calvin.*   [4] Or, "utter this proverb."—*Calvin.*

[5] That is, "are my own."—*Calvin.*   [6] That is, "are my own."—*Calvin.*

| soul of the son is mine: the soul that sinneth, it shall die. | Anima quæ peccaverit ipsa morietur. |

We may collect from this rebuke that the Jews were perverse interpreters of the best teaching; yea, they purposely reviled the Prophet's expression, and drew it to a contrary meaning. For it is far commoner than it ought to be among unbelievers, always to take occasion of turning backwards, twisting, distorting, and tearing the teaching of heaven. And at this time we see this impudence increasing greatly in the world. For the world is full of buffoons and other deceivers, who wickedly sport with God, and seek material for joking from the law and the gospel: and so also it appears to have been in the Prophet's time; for although they listened to the wrath of God hanging over them, they did not cease to provoke him, and that too for many years. And not only were their own iniquities set forth against them, but also those of their fathers: hence the occasion for cavil when they heard—For so many ages ye do not cease your warfare against God: he has borne with you patiently unto this day. Do you think that you can carry on your audacity with impunity? God wished hitherto to tame you by his forbearance; but your obstinacy is not to be subdued. Since, therefore, not only for one or two generations, but for four and five, your obstinacy has wrestled with God's goodness, he cannot any longer pardon you. Since the prophets thus gathered up the iniquities of their fathers, impious men scattered abroad their witticisms—then we are to pay the penalty of our fathers' sins: they provoked God, but we suffer the punishment which they deserved. The Prophet now convinces them of this unfairness, and shows that they had no reason for transferring their faults to others, or to thrust them away from themselves, since God was just in taking vengeance on them. We know that men willingly shuffle so as to free themselves from blame, and then afterwards accuse God of cruel injustice. It is true, indeed, that they are held in such constraint by their own consciences that they are compelled, whether they will or not, to feel that they are suffering punishment justly; but afterwards they become refractory, and suffocate their conscience, and strive pettishly with God. Hence these words—

> Though guiltless of your fathers' crimes,
> Roman, 'tis thine to latest times
> The vengeance of the gods to bear,
> Till you their awful domes repair.
> *Horace,* lib. iii., *Od.* vi., *as translated by Francis.*

Since so many crimes were rife at Rome, why does that trifler say that the men of his own age were undeservedly paying the penalty due by their ancestors? But, as I have said, this is the testimony of a corrupt nature, because we desire to throw off the blame as far from ourselves as we possibly can. Hence we begin to strive with God, and to rebel against his judgments. And hence this instruction is the more useful to us, since it is proposed as a remedy for a disease by far too common. Whatever the meaning is, this sentiment came into common use like a proverb—*that the children's teeth were set on edge, because their fathers had eaten sour grapes.* By these allegorical words they wished to free themselves from blame, as if God was unjustly charging the wickedness of their fathers against them. For to eat the sour grape or wild grape has the same meaning as to set the teeth on edge; for we know this to be the effect of acidity. If any one eats a sour grape, his teeth will suffer from its unripeness. To eat then is to cause this effect on the teeth—referring to sin: for they said that their own teeth suffered, not through their own eating the sour grapes, but through its flowing down from their fathers. On the whole, they wished to contend with God, as if he were afflicting the innocent, and that, too, under the fallacious pretext which I have mentioned, as God announced that he would avenge the wickedness which had been perpetrated in former ages.

Ye, says he, *use this proverb; but as I live, says the Lord Jehovah, ye shall not use this proverb any more.* He does not mean, by these words, that the Jews should repent and become more modest, and not dare to vomit forth such blasphemy against him; for he is not treating of repentance here; but it is just as if he said, I will strike from under you this boasting, since your iniquity shall be made manifest, and the whole world shall acknowledge the justice of your punishment, and that you have deserved it yourselves, and cannot throw it upon your fathers, as you have hitherto endeavoured to do. The Jews indeed did not cease their rebellion against God, and there is no doubt that they were more and more exasperated, so as to expostulate with audacity against him; but because their wickedness was really apparent, and God was not hostile to them in vain, or for trifling reasons; and although he was severe, yet they had arrived at the highest pitch of impiety, so that no punishment could be sufficient or too oppressive. We now understand the meaning of the Prophet, or rather of the Holy Spirit, since God took away all pretence for shuffling from the Jews when he detected their impiety, and made it conspicuous that they were only suffering the due reward of their crimes. But God swears by himself, whence we gather how abominable was their blasphemy; and truly men cannot absolve themselves without condemning God; for God's glory then shines forth, when every mouth is stopped, as we saw before. (Ezek. xvi. 63; Rom. iii. 19.) As soon as men descend into that arena, through wishing to show their innocence, it is just as if they wished to reduce God's justice to nothing. Hence it is not surprising that God is very angry when he is despoiled of his justice; for he cannot exist without this attribute.

We now see why an oath is interposed, while he pronounces that he will take care that the Jews should not ridicule any longer. *Behold,* says he, *all souls are mine; as the soul of the son so the soul of the father, all souls are mine; the soul, therefore, which has sinned it shall die.* Some interpreters explain the beginning of the verse thus: that men vainly and rashly complain when God seems to treat them too severely, since the clay does not rise against the potter. Since God is the maker of the whole world, we are his workmanship: what madness, then, to rise up against him when he does not satisfy us: and we saw this simile used by Jeremiah. (Chap. xviii. 6.) The sentiment, then, is true in itself, that all souls are under God's sovereignty by the right of creation, and therefore he can arbitrarily determine for each whatever he wishes; and all who clamour against him reap no profit: and this teaching it is advantageous to notice. But this passage ought to be understood otherwise; namely, that nothing is more unworthy than that God should be accused of tyrannizing over men, when he rather defends them, as being his own workmanship. When, therefore, God pronounces *that all souls are his own,* he does not merely claim sovereignty and power, but he rather shows that he is affected with fatherly love towards the whole human race since he created and formed it; for, if a workman loves his work because he recognises in it the fruits of his industry, so, when God has manifested his power and goodness in the formation of men, he must certainly embrace them with affection. True, indeed, we are abominable in God's sight, through being corrupted by original sin, as it is elsewhere said, (Ps. xiv. 1, 2;) but inasmuch as we are men, we must be dear to God, and our salvation must be precious in his sight. We now see what kind of refutation this is: *all souls are mine,* says he: I have formed all, and am the creator of all, and so I am affected with fatherly love towards all, and they shall rather feel my clemency, from the least to the greatest, than experience too much rigour and severity. At length he adds, *the soul which sinned it shall die.* Now, Ezekiel expresses how God restrains the Jews from daring to boast any longer that they are afflicted undeservedly, since no innocent person shall die; for this is the meaning of the sentence; for he does not mean that every guilty person should die, for this would shut against us the door of God's mercy, for we have all sinned against him: so it would follow that there is no hope of safety, since every man must perish, unless God freed sinners from death. But the Prophet's sense is not doubtful, as we have said, since those who perish are not without fault; neither can they bring up their innocence to God, nor complain of his cruelty in punishing them for the sins of others. Although here a question may arise, since no one at this day perishes who does not partly bear the fault of another, namely, of Adam, by whose fall and revolt the whole human race actually perished. Since therefore Adam, by his fall, brought destruction upon us, it follows that we perish through the fault of another. Since this question will be treated again in its own place, it will now be sufficient to say, in three words, that although we perish through the fault of another, yet the fault of each individual is joined with it. We are not condemned in Adam as if we were innocent in ourselves, but we have contracted pollution from his sin; and so it has come to pass that each must bear the punishment of his own crime, since the punishment which he deserved first is not simply inflicted on the whole human race, but we have been tainted with his sin, as will afterwards be said. Whatever the meaning, we shall not die innocent, since each is held convicted by the testimony of his own conscience. As far as relates to young children, they seem to perish, not by their own, but for another's fault; but the solution is twofold; for although sin does not appear in them, yet it is latent, since they carry about with them corruption shut up in their soul, so that they are worthy of condemnation before God. This does not come under the notice of our senses; but we should consider how much more acutely God sees a thing than we do: hence, if we do not penetrate into that hidden judgment, yet we must hold that, before we are born, we are infected by the contagion of original sin, and therefore justly destined to ultimate destruction:—this is one solution. But as far as concerns the Prophet's expression, the dispute concerning infants is vain and out of place, since the Prophet only wished to refute that impious perverseness, as I have said, so that the people should no longer charge God with cruelty. *The soul,* says he, *which has sinned;* that is, none of you can boast of innocence when I punish you: as when it is said, He who does not labour, neither let him eat. (2 Thess. iii. 10.) Surely this cannot be extended to infants. Nature teaches us that they must be nourished, and yet sure enough they do not acquire their food by labour: but this is said of adults, who are old enough to acknowledge the reason why they were created, and their fitness for undergoing labour. So also, in this place, we are not treating of the tender young when newly born, but of adults, who wish to charge God instead of themselves, as if they are innocent; and so, when they cannot escape punishment, they are anxious to transfer the fault elsewhere—first upon others, and then upon God himself.

PRAYER.

Grant, Almighty God, since thou hast not only created us out of nothing, but hast deigned to create us again in thine only-begotten Son, and hast taken us from the lowest depths, and deigned to raise us to the hope of thy heavenly kingdom:—Grant, I say, that we may not be proud or puffed up with vainglory; but may we embrace this favour with becoming humility, and modestly submit ourselves to thee, until we become at length partakers of that glory which thine only-begotten Son has acquired for us.—Amen.

Lecture Fifty-Fourth.

5. But if a man be just, and do that which is lawful and right,

6. *And* hath not eaten upon the mountains, neither hath lifted up his eyes to the idols of the house of Israel, neither hath defiled his neighbour's wife, neither hath come near to a menstruous woman,

7. And hath not oppressed any, *but* hath restored to the debtor his pledge, hath spoiled none by violence, hath given his bread to the hungry, and hath covered the naked with a garment;

8. He *that* hath not given forth upon usury, neither hath taken any increase, *that* hath withdrawn his hand from iniquity, hath executed true judgment between man and man,

9. Hath walked in my statutes, and hath kept my judgments, to deal truly; he *is* just, he shall surely live, saith the Lord God.

5. Et vir si fuerit justus, et fecerit judicium et justitiam,

6. Super montes non comederit, et oculos suos non extulerit ad idola[1] domus Israel, et uxorem socii sui[2] non polluerit, et ad mulierem menstruatam non accesserit,

7. Et neminem afflixerit,[3] pignus suum reddiderit debitori, prædam non rapuerit,[4] panem suum famelico dederit, et nudum texerit vestimentis;

8. Cum usura non dederit et incrementum[5] non acceperit, ab iniquitate retraxerit manum suam, judicium fideliter fecerit inter virum et virum,

9. In statutis meis ambulaverit, et judicia mea custodierit ad faciendum veritatem,[6] justus est, vivendo vivet, dicit Dominator Iehovah.

HERE the Prophet confirms his former teaching by examples. For he first says, if any one faithfully keep the law, he shall prosper, since God will repay the reward of justice: afterwards he adds, if the just man beget a son unlike himself, the justice of the father shall not profit the

---

[1] Properly, "to the filthiness."—*Calvin.*
[2] Or, "of his neighbour."—*Calvin.*   [3] Or, "oppressed."—*Calvin.*
[4] Verbally, "has not seized booty."—*Calvin.*
[5] Or, "reward, gain."—*Calvin.*
[6] That is, "to conduct himself faithfully."—*Calvin.*

degenerate son, but he shall receive the reward of his iniquity. But if this second person should beget a son who does not imitate his father, God promises that this third person shall be acceptable by him, because he is just, and therefore enjoys prosperity and happiness. We see, then, that the grandfather and grandson are here spoken of, and that the son of the first, and father of the third, is placed between them. But this is the Spirit's intention, that God has prepared a reward for each according to their lives, so that he does not permit them to be deprived of their promised blessing, nor let the impious and despisers of his law escape. Now let us come to the words, *if any one has been just,* says he, *he shall be just, therefore he shall live.* He speaks generally first: he afterwards enumerates certain species under which he embraces the sum of the whole law. The full sentence is, if any one has been just, he shall live in consequence of his justice. But the Prophet defines what it is to be just, and he there chooses certain parts of the law: by putting a part for the whole, as I have said, he signifies, that whoever faithfully observes the law is esteemed just before God. Now we must examine each of these kinds of justice, and afterwards come to the general doctrine. He says first, *that he is just who does justice and judgment.* By the word judgment holy Scripture signifies rectitude; but when the two words are joined together, judgment seems to express more than justice: for justice is nothing but equity, fidelity, integrity, when we abstain altogether from fraud and violence, and deal with our brethren as we wish them to deal with us. Whoever so conducts himself is said to do justice; but judgment is extended further, namely, when we not only desire to benefit but defend our brethren, when unjustly oppressed, as far as we can, and when we oppose the lust and violence of those who would overthrow all that is right and holy. Hence to do judgment and justice is nothing else than to abstain from all injury by cultivating good faith and equity with our neighbours: then to defend all good causes, and to take the innocent under our patronage when we see them unjustly injured and oppressed. But these duties belong properly to the second table of the law. But it is clear from this that we fear God when we live justly with our brethren, for piety is the root of charity. Although many profane persons seem blameless in their life, and manifest a rare integrity, yet no one ever loves his neighbour from his heart, unless he fears and reverences God. Since, therefore, charity flows from piety and the fear of God, as often as we see the duties of the second table placed before us, we should learn them to be the testimonies to the worship of God, as in this place: but then the Prophet also adds certain parts of the first table.

He says then, *if he has not eaten upon the mountains, and not raised his eyes to the abominable deeds of the house of Israel.* These two points respect the worship of God: for by the figure " a part for the whole" to eat, means to offer sacrifices: he refers to those to which banquets were added as appendages. And truly when Paul speaks of idolatry, he does not say, if any one bends his knees before stone or wood, but he quotes the words of Moses, that the people rose up to play after eating, that is, after banqueting. (1 Cor. x. 7 ; Exod. xxxii. 6.) Hence a feast is there taken for that sacrilegious profaneness when the people made for themselves a calf, and wished to worship God before it. When, therefore, it is now said, *if any one has not eaten upon the mountains :* by a feast, as I have said, a sacrifice offered to idols is intended. Now we know that altars were raised on high in every direction, because they thought that they were near God when they ascended to an elevated spot. Because, therefore, superstitions were so exercised on the mountains, hence the Prophet relates what was customary, *if any one has not eaten upon the mountains :* then he explains himself more clearly, *if any one has not raised his eyes to the idols of the house of Israel.* To raise the eyes is here taken by a figure of speech for to be urged with eagerness towards superstitions : for we know that eyes are the principal outlets to the affections ; for when the affections burst forth in the eyes, and are conspicuous there, it is not surprising if all our desires are marked by this form of speech. Thus a person is said to raise his eyes to the house of his neighbour when he covets it, and also towards his wife, or anything else, when he is seized by a depraved lusting. The meaning is, then, that those who do not contaminate themselves with idols are thought just before God, as far as concerns the first table of the law, since they are content with the simple and lawful worship of God, and do not incline from it in any direction; nor, like the superstitious, allow their eyes to be wandering and erratic: and so they are compared with harlots who seek lovers on all sides. I repeat it again—the meaning is, that the true worshippers of God are those who are content with his doctrine, and are not carried hither and thither by a perverse appetite, and so fabricate for themselves idols. Besides, the Holy Spirit calls idols גִלּוּלִים, *gelolim*, "defilements,"[1] since all superstition should be detested by us; for as we are prone by nature to all kinds of error, we cannot be sufficiently restrained within the true and pure worship of God. Since, then, unbelievers imagine their gods to be sacred, the Holy Spirit, on the other hand, pronounces them to be defiling, since their profane worship is disgusting and abominable. But he says, *the idols of the house of Israel*, so that all shuffling must cease: because, if he had spoken of idols only, they might have objected that they detested the false and foolish gods of the Gentiles; but since many ceremonies were through long use received among the elect people, these ought not to be condemned like the impious rites of the heathen. The Holy Spirit refutes this cavil, and says, that though the house of Israel has approved such defilements, yet they are not to be excused for setting aside the law of God, and devoting themselves to human fictions.

And has not polluted his neighbour's wife. The Prophet now returns again to the second table, and treats here of adultery; and the language must be noticed, since such contamination shows how holy God considers the marriage tie: hence we see the atrocity of the sin, and the detestable nature of adultery; for both parties are equally polluted, though it appears stronger in the female sex through their

[1] The older lexicons connect this word with that for filth, *dii stercorii*, following the Jewish commentators: it occurs forty-seven times in the Old Testament, and our translators have always translated it "idols." The margin of Deut. xxix. 17, has *dungy gods*.

natural modesty. We must hold, then, that the very body is engrained with disgrace and infamy, as Paul says, when such sins are committed. Other sins, says he, are without the body; but this is a sin against the body itself which thus bears the marks of shame and infamy. (1 Cor. vi. 18.) Here, as I have said, Ezekiel treats the case of the woman, since the offence is in her case more pernicious. It follows —and *has not approached a female when legally unclean:* for we know this to be prohibited under the law, as being contrary to nature; for it was not necessary to define the matter by written law, as it speaks for itself: and God detests such crimes, not only because their offspring would contaminate cities and the nation at large, but because they are adverse to the instincts of human nature. (Lev. xviii. 19; xx. 18.) He afterwards adds, *if he has not oppressed* or afflicted *any one.* This is general, just as if the Prophet had said, if he has abstained from all fraud, violence, and injustice. But this is a great point to live so innocently among men, that no one should complain of any injury done to him, nor of any loss sustained. But it is not enough to preserve this self-restraint unless we desire to profit our brethren, since God wishes the good offices of life to be reciprocal: although, indeed, to take care to be free from all injustice ought to precede other duties. He says, *if he has returned his pledge to the debtor.* This ought not to be taken generally, but depends on the precept of the law; for we have often said, that the prophets are the interpreters of Moses, and so they often touch briefly on what Moses expresses more clearly. But if we wish to occupy ourselves usefully in reading them, we ought to determine the meaning of the law, and then to accommodate what we read in the prophets to what is there contained.[1] So, in this passage, *to restore the pledge to the debtor,* is restricted to the

[1] This canon of sacred criticism was not received by the Jews. The Talmud informs us of discussions among their doctors, pointing out the discrepancy between this chapter of Ezekiel and the Pentateuch, and objecting to the writings of this prophet being received into the Canon. See Bartolocci Biblioth. Heb., vol. ii. pp. 847, 848, and Wolf. Bibl. Heb., vol. ii. p. 156, as quoted in Norton's Genuineness of the Gospels, vol. ii. Additional Notes, p. cxli.; and also the Dissertation on this chapter at the end of this volume.

poor and needy, who had pledged either their garments, or their beds, or the tools by which they acquired a livelihood: for God forbids taking a pledge of a widow or a poor person: then he forbids taking a millstone, that is, any tool which a workman uses to get his living; for if any one empties the workshop of the miserable, he might just as well take his life. Hence Moses says, His life is in the pledge, (Deut. xxiv. 6,) that is, if any one pledges his tools, it is like having his hands cut off, since he cannot carry on his trade without his tools: hence thou takest away his life. Hence God forbids taking a coverlet, or garments, or bedding, for a wretched man would perish with cold were he to pledge either his coverlet or his bedding. But if, on the other hand, men of this kind are assisted without taking a pledge, they will bless those who abstain from too much rigour. Lastly, God forbids the destruction of the poor man's house, lest he should be ashamed of his poverty, and then because it is too cruel to penetrate into the house of another, and inquire for its contents; nay, this is a species of robbery. We see now how Ezekiel ought to be understood, *if he has restored a pledge to the debtor*, that is, to the poor debtor, or the necessary pledge, as I have said, such as tools and needful furniture, without which a person cannot exercise his trade. *He has not seized a prey*, that is, has not preyed upon his neighbours. For every kind of robbery is here marked by the word גזל, *gezel*, violence. *And has given his bread to the hungry.* Here the Prophet teaches what I have lately touched on, that cautious self-restraint from all injury is not sufficient, and sparing our neighbours; but that more is required, since we ought to assist them as far as we possibly can. Unless this had been added, many might object that they injured no one, never defrauded any, nor took advantage of the simple. But since God has united men in the bonds of mutual society, hence they must mutually perform good offices for each other. Here, then, it is required of the rich to succour the poor, and to offer bread to the hungry. But it is said, His bread, lest any one should object, through his habit of being too restricted; but there is no reason to bind me to bestow *my* goods on others: this is my bread, and so I have a right to possess what is my own: if any one is oppressed by want, I confess it to be praiseworthy to succour him, but no one is compelled to this act of liberality. Lest any one should escape thus, *behold,* says the Holy Spirit, *although you rightly call the bread yours,* yet it is not so yours that you ought to refuse your brother when his hunger provokes you to pity. *And has covered the naked with a garment:* the rule for garment and for bread is the same. The substance is, that others are not deemed just before God unless they are inclined to benevolence, so as to supply the necessities of their brethren, and to succour them in their poverty. It follows, *since he has not given on usury and has not received increase.* Here, among other crimes, Ezekiel enumerates usury—though the word usury is not properly suitable to this passage: נשך, *neshek,* is deduced from biting, and so the Hebrews name usury, because it gnaws and by degrees consumes the miserable. Ezekiel then says, that they are considered observers of the law who abstain from usury. But because men are very acute and cunning on this point, and devise subterfuges by which they may hide their cruelty, he adds, *and has not received increase:* for we know how various are the schemes for gain: for whoever devotes his attention to unlawful gains, will find out many monstrous things which no one would ever have thought of. Thus it happens that the usurer will deny that he exacts usury, and yet he will spoil the wretched and even suck out their blood. Under the name תרבית, *ther-bith,* Ezekiel comprehends those more secret kinds of usury which the avaricious use with many disguises, and when they spread such coverings before them, think themselves free from all blame. Hence the Prophet says, even if the name of usury is removed and is not taken into account, yet it is sufficient to condemn men if they receive increase, that is, make a profit at the expense of others. A question arises here, whether usury be in itself a crime, since God formerly permitted his people to take interest of strangers, and only forbade it among themselves. And there was the best reason for that law. For if its just proportion had been overthrown, there would have been no reciprocity, since the Gentiles could exact interest of the Jews; and unless that right had been mutual and reciprocal, as the phrase is, the condition of God's people would have been worse than that of the Gentiles. God therefore permitted his people to take interest, but not among each other, as I have said: this was only allowable with strangers. Besides, the law itself was political: but in this case the Prophet seems to condemn all kinds of interest, and exaggerates the weight of the sentence, when he adds increase, that is, whatever gains the avaricious mutually strive for. So also in the 15th Psalm, where a just mode of living is proscribed for us, David mentions, among other things—who has not lent his money on usury, (ver. 5.) It seems, then, from these two places, that usury is in itself unlawful. But because God's law embraces complete and perfect justice, hence we must hold that interest, unless it is opposed to God's law, is not altogether to be condemned, otherwise ignominy would clearly attach to the law of God if it did not prescribe to us a true and complete rule of living justly. But in the law there is that perfection to which nothing can be added. If then we wish to determine whether interest is unlawful we must come to the rule of the law, which cannot deceive us: but we shall not find all interest contrary to the law, and hence it follows that interest is not always to be condemned. Here, too, we must remember that we must regard the subject rather than the words, for men trifle by their own cavillings, but God does not admit of such fallacies. Hence, as I said, the substance ought to be weighed, because the words alone will not enable us to decide whether interest be sometimes lawful or not. For example, among the Latins the word for interest is honourable in itself and has no disgrace attached to it, but that for usury is odious. What causes disgrace to be thus hidden under it? they fancied that they abhorred usurers, hence the general term interest contains within it all kinds of usury, and there was nothing so cruel, so unjust, and so barbarous, which was not covered by that pretence. Now since the name for interest was unknown to the French, that for usury became detestable: hence the French devised a new craftiness by which they could deceive God. For since no one could bear the name of usury, they used " interest" instead: but what does this mean but something which interests us, and thus it signifies all kinds of repayment for loans, for there was no kind of interest among the ancients which is not now comprehended in this word. Now since we have said that interest cannot be totally and without exception condemned, (for we must not play upon words, but treat the real point,) we must see how far it can be proved not to be reckoned a crime. First of all, in a well regulated state, no usurer is tolerated: even the profane see this: whoever therefore professedly adopts this occupation, he ought to be expelled from intercourse with his fellow-men. For if any illiberal pursuits load those who pursue them with censure, that of the usurer is certainly an illiberal trade, and unworthy of a pious and honourable man. Hence Cato said that to take usury was almost the same as murder. For when asked concerning agriculture, after he had given his opinion, he inquired, But what is usury? Is it not murder? says he. And surely the usurer will always be a robber; that is, he will make a profit by his trade, and will defraud, and his iniquity will increase just as if there were no laws, no equity, and no mutual regard among mankind. This is one point: but there is another part of the occupation besides that of taking interest. When any one sets up his table he uses the same art as a farmer does in employing his labour in cultivating the fields. But any one may receive interest without being a professed usurer. For example, a person may have capital and put out a part of it on loan, and thus receive interest: and if he do that once, he will not be called a usurer; so that we must consider when and from whom a person exacts interest. But this sentiment ought to prevail here: " neither everywhere, nor always, nor all things, nor from all." This indeed was said of offices, and that law was imposed upon the governors of provinces: but it agrees best with this subject. It is not suitable then to receive "all things," because if the profit exceed moderation it must be rejected, since it is contrary to charity: we said also that the continual habit and custom is not without fault. Neither "everywhere," since the usurer, as I have said, ought not to enter or be brought into the Church of God. Then again, not "from all," because it is always wrong to exact usury from a poor man; but if a man is rich, and has money of his own, as the saying is, and has a very good estate and a large patrimony, and should borrow money of his neighbour, will that neighbour commit sin by receiving a profit from the loan of his money? Another borrower is the richer of the two, and might do without it and yet suffer no loss: but he wishes to buy a farm and enjoy its fruits: why should the creditor be deprived of his rights when his money brings profit to a neighbour richer than himself? We see, then, that it may sometimes happen that the receiver of interest is not to be hastily condemned, since he is not acting contrary to God's law. But we must always hold that the tendency of usury is to oppress one's brother, and hence it is to be wished that the very names of usury and interest were buried and blotted out from the memory of men. But since men cannot otherwise transact their business, we must always observe what is lawful, and how far it is so. I know that the subject might be treated at greater length, but I have shortly expressed what is sufficient for our purpose.

It follows, *And hath withdrawn his hand from iniquity.* Here again the Prophet commends innocency, when we are cautious that our neighbour should not receive any damage or injury through our fault. Hence abstaining from injury is again praised here, but a new form of speech is used, since if men are not very anxious and careful they easily extend the hand to iniquity: and why so? various means of gain from many quarters present themselves to us, and we are easily led captive by such enticements. Hence the Prophet, not without reason, here commends *the servants of God to withdraw the hand from iniquity,* that is, not only to abstain from injury, but when the sweetness of gain entices us, and some plausible means of profit is proposed, that they should refrain themselves: this is the meaning of *to withdraw the hand from iniquity.* The rest I leave for tomorrow.

PRAYER.

Grant, Almighty God, since thou hast so instructed us by thy law in the rules of living justly, that we have no excuse for error or ignorance: Grant, I say, that we may be attentive to that teaching which thou prescribest for us; and so anxiously exercise ourselves in it, that each of us may live innocently among the brotherhood: and then may we so worship thee with one consent and so glorify thy name, that we may at length arrive at that happy inheritance which thou hast promised for us in thine only-begotten Son.—Amen.

Lecture Fifty-Fifth.

WE yesterday explained why the Prophet says that no one is just unless *he withdraw his hands from iniquity*, because many occasions tempt us to injure others: unless we restrain ourselves in a middle course we often hurt our neighbours. Now among the virtues of a just man he puts, *to judge according to truth: to act truthfully*, says he, *between man and man*. This seems indeed to be the proper duty of judges who discharge a public office, but yet it is suitable to private persons; for although no one argues his own cause except before some one endued with power to decide it, yet we see that the inclinations of men often pervert equity and rectitude in judgments. Again, many are chosen arbitrators who do not hold any public office. The meaning is, that what Ezekiel previously taught concerning equity is extended to the causes of others, that no one should turn aside from right and equity through private friendship. Afterwards it follows, *if he has walked in my statutes and kept my judgments, in acting with truthfulness*. Again, the Prophet returns to general remarks: for he has recorded certain kinds of justice, as we said yesterday, whence its nature may be more clearly perceived. Besides, because God's law contains within it more than the Prophet has thus far mentioned; hence it was necessary to add this clause, *who has walked in my decrees*, says he. It is too cold to restrict this to ceremonies, as is sometimes done; hence I interpret it of edicts or decrees. The metaphor of walking does not require a long explanation, as it is very common in Scripture. Hence, *to walk in God's precepts* is nothing else than to form his life and morals according to the rule which has been prescribed by God ; or, what is the same thing, so to conduct oneself, that in desiring to be deemed just a man should attempt nothing but what is agreeable to God's precepts. But since the observance of the law is difficult, first, because we are not only of a frail disposition, but prone to sin ; hence the word " serving " is added, by which the Prophet commends diligence. Whoever wishes to direct his life according to God's precepts should attentively keep them, since nothing is more natural than to transgress and fall. He now adds, *for acting truthfully.* Integrity is here denoted by the word truthfulness. We gather, then, from this word the fruitful teaching, that the object of God's whole law is to conduct ourselves without deceit or fraud, and study to assist one another in simplicity, and to conduct ourselves with sincerity in every duty. If any one, then, asks the object of the law, the Prophet here describes it to us— *the performance of truth ;* and this is said rightly of the second table. But this may be adapted to the former table, since the Scripture teaches us that no dissembling can be pleasing to God. And we see also what Paul says when he briefly defines the end of the law to be charity out of any pure heart, and faith unfeigned. (1 Tim. i. 5.) But the word truth in this passage is, in my judgment, referred to that sincerity which we must cultivate, so that no one should deceive another, nor act fraudulently or knowingly, but be really simple and sincere. He adds, *he is just, and in living he shall live, says the Lord Jehovah.* At length he pronounces, as we said, that he is just who has faithfully observed God's law ; then that a recompense is prepared for all the just who thus sincerely worship God. Now let us come to the second example.

10. If he beget a son *that is* a rob-   10. Et genuerit filium prædonem,[1]

---

[1] Or, " a destroyer :" פָּרִיץ, *pheretz*, signifies to corrupt, destroy ; whence פָּרִיצִים, *pher-tzim,* means thieves who dig through the walls of houses. But that derivation seems to me forced : I rather interpret the word as " a violent man," and one who breaks through all rectitude.—*Calvin.*

ber, a shedder of blood, and *that* doeth the like to *any* one of these *things*,

11. And that doeth not any of those *duties*, but even hath eaten upon the mountains, and defiled his neighbour's wife,

12. Hath oppressed the poor and needy, hath spoiled by violence, hath not restored the pledge, and hath lifted up his eyes to the idols, hath committed abomination,

13. Hath given forth upon usury, and hath taken increase: shall he then live? he shall not live: he hath done all these abominations; he shall surely die; his blood shall be upon him.

qui sanguinem effundit, et facit fratri:[1] fratri (*ergo*) unum ex his.[2]

11. Et ipse hæc omnia[3] non fecerit, quin potius omnia in montibus comederit, et uxorem proximi sui corruperit.[4]

12. Pauperem et egenum oppresserit, prædas rapuerit, pignus non reddiderit, et ad idola oculos suos extulerit, abominationem fecerit.

13. Cum usura dederit, et incrementum acceperit: et vivet?[5] non vivet: abominationes cunctas has patravit, moriendo morietur, sanguis ejus in eo erit.[6]

He has oppressed the poor and needy : he had simply said, he had oppressed a man; but now to make the greatness of the crime appear, he speaks of the poor and needy: for cruelty in oppressing them is less tolerable. Whatever the condition of the person whom we treat with injustice, our wickedness is in itself sufficiently worthy of condemnation; but when we afflict the wretched, whose condition ought to excite our pity, that inhumanity is, as I have said, far more atrocious. Hence this circumstance exaggerates what Ezekiel had formerly simply expressed. In the phrase for *seizing booty*, the word for booty is in the plural: in the next phrase he omits the word for debtor, because it is sufficiently understood: in the next, he does not add "of the house of Israel" to the word "idols;" and in the last clause the word "abomination" seems to refer to one kind of grossness only: but if any wish to extend its meaning further, I do not object; but since he lately used the word in the plural, I rather take this word in its restricted sense. I pass thus rapidly over this second example, as I shall over the third, because Ezekiel preserves the same sentiments, and repeats

[1] So I interpret it: others read "one thing;" but we shall afterwards see that the word brother is better.—*Calvin*.

[2] That is, "any one."—*Calvin*. Three manuscripts with the Syriac version omit the word אח, *ach*, brother; but the Chaldee, and Houbigant, with Archbishop Newcome, all agree with Calvin in inserting it.

[3] The precepts of the law, which he had mentioned before.—*Calvin*.

[4] "Polluted," as we said yesterday.—*Calvin*.

[5] That is, "shall he live?"—*Calvin*.

[6] That is, "shall rest upon himself."—*Calvin*.

almost the same words as he had just used. Hitherto he has taught that life is laid up for all the just as the reward of their justice: but he now sets before us a degenerate son, sprung from a just father, running headlong into all kind of wickedness. He says, then, if a man who desires to obey the law beget a son of a perverse disposition, who rejects the discipline of his father, and at the same time violates the whole law of God, *shall he surely live?* No, says he, *he shall die, his blood shall be upon him;* that is, he cannot escape God's judgment, because his crimes cry out, and are heard. Hence none who turn aside from the right way shall remain unpunished: this is the simple meaning of the Prophet. Let us now come to the third member.

14. Now, lo, *if* he beget a son, that seeth all his father's sins which he hath done, and considereth, and doeth not such like,	14. Et ecce genuerit filium, et viderit cuncta scelera patris sui quæ perpetravit, et timuerit, et non fecerit secundum ipsa,
15. *That* hath not eaten upon the mountains, neither hath lifted up his eyes to the idols of the house of Israel, hath not defiled his neighbour's wife,	15. Super montes non comederit, et oculos suos non extulerit ad idola [1] domus Israel [2] uxorem proximi sui non polluerit,
16. Neither hath oppressed any, hath not withholden the pledge, neither hath spoiled by violence, *but* hath given his bread to the hungry, and hath covered the naked with a garment,	16. Et neminem oppresserit, pignus non pigneraverit,[3] et rapinam [4] non rapuerit: panem suum famelico dederit,[5] et nudum operuerit vestimento.
17. *That* hath taken off his hand from the poor, *that* hath not received usury nor increase, hath executed my judgments, hath walked in my statutes; he shall not die for the iniquity of his father, he shall surely live.	17. Ab egeno retraxerit manum suam, fœnus et incrementum non acceperit, judicia mea fecerit, in decretis meis ambulaverit, ipse non morietur in iniquitate patris sui, vivendo vivet.

In this third example Ezekiel announces, that if a man be born of a wicked father, he may nevertheless be pleasing to God, if he be unlike his father: and thus he refutes the proverb that was so common in Israel—that the father ate the sour grapes, and the children's teeth were set on edge.

[1] Or, "pollutions."—*Calvin.*

[2] The house of Israel is expressed here as in the first set.—*Calvin.*

[3] Verbally; but because there is a difference between the Latin words for to give and receive a pledge, it makes the sense clearer to say, not to receive a pledge.—*Calvin.*

[4] He now uses the singular number, "a prey."—*Calvin.*

[5] Or, "distributed."—*Calvin.*

For if the sons were sufferers through the father's eating the sour grapes, then the pious who drew their origin from wicked despisers of God would be freed from all their sins. Thus Ezekiel would have been punished instead of his father, Ahaz, and Josiah instead of Manasseh. But here the Prophet bears witness that the good, however they may have been born from wicked parents, should receive the reward of righteousness no less certainly and faithfully than if they had come down from heaven, and if their family had always been without the commission of any crime. Since, therefore, God does not punish them for their fathers' crimes, it follows that the Israelites uttered this taunt not only foolishly, but impiously, saying that their own teeth were set on edge, because their fathers had eaten the sour grapes. Besides, as there is a difference in the phrase, I shall notice briefly what is worthy of remark : *if he begat a son who saw all that his father had done, and was afraid.* Here the Prophet teaches that it needed the greatest attention for the son to forsake the example of a bad father. For sons are blind to their fathers' vices ; and although, when duty is set before them, they carelessly despise it, yet they fancy themselves held so far by pious reverence, that they dare not condemn their fathers. Hence it happens that sons do not acknowledge their fathers' crimes, and thus a wicked father corrupts his son willingly. Bad discipline, therefore, is added to this, so that it is not surprising if the offspring is worse than his ancestors. For this reason the Prophet says, *if he has seen*, that is, if a righteous child has observed his father's sins, since sons shut their eyes as much as possible to all their fathers' crimes ; nay, they embrace their vices for the greatest virtues.

He then adds, *if he have feared.* It would not be sufficient to take notice of this without adding the fear of God. It is true, indeed, that many were unlike their parents, through being restrained by shame ; for when they heard the reproaches of their parents, they were touched with ingenuous modesty, so as to be on their guard against such enormities. But all these followed the empty shadow of justice ; and here the serious observance of the law is treated, which cannot flow from anything else but the fear of God, and this, as Scripture says, is the beginning of wisdom. (Ps. cxi. 10; Prov. i. 7.) A person thus may be blameless through his whole life, and yet not touch on any part of justice, since righteousness flows from only one principle—the fear of God. He afterwards adds, *and has not done according to them.* We see, therefore, that those who implicate themselves in others' crimes are not otherwise deceived, unless they purposely stifle all difference between good and evil; for if they had attended to this, they would doubtless have been touched with some fear, and thus have governed their life according to God's precepts: but scarcely one in a hundred thinks of this, and hence every one mingles freely with his neighbours, and so all perish together. He afterwards adds, *he has not eaten upon the mountains, has not raised his eyes to the idols of the house of Israel:* we have explained all these: *and has not oppressed any one, and has not received a pledge.* We said that this ought not to be explained of every pledge; for it was lawful for any one, on giving money, to receive a pledge for its return, but not from one who is destitute of either garments or the necessary implements of trade: so I pass this by. *He has not received a prey, has distributed his bread to the hungry.* He adds, what he had not touched on previously, *he has withdrawn his hand from the poor.* This seems to differ from the opinion which we had in the sixteenth chapter, (ver. 49.) Among the sins of Sodom, the Prophet there puts this also, that they withdrew their hand from the poor and needy; and surely, when we stretch forth the hand for the sake of help, it is a true proof of charity; but if we withdraw the hand, it is a proof of cruelty, since we do not deign to aid a brother who ought to obtain some favour from us. But we must bear in mind that there are two senses in which the hand is either extended or withdrawn. If I extend my hand to the poor to supply what is wanting, and to the weak to render him aid, this is the duty of charity. If, on the contrary, I withdraw my hand, I unjustly turn away from him who implores my confidence, and whose misery ought to win for him some favour. But we extend the hand when we seize on a neighbour's goods, and violently deprive him of them, and despoil the innocent of their rights. On the contrary, he who withdraws his hand is humane in sparing his brethren, and not enriching himself at their expense, and profiting by their oppression. In this sense the Prophet now enumerates *withdrawing the hand from the poor* in the list of virtues, because the poor are subject to all kinds of injury. If, therefore, when we see booty already prepared for us, and yet we refrain from it, this is a proof of true charity. But again, we must remark upon what I treated but briefly yesterday, namely, that *we must withdraw our hands from the poor*, because nothing is more easy than to be enticed to make a gain of the poor; and wherever occasion and impunity offer themselves, avarice so seizes us, that we neither discern nor consider what is right and fair. Every one who wishes to preserve his self-restraint, and to subdue his affections, ought to attend to this with all his strength and with constant struggling: thus the Prophet says, *we must withdraw the hand.*

Now at last he concludes: *he shall not die through his father's iniquity; he shall surely live.* He does not repeat that this is just, yet we must understand it so; but he stops at the immediate effect, since God's blessing awaits all the just, as Isaiah says: surely there is a reward to the just, (chap. iii. 10;) and the Prophet exclaims as if it were believed with difficulty: for, since we see all things revolving promiscuously in the world, we directly imagine either that God is at rest in heaven, or that chance governs all things here on earth. But we must strive against this perverse supposition, and determine, as Isaiah teaches, that there is a reward for the just. The Prophet now expresses this, while a difficult question arises from the passage; for he says *that he is just who has kept the law,* and so God will bestow a recompense upon him: hence these two things are connected together, and the question which I mentioned arises from the former clause; for the whole Scriptures teach that no one is just, and that none can be justified by the law. But these things are contrary to each other; to be just and worthy of reward through keeping the law, since none is just, all are transgressors, all devoid of justice, and so but one remedy remains—that of seeking our safety from the gratuitous mercy of God. But although, at first sight, this kind of inconsistency disturbs the rude and partially-exercised commentator, yet this solution is easy, since, strictly speaking, justice is the observance of the law. If any one asks, then, what justice is, the proper definition is, the observance of law. Why so? Because the law, as I said yesterday, lays down the solid rule of justice; whoever observes it will be esteemed just; and thus justification is properly said to be placed in works. But, on the other hand, Scripture pronounces what is very true, and entirely confirmed by experience, that no one can satisfy the law, and, on account of this defect, we are all deprived of justification by works. What I have said may be made much clearer by many testimonies of Scripture. Not the hearer of the law, says Paul, in the second chapter of the epistle to the Romans, but the doer of the law, shall be justified, (ver. 13.) There Paul speaks naturally, that those are just who conform their whole life to the obedience of God's law. So also John, in his canonical epistle: He who doeth righteousness is righteous. (1 John iii. 7.) Now, if any one asks whether any perfect observer of the law can be found, or one who does justice in every respect, the answer is at hand, that we are all by nature very far gone from all righteousness, and all our senses and affections are enemies which contend against God's law, as Paul teaches: The whole soul of man is perverse, and we are not fit to think anything of ourselves, and that all our sufficiency is of God, since we are slaves of sin. (Rom. viii. 7; 2 Cor. iii. 5; Rom. xi.) But it would be superfluous to heap together many testimonies. Let it suffice, then, that we are by nature all together rebels against God, so that not the slightest particle of good can be found in us. As far as concerns the faithful, they aspire indeed to righteousness, but lamely, and at a great distance from their aim; they often wander from the way, and they often fall, so that they do not satisfy the law, and hence require God's pity. Hence we must come to the second kind of righteousness, which is improperly so called, namely, that which we obtain from Christ. He who doeth righteousness is righteous. (1 John iii. 7.) None of us does it; but Christ, who fulfilled the law, is esteemed just before God. Hence it is necessary that we should be approved by God through his righteousness; that is, it is imputed to us, and we are accepted through his righteousness. Hence justification by faith, as it is called, is not properly righteousness; but on account of the defect of true righteousness, it is necessary to fly to this as to a sacred anchor; and Paul, in the tenth chapter to the Romans, explains this briefly and clearly. The righteousness of the law, says he, thus speaks: He who has done these things shall live in them; but the righteousness of faith says, He who has believed shall be just. The Apostle here speaks of a double righteousness—that of the law and of faith: he says, that the righteousness of the law is situated in works, since no one is thought just unless he fulfils the law. (Rom. x. 5-8.) Since all are far distant from this standard, another is added and substituted, namely, that we may embrace the righteousness of Christ by faith, and so become just, by another righteousness without us: for if any one again objects that justification by the law is superfluous, I answer, that it profits us in two ways; first, because the law brings in those convicted of their own unrighteousness to Christ. This, then, is one fruit of the law, that we renounce our own righteousness, when our iniquity so discloses itself, that it compels us to be silent before God, as we formerly saw. A more fruitful result follows; because, when God regenerates his elect, he inscribes a law on their hearts and in their inward parts, as we have elsewhere seen, and shall see again in the thirty-sixth chapter. (Jer. xxxi. 33; Ezek. xxxvi. 26, 27.) But the difficulty is not yet solved; because the faithful, even if regenerated by God's Spirit, endeavour to conform themselves to God's law, yet, through their own weakness, never arrive at that point, and so are never righteous: I answer, although the righteousness of works is mutilated in the sons of God, yet it is acknowledged as perfect, since, by not imputing their sins to them, he proves what is his own. Hence it happens, that although the faithful fall back, wander, and sometimes fall, yet they may be called observers of the law, and walkers in the commandments of God, and observers of his righteousness. But this arises from gratuitous imputation, and hence also its reward. The works of the faithful are not without reward, because they please God, and pleasing God, they are sure of remuneration. We see, then, how these things are rightly united, that no one obeys the law, and that no one is worthy of the fruits of righteousness, and yet that God, of his own liberality, acknowledges as just those who aspire to righteousness, and repay them with a reward of which they are unworthy. When, therefore, we say that the faithful are esteemed just even in their deeds, this is not stated as a cause of their salvation, and we must diligently notice that the cause of salvation is excluded from this doctrine; for, when we discuss the cause, we must look nowhere else but to the mercy of God, and there we must stop. But although works tend in no way to the cause of justification, yet, when the elect sons of God were justified freely by faith, at the same time their works are esteemed righteous by the same gratuitous liberality. Thus it still remains true, that faith without works justifies, although this needs prudence and a sound interpretation; for this proposition, that faith without works justifies is true and yet false, according to the different senses which it bears. The proposition, that faith without works justifies by itself, is false, because faith without works is void. But if the clause "without works" is joined with the word "justifies," the proposition will be true, since faith cannot justify when it is without works, because it is dead, and a mere fiction. He who is born of God is just, as John says. (1 John v. 18.) Thus faith can be no more separated from works than the sun from his heat: yet faith justifies without works, because works form no reason for our justification; but faith alone reconciles us to God, and causes him to love us, not in ourselves, but in his only-begotten Son. Now, therefore, that question is solved, when the Prophet teaches that life is reposed in the just, even if they are born of wicked and unholy parents.

Lastly, we must notice the word "life," since the word "living" ought not to be understood only of life on earth, but looks to eternal life: and here some expositors are mistaken: for because they could not free themselves from those difficulties which I lately explained, they interpreted the words of Moses in a civil sense—He who has done these things shall live in them. But Moses is speaking of life eternal. Hence we must hold, not only that a reward is promised in this life to the just observers of the law, but that eternal life is also a promised reward. Besides, as I have said, since we are all destitute of righteousness, so we ought not to hope for any reward, since we are all under the law and under the curse, as Paul says: neither is there any means of escape, as Paul again says, (Gal. iii. 10, 13,) unless we fly with complete and abject faith to the mercy of God alone, and to the satisfaction by which Christ has reconciled us to his Father. Here I shall finish.

PRAYER.

Grant, Almighty God, since thou hast pointed out to us the true way of safety, since thou didst perceive us all deficient in this respect, and since the law which ought to have given us life brought death through our transgressing it: Grant, I pray thee, since thou hast set before us thine only Son in whom we may be reconciled and obtain the perfect righteousness which we need, that we may so embrace the grace which is offered to us in the gospel, that we may strive more and more to proceed in the pursuit of piety, till we arrive at length at the blessed inheritance which the same, thine only-begotten Son, has acquired for us.—Amen.

Lecture Fifty-Sixth.

18. *As for* his father, because he cruelly oppressed, spoiled his brother by violence, and did *that* which *is* not good among his people, lo, even he shall die in his iniquity.

19. Yet say ye, Why? doth not the son bear the iniquity of the father? When the son hath done that which is lawful and right, *and* hath kept all my statutes, and hath done them, he shall surely live.

18. Pater ejus quia opprimendo oppressit, et rapuit prædam a fratre, et quod non est bonum fecit in medio populi sui: ecce is morietur in iniquitate sua.

19. Et dicitis, Quare non portabit filius iniquitatem patris? eo quod filius fecit judicium et justitiam, et custodivit omnia statuta mea fecitque ea: ideo vivendo vivet.

HE inculcates the same thing more at length, not for the sake of ornament so much as to refute that impious saying in which the Israelites so pertinaciously persisted. Since then it was difficult to tear from their minds what was so deeply rooted in them, the Prophet often exclaims that no one was punished except he deserved it for his crimes. He adds in the next verse what seems superfluous and absurd: for the Israelites did not contend with God for sparing the innocent: but here Ezekiel represents them speaking as if they wished the innocent son to be punished equally with the wicked father. But he does not mean that they contended about the right, but about the fact, as we usually say. For since they were imbued with that error, that punishments extended beyond the criminals, on the other hand he pronounces that the just were not absolved by their own goodness, if they sprang from impious parents, although the people supposed so; for they were buried under their own depraved judgment, otherwise they must have perceived that justice is never deprived by God of its reward of life.

20. The soul that sinneth, it shall die. The son shall not bear the iniquity of the father, neither shall the father bear the iniquity of the son: the righteousness of the righteous shall be upon him, and the wickedness of the wicked shall be upon him.	20. Anima quæ peccaverit ipsa morietur: filius non portabit iniquitatem patris, et pater non portabit iniquitatem filii: justitia justi super eum erit, et impietas impii super eum erit.

Ezekiel still pursues the sentiment which we have explained, namely, that God is a just judge and treats every one according to his conduct; as Paul says, As each has lived in the flesh, so God lays up a reward for him. (Rom. viii. 13.) But he more clearly refuted the proverb, that the sons should suffer for their fathers' sins. He says, then, that each when he comes before God's tribunal should be judged by his works. As far then as the general sentiment is concerned, it is in accordance with common sense that God should exact punishment of the wicked, and that they should receive the just reward of their works. But in the next clause, the question arises how the Spirit here pronounces that the son should not pay the penalty due to the father, when God so often declares that he visits the sins of the fathers upon the children unto the third and fourth generation. (Exod. xx. 5.) That sentiment often occurs: but there are two passages peculiarly remarkable, where it is annexed to the second precept of the law, (Deut. v. 9,) and then in that remarkable vision which occurred to Moses, God pronounces the same thing as before, namely, that the iniquity of the fathers should fall upon the sons. (Exod. xxxiv. 7.) These passages seem opposed to each other, but it will be easy to remove the contradiction by beginning with the fall of Adam, since if we do not consider the whole race fallen in Adam, we can scarcely extricate ourselves from that difficulty which we often feel as causing pungent scruples. But the principle of one universal fall in Adam removes all doubts. For when we consider the perishing of the whole human race, it is said with truth that we perish through another's fault: but it is added at the same time, that every one perishes through his own iniquity. If then we inquire into the cause of the curse which presses upon all the posterity of Adam, it may be said to be partly another's and partly our own: another's, through Adam's declension from God, in whose person the whole human race was spoiled of righteousness and intelligence, and all parts of the soul utterly corrupted. So that every one is lost in himself, and if he wishes to contend with God, he must always acknowledge that the fountain of the curse flows from himself. For before the child was born into the world, it was corrupt, since its mental intelligence was buried in darkness, and its will was perverse and rebellious against God. As soon as infants are born they contract pollution from their father Adam: their reason is blinded, their appetites perverted, and their senses entirely vitiated. This does not immediately show itself in the young child, but before God, who discerns things more acutely than we do, the corruption of our whole nature is rightly treated as sin. There is no one who during the course of his life does not perceive himself liable to punishment through his own works; but original sin is sufficient for the condemnation of all men. When men grow up they acquire for themselves the new curse of what is called actual sin: so that he who is pure with reference to ordinary observation, is guilty before God: hence Scripture pronounces us all naturally children of wrath: these are Paul's words in the second chapter of the epistle to the Ephesians, (ver. 3.) If then we are children of wrath, it follows that we are polluted from our birth: this provokes God's anger and renders him hostile to us: in this sense David confesses himself conceived in sin. (Ps. li. 5.) He does not here accuse either his father or his mother so as to extenuate his own wickedness; but when he abhors the greatness of his sin in provoking the wrath of God, he is brought back to his infancy, and acknowledges that he was even then guilty before God. We see then that David, being reminded of a single sin, acknowledges himself a sinner before he was born; and since we are all under the curse, it follows that we are all worthy of death. Thus, the son properly speaking shall not die through the iniquity of his father, but is considered guilty before God through his own fault.

Now let us proceed further. When God pronounces that the iniquity of the father returns into the bosom of the son, we must remember that when God involves the son in the same death with the father, he does so principally because the son of the impious is destitute of his Spirit: whence it happens that he remains in the death in which he was born. For if we do not consider any other punishments than those which are openly inflicted, a new scruple will again arise from which we cannot free ourselves, since this inquiry will always recur, how can the son perish by his own fault, if he can produce good fruit and so reconcile himself to God? But the first punishment with which God threatens the reprobate is that which I have mentioned, namely, that their offspring are destitute and deprived of spiritual gifts, so that they sink deeper and deeper into destruction: for there are two kinds of punishment, the one outward and the other inward, as we express it. God punishes the transgressors of his law by either the sword, or by famine, or by pestilence, as he everywhere denounces: he is also armed with other means of slaughter for executing his wrath, and all these punishments are outward and openly apparent. But there is another sort inward and hidden, when God takes away the spirit of rectitude from the reprobate, when he gives them up to a reprobate mind, subjects them to foul desires, and deprives them of all his gifts: hence God is said to cause the fathers' iniquity to recoil upon the children not only when he outwardly punishes the little ones, but because he devotes a cursed offspring to eternal destruction, through being destitute of all the gifts of the Spirit. Now we know that God is the fountain of life, (Ps. xxxvi. 9,) whence it follows that all who are separated from him are dead. Now therefore it is evident how God throws the iniquity of the fathers upon the children, since when he devotes both father and son to eternal destruction, he deprives them of all his gifts, blinds their minds, and enslaves all their appetites to the devil. Although we may, in one word, embrace the whole matter of the children suffering for the fathers when he leaves them to simple nature, as the phrase is, since in this way he drowns them in death and destruction. But outward punishments also follow afterwards, as when God sent lightning upon Sodom many young children perished, and all were absorbed with their parents. (Gen. xix. 24.) If any one asks by what right they perished, first they were sons of Adam and so were accursed, and then God wished to punish the Sodomites through their offspring, and he could do so deservedly. Concerning the young who thus perished with their fathers, it is said, happy is he who dashes thy young ones against the stones or the pavement. (Ps. cxxxvii. 9.) At first sight, indeed, that atrocity seems intolerable that a child whose age and judgment is thus tender should be so cruelly slain: but as we have already said, all are naturally children of wrath. (Eph. ii. 2.) No wonder, therefore, that God withdraws his favour from the offspring of the reprobate, even if he executes these outward judgments. But how will this now be suitable, *shall not the son bear the iniquity of the father?* for Ezekiel here speaks of adults, for he means that the son shall not bear his father's iniquity, since he shall receive the reward due to himself and sustain his own burden. Should any one wish to strive with God, he can be refuted in a single word: for who can boast himself innocent? Since therefore all are guilty through their own fault, it follows that the son does not bear his father's iniquity, since he has to bear his own at the same time. Now that question is solved.

He now adds, *the righteousness of the righteous shall be upon him, and the impiety of the impious shall be upon him.* We said that this was the legal sentence: if God used the same language everywhere, no hope of safety would be left to us. For who would be found just if his life were judged strictly by the law? But it has already been said, speaking accurately, that God rewards those worshippers who observe his law, and punishes those who transgress it. But since we are all far from perfect obedience, Christ is offered to us, from whom we may partake of righteousness, and in this way be justified by faith. Meanwhile it is true, according to the rule of the law, *that the righteousness of the righteous shall be upon him,* since God will not disappoint any, but will really perform what he has promised. But he promises a reward to all who observe his law. If any one object that this doctrine is useless and superfluous, we have an answer at hand, that it is in many ways useful, since, first of all, we acknowledge that God, although he owes us nothing, yet willingly binds himself to be reconciled to us; and thus his surprising liberality appears. Then we again collect, that by transgression we cannot profit or obtain any advantage when God offers a reward to all who observe his law. For what can we demand more equitable than that God should of his own accord be our debtor? and should reward us while he holds us bound to himself, and completely subject to him with all our works? And that pattern of Christ must be considered, When ye have done all that was commanded you, say, We are unprofitable servants. (Luke xvii. 10.) Why so? for we return nothing but what God has justly required of us. We gather, then, from this sentence, that we cannot expostulate with God, or complain of anything while the fault of our own condemnation resides in us for not keeping the law. Thirdly, we acknowledge another instance of God's mercy in his clothing us in the righteousness of his Son, when he sees us in want of a righteousness of our own, and altogether destitute of everything good. Fourthly, we said that they are esteemed just who do not satisfy the law, since God does not impute their sins to them. Hence the righteousness of the law is not without fruit among the faithful; since on account of that blessedness which is described in Psalm xxxii. 2, their works are taken into account and remunerated by God. So *the righteousness of the righteous is upon him, just as the impiety of the impious is upon him, and it shall recoil upon his own head.* It follows—

21. But if the wicked will turn from all his sins that he hath committed, and keep all my statutes, and do that which is lawful and right, he shall surely live, he shall not die. 22. All his transgressions that he hath committed, they shall not be mentioned unto him: in his righteousness that he hath done he shall live.	21. Et si impius reversus fuerit ab omni iniquitate sua quam fecit, et servaverit omnia edicta mea, et fecerit judicium et justitiam, vivendo vivet, non morietur. 22. Omnes transgressiones quas fecit non venient in memoriam ei,[1] sed in justitia sua quam fecit vivet.

In this sentence God proposes the hope of pardon, and invites and exhorts to penitence all the transgressors of his law. But this doctrine is specially worthy of notice, that God extends his arms, and is prepared to meet and receive all who betake themselves to good fruits: for despair hurls us into madness, and then hardens our hearts by abandoned obstinacy. Hence it is necessary that God should extend his hand towards us, and animate us to penitence. This is the meaning of this passage of the Prophets, *as soon as the impious is turned away from his impiety, God will be at peace with him.* Now we see that no excuse remains for us if this humane invitation of God does not stir us up when he bears witness that he is propitious to us when we heartily desire to be reconciled to him. But he here requires serious repentance when he says, *if the impious has turned away from his impiety, and has kept my statutes, and done justice and judgment, he shall live,* says he. For a sort of half conversion is discerned in many who think that in this way they are safe before God, but they are greatly deceived; for many mingle virtues with vices, and imagine their guilt blotted out, if they can only bring forward something as worthy of praise. But this is just as if any one should offer

[1] That is, "against him."—*Calvin.*

muddy wine to his master, because he had mixed it not only with dregs, but even with filth: so are all the works of those who do not put away all depraved desires, and strive to free themselves from all the corruptions of the flesh. Thus what is here taught is worthy of notice, namely, that the beginning of conversion is, when any one renounces himself and his own lusts. But it is necessary to add another part of duty, that when any one bids farewell to his vices, he must devote himself obediently to God. The Prophet joins the two together, therefore, since one cannot be separated from the other. Hence the Spirit here shortly defines what true and legitimate conversion is. He says, that when any one is thus converted, that his life is prepared for God, since God will forget all his sins. This is a confirmation of the doctrine; for God cannot be entreated as long as he imputes our sins to us: hence, that we may determine him to be propitious to us, he promises, as soon as we repent, that all our sins shall be buried, and no longer come into remembrance. But this is the incomparable goodness of God, since he deigns to forget all our sins as soon as he sees us earnestly desirous of returning to him. On the whole, Ezekiel pronounces that all the penitent pass at once from death to life, since God blots out all their transgressions by voluntary oblivion. It afterwards follows—

| 23. Have I any pleasure at all that the wicked should die? saith the Lord God; *and* not that he should return from his ways, and live? | 23. An cupio cupiendo mortem impii, dicit Dominator Iehovah? An non ut convertatur a viis suis, et vivat? |

He confirms the same sentiment in other words, that God desires nothing more earnestly than that those who were perishing and rushing to destruction should return into the way of safety. And for this reason not only is the Gospel spread abroad in the world, but God wished to bear witness through all ages how inclined he is to pity. For although the heathen were destitute of the law and the prophets, yet they were always endued with some taste of this doctrine. Truly enough they were suffocated by many errors: but we shall always find that they were induced by a secret impulse to seek for pardon, because this sense was in some way born with them, that God is to be appeased by all who seek him.

Besides, God bore witness to it more clearly in the law and the prophets. In the Gospel we hear how familiarly he addresses us when he promises us pardon. (Luke i. 78.) And this is the knowledge of salvation, to embrace his mercy which he offers us in Christ. It follows, then, that what the Prophet now says is very true, that God wills not the death of a sinner, because he meets him of his own accord, and is not only prepared to receive all who fly to his pity, but he calls them towards him with a loud voice, when he sees how they are alienated from all hope of safety. But the manner must be noticed in which God wishes all to be saved, namely, *when they turn themselves from their ways.* God thus does not so wish all men to be saved as to renounce the difference between good and evil; but repentance, as we have said, must precede pardon. How, then, does God wish all men to be saved? By the Spirit's condemning the world of sin, of righteousness, and of judgment, at this day, by the Gospel, as he did formerly by the law and the prophets. (John xvi. 8.) God makes manifest to mankind their great misery, that they may betake themselves to him: he wounds that he may cure, and slays that he may give life. We hold, then, that God wills not the death of a sinner, since he calls all equally to repentance, and promises himself prepared to receive them if they only seriously repent. If any one should object—then there is no election of God, by which he has predestinated a fixed number to salvation, the answer is at hand: the Prophet does not here speak of God's secret counsel, but only recalls miserable men from despair, that they may apprehend the hope of pardon, and repent and embrace the offered salvation. If any one again objects—this is making God act with duplicity, the answer is ready, that God always wishes the same thing, though by different ways, and in a manner inscrutable to us. Although, therefore, God's will is simple, yet great variety is involved in it, as far as our senses are concerned. Besides, it is not surprising that our eyes should be blinded by intense light, so that we cannot certainly judge how God wishes all to be saved, and yet has devoted all the reprobate to eternal destruction, and wishes them to perish. While we look now through a glass darkly, we should be content with the measure of our own intelligence. (1 Cor. xiii. 12.) When we shall be like God, and see him face to face, then what is now obscure will then become plain. But since captious men torture this and similar passages, it will be needful to refute them shortly, since it can be done without trouble.

God is said *not to wish the death of a sinner*. How so? since he wishes all to be converted. Now we must see how God wishes all to be converted; for repentance is surely his peculiar gift: as it is his office to create men, so it is his province to renew them, and restore his image within them. For this reason we are said to be his workmanship, that is, his fashioning. (Eph. ii. 10.) Since, therefore, repentance is a kind of second creation, it follows that it is not in man's power; and if it is equally in God's power to convert men as well as to create them, it follows that the reprobate are not converted, because God does not wish their conversion; for if he wished it he could do it: and hence it appears that he does not wish it. But again they argue foolishly, since God does not wish all to be converted, he is himself deceptive, and nothing can be certainly stated concerning his paternal benevolence. But this knot is easily untied; for he does not leave us in suspense when he says, that he wishes all to be saved. Why so? for if no one repents without finding God propitious, then this sentence is filled up. But we must remark that God puts on a twofold character: for he here wishes to be taken at his word. As I have already said, the Prophet does not here dispute with subtlety about his incomprehensible plans, but wishes to keep our attention close to God's word. Now, what are the contents of this word? The law, the prophets, and the gospel. Now all are called to repentance, and the hope of salvation is promised them when they repent: this is true, since God rejects no returning sinner: he pardons all without exception; meanwhile, this will of God which he sets forth in his word does not prevent him from decreeing before the world was created what he would do with every individual: and as I have now said, the Prophet only shows here, that when we have been converted we need not doubt that God immediately meets us and shows himself propitious. The remainder to-morrow.

PRAYER.

Grant, Almighty God, since we are all lost in ourselves, that we may desire to obtain life where it is laid up for us, and where thou dost manifest it, namely, in thy Son : and grant that we may so embrace the grace which has been exhibited to us in the sacrifice of his death, that we may be regenerated by his Spirit; and thus being born again, may we devote ourselves wholly to thee, and so glorify thy name in this world, that we may at length be partakers of that glory which the same, thine onlybegotten Son, has acquired for us.—Amen.

Lecture Fifty-Seventh.

24. But when the righteous turneth away from his righteousness, and committeth iniquity, *and* doeth according to all the abominations that the wicked *man* doeth, shall he live ? All his righteousness that he hath done shall not be mentioned : in his trespass that he hath trespassed, and in his sin that he hath sinned, in them shall he die.

24. Et si aversus fuerit justus à justitia sua, et fecerit iniquitatem, secundum omnes abominationes quas facit impius fecerit, an vivet ? Omnes justitiæ ejus quas fecit non venient in recordationem :[1] in transgressione qua transgressus est, et in scelere, quo scelerate egit, in ipsis morietur.

As in the last lecture the Prophet offered to sinners a sure hope of pardon if they heartily repented, and promised that God would be propitious to them as soon as they shall seek reconciliation with him ; so now, on the other hand, he pronounces, *if the just shall decline from his justice*, whatever he has hitherto done, shall not come into the account before God. He urged sinners to repentance when he assured them that God was prepared to pardon them : but he now frightens those who profess for the occasion to be pure and sincere worshippers of God, if they fall back in the midst of their course ; as Paul says, Let him who stands take heed lest he fall. (1 Cor. x. 12.) Besides, we gather from this passage, as Christ teaches, that those only are happy who persevere, (Matt. xxiv. 13 ;) since a temporary righteousness will never profit those apostates who afterwards turn aside from God. We see, then, how these two clauses unite together, namely, that God invites all who are

---

[1] That is, " be taken into account."—*Calvin.*

in danger of perdition with extended arms, and promises them salvation if they heartily return to him. Again, that he may restrain within the bounds of duty those who have made some progress, and correct their sloth, and stir up their anxiety, he threatens, that unless they pursue the course of a holy and pious life to the end, their former righteousness will not profit them. But here a question arises, Can a truly just person deflect from the right way? for he who is begotten of God is so free from the tyranny of sin that he devotes himself wholly to righteousness: and then if any do turn aside, they prove that they were always strangers to God. If they had been of us, says John, they would never have gone out from us. (1 John ii. 19.) And regeneration is an incorruptible seed: so we must determine that the faithful who are truly regenerate never fall away from righteousness, but are retained by God's unconquered power: for God's calling in the elect is without repentance. (Rom. xi. 29.) Hence he continues the course of his grace even to the end. Nor are they to be listened to, who, in contradiction to Scripture, teach that faith is extinct in the elect, when, through its barrenness, they bring forth no fruit. In what sense, then, does Ezekiel mean that the just fall away? That question is easily answered, since he is not here treating of the living root of justice, but of the outward form or appearance, as we commonly say. Paul reminds us that God knows us, but adds, that this seal remains. (2 Tim. ii. 19.) God therefore claims to himself alone the difference between the elect and the reprobate, since many seem to be members of his Church who are only outwardly such. And that passage of Augustine is true, that there are many wolves within, and many sheep without.[1] For before God demonstrates his election, the sheep wander, and seem altogether strangers to the hope of salvation. Meanwhile many hypocrites make use of the name of God, and openly boast themselves pre-eminent in the Church, but inwardly they are wolves. But because it often happens that some make the greatest show of piety and justice, the Prophet very properly says, that if such fall away, they cannot boast of their

---

[1] Augustin. Comment. in Joan., cap. x. 16.

former righteousness before God, since its remembrance will be blotted out.

In fine, we see that the word righteousness is referred to our senses, and not to God's hidden judgment; so that the Prophet does not teach anything but what we perceive daily: for those who seem to excel others desert their calling, shake off every yoke, and cast away the fear of God, and sometimes rush on with diabolical fury. When this result occurs we hear what the Spirit pronounces by the mouth of the Prophet, *that none of their righteousness shall be taken into account.* But weight is added to his words when he says, *if he have turned aside from righteousness, and done according to all the abominations of the impious,* (or wicked,) *shall he live?* For the Prophet separates those who desert God and rush into every wickedness from those who fall through infirmity or want of thought, and from those also who would fall headlong into ruin, unless God preserved them, yet do not utterly cast off his fear, and the desire of living piously and righteously. For example—every one is occasionally off his guard; and hence, in numberless ways, we offend God through error: and hence David exclaims, Who can understand his faults? (Ps. xix. 12.) We fall of our own accord, since we are often conquered by temptations, even when our consciences accuse us; so that, although sanctified, we decline from the path of uprightness through ignorance, and depart from duty through infirmity. But what is far worse, the saints sometimes rush headlong, as though utterly desperate. For the example of David shows that the elect, although regenerated by God's Spirit, not only sin to a small extent, but, as I have said, plunge into the very lowest abyss. David became a perfidious homicide, and a traitor to the army of God; then that wretched king fell into a series of crimes: yet he failed in only one thing, and showed that God's grace was only suffocated within him, and not altogether extinguished. For as soon as Nathan reproves him, he confesses that he had sinned, and is prepared to undergo any punishment which God may inflict. Since, therefore, the saints sometimes fall, the Prophet here stretches forth his hand, lest they should despair, and bears witness that God does not reject them unless *they turn aside from their righteousness and commit all the abominations which the impious do.* By these words, as we see, he expresses a complete revolt, and he so mitigates the severity of the sentence, lest the minds of those who had only partially relapsed should despond. Now we see the meaning of this language: *If he has done according to all the abominations of the wicked, shall he live?* says he; *all the righteousness which he has done shall not be remembered, because he shall perish.* Here the Prophet shows that a mere temporary righteousness will not profit us unless we persevere unto the end in the fear of God.

Here again the contrast is worthy of notice, because it enables us to refute a fiction which is current in the schools of the papacy. They say that guilt is remitted by God, but the punishment is retained. Now what says our Prophet? *If the impious turn away from his impiety, I will no longer remember any of his iniquities.* Here the papists thrust forward the foolish distinction, that God does not remember them as to their guilt, but he does as to their punishment. But what follows a little afterwards? *If the just turn away from his justice, his justice shall not be taken into account.* But if they do not come into the account as to merit, and yet do as to reward, what is the meaning of the passage? how will the Prophet's meaning stand? But it is necessary thus to receive what the Prophet says; because, if the distinction of guilt and punishment avails, that of merit and reward will avail also. Hence it will follow, that as to merit God forgets all acts of righteousness; but as far as reward is concerned, they are remembered since they are not abolished. Since, then, it is sufficiently clear that the righteousness of the backslider is not taken into account, so as to lead him to hope for reward, it follows, on the other hand, that his sins are abolished not only as to guilt, but also as to punishment. It now follows—

25. Yet ye say, The way of the Lord is not equal. Hear now, O house of Israel, Is not my way equal? are not your ways unequal?	25. Et dixistis, Non rectificata est via Domini: audite agedum domus Israel, Via mea non rectificabitur?[1] An non viæ vestræ non sunt rectæ?[2]

[1] That is, "is not straightforward."—*Calvin.*

[2] תכן, *theken,* signifies "to weigh;" but it means also "to balance accurately."—*Calvin.*

The Prophet here shows that those who used the vulgar taunt—that the children's teeth were set on edge, because their fathers had eaten sour grapes—had broken away from all restraint; and nothing further remained to hinder them from uttering their blasphemies arrogantly against God: but their insolence and madness now increases when they say *that God's ways are not equal.* And this is discerned in almost all hypocrites: at first they indirectly find fault with God, and yet pretend not to do so: while they endeavour to excuse themselves, they accuse him of injustice, and of too much rigour, yet they do not openly break out into such impiety as to dare to charge God with this crime: but after they profit nothing by their double dealing, the devil enflames them to such a pitch of boldness that they hesitate not openly to condemn God himself. The Prophet refers to this when he says that this disgraceful saying was bandied about among the Israelites, *that the ways of the Lord are unequal.* Lest, therefore, we should happen to resist God, and to contend with him, let us learn to restrain our rashness in good time before he becomes enraged against us. As soon as any thoughts spring up, tending to reflect upon the character of the Almighty, let us quickly restrain them; for if we do not, they will entangle us by degrees, and draw us into the extremity of folly, and then no sense of either religion or shame will deter us from open rebellion against God. But it is worth while noticing the source of this impiety: first of all, when we think of men's relation to God, they should be ashamed to rise up against their Maker: for the clay does not cry out against the potter; and we are a hundredfold more insignificant than the clay, with reference to God. (Is. xlv. 9; Rom. ix. 20, 21.)

But let us come to another consideration. We know with how much greater clearness the angels are able reverently to adore God's wisdom than the human race. What, therefore, must we do? Not only is God's wisdom incomprehensible, but his justice is the most perfect rule of all justice. Now, if we desire to pass opinions upon God's works according to our own perceptions, and to weigh them in our balance, what else are we doing but passing judgment upon him?

But we must remember that passage of Isaiah, As I live, saith Jehovah, every knee shall bend before me, and every tongue shall swear by me. (Chap. xlv. 23.) Paul, too, is a faithful interpreter of this sentiment, when he forbids mortals to judge arrogantly, by saying, we shall all stand before the judgment-seat of Christ. (Rom. xiv. 10, 11.) Since, then, it will be necessary for us to render an account before Christ's heavenly tribunal, we must now acquiesce in God's judgments; because, when at length our license has entirely spent itself, and our petulance has had its full scope, God will be our judge. We see, therefore, that when men claim to themselves the right of daring to pronounce their own opinions on God's work, they first subject his wisdom to their own fictions, and then feel too much hostility and contempt towards his justice. But this one thing ought to be sufficient, that men are too forgetful of their own condition when they dare to open their mouth against their Maker, not only to murmur, but openly to condemn him, as if they were his superiors. Let us then obey the contrary rule; let us with sobriety and modesty learn to look upon those works of God which are unknown to us, and to concede to him the praise of supreme wisdom, although his counsels seem at first sight contradictory. Hosea also briefly reminds us of this. For after God had promised that he would be merciful to the people, and when he had discoursed on the slaughter which he had inflicted, he says, that at length he would heal them: he adds, Who is wise, and he shall understand these things? (chap. xiv. 9;) because many might have thought it inconsistent to remit so many sins for the abandoned people; and others might object that what they heard was utterly incredible and absurd, since God suffered the people to be utterly torn to pieces, so that no hope remained. For this reason, then, the Prophet exclaims, that we have need of rare and singular prudence to comprehend and embrace that teaching. When he says, "who is wise?" it signifies that the number is but small of those who will wait patiently till God really fulfils his promises. Yet he adds, because the ways of the Lord are right, and the just shall walk in them; but the impious shall stumble and perish.

When he speaks here of the ways of the Lord, he does not mean only precepts, though the Scriptures often take the word in this sense; but he means the whole order of government which God upholds, and all the judgments which he exercises. He says, therefore, that all the ways of the Lord are right, and the just shall walk in them, since the just will give God the glory calmly, and with the proper docility; and when they are agitated by various doubts, and through their infirmity are ever in a ferment through the force of many temptations, yet they will always repose on the providence of God, and briefly determine, by cutting off every occasion for long and perplexing and thorny questions, that God is just. Thus the just walk in the ways of the Lord, because they submit to all his works.

He says also, that the impious stumble and fall; for as soon as they begin to think that God does not act rightly or prudently, they are rebellious, and are carried away by blind impulse, and their pride at length hurries them headlong into madness. Thus they stumble in the ways of the Lord, because, as we see in this passage, they vomit forth their blasphemies against God. Hence we ought to be influenced by this course of action, namely, adoring with humility the counsel of God, although to us incomprehensible, and attributing the praise of justice to all his works, though in our opinion they may not correspond, or be consistent with each other.— This, then, is the sum of the whole. Although the Prophet speaks of the penalties which God inflicts on the reprobate, and of the reward which he has laid up for the just, yet we ought to ascend still higher; and if God in his deeds seems to pervert the whole course of justice, yet we should always be sustained by this bridle—he is just; and if his deeds are disapproved by us, it arises from our error and ignorance. For example, we not only contend with God when he seems not to repay us a just reward for our good works, or when he seems too severe towards us; but when his eternal election is discussed, we immediately roar out, because we cannot penetrate to so great a height: the pious, indeed, are not altogether free from perplexing doubts which disturb them, but they restrain themselves directly as I have said. But some restive men break out in this way,—I do not comprehend—I do not understand: hence God is unjust. We see how many blusterers in the present day betray their desperate impudence, whence this teaching should recur to our minds—*the ways of God are right.* But since we do not perceive how it is so, another clause is added, *that our ways are not right;* that is, that all our senses are defective, and our intellect blinded, and that we are all so corrupt that our judgment is perverted. If, therefore, we conclude with the Prophet, *that our ways are not right,* the glory of God's justice will remain untarnished and entire. Afterwards he adds—

26. When a righteous *man* turneth away from his righteousness, and committeth iniquity, and dieth in them; for his iniquity that he hath done shall he die.
27. Again, when the wicked *man* turneth away from his wickedness that he hath committed, and doeth that which is lawful and right, he shall save his soul alive.
28. Because he considereth, and turneth away from all his transgressions that he hath committed, he shall surely live, he shall not die.

26. Si aversus fuerit justus a justitia sua, et fecerit iniquitatem et mortuus fuerit in illis,[1] in iniquitate sua quam patravit morietur.
27. Et si conversus fuerit sceleratus a sceleribus suis quæ fecit, et fecerit judicium et justitiam, ipse animam suam vivificabit.[2]
28. Et viderit, et conversus fuerit ab omnibus sceleribus quæ patravit, vivendo vivet, non morietur.

The Prophet repeats what we formerly saw, namely, that the state of the case turned upon this, Whether the people had any cause of complaint when God absolves those who repent, and condemns the just who desert the course of a pious and holy life? Now, we must always return to this cardinal point, that God rewards every one according to his works, since he offers mercy to all the lost, and demands nothing else but a sincere and hearty return to him. Since, then, God treats the impious with such clemency, and is so ready to pardon them, what is the reason why men contend with him? If the just should retrace his steps, and after having shown some signs of the fear of God, throw off all obedience, who can object when God punishes him, and blots out the remembrance of his former righteousness? God,

[1] The number is changed from singular to plural, " in his wickedness."—*Calvin.*
[2] That is, "he shall snatch from death, or restore to life."—*Calvin.*

therefore, determines the result fairly in each case. We have explained how the phrase, *the just should turn aside from their righteousness*, ought to be understood, not that the elect ever utterly fall away, as many think their faith is extinguished, and every root of piety also in the sons of God; that is too absurd, because, as I have said, the gift of regeneration has perseverance always annexed to it: but here that righteousness which mankind recognise is intended. But we know how frequently it happens that what seemed entirely pure and perfect is deficient. Now, God pronounces that he would punish all who fall away from him, and would be accessible and propitious to miserable sinners who desire to be reconciled to him; and he repeats again, if *the wicked has seen and turned away from his wickedness*. We must mark this phrase, for it shows that thinking rightly is the commencement of repentance; because, though the reprobate knowingly and willingly transgress God's law, it is certain that they labour under blindness and madness, so that the Scripture does not call them foolish and beside themselves in vain. He does not extenuate their faults, as if they sinned ignorantly; but he means that they were so blinded by diabolical madness as to think of nothing; for surely horror would immediately possess their minds if they only perceived God to be their adversary, and themselves to be making war with him. For this reason, therefore, when the Prophet describes to us the conversion of the wicked, he says, *if he has seen;* that is, if at length he has returned to a sound mind, and collected his senses, so that he may not rush on madly, as he has been accustomed to do, but may look upon both God and himself. It now follows—

29. Yet saith the house of Israel, The way of the Lord is not equal. O house of Israel, are not my ways equal? are not your ways unequal?   29. Et dixerunt domus Israel,[1] non rectificata est[2] via Domini: An viæ meæ non rectæ sunt, domus Israel? An non viæ vestræ non rectæ sunt?

Here God briefly shows how furious those are who dare to rebel against him even when his justice is manifest: for what can be desired more justly than that God should punish all the transgressors of his law? and also, if sinners repent,

[1] That is, "the Israelites said."—*Calvin*.
[2] The tense is future, but continued action is intended.—*Calvin*.

that he should be prepared to pardon them? But if it seems hard that punishment should overtake the just if they fall away, common sense dictates that no virtue can be approved without perseverance. Since, therefore, it is very clear throughout this course of action, that God is just and without blame, what madness it is to vomit forth blasphemies against him, as if his ways were unjust! But God shows in one word, as I have mentioned, that the Israelites had no excuse for such dishonesty and impudence; and he repeats what he had formerly said, that men would always be guilty of rashness in insolently cursing God when their own ways are found oblique and perverse: but God will sufficiently vindicate his own ways. But we must add what follows—

| 30. Therefore I will judge you, O house of Israel, every one according to his ways, saith the Lord God. Repent, and turn *yourselves* from all your transgressions; so iniquity shall not be your ruin. | 30. Propterea quemque[1] secundum vias ejus judicabo in vobis,[2] domus Israel, dicit Dominator Iehovah. Convertimini et redire vos facite[3] ab omnibus sceleribus vestris, et non erit vobis in laqueum iniquitas. |

Here God precisely points out that he would discharge the office of judge, and then he reduces the Israelites to order, and refutes their audacity: for, as long as men do not feel God's judgments hanging over them, and are not held completely in check, they grow restive in their petulance. We see how ferocious and wanton the reprobate are, because they are not held in by the fear of punishment, nor do they dread the judgments of God. Hence that he may take away every vestige of excuse, he says, *I will be your judge:* plead now; but I will decide your strifes in one word, since each of you shall be judged by my will. It is certain, then, that God here asserts for himself the praise of justice and rectitude; but at the same time he brings forward his own authority, that he may strike terror into those who thus madly dare to oppose his sway, and call upon him to render an account. Now, therefore, we understand in what sense he says that *he will judge them all according to their ways;* that is, although ye do not confess yourselves worthy of destruction, it is sufficient that I, as the lawful judge, pro-

---

[1] Verbally, " each man."—*Calvin.*   [2] Or, " between you."—*Calvin.*
[3] " And bring you back:" others, " bring your neighbours back;" but this is far-fetched. I prefer " bring yourselves back."—*Calvin.*

nounce you so. *I will judge you justly*, therefore, since I pronounce sentence *according to your ways* and to my supreme power, that all your complaints and murmurs may cease. He afterwards exhorts them to repentance, and signifies that they have no other remedy than being dissatisfied with their sins, and deprecating his wrath. Hence we collect that men rebel so extravagantly against God, while they wander away from themselves, since, if they descended within themselves, and sincerely examined their whole life, they would be instantly humbled before God; hence that thought should stimulate them to repentance: but because their conscience is stupid, and they are willingly brutish, they boldly blaspheme God. On the other hand, God now offers a remedy on their repentance and return from their wickedness. The word being converted, or return, refers to the renovation of the mind and heart: for this also is the beginning of repentance, that we should be inwardly renewed in mind, as Paul says, and so be made new men. (Eph. iv. 22, 23.) And this deserves notice, because many, when repentance is spoken of, fix their eyes only on the outward fruits of penitence. But we must begin at the root, as the Prophet teaches, by saying *be ye converted*. But he afterwards adds, והשיבו, *veheshibu, and return*. This second word ought to be referred to the fruits of penitence; for as interior conversion comes first in order, when we leave off our peculiar vices, and renounce flesh and blood, the fruits and proofs of repentance ought to follow, as John said, Bring forth fruits as witnesses to your repentance. (Matt. iii. 8; Luke iii. 8.) We see, then, that the Prophet begins with purity of heart, and then comes to hands, as the Scripture elsewhere says, that is, to outward works. He says, *from all your iniquities* or crimes, to show that a partial repentance is not approved by God. It is true, indeed, that even those who strive with all their might to act rightly, do not succeed in discharging their duty without many faults remaining; but we are not treating here of perfection, but only of sincere affection and serious endeavours. Let us then only strive seriously to return into the way, and to humble ourselves calmly and sincerely: this is the integrity which the Prophet now requires.

PRAYER.

Grant, Almighty God, since nothing is more frail than we are, and even when thou hast once stretched forth thine hand to us, we labour under such infirmity, that numberless falls await us unless thou dost succour us: Grant, I say, that being propped up by thine unconquered strength, we may proceed in the course of thy holy calling, and may so bravely and perseveringly make war against all temptations, that we may at length enjoy in heaven the fruit of our victory, through Christ our Lord.—Amen.

Lecture Fifty-Eighth.

31. Cast away from you all your transgressions, whereby ye have transgressed; and make you a new heart and a new spirit: for why will ye die, O house of Israel?	31. Projicite a vobis omnes iniquitates in quibus inique egistis: et facite vobis cor novum, et spiritum novum: et quare moriemini domus Israel?

EZEKIEL again exhorts the people to leave off complaining, and to acknowledge that there is no remedy for their evils but to be reconciled to God. But that cannot be done unless they repent. For God was not hostile to them in vain; nor did he, after the manner of men, persecute with hatred the innocent, and those who did not deserve it. Hence it was necessary to seek God's pardon suppliantly. Ezekiel had already touched upon this, but he now confirms it more at length. He says, therefore, that they not only lost their labour, but increased the flame of God's wrath by striving with him, and complaining that they were unworthily treated by him: *cast forth,* says he, *your iniquities from you.* He shows that the cause of all evils is within themselves: so that they have no excuse. But he afterwards expresses more clearly that they were entirely imbued with contempt of God, impiety, and depraved desires. For if he had only spoken of outward wickedness, the reproof would have been partial, and therefore lighter; but after he commanded them to bid farewell to their sins, he adds, *make yourselves a new heart and a new spirit.* He requires, therefore, from them a thorough renewal, so that they should not only conform their life to the rule of the law, but should fear God sincerely, since no one can produce good fruit but from a living root. Outward works, then, are the fruits of repentance, which must spring from some root; and this is the inward affection of the heart. What is added is to refute their impiety, for they wished their destruction to be ascribed to God. Here God takes up the character of a mourner, saying, *Why will ye die, O house of Israel?* while the next verse confirms this more clearly.

| 32. For I have no pleasure in the death of him that dieth, saith the Lord God: wherefore turn *yourselves*, and live ye. | 32. Quia non oblector morte morientis, dicit Dominator Iehovah : convertimini itaque, et vivite. |

We see, therefore, how God throws off that false reproach from himself with which the children of Israel taunted him, saying, that they perished by his immoderate rigour, and could find no reason for his severity against them. He announces, on the other hand, that the cause of death rested with themselves; and then he points out the remedy, that they should amend their life, not only in outward appearance, but in sincerity of heart: and at the same time he testifies his willingness to be entreated; nay, he meets them of his own accord, if they only repent heartily and unfeignedly. We now understand the Prophet's meaning. We said, that we are admonished in this way, that if we desire to return to God we must begin at the beginning, namely, renewal of the heart and spirit; because, as Jeremiah says, he looks for truth and integrity, and does not value outward disguises. (Chap. v. 3.) But it may seem absurd for God to exhort the Israelites *to form their hearts anew:* and men badly trained in the Scriptures erect their crests under the pretence of this passage, as if it were in the power of man's free will to convert himself. They exclaim, therefore, either that God here exhorts his people deceitfully, or else that when alienated from him we can by our own movement repent, and return into the way. But the whole Scripture openly refutes this. It is not in vain that the saints so often pray that God would renew them; (Ps. li. 12, and very often elsewhere;) for it would be a feigned and a lying prayer, if newness of heart were not his gift. If any one requests of God what he is persuaded that he has already, and by his own inherent virtue, does he not trifle with God?

But nothing occurs more frequently than this mode of entreaty. Since, therefore, the saints pray to God to renew them, they doubtless confess that to be his peculiar gift; and unless he moves his hand, they have no strength remaining, so that they can never rise from the ground. Besides, in many passages God claims the renewal of the heart as peculiar to himself. We noticed that remarkable passage in the eleventh chapter of this Prophet, (ver. 19,) he will repeat the same in the thirty-sixth chapter, (ver. 26, 27;) and we know what Jeremiah says in his thirty-first chapter, (ver. 33.) But Scripture is everywhere full of testimonies of this kind, so that it would be superfluous to heap together many passages; nay, if any one denies that regeneration is a gift of the Holy Spirit, he will tear up by the roots all the principles of piety. We have said that regeneration is like another creation; and if we compare it with the first creation, it far surpasses it. For it is much better for us to be made children of God, and reformed after his image within us, than to be created mortal: for we are born children of wrath, corrupt and degenerate; (Eph. ii. 3;) since all integrity was lost when God's image was removed. We see, then, the nature of our first creation; but when God refashions us, we are not only born sons of Adam, but we are the brothers of angels, and members of Christ; and this our second life consists in rectitude, justice, and the light of true intelligence.

We now see that if it had been in man's free will to convert himself, much more would be ascribed to him than to God, because, as we have said, it was much more valuable to be created sons of God than of Adam. It ought, then, to be beyond all controversy with the pious that men cannot rise again when they are fallen, and turn of themselves when alienated from God; but this is the peculiar gift of the Holy Spirit. And the sophists, who in all ways endeavour to obscure God's grace, confess that half the act of conversion is in the power of the Holy Spirit: for they do not say that we are simply and totally converted by the motion of our own free will, but they imagine a concurrence of grace with free will, and of free will with grace. Thus they foolishly represent us as co-operating with God: they confess, indeed, that God's grace goes before and follows; and they seem to themselves very liberal towards God when they acknowledge this twofold grace in man's conversion. But God is not content with that partition, since he is deprived of half his right: for he does not say that he would assist men to renew themselves and to repent; but he attributes the work to himself entirely: I will give you a new heart and a new spirit. (Ezek. xxxvi. 26.) If it is his to give, it follows that the slightest portion of it cannot be transferred to man without diminishing something from his right. But they object that the following precept is not in vain, *that men should make for themselves a new heart.* Now their deception arises through ignorance, from their judging of the powers of men by the commands of God; but the inference is incorrect, as we have said elsewhere: for when God teaches what is right, he does not think of what we are able to do, but only shows us what we ought to do. When, therefore, the power of our free will is estimated by the precepts of God, we make a great mistake, because God exacts from us the strict discharge of our duty, just as if our power of obedience was not defective. We are not absolved from our obligation because we cannot pay it; for God holds us bound to himself, although we are in every way deficient.

They object again, God then deludes men when he says, *make yourselves a new heart.* I answer, we must always consider to what purpose God thus speaks, namely, that men convicted of sin may cease to throw the blame on any one else, as they often endeavour to do; for nothing is more natural than to transfer the cause of our condemnation away from ourselves, that we may seem just, and God appear unjust. Since, then, such depravity reigns among men, hence the Holy Spirit demands from us what all acknowledge they ought to pay: and if we do not pay it, still we are bound to do so, and thus all strife and complaint should cease. Thus, as it concerns the elect, when God shows them their duty, and they acknowledge that they cannot discharge it, they fly to the aid of the Holy Spirit, so that the outward exhortation becomes a kind of instrument which

God uses to confer the grace of his Spirit. For although he gratuitously goes before us, and does not need outward channels, yet he desires exhortations to be useful to this end. Since, therefore, this doctrine stirs up the elect to deliver themselves up to be ruled by the Holy Spirit, we see how it becomes fruitful to us. Whence it follows, that God does not delude or deceive us when he exhorts *each of us to form his heart and his spirit afresh*. In fine, Ezekiel wished by these words to show that pardon would be prepared for the Israelites if they seriously repented, and showed its effects through their whole life. That was most true, because the elect did not embrace this doctrine in vain, when at the same time God worked in them by his Spirit, and so turned them to himself. But the reprobate, though they do not cease to murmur, yet they are rendered ashamed, since all excuse has been removed, and they must perish through their own fault, since they willingly remained in their wickedness, and by self-indulgence they cherished the old man within themselves,—a fountain of all injustice. Whenever such passages occur, let us remember that celebrated prayer of Augustine: Grant us what you command, and command what you wish, (Epist. xxiv. ;) for otherwise, if God should lay upon us the slightest burden, we should be unable to bear it. Besides, our strength will be sufficient to fulfil his requirements, if only he supply it, and we are not so foolish as to think anything comprehended in his precepts which he has not granted to us ; because, as I have said before, nothing is more perverse than to measure the angelic righteousness of the law by our strength. By the word *heart*, I understand him to mean the seat of all the affections ; and by *spirit*, the intellectual part of the soul. The heart is often taken for the reason and intelligence ; but when these two words are joined together, the spirit relates to the mind, and so it is the intellectual faculty of the soul ; but the heart is taken for the will, or the seat of all the affections. Hence we see how very corrupt the Israelites were, since they could not be otherwise reconciled to God, unless by being renewed in both heart and mind. Hence also we may gather the general doctrine, that nothing in us is sound and perfect, and hence an entire renovation is necessary that we may please God.

The subjoined phrase, *why will ye die, O house of Israel?* suggests many questions. Here unskilful men think that God speculates on what men will do, and that the salvation or destruction of each depends on themselves, as if God had determined nothing concerning us before the foundation of the world. Hence they set him at nought, since they fancy that he is held in suspense and doubt as to the future end of every one, and that he is not so anxious for our salvation, as to wish all to be saved, but leaves it in the power of every one to perish or to be saved as he pleases. But as I have said, this would reduce God to a spectre. But we have no need of a long dispute, because Scripture everywhere declares with sufficient clearness that God has determined what shall happen to us: for he chose his own people before the foundation of the world and passed by others. (Eph. i. 4.) Nothing is clearer than this doctrine; for if there had been no predestination on God's part, there had been no deity, since he would be forced into order as if he were one of us: nay, men are to a certain extent provident, whenever God allows some sparks of his image to shine forth in them. If, therefore, the very smallest drop of foresight in men is laid hold of, how great must it be in the fountain itself? Insipid indeed is the comment, to fancy that God remains doubtful and waiting for what will happen to individuals, as if it were in their own power either to attain to salvation or to perish. But the Prophet's words are plain, for God testifies with grief that he *willeth not the death of a mortal.* I answer, that there is no absurdity, as we said before, in God's undertaking a twofold character, not that he is two-faced himself, as those profane dogs blurt out against us, but because his counsels are incomprehensible by us. This indeed ought to be fixed, that before the foundation of the world we were predestinated either to life or death. Now because we cannot ascend to that height, it is needful for God to conform himself to our ignorance, and to descend in some way to us since we cannot ascend to him. When Scripture so often says that God has heard, and inquires, no one is offended:

all pass over those forms of speech securely, and confess them adopted from human language. (Gen. xvi. 11, and often.) Very often, I say, God transfers to himself the properties of man, and this is admitted universally without either offence or controversy. Although this manner of speaking is rather harsh: God came to see, (Gen. xi. 5,) when he announces that he came to inquire about things openly known; it is easily excused, since nothing is less in accordance with his nature: for the solution is at hand, namely, that God speaks metaphorically, and adapts his speech to the convenience of men. Now why will not the same reasoning avail in the present case? for with respect to the law and the whole teaching of the prophets, God announces his wish that all should be saved. And surely if we consider the tendency of the heavenly teaching, we shall find that all are promiscuously called to salvation. For the law was a way of life, as Moses testifies, This is the way, walk ye in it: again, Whosoever has done those things shall live in them: and, again, This is your life. (Deut. xxx. 15, 19; xxxii. 47; Lev. xviii. 5; Is. xxx. 21.) Then of his own accord God offers himself as merciful to his ancient people, so that this heavenly teaching ought to be life-giving. But what is the Gospel? It is God's power unto salvation to every believer, says Paul. (Rom. i. 16.) Therefore God *delighteth not in the death of him who dieth*, if he repent at his teaching. But if we wish to penetrate to his incomprehensible counsel, this will be another objection: Oh! but in this way God is chargeable with duplicity;—but I have denied this, though he takes up a twofold character, because this was necessary for our comprehension. Meanwhile Ezekiel announces this very truly as far as doctrine is concerned, *that God willeth not the death of him that perisheth:* for the explanation follows directly afterwards, *be ye converted and live.* Why does not God delight in the death of him who perishes? Because he invites all to repentance and rejects no one. Since this is so, it follows that he is not delighted by the death of him who perishes: hence there is nothing in this passage doubtful or thorny, and we should also hold that we are led aside by speculations too deep for us. For

God does not wish us to inquire into his secret counsels: His secrets are with himself, says Moses, (Deut. xxix. 29,) but this book for ourselves and our children. Moses there distinguishes between the hidden counsel of God, (which if we desire to investigate too curiously we shall tread on a profound abyss,) and the teaching delivered to us. Hence let us leave to God his own secrets, and exercise ourselves as far as we can in the law, in which God's will is made plain to us and to our children. Now let us go on.

CHAPTER XIX.

1. Moreover, take thou up a lamentation for the princes of Israel,
2. And say, What *is* thy mother? A lioness: she lay down among lions, she nourished her whelps among young lions.
3. And she brought up one of her whelps: it became a young lion, and it learned to catch the prey; it devoured men.
4. The nations also heard of him; he was taken in their pit, and they brought him with chains unto the land of Egypt.

1. Et tu tolle lamentum[1] super[2] principes Israel,
2. Et dices, Quare mater vestra leæna inter leones occubuit? in medio leonum educavit catulos suos.
3. Et sustulit unum è catulis suis, leo factus est, et didicit prædari prædam, homines comedit.[3]
4. Et audierunt de ipso Gentes, in fovea ipsarum captus est; et abduxerunt in cathenis in terram Ægypti.

Here the Prophet, under the image of a lion, informs us that whatever evils happened to the Israelites could not be imputed to others. We must understand then his intention: it is not surprising that the Spirit of God insists on a matter not very obscure, since nothing is more obstinate than the pride of men, especially when God chastises them, although they pretend to humility and modesty, yet they swell with pride and are full of bitterness, and, lastly, they can scarcely be induced to confess God to be just, and that they deserve chastisement at his hand. For this reason, therefore, Ezekiel confirms what we formerly saw, that the Jews were not afflicted without deserving it. But he uses, as I have said, a simile taken from lions. He calls *the nation itself a lioness:* for when he treats of the mother of the people, we

---

[1] Or, " a mournful song."—*Calvin.*
[2] Or, " against."—*Calvin.*
[3] Or, " devoured."—*Calvin.*

know that the offspring is considered. He says, therefore, that the people was full of insolence. The comparison to a lion is sometimes taken in a good sense, as when Moses uses it of the tribe of Judah, as a lion's whelp shall he lie down, (Gen. xlix. 9,) a phrase used in a good sense. But here Ezekiel denotes cruelty, as if he had said that all the Jews were fierce and savage beasts. For under the name of mother, as I said, he embraces the whole nation. At the beginning he orders his Prophet to take up *a mournful wailing:* for thus I interpret the word קִינָה, *kineh,* but there is in my judgment an indirect opposition between this lamentation which God dictated to them by his Prophet, and the common complaints which sounded constantly from their tongues. For when their condition was not only ruinous, but utterly deplorable, they made many groanings and bewailings. But at the same time no one extended his thoughts beyond the pressure of present evils: they all exclaimed that they were wretched, but no one was anxious to inquire why they were so or whence their miseries arose; nay, they avoided this contemplation. The Prophet then indirectly reproves them, by stating that this mournful complaint was suggested by God, but yet was very different from that ordinary lamentation and howling in which the Jews stopped at blind grief, and never inquired why God was so hostile to them. *Take up,* therefore, *a lamentation,* says he, *regarding* or against *the princes of Israel.* In this way God does not excuse the people from blame, he only means that not only the common people were lost, but the very flower of the nation and all who were held in honour.

He says next, *that their mother lay down among lions,* alluding to the people's origin from lions, as we said before, when the Prophet calls Judah the descendant of Canaan, and the sister of Sodom and Samaria. When he now says, *their mother lay down among lions,* he means that they were shamefully mixed with the corruptions of the Gentiles, so that they did not differ from them. But God had chosen them as his peculiar people on the very condition of being separate from all the filth of the Gentiles. There was, therefore, a certain withdrawing of God's favour *when the mother of the people lay down among the lions,* that is, when they all promiscuously gave themselves up to the perverse morals and superstitions of the Gentiles. He says, *that she brought up whelps,* or young lions, which she produced to these lions; since their origin was impure, being all Abraham's children, but, as I have said, a degenerate race. He afterwards adds, *that the lion's whelp,* or young lion, *grew up till it became a lion: then it learnt to seize prey,* says he, *and to devour men.* He refers to King Jehoahaz, son of Josiah, (2 Kings xxiii. 30-32:) but he had before asserted that the whole people had a lion's disposition, and that the princes, who were more exalted, were like whelps. As only one lion is here brought forward, it ought to be referred to the violence by which that wicked king manifested his real disposition. But if it be asked whence the lion went forth, the reply is, from amidst his brethren, for they were all lions' whelps, or young lions. They could not administer the government either together or singly, but each devoured his brother, and was devoted to robbery and rapine. The king only, because freed from all fear, could surpass the rest in rapine and robbery with impunity. We see, then, that not only the king was here condemned, but that he becomes the type of the whole nation; because, since no one could restrain his passions, he could rob and devour mankind with unbridled freedom.

He afterwards adds, *that the nations had heard, and were taken in their pit-fall.* Here Ezekiel states that Jehoahaz was hurled from the royal throne, and taken captive by the Egyptians, not only because God had beheld his cruelty, but because the Gentiles had observed it; and it was notorious among them all. In this way he signifies that the cruelty of King Jehoahaz was intolerable: and he mentions him, since all the neighbouring nations had heard of his fame, and had conspired to destroy him; and so *he was taken in their pit, and confined by chains, and led away into Egypt.* He means, as I said, Jehoahaz, whom King Pharaoh-nechoh took captive. (2 Kings xxiii; 2 Chron. xxxvi.) For when he thought that the Egyptians were distracted by foreign wars, he took the opportunity of collecting an army, and endeavoured to seize on certain neighbouring cities. But

Pharaoh, after he was disengaged from other business, entered Judæa, and since Jehoahaz was unable to resist, he was taken. We now understand the Prophet's meaning, namely, when this first calamity and destruction happened to the Jews they were justly chastised, because they were young lions; and a lion had sprung from them whose cruelty was already intolerable to the profane Gentiles: this is the sense of the passage. Now if we consider who was the father of Jehoahaz this will be more detestable. For we know, that if ever any king excelled in piety and every virtue, Josiah was among the number: and from the son being so unlike his father, we perceive his perverse disposition. There can be no doubt that his father desired to instruct him in the fear and worship of God, and to train him to the discharge of the royal office. But if we descend to the whole people, the prodigy will be yet more detestable. For we know with what fervour and zeal Josiah strove to form the morals of the people, so that the kingdom should be entirely renewed. But the people soon declined, so that the Holy Spirit says, *their mother was a lioness, and lay down among lions*, whence we see their depraved nature. It now follows—

5. Now, when she saw that she had waited, *and* her hope was lost, then she took another of her whelps, *and* made him a young lion.	5. Et vidit quod sperasset, perdita esset[1] spes ejus: et sumpsit unum ex catulis suis leonem constituit eum.[2]

I cannot proceed further.

PRAYER.

Grant, Almighty God, since we are all so depraved by nature that we are not only most deserving of being cast into the midst of lions, but are unworthy of being reckoned among thy creatures, that thou mayest extend thy hand to us, and manifest thy wonderful power in reforming us; and may thine image be so renewed in us, that we may daily make more and more progress in true piety and righteousness, until at length all the corruptions of the flesh may be abolished, and we may be partakers of that eternal glory which thine only-begotten Son has acquired for us.—Amen.

[1] " Had perished."—*Calvin.*
[2] That is, " educated or brought him up till he was a lion."—*Calvin.*

Lecture Fifty-Ninth.

WE yesterday read over that sentence in which the Prophet says that Judæa produced another lion after the former had been captured and led into Egypt. Now this ought to be referred to King Jehoiakim, who was appointed by King Nebuchadnezzar, when he had laid waste a part of Egypt, possessed the whole of Judæa, and imposed laws by establishing a king, according to the rights of conquest. But since he also acted perfidiously, he was led away into captivity. The Prophet, therefore, means that the nation did not repent through this single chastisement; nor did it change its disposition, since its mother was a lioness: and not only did it bring forth young lions, but taught them to seize upon their prey till they became grown up. He says, therefore, that *she saw what she had hoped, and her hope was futile*. Some think that the noun "hope" is here repeated by the Prophet—she saw that her hope was lost; lost hope, I say. But the other reading is better—*she saw what she had hoped;* that is, she saw that her hope had not produced any fruit for some time, because the royal throne remained deserted; *therefore she took another of her whelps,* says he, *and made him a lion.* The Prophet again briefly teaches that the whole royal offspring was like young lions. Although, therefore, the lion alone is called king, yet he is said to be taken from a number of whelps; and hence it follows that this denotes the depraved and cruel nature of all. Thus we see that the Jews are indirectly reproved for not returning to soundness of mind, when God punished them severely, and King Jehoahaz was taken. Since, therefore, that punishment did not result in their correction, it follows that their dispositions were depraved; and the Prophet means this when he says, *that she took one of her whelps, and again made it a lion.* It follows—

6. And he went up and down among the lions, he became a young lion, and learned to catch the prey, *and* devoured men.

6. Et incessit in medio leonum, leo fuit, et didicit prædari prædam,[1] homines voravit.

[1] Or, "to seize booty"—an expression more in agreement with the Latin idiom.—*Calvin.*

Ezekiel confirms what I have already briefly touched on, that this second lion was no less savage and cruel than the former, of which he had spoken. As to the phrase, *he walked among lions*, it means that his government was tyrannical, since there was then such foul barbarity in those regions, that kings were scarcely human in their conduct. Since, therefore, kings were then everywhere like lions, the Prophet says that Jehoiakim was not different from them, but in every sense their ally. *He walked*, therefore, he says, *in the midst of lions*, since he imitated their ferocity, which at length he expresses more clearly, *that he became a lion, and was taught to seize his prey*, so as to devour not only animals, but men, thus marking his extreme cruelty. He afterwards adds—

7. And he knew their desolate palaces, and he laid waste their cities; and the land was desolate, and the fulness thereof, by the noise of his roaring.

7. Et contrivit,[1] palatia ejus, et urbes eorum destruxit, et redacta fuit in solitudinem terra, et plenitudo ejus à voce rugitus illius.

He again confirms what he said of the cruelty of King Jehoiakim: but the phrase is mixed, since he retains but a part of the simile, and then speaks without a figure of palaces and cities. Although interpreters incline to a different opinion, and translate—and took notice of his widows: and if the remaining words had suited, this reading would have been better; but I do not see how things so different can be united, as destroying cities and noticing widows. First, those who adopt this comment are obliged to adopt the notion that Jehoiakim destroyed the men and deflowered their widows, since he could not possess them in freedom till they were widows. Every one will admit that this is far-fetched. But the word "afflict" suits tolerably well. And truly the 53d chapter of Isaiah, where Christ is said to be bruised for our griefs, cannot be better explained, (ver. 3.) Some translate, that he experienced sorrows, or knew them, or was acquainted with them, in the passive signification. But those who say that he saw sorrows, or experienced them, do not consider how it suits the passage; and those who say that he was cognisant of griefs, meaning his own, also distort the Prophet's words. I doubt not, therefore, that in this passage it means to afflict. Respecting the noun, I suppose the

[1] Or, "afflicted."—*Calvin.*

letter ל (*l*) taken for ר (*r*); and in Isaiah (chap. xiii. 22) this word is used for palaces: wild beasts shall howl, says the Prophet, בְּאַלְמְנוֹתָיו, *bal-meno-thiv*, that is, in her palaces. The word cannot here mean widows, and all are agreed to take it for palaces; and when the Prophet adds, *that he destroyed cities,* the subject shows us that in the former clause the palaces were afflicted, and then the cities destroyed: the Prophet asserts this simply, and without a figure, though he soon returns to the simile, *that the land was reduced to a desert by the voice of roaring.* Again, he compares King Jehoiakim to a lion; whence it follows, as I said, that the Prophet's language is mixed. Elsewhere, also, the prophets reprove the pride of their king. (Jer. xxii. 15; xxxvi. 30.) For although he was contemptible, yet he raised himself above other kings; hence he is derided, since he was not content with the condition and moderation of his father, who ate and drank,—that is, lived like mankind,—but he desired to raise himself above the race of men. For this cause the Prophet now says, *that cities were destroyed by him, and palaces afflicted by him.* There is a change of number in the pronouns, because the singular number is put in the word "palaces," and the plural in "cities." But we know how frequently this change occurs in the Hebrew language; while as to the sense there is no obscurity, for King Jehoiakim was like a fierce and cruel beast, *because he destroyed cities and pulled down palaces.* But afterwards he adds, *the land was laid waste and made solitary by the voice of his roaring.* Here the Prophet enlarges upon the atrocity of that king, since by his roaring alone he had reduced the land to a desert. He does not speak of claws or teeth, but says that they were all so frightened at the sound of his roaring that the land was waste and solitary. He adds, *the fulness of the land,* by which expression Scripture usually denotes the ornaments of a country. The word comprehends trees, and fruits, and animals, as well as inhabitants; for a land is empty and bare without that clothing; that is, if trees and fruits are taken away as well as men and animals, the face of the land is deserted and deformed, and its state displays its emptiness. It afterwards follows—

8. Then the nations set against him on every side from the provinces, and spread their net over him: he was taken in their pit.

8. Et posuerunt[1] super eum gentes in circuitu, et regionibus, et expanderunt super ipsum rete suum: in fovea ipsarum captus est.

Since the word נתן, *nethen*, is often taken for " to utter a voice," some explain this passage, that the nations came with great clamour against King Jehoiakim, as when an attack is made against a wild beast, the assailants mutually excite and encourage each other. They understand it, that such a clamour was raised on all sides that they rushed with one consent against King Jehoiakim. But since the same word means " to put," it may, in my opinion, be properly applied to counsel, since they took counsel, that is, determined among themselves to take him captive. The passive sense does not suit at all. Now, then, we understand the Prophet's meaning when he says, that *the Gentiles had resolved against him*, that is, had conspired to take him. No doubt the Chaldæans were assisted by all their neighbours. First, we know that the Jews were hated by other nations; then the audacity and rashness of this king provoked many to send for the Babylonians, and eagerly to assist them; and because they scarcely dared to engage in the war by themselves, they conspired against King Jehoiakim under the protection of others. Thus far concerning other nations, for this cannot be meant of the Chaldæans alone; because, although they had other tribes under their sway, yet that monarchy had devoured the Assyrians, whose people made a portion of the Chaldæan army. Then the Prophet speaks of a circuit, and says, that King Jehoiakim was shut in on all sides: hence this must be ascribed to the neighbouring nations, who not only favoured the Babylonians, but assisted them with troops and wealth, as is sufficiently gathered from other passages.

At length he says, *they expanded their net*, by which metaphor he means plans, desires, and efforts. For before the neighbouring nations openly declared war against the Jews, there is no doubt that they took secret counsel as to the best way of attracting the Chaldæans to their side, and

---

[1] Or, " uttered a cry;" some take it passively, " were set against."—*Calvin.*

of insinuating themselves by various arts, as if they were laying snares; although by the word *net* we may also understand whatsoever apparatus they used for destroying King Jehoiakim. In fine, he says that he was *taken in the pit of the nations*, that is, was oppressed as well by snares as by open violence. He uses the word *pitfall*, in accordance with the resemblance of the king to a lion; but there is nothing absurd in extending the phrase to any hostile violence by which Jehoiakim was oppressed. It follows—

9. And they put him in ward in chains, and brought him to the king of Babylon: they brought him into holds, that his voice should no more be heard upon the mountains of Israel.	9. Et posuerunt eum in clausuran,[1] et adduxerunt in cathenis ad regem Babylonis, deduxerunt in munitiones[2] ut non audiatur vox ejus amplius in montibus Israel.

He pursues the same subject, saying, that King Jehoiakim, after being taken captive, was bound with fetters and chains, adding, that he was brought to the king of Babylon; and thirdly, was cast into prison. He shows, therefore, how severely God punished the vicious obstinacy of that nation: for when King Jehoiakim was chastised, it ought to have been enough to correct them; but since the people were not improved by this, the severity was doubled; and here Ezekiel says, *that King Jehoiakim was cast into a fortified dungeon.* He adds, *that his voice*, that is, his roaring, *should be no longer heard in the mountains of Israel.* For although he was reduced to straits, through a great part of his kingdom being cut off, yet he did not desist from his ferocity. The Prophet, therefore, sharply derides his insolence, since he did not cease to cry out, and to roar even in the mountains of Israel. It follows—

| 10. Thy mother *is* like a vine in thy blood, planted by the waters: she was fruitful, and full of branches, by reason of many waters. | 10. Mater tua tanquam vitis in sanguine tuo super aquas plantata fuit: fructifera et ramosa[3] fuit ob aquas multas. |
| 11. And she had strong rods for the sceptres of them that bare rule, and her stature was exalted among the | 11. Et fuerunt illi virgæ roboris[4] ad sceptra dominantium: et elevata fuit statura ejus supra,[5] et apparuit |

---

[1] " In ward, or custody, or prison:" an old interpreter translates " into a cave."—*Calvin.*

[2] That is, " into a close and well-guarded prison."—*Calvin.*

[3] Or, " leafy," as some translate it.—*Calvin.*

[4] That is, " strong or robust."—*Calvin.*

[5] That is, " on high among the boughs or vine-branches."—*Calvin.*

thick branches, and she appeared in her height with the multitude of her branches.	in altitudine sua, in multitudine ramorum suorum.
12. But she was plucked up in fury, she was cast down to the ground, and the east wind dried up her fruit; her strong rods were broken and withered, the fire consumed them.	12. Et evulsa fuit in furore,[1] in terram projecta: et ventus Orientalis arefecit fructum ejus discerpti sunt,[2] et arefacti; virga robusta,[3] ignis voravit eas.

Here Ezekiel places before our eyes the twofold state of the Jews, that they may acknowledge themselves fallen into extreme misery, because they had provoked God. For they did not sufficiently consider their present state, unless the former dignity and happiness with which they were adorned was brought to their remembrance. Now, in some way they had grown callous to all evils: although scarcely anything remained safe but Jerusalem, they did not look back, but were just as wanton as when their affairs were prosperous. Since they had not yet been humbled by so many slaughters, the Prophet, therefore, on the one hand, reminds them of their former condition, and then shows them how they had fallen. This comparison, then, ought to prick their consciences sharply, that they may at length feel that God was hostile to them. We now understand the Prophet's intention in saying, that *the people's mother was at first like a flourishing and fruit-bearing vine.* It is not surprising that he says, *the vine was planted near the waters:* for there the vines do not require lofty and dry situations, as in cold climates, but rather seek their nourishment from water, as we gather from many passages of Scripture. The Prophet, therefore, says, that the people at the beginning was like a vine planted in a mild and choice situation. He says, that *the vine was flourishing,* or branching, *and fruitful,* since it drew its juices from the waters.

Respecting the word "blood," I think those who take it for vigour are mistaken; it rather refers to birth: he says, *the mother of the people in her blood,* that is, in bringing forth the people. Thus Ezekiel recalls the Jews to their first origin, as we previously saw the word used in this sense. When thou wast in thy blood, meaning, when thou wast

[1] Or, "burning wrath."—*Calvin.* [2] Or, "broken up."—*Calvin.*
[3] "Its twigs were broken up and withered."—*Calvin.*

born, as we know this to be the state of the young offspring, as the metaphor was explained in the sixteenth chapter. Live in thy blood, said God, (ver. 6,) since the Jews were still defiled through not being cleansed from pollution. In fine, blood is taken for birth, as if it had been said, that the Jews, when first brought to light, were planted so as to take root, since God led them into the land of Canaan. Here he says they were brought to light when God restored them. He omits the intervening space of time which we saw elsewhere, because he passes directly from the end to the beginning. On the whole, he means that the Jews at their nativity were placed in the land of Canaan, which was very fruitful, so that they should bring forth their own fruit, that is, spend their time happily, and enjoy an abundance of all things. Now we understand the meaning of the phrase, *the mother of the people was planted near the waters, as a flourishing and fruitful vine.*

He adds, *she had branches,* that is, vine twigs, *for the sceptres of those who bear rule.* Those who translate with or above the sceptres of rulers do not seem to me to comprehend the Prophet's meaning. I have no doubt he intends that sceptres were gathered from these vine branches, or rather that they were so formed as to be like royal sceptres. Although this translation seems rather rough, yet the sense is not doubtful; because the Prophet means that kings were taken from the people just as branches from the vine, as God chose kings from David to Zedekiah. In this sense he says that *the vine branches became sceptres of the rulers.* He afterwards adds, *her stature was conspicuous, that she was remarkable for her loftiness even in the multitude of the vine branches.* This is extended to the whole body of the people. Since mention is made of the king, there is no doubt that God commends his grace towards the whole people, whose safety and happiness were placed in the king, as we saw elsewhere. But he asserts more clearly that the people had increased, so that they excelled in population, power, and wealth. On the whole, the Prophet teaches that the Jews were adorned from the beginning with all kinds of advantages, since God's best gifts shone forth there, and their dignity was conspicuous, and their opulence great, since he unites *the multitude of the boughs* or vine branches with their height.

Let us come now to the second clause. He says *that the vine was torn away in wrath, thrown on the ground, and dried by the east wind, and that its boughs were broken off and withered, and consumed by fire.* I have now briefly explained the Prophet's meaning. As the Jews had grown stupid in their calamity, and were not humbled so as suppliantly to fly to God's mercy, the Prophet corrects their torpor when he shows them their origin. He now says that they were reduced to extreme wretchedness by a sudden assault; for a change which took place in a short space of time ought to affect them to the quick; but if they had been slowly diminished, the change had not been so remarkable: but when the vine was struck by lightning, torn up, withered, and burnt, that instantaneous slaughter, as I have said, showed that it was not by chance, but by the evident wrath of God. For this reason he says that *the vine was violently torn up, and cast upon the ground.* If the vine had been dried up by degrees, it would not have been so wonderful; but its sudden tearing up ought to have made them sensible of the wrath of God, towards which they had grown callous. This is the reason why the Prophet adds one simile to another. The plucking up would have been sufficient; but he adds, *it was cast upon the ground,* that it should wither away completely. He adds, *the east wind,* which destroys both fruits and trees, as is sufficiently evident from many passages; and not only so, but he says *that the boughs were broken,* or plucked off, *and withered:* lastly, *they were consumed with fire.* In fine, the hand of God appeared visibly in that horrible slaughter of the people, when they were torn up, cut off, withered, and burnt. It follows—

13. And now she *is* planted in the wilderness, in a dry and thirsty ground.   13. Et nunc plantata est in deserto, in terra siccitatis et sitis.[1]

The Prophet seems here inconsistent with himself, since these two clauses are openly at variance, that the vine was not only withered, but burnt up, and yet planted in a desert

---

[1] That is, "dry and barren."—*Calvin.*

place; for if it was withered, it could not take root again; but the burning removed the slightest hope; for when the twigs were reduced to ashes, who ever saw a vine spring up and grow from its ashes? But when the Prophet says that the vine was *withered and burnt up*, he refers to the conclusion which men must arrive at by their own senses when the city was utterly ruined; for that was in truth a horrible spectacle, when the people were made tributary after their king was taken, the temple plundered, the city ruined, and their safety dependent on the lust of their conqueror. Since, therefore, neither the royal name and dignity, nor freedom and security, remained, and especially when they were led to the slaughter-house, was not their ruin very like a burning? Now, therefore, we see why the Prophet said that the vine was torn and burnt up, for that most severe destruction took away all hope of restoration for a short time. Hence he spoke according to common sense: then he kept in view that form of horrible ruin, or rather deformity, which was like a burning and a final destruction of the people. But now, when he says that the vine was planted again, he commends the mercy of God, who wished some seed to remain for the production of young plants; as it is said in the first chapter of Isaiah, Lest ye should be like Sodom and Gomorrah, some small seed has been wonderfully preserved. Although, therefore, the people were burnt up after being violently plucked up, and all their lives subjected to the will of the proudest of conquerors, yet God took some twigs or vine branches, which he planted, that he might propagate a new nation, which was done at the people's return.

But he says *that those vine branches were planted in the desert in the dry and thirsty land,* since God preserves the religion of his people even in death. Hence he compares their exile to a desert and a wilderness. It may seem absurd at first sight that Chaldæa should be likened to a desert, since that district we know to be remarkable for its fertility and other advantages; we know, too, that it was well watered, though called dry. But the Prophet here does not consider the material character of the country, but the condition of the people in it. Although Chaldæa was most lovely, and full of all kinds of fruits, yet, since the people were cruelly oppressed and contemptuously treated, hence the land was called a desert. We say that no prison is beautiful, so that their exile could not be agreeable to the children of Israel; for they were ashamed of their life, and did not dare to raise their eyes upwards. Since, then, they were drowned in a deep abyss of evils, the land was to them a desert; hence there was no splendour, dignity, or opulence; and liberty, the most precious of all boons, was wrested from them. Now we see the sense of the words. It follows at length—

14. And fire is gone out of a rod of her branches, *which* hath devoured her fruit, so that she hath no strong rod *to be* a sceptre to rule. This *is* a lamentation, and shall be for a lamentation.

14. Et egressus est ignis a virga ramorum ejus, fructum ejus voravit,[1] et non fuit in ea virga fortitudinis,[2] sceptrum ad dominandum. Lamentatio hæc, et erit in lamentationem.

Here the Prophet comes down to the close of their woes, when Zedekiah was dragged into captivity, and so the people's independence was abolished. God had formerly planted that vine, or at least some of the branches, in a desert spot, since first four tribes, and afterwards seven, were led away, and last of all, the greater part of the tribe of Judah; but the little that remained with King Zedekiah perished. He says, therefore, *that the fire went forth from the vine branches:* thus he shows that the last slaughter proceeded only from the people themselves; and lest they should utter their accustomed complaints, the Prophet meets them by saying that they were consumed by intestine fire; that is, their slaughter could not be ascribed to their Chaldæan conquerors, but to themselves; because King Zedekiah, by his own perfidy, had stirred up the king of Babylon against himself; for he might have spent his time in his kingdom, but he could not refrain himself from throwing off the yoke; for this reason he armed himself against the king of Babylon, because he was a breaker of treaties: and thus the Prophet says, with propriety, *that a fire went forth from one rod,* or twig of its branches, and hence *the fruit of the whole vine was consumed;* that is, the remnant was lost by the fault of that perfidious king. He now adds, *there was no sceptre for ruling among its rods.*

[1] Or, "consumed."—*Calvin.* [2] That is, "strong."—*Calvin.*

Hence it appears that the exposition which I have advanced suits best, and is entirely genuine. He said first that the rods were for a sceptre of the rulers; but he here says there was no sceptre for them among these rods. What follows we will treat to-morrow.

PRAYER.

Grant, Almighty God, since thou hast once deigned to insert us into the body of thy Son, that we may be such vine-branches as thou hast undertaken to cultivate: that by the power of thy Spirit we may be so watered as never to be deficient in spiritual vigour: and may we so bear fruit to the glory of thy name, that we may at length arrive at the fountain of our faith, when we enjoy the celestial glory to which thou hast adopted us in the same, thine only-begotten Son.—Amen.

Lecture Sixtieth.

TIME did not permit us yesterday to explain the words at the close of this nineteenth chapter: *this is a lamentation, and it shall be a lamentation.* Some think this to be said of the Jews, that is, of all the Israelites, since they should all be lamentable, because God would not cease to inflict his judgments upon them until he had utterly consumed them. But I had rather refer it to the prophecy, and this is the more correct sense. *This lamentation:* thus the Prophet designates this sad and mournful prophecy because it contains the last slaughter of the people. Secondly, he adds, *it shall be for a lamentation,* because it suggests material for wailing, since remarkable miseries are accustomed to be more celebrated. If anything usual occurs, men soon forget it; but if any slaughter happens worthy of notice and of remembrance it is everywhere spread abroad, nay, it supplies posterity with material for their poems. Hence the Prophet signifies not only that this prophecy was mournful, but that God's wrath would fly about in common conversation through so rare and memorable an example. I now come to the twentieth chapter.

CHAPTER XX.

1. And it came to pass in the seventh year, in the fifth *month*, the tenth *day* of the month, *that* certain of the elders of Israel came to enquire of the Lord, and sat before me.	1. Et fuit anno septimo, quinto mense, decimo mensis venerunt viri e senioribus Israel ad consulendum Jehovam: et sederunt coram facie mea.[1]

Here he does not narrate a vision but an event which really happened. It is a simple historical narrative, that some of the elders of Israel were chosen to interrogate him. We know this to be customary, and when God separates his people from the profane nations, he opposes his prophets to the soothsayers and magi, augurs and astrologers. For he says that the Gentiles inquire what concerns them in various ways, and so interrogate their deities; but that he prescribes to the chosen people but one method: I will raise for them a prophet from the midst of their brethren, says Moses, (Deut. xviii. 18;) that is, they need not wander about, like the wretched Gentiles, destitute of counsel, first to their soothsayers, then to magi, and then to astrologers: there is no end to them: but I will meet them, says he, by my prophets, who shall always exist among the people. In this sense Ezekiel says *that the elders of Israel came to consult God.* The verb דרש, *deresh*, properly signifies "to seek," but it is here received for "to consult" or "inquire into," as in many other places. Now it is not surprising that the elders came by public consent to the Prophet: for the Israelites were already worn out by long weariness, and thought that they had almost perished through their long exile. But there was another reason, since false prophets, as we saw, tickled the ears of the simple by offering them daily some new hope. Since therefore they were agitated between hope and fear, and the devil scattered false prophecies which distracted the minds of the vulgar, it is probable that the elders of Israel came and were sent to inquire concerning either the prosperous or disastrous event of their captivity. They come therefore to the prophets; he says *it happened in the seventh year*, that is, after the captivity of Jehoiakim. They reckoned the years from that change, and deservedly

---

[1] Or, "before me."—*Calvin*.

so : for so remarkable an act of God's vengeance ought to be kept constantly in remembrance. There was also another reason, since God gave some hope of restoration. The reckoning of the years, then, which the Israelites dated from Jehoiakim's exile, had a twofold use and end, first, that God's judgment might remain fixed in their minds, and next, that they might nevertheless refresh their spirits by the hope of good. Hence as often as they dated the first year or the second, it was just as if they kept before their eyes that slaughter by which God testified himself grievously offended. But for another reason they ought to cheer their spirits by good hopes, because if the kingdom had been utterly abolished and no promise added to lighten their sorrow, that reckoning was superfluous, since in a state of desperation we do not take an account of years : but when seventy years were fixed, they nourished and cherished hope in this way, because they renewed the remembrance of their liberty, which had been promised them by the mouth of Jeremiah. (Chap. xxv. 12, 13, and xxix. 10.) Now therefore we understand why he simply says *the seventh year :* he mentions also the day and the month.

Now the clause which I have noticed contains some useful instruction,—*the elders of Israel came to consult God and sat before the Prophet.* We see, then, as far as concerns outward forms, that they followed what God had commanded in his law ; lest thou shouldst say, Who shall ascend above the clouds ? who shall descend into the abyss ? who shall cross the sea ? The word is ever there, in thy heart and in thy mouth. (Deut. xxx. 12-14 ; Rom. x. 6-8.) Since therefore God in some way brought himself forward whenever he instructed his servants by the spirit of prophecy, so when the elders of Israel came to the Prophet, they are said to come to God himself, because God was unwilling to utter his own oracles either from heaven or by means of angels, but he appointed his servant by whom he would speak, and suggested what he should say. Hence we gather that our faith is not rightly founded unless when we listen to God alone, who only deserves and claims us as listeners. But at the same time, we must remark that faith was joined with humility and modesty. Hence if any one desires to ascend to the clouds to inquire what God will answer, he departs far from him, although he pretends to approach him. Hence this moderation is to be observed, that our faith may acquiesce in the authority of the one God, and not be carried hither and thither by the will of men; and yet it should not object to hear God speak through his servants, but calmly submit itself to the prophets. It now follows—

2. Then came the word of the Lord unto me, saying,	2. Et fuit sermo Iehovæ ad me dicendo.
3. Son of man, speak unto the elders of Israel, and say unto them, Thus saith the Lord God, Are ye come to enquire of me? *As* I live, saith the Lord God, I will not be enquired of by you.	3. Fili hominis, loquere ad seniores Israel, et dic illis, Sic dicit Dominator Iehovah, An ad quærendum me,[1] venistis? Vivo ego si quærar a vobis, dicit Dominator Iehovah.

Here the Prophet is ordered to blame those elders, although they pretended to rare piety in inquiring of him: God says that they did not come with a right disposition. Many translate otherwise—if I shall be found, or be entreated by you, or if I shall answer: thus they take the word דרש, *deresh*, in a double sense: in the first clause, for to seek or interrogate; but when it is added, as I live, &c., they do not take the word by "to be sought" or "interrogated," but by "to answer" or "be entreated." But this seems far-fetched: and in chapter xiv. 3, a phrase not unlike this was explained; and hence we may gather, that God rather inveighs against the people's hypocrisy than rejects them, and refuses to answer. There the Prophet said that the elders came to consult him, as if they had been his best disciples; but as Ezekiel might be deceived by that deceptive picture, God meets him, and says, Do you think that they come to inquire of me? They are fixed upon their idols; for their heart is towards them, and they raise their eyes to their own abominations: As I live, if they seek me, says he; that is, it is easy to convict them of bad faith, when they come suppliantly to inquire of thee. For if they truly and heartily sought me, they would renounce their idols, and would no longer partake of their abominations; but they do not repent, but remain obstinate in their wickedness.

[1] That is, "to consult me."—*Calvin*.

It is certain, therefore, that they are by no means sincere: there is no reason why you should delay them, or trouble yourself about them, since their conduct is mere dissimulation. So, therefore, in this passage God pronounces by his Prophet, *are ye come to seek me?* that is, to consult me. *I will not be inquired of by you*, says he: the reason is, because, as we saw in the 14th chapter, they always remained the same, since therefore they were at the greatest distance from God, and remained wrapt up in their own abominations, their seeking God was only fallacious. The conclusion is, that God rejected them, because, though they pretended a holy zeal, they were still perverse in their disposition; hence God refuses to discharge the office of a master towards them since they did not come to learn: this is one point. He then says, *if I shall be inquired of by you.* And because their hypocrisy was stained by various colours, God swears that their disposition was perverse, and that they did not come with pious and holy affections, and were neither docile nor obedient, nor desirous of making progress, and hence were unworthy of having him for a teacher. Now let us go on.

4. Wilt thou judge them, son of man? wilt thou judge *them?* cause them to know the abominations of their fathers.

4. An judicabo eos? an judicabo eos, fili hominis? abominationes patrum ipsorum indica[1] illis.

The context flows very well if we embrace this sense, that God swears that the Israelites did not come to be subject to his Prophet, and to submit themselves modestly to his instructions. If this sense pleases, it is well added, *shalt thou judge them?* that is, shalt thou spend thy breath in arguing with them? He means that they are rather to be dismissed than instructed; as Christ says, Thou shalt not cast pearls before swine. (Matt. vii. 6.) And we know what God pronounces: My Spirit shall not always strive with man, because he is flesh. (Gen. vi. 3.) He now means that there was no need of any dispute, since there was no means of carrying it on; so in this passage, since the Prophet was dealing with men utterly broken down, who never listened to wise counsels, nor obeyed any admonitions, nor were softened by any chastisement, he adds, therefore, *shalt thou*

[1] Or. "explain."—*Calvin.*

judge them? Some indeed coldly and insipidly explain this of taking away the part of a judge, since God rather wishes them to be called to repentance than to be condemned. But here *judging* embraces within itself all reproaches and threats. On the whole, since they acted deceitfully, and by no means proposed to submit themselves to God, hence he uses this bitterness, What! are they worthy of your judging them? that is, of your contending with them? for the Prophet's duty is to argue with sinners, to threaten them, and to cite them to God's tribunal. God, therefore, pronounces them unworthy of such disputing, because they are not only deaf, but hardened by abandoned obstinacy. Now, therefore, we understand the sense of the words, *wilt thou judge them? wilt thou judge them?* The repetition is emphatic, that God may strongly express the obstinacy of that desperate people. He afterwards adds, *If this be done, then show them the abominations of their fathers.* God here mitigates the asperity which he had used, and by means of a correction descends to a reason for it, namely, that he may for once try whether or not they are curable. If then they are to be judged, that is, if he chooses to enter into any dispute, and to argue with them, he says that he ought to begin not with themselves, but with their fathers. God wishes them to be judged, not only on account of the wickedness of a few years, but because before they were born their fathers were obstinately attached to their abominations. In fine, God shows that the wound was deep, and could not be cured, unless the hidden poison was carefully examined, which otherwise would cause putrid matter, from which at length inflammation would arise. For many think that they have properly discharged their duty when they have but lightly probed their wounds: but sometimes it is necessary to penetrate to the inmost parts, as the people had not only provoked God lightly, and for a short time, but their impiety had been growing for ages, and their sins had become a kind of inheritance to them. Since, then, this hidden poison existed, which could not be cured either easily or by any slight remedy, hence God orders them to begin with their fathers. *Show them, therefore, the abominations of their fathers.* It follows—

And say unto them, Thus saith Lord God, In the day when I chose Israel, and lifted up mine hand unto the seed of the house of Jacob, and made myself known unto them in the land of Egypt, when I lifted up mine hand unto them, saying, I *am* the Lord your God;	5. Et dices illis, Sic dicit Dominator Iehovah, Die quo elegi Israelem, et sustuli manum meam ad semen domus Iacob, et cognitus fui illis in terra Ægypti, et sustuli manum meam illis dicendo, Ego Iehovah Deus vester;
6. In the day *that* I lifted up mine hand unto them, to bring them forth of the land of Egypt into a land that I had espied for them, flowing with milk and honey, which *is* the glory of all lands:	6. Die illo sustuli manum meam ad ipsos, ut educerem eos e terra Ægypti in terram quam prospexi illis fluentem lacte et melle, desiderium[1] præ omnibus terris:
7. Then said I unto them, Cast ye away every man the abominations of his eyes, and defile not yourselves with the idols of Egypt: I *am* the Lord your God.	7. Et dixi illis, Quisque spurcitias oculorum suorum projicite et in idolis[2] Ægypti ne polluamini: ego Iehovah Deus vester.
8. But they rebelled against me, and would not hearken unto me: they did not every man cast away the abominations of their eyes, neither did they forsake the idols of Egypt; then I said, I will pour out my fury upon them, to accomplish my anger against them in the midst of the land of Egypt.	8. Et rebelles fuerunt mihi, et noluerunt audire me, *et quæ sequuntur.*

God confirms what I said before, that the Jews were not to be reproved for beginning lately to sin: it was not sufficient to bring recent offences before them; but God orders the Prophet to begin with their fathers, as if he had said that the nation was abandoned from the very beginning, as Stephen reproaches them: Uncircumcised in heart, ye still resist the Holy Spirit, as your fathers always did. (Acts vii. 51.) And Christ had said the same thing before: Ye fill up the measure of your fathers. (Matt. xxiii. 32.) We know also how frequently rebukes of this kind occur in the Prophets. God therefore says, that from the time when he chose the seed of Israel, he had experienced both the wickedness and obstinacy of the people; for he says that they were not drawn aside by either error or ignorance, but because they were unwilling to hear, when they were over and over again admonished as to their duty. Hence three things are to be marked, namely, that the people were bound to God, since he had gratuitously adopted them; for God here

---

[1] That is, "which is a desire, or desirable."—*Calvin.*

[2] Though it signifies also "foulness or pollution."—*Calvin.*

commends his gratuitous election, together with the singular benefits which he had conferred on that people: this is one point. The second is, that he not only took them once to himself, but showed them what was right, so that they could not mistake, except knowingly and wilfully: this is the second point. Then the third is, that they rebelled purposely, because they would not listen: for if they had been left at the meeting of two roads, their error had been excusable if they had turned to the left instead of the right. But if God by his law so shone before them, that he was prepared to direct them straight to the mark, and they turned aside; thus their obstinacy and rebellion is plainly detected. This is the sense.

Now as far as words are concerned, he says, *that he had chosen Israel.* But election, as I have already briefly touched upon, is opposed to all merits: for if anything had been found in the people which should cause them to be preferred to others, it would be improperly said that God had elected them. But since all were in the same condition, as Moses says in his song, (Deut. xxxii. 8, 9,) there was scope for God's grace, since he separated them from others of his own accord: for they were just like the rest, and God did not find any difference between them; we see, then, that they were bound to God more sacredly, since he had joined them to himself gratuitously. He now adds, *that he lifted up his hand to the seed of Jacob.* The lifting up the hand seems to be taken here in different senses. Since it was a customary method of swearing, God is said sometimes to lift up his hand when he swears. That is indeed harsh, since the lifting up the hand does not suit God: for we lift up the hand when we call God to witness; but God swears by himself, and cannot raise his hand above himself. But we know that he uses forms of speech according to the common customs of men: hence there is nothing absurd in this phrase, *he lifted up his hand,* that is, he swore. Hence, if we may so explain it, this was a confirmation of the covenant, when God by interposing an oath promised himself to be Israel's God. But since he shortly afterwards adds, *that he was known,* the other sense suits pretty well, since it refers to the benefits which he had conferred upon the people. And truly experimental knowledge is intended, since God really proved himself to be worthy of credit, and thus illustrated his own power in preserving the people. Hence I said that to lift up the hand is to be received variously in this chapter, since, if we read the two clauses conjointly, *I lifted up my hand unto the seed of the house of Jacob, and was made known to them,* truly the lifting up the hand will imply a display of power. That also has been said by means of a simile; but shortly afterwards the lifting up of the hand must be taken for to swear, by the figure of rhetoric called *catachresis,* which is the use of a word in a different signification, and yet there is no absurdity. *I have raised my hand,* therefore, *to the seed of the house of Jacob, saying, I Jehovah am your God.* (Ver. 15.) We see, then, that God raised his hand to sanction the covenant which he had made; for when he pronounces himself their God, he binds them to himself, and claims them for his peculiar people, and thus confirms his covenant. But at the same time he had raised his hand or arm by so many miracles performed in freeing the people. He says, *in that day I raised my hand to,* or towards *them, to bring them out.* Again, the raising the hand refers to God's power, since he brought them forth by an extended arm from that miserable slavery. Since, therefore, he so raised his hand, he acquired them as his own, that they should no longer be free, but belong altogether to him. He afterwards adds other benefits, since he not only snatched them from the tyranny of Pharaoh, *but brought them into a land flowing with milk and honey, which he had espied for them.* We see how briefly God enlarges upon that remarkable benefit which he had bestowed upon his people. Not only was he their Redeemer, but he looked out for a place of residence for them, not only commodious, but abounding with plenty; for this phrase is common enough with Moses. *In that same day in which I led them out of Egypt, I brought them into a land, the desire of all lands;* that is, which is desirable and superior to all other lands. It is true, indeed, that other nations were not less fruitful; but God, in thus praising the land of Canaan, considers it clothed and adorned by his bounty. But there was no region under heaven to be compared with the land of Canaan in one point, namely, God's choosing it as his earthly dwelling-place. Since the land of Canaan excelled all others in this respect, it is deservedly called the desire of all lands, or desirable beyond all lands.

Another clause now follows, that God instructed the Jews in piety, and withdrew them from all the idolatries to which they had been devoted. Instruction then went before, which showed them the right way of salvation, and recalled them from their superstitions. The meaning is, that when God adopted the people, he gave them the rule of living piously, that they should not be tossed about hither and thither, but have an aim, to which they might direct the whole course of their life. *I said,* therefore, *to each of them:* this seems more emphatic than if he had spoken to all promiscuously and generally: but this familiar invitation ought to penetrate more into their minds, when he speaks *to each* individually, just as if he said, let each of you cast away your abominations, and *not pollute himself any more with the idols of Egypt.* When therefore God thus attached them to himself, he shows that he could not be rightly worshipped by them unless they bid their idolatries farewell, and formed their whole life according to the rule of his law. He calls their enticements defilements or idols of the eyes: but we know that the Prophet often speaks thus, that unbelievers should consider their idols. Hence it is just as if God recalled them from all the wiles of Satan in which they were enticed, and were so devoted to them as to have their eyes exclusively fixed on them. He speaks by name of the idols of Egypt: whence it easily appears that they were corrupted by depraved desires, so as for the most part to worship the fictitious gods of Egypt. Yet they knew themselves elected by the true God, and boasted in circumcision as a symbol of divorce from all nations. Yet though they wished to be thought illustrious on the one hand, they afterwards prostituted themselves so as to differ in nothing from the Egyptians. We see then that the desire of piety was almost extinct in their hearts, since they had so contaminated themselves with the superstitions of Egypt. That he might retain them the better, he says at the same time *that he was their God*: for without this principle men are tossed hither and thither, for we know that we are lighter than vanity. Hence the devil will always find us subject to his fallacies unless God restrains us in our duty, until he appears to us and shows himself the only God: we see then the necessity for this remedy, lest men should be carried away by idolatries, namely, the knowledge of the true God. The third clause will follow afterwards, but we shall explain it in its turn.

PRAYER.

Grant, Almighty God, since thou hast once stretched forth thine hand to us by thine only-begotten Son, and hast not only bound thyself to us by an oath, but hast sealed thine eternal covenant by the blood of the same, thy Son: Grant, I pray thee, that we in return may be faithful to thee, and persevere in the pure worship of thy name, until at length we enjoy the fruit of our faith in thy heavenly kingdom by the same Christ our Lord.—Amen.

Lecture Sixty-First.

In the last lecture I began to explain the eighth verse, where God complains that he was exasperated by the children of Israel when he had begun to extend his hand to free them. He says, then, that they had rejected his grace. But at the same time we see that all pretence of ignorance was removed, because unless Moses had exhorted them to good hope, they would have pretended to be so deserted through two centuries, that they had hoped for help from God in vain. But since Moses was a witness of their redemption, hence their ingratitude was the more without excuse, since they were unwilling to embrace the message which they had so greatly desired. Nor is the language of Moses vain, that they often cried out in their calamities. Although their clamour was turbulent, yet they doubtless remembered what they had heard from their fathers, that the end of those evils was at hand to which God had fixed an appointed time. But more is expressed in this passage than Moses relates, who simply says, because they saw themselves treated too roughly, that they were worn down and disgusted : hence those expostulations—Ye have made our name to stink before Pharaoh : God shall judge between you and us: get ye gone from us. (Exod. v. 21.) We do not then clearly collect from Moses that they were rebels against God, since they had not cast away their idols and superstitions, but the probable conjecture is that they were so rooted in their filth, that they repelled God's hand from succouring them. And truly if they had promptly embraced what Moses had promised them in God's name, the accomplishment would have been readier and swifter : but we may understand that their sloth was the hinderance to the exertion of God's hand in their favour and to the real fulfilment of his promises. God ought indeed to contend with Pharaoh, that his power might be more conspicuous : but the people would not have been so tyrannously afflicted, unless they had closed the door against God's mercy. They were, as we have said, immersed in their defilements from which God wished to withdraw them. He now accuses them of ingratitude, *because they did not cast away their idols,* but obstinately persisted in their usual and customary superstitions. He speaks of the time of their captivity in Egypt, and this passage assures us that while there they were infected and polluted by Egyptian defilements. For the contagion of idolatry is wonderful : for since we are all naturally inclined to it as soon as any example is offered to us, we are snatched in that direction by a violent impulse. It is not surprising then that the children of Israel contracted pollution from the superstitions of Egypt, especially as they lived there as slaves, and were desirous of gratifying the Egyptians : for if they had been treated liberally, they might have lived freely after their custom, but since they were not free and were oppressed as slaves, it happened that they pretended to worship the gods of Egypt according to the will of those by whom they saw themselves oppressed : and not only did they sin by pretending, but it is probable that they were impelled by their own lusts as well as by fear: for it will soon be evident that they were too inclined to impiety of their own accord.

On the whole, Ezekiel here testifies that they were rebels

against God, *because they did not listen to God by casting away the idols of their eyes,* that is, to the worship of which they were too attentive, *nor did they desert the idols of Egypt.* When he speaks of *the idols of their eyes,* we gather what I have touched upon, that they were not impelled to idolatry by fear and necessity, but by their own depraved appetites: For unless they had been eagerly devoted to Egyptian superstitions, Ezekiel would not have called them idols of the eyes. Hence by this word he means that they were not only superstitious through obedience to the Egyptians, but were spontaneously inclined towards them. Besides, when he adds *the idols of Egypt,* he points out as the occasion of their corruption their spending time under that tyranny, and their being compelled to bear many evils, since slavery commonly draws with it dissimulation. It now follows, *And I said I would pour forth,* that is, I determined to pour forth. God here signifies that he was inflamed by anger, and unless they had respect to his name he would not withdraw his hand from the vengeance to which it was armed and prepared. We know that this does not properly belong to God, but this is the language of accommodation, since first of all, God is not subject to vengeance, and, secondly, does not decree what he may afterwards retract. But since these things are not in character with God, simile and accommodation are used. As often as the Holy Spirit uses these forms of speech, let us learn that they refer rather to the matter in hand than to the character of God. God determined to pour forth his anger, that is, the Israelites had so deserved it through their crimes, that it was necessary to execute punishment upon them. The Prophet simply means that the people's disposition was sinful, and hence God's wrath would have been poured out, unless he had been held back from some other cause. I have already touched upon the obstacle, because he consulted his honour *lest it should be profaned.*

I have decreed, therefore, *to pour forth my burning fury upon them in the midst of the land of Egypt.* Some translate, to consume them, but improperly, for the word כלה, *keleh,* signifies to fill up or accomplish, as well as to consume.

But although God sometimes says that he consumes all his weapons or scourges in the punishment of men's sins, yet it is not suitable to transfer this to his wrath itself. Hence another sense will suit better, namely, that *God decreed to pour out his wrath* until he satisfied himself. For here, as we have said, he puts on the character of an angry man, who cannot appease his mind otherwise than by satiating it by the exaction of punishment: for anger is usually inexhaustible. But God on the whole here expresses that such was the atrocity of their wickedness, that the Israelites deserved destruction through the pouring forth of God's wrath and the filling up of the measure of his indignation; *and that in the midst of the land of Egypt;* because they had shown themselves unworthy of his redemption, and hence it was enough for them to perish in the midst of the land of Egypt. But he afterwards added—

9. But I wrought for my name's sake, that it should not be polluted before the heathen, among whom they *were,* in whose sight I made myself known unto them, in bringing them forth out of the land of Egypt.	9. Et feci propter nomen meum ne profanaretur in oculis gentium, in quibus ipsi in medio eorum, quibus cognitus fui ipsis in oculis eorum, ad educendum eos e terra Ægypti.

Here God signifies that he was restrained for one reason only from entirely blotting out so ungrateful and wicked a nation, namely, since he saw his own sacred name would be exposed to the Gentiles as a laughing-stock. He teaches, therefore, that he spared them, and suspended his rigour for the time, rather through being induced by regard to his own glory than by pity to them. Hence, by the word *I did it,* we ought to understand what will be more clearly explained. The sense is, that he abstained from the final act of vengeance for his name's sake, that it should not be profaned among the Gentiles. Although God here pronounces that he had respect rather to himself than to them, yet there is no doubt that he spared them, because he saw that they could not be otherwise preserved than by his pardoning them even in such hardness and obstinacy; and certainly God's glory and the salvation of the Church are things almost inseparably united. When I speak of the salvation of the Church, I do not comprehend all those who profess to be its members, but

I mean only the elect. Since, therefore, God had adopted that nation, he must preserve the remnant in safety, otherwise his truth would have failed, and thus his name would have been much more severely profaned. Hence we may gather, whenever God pardons us, though he regards himself, and wishes in this way to exercise his clemency, yet his pity towards us is another reason for his pardoning us: but when he says that he has withdrawn his hand from vengeance through regard for his own glory, he in this way prostrates still more the pride of this nation, since, whenever he had pity on them, they thought it a concession to their own worthiness and merits. The Prophet therefore shows here that they were snatched from destruction, while they were remaining in the land of Egypt, for no other reason than this, that God was unwilling to expose his name to the contempt of the nations. He says, therefore, *in the eyes of the Gentiles, among whom they were*, regarding not the Egyptians only, but others.

Yet the question arises, in what sense, he adds by and bye, *that he was known to them?* for as yet he had given no specimen of his power among the Gentiles. He had borne witness by two miracles that Moses should be the agent in their redemption, (Exod. iv. 2, and following:) afterwards Moses approached Pharaoh himself: there God put forth the signs of his power, which deservedly frightened all the Egyptians; but his fame had not yet reached other nations. But this knowledge ought not to be simply restricted to past time; for God only means that he had already begun to show, by certain and remarkable proofs, that Moses was chosen, by whose hand he wished to redeem his own people. Since, therefore, God had already come forward with those remarkable signs, he says, *that he was known to those nations*, not that his fame had reached them, but because he had gone there himself, so that the event could not be in obscurity, and all must know that miracles had been performed by the hand of Moses, by which it was evident that he wished to claim the Israelites as his own. Now, therefore, we understand in what sense Ezekiel says *that God was known*. Some explain this relatively thus: I was known to them meaning the Israelites, in their eyes, meaning the Gentiles: but this sense seems to me forced; for in my opinion this one word "their," in the Prophet's language, is superfluous. He simply means that God was manifested in the eyes of all the nations *in leading them forth.* This clause shows the kind of knowledge intended, since God showed his power in liberating the people by remarkable miracles. It follows—

10. Wherefore I caused them to go forth out of the land of Egypt, and brought them into the wilderness.	10. Et eduxi (*eduxi ergo*) eos e terra Ægypti, et adduxi in desertum.

After Ezekiel had taught that the Israelites deserved to perish in Egypt, unless God had spared them for his name's sake rather than for their own, he now adds the cause of their coming forth, which was the promotion of his own glory. Hence, therefore, we gather that the Israelites falsely imagined any other cause of their deliverance than that respect of which the Prophet now speaks. But this is more than if he had simply said that they were snatched from the tyranny of Egypt by God's gratuitous pity, since God gratuitously stretched out his hand towards them, and was so induced by feelings of humanity and clemency as to snatch away from their miseries the innocent who were unjustly afflicted; but he here excludes them from God's clemency, because they were unworthy of his notice. I said, indeed, that two things were united, the salvation of the Church and the glory of God; but at the same time I noticed that the Prophet's intention must be considered, since he wished to withdraw all confidence from such a proud people, and to show that, as far as they could, they had always repelled God's favour by their obstacles, unless he had overcome their wickedness by his untiring goodness. It follows—

11. And I gave them my statutes, and shewed them my judgments, which *if* a man do, he shall even live in them.	11. Et dedi illis decreta mea,[1] et judicia mea patefeci ipsis, quæ qui fecerit homo vivet in ipsis.

Here God enlarges upon his favours, since he had given his law to the Israelites, as if he would prescribe to them a certain rule of living. If they had only been brought out of Egypt, that would have been an inestimable benefit: but God was much more generous, since he deigned to rule them

[1] "Statutes."—*Calvin.*

familiarly with his doctrine, lest they should wander to one side or the other; and in this way he testified that he would be their God. He adds a promise: for God might precisely enjoin what he wished on the people of his choice; but he spontaneously adopts the method of indulgence by promising them life. Now, then, we understand why this promise is mentioned; for God might simply command anything, and say, this pleases me, and use but a monosyllable, after the manner of kings issuing a command. Since, then, God not only exacted of the Israelites what he might justly require, but, by annexing a promise, enticed them gently to the pursuit of obedience, this was certainly a mark of his fatherly indulgence. Hence he now exaggerates the people's ingratitude by this circumstance, that neither by commands nor by kindnesses could he induce these obstinate and perverse dispositions to bend to the yoke. *I gave them, therefore,* my statutes and my laws; and afterwards, *which if a man do, he shall live in them.* He thus briefly reminds them, that it was not his fault if the Israelites were not in any sense happy; for when he stipulated with them for the observance of his law, he bound them in turn to himself, that they should want nothing which contributed to a good and happy life; for in the name of life solid happiness is comprehended.

Yet it is here asked how the Prophet testifies *that men should live by the works of the law,* when the law, on the testimony of Paul, can only bring us death. (Rom. iv. 15; Deut. xxx. 15.) He took this testimony from Moses, and we shall see immediately that he cites it in a different sense. Moses there pronounces that the life of man rests on the observance of the law; that is,—life was surely to be expected through satisfying the law. Some think this absurd, and so restrict what is said to the present life, taking *he shall live in them* politically or civilly: but this is a cold and trifling comment. The reasoning which influenced them is readily answered: they object, that we owe all things to God; that we ourselves and our possessions are all his by the right of possession; so that if we keep the law a hundred times over, still we are not worthy of such a reward. But the solution is at hand, that we deserve nothing, but God graciously binds himself to us by this promise, as I have already touched upon. And from this passage it is easy to infer that works are of no value before God, and are not estimated for their intrinsic value, so to speak, but only by agreement. Since, then, it pleased God to descend so far as to promise life to men if they kept his law, they ought to accept this offer as springing from his liberality. There is no absurdity, then, if men do live, that is, if they deserve eternal life according to agreement. But if any one keeps the law, it will follow that he has no need of the grace of Christ. For of what advantage is Christ to us unless we recover life in him? but if this is placed in ourselves, the remedy must not be sought anywhere but in ourselves. Every one, then, may be his own saviour if life is placed in the observance of the law. But Paul solves this difficulty for us when he determines for us a twofold righteousness of the law and of faith. (Rom. x. 5, 6.) He says that this righteousness is of the law when we keep God's precepts. Now, since we are far distant from such obedience, nay, the very faculty of keeping the law is altogether defective in us: hence it follows that we must fly to the righteousness of faith. For he defines the righteousness of faith, if we believe Christ to be dead, and to be risen again for our justification. We see, therefore, although God promised salvation to his ancient people, if they only kept the law, yet that promise was useless, since no one could satisfy the law and perform God's commands. Here another question arises. For if this promise does not take effect, God vainly reckons that as a benefit to the Israelites which we see was offered them in vain: hence no utility or fruit would arise from it. But some one may say that the imagination was fallacious, when God promised life, and now by his Prophet blames the Israelites for despising such a benefit. But the reply is easy: although men are not endued with the power of obeying the law, yet they ought not on that account to depart from the goodness of God; for men's declension by no means hinders them from estimating the value of so liberal a promise: God is treating with men: he might then, as I have said, imperiously demand whatever he pleased, and exact it with the utmost rigour; but he treats according to an agreement, and so there is a mutual obligation between himself and the people. No one will surely deny that God here exhibits a specimen of his mercy when he deigns thus familiarly to make a covenant with men. "Ah! but this is all in vain: God's promise is of no effect, because no one is able to keep his law." I confess it: but man's declension cannot, as I have said, abolish the glory of God's goodness, since that always remains fixed, and God still acts liberally in being willing thus to enter into covenant with his people. We must then consider the subject simply, and by itself: man's declension is accidental. God then put forth a remarkable proof of his goodness, in promising life to all who kept his law: and this will remain perfect and entire. It now follows—

12. Moreover also, I gave them my sabbaths, to be a sign between me and them, that they might know that I *am* the Lord that sanctify them.

12. Atque etiam sabbatha mea dedi ipsis, ut essent in signum inter me et ipsos, ut cognoscerent quod ego sim (*vel, ego sum*) Iehovah, qui ipsos sanctifico.

Besides the law God here commends his Sabbaths, which we know to be only a part of his law: nay, whoever compares the commandments one by one, will at first sight perceive more weight in others than in the fourth. For what is the meaning of that commandment, Thou shalt not have any strange god? Thou shalt not make any idols? Afterwards, Do not take God's name in vain? (Exod. xx. 3, 4, 7; Deut. v. 7, 8, 11.) I answer, that the Prophet takes one precept of the law the better to explain what I have already touched on before, namely, that the law was given to the Israelites to bind them more and more to their benefactor. For God was unwilling to cast them away after redeeming them: but he testified by his law that he would be the guide of their whole life. Still the Prophet looked further, meaning, that the law consisted not only of the commandments, but embraced the whole grace of God, on which the adoption of the nation depended. For if God had simply commanded either one thing or another, it would not have been easy to perceive and taste his goodness. Why so? because when he calls upon us to discharge a duty, every one feels that a greater burden is imposed on him than he can bear. Even if the promise should entice us by its sweetness, —he who does these things shall live in them; yet when we try, we are deficient through being destitute of all power. But the Prophet means that something else was intended by the Sabbath, that the Israelites might acknowledge themselves separated by God, so as to experience him for their Father in all things. Hence, though the precepts of the law were somewhat distasteful; yet, as the fourth commandment has in it a gratuitous promise, it has a different savour, since the people thus recognises itself as elected by God for a peculiar nation: and this the Prophet sufficiently expresses by the word *sanctifying,* for it means that the people were separated from the profane nations to be God's peculiar inheritance. If any one wishes to render sanctify by one word it will be, "to separate." But the meaning of separation ought to be explained. How, then, did God separate a certain people from the whole world? Why, by promising to Abraham that he would be a God to his seed. (Gen. xxii. 17.) Then he could not otherwise be their God than by gratuitously loving his elect, by regenerating them by his Spirit, and becoming propitious and easily entreated: and besides, a single people could not be separated from others without a mediator. For separation cannot last unless the people be united to God; and what bond of union is there without a mediator?

Now, therefore, we understand why the Prophet speaks of the Sabbath, since he had formerly commended the whole law, of which the Sabbath was a part, namely, because it displayed God's gratuitous adoption; and at the same time the Israelites might acknowledge that the way of approach to God was open to them, and he was rendered placable; then that they were not adopted in vain, but were sought by God, that he should renew them by his Spirit, and rule the whole course of their life. It was, then, the greatest ingratitude to break the Sabbath, as will be said shortly afterwards. But this passage teaches that God was not pleased with the people's quiet or ease when he commanded them to keep the seventh day holy, but he has another intention. Whence we gather that that precept was shadowy: for there are some things which please God of themselves, and must be performed ; but others have a different object. For to worship one God, to abominate idols, to use God's name reverently, these things are, as I have said, the simple duties of piety in themselves : so the honour which sons pay to their parents is a duty pleasing to God in itself, like chastity, abstinence, and such like. But Sabbaths do not please God simply and by themselves. We ought, therefore, to look for another purpose, if we wish to understand the reason of this precept. And hence Paul says, that Sabbaths were shadows of those things of which Christ is the substance. (Col. ii. 16, 17.) This, therefore, is one point. Ezekiel is not the first who says so, though he took it from Moses ; for though he does not clearly say in so many words that the Sabbath was the symbol of sanctification, yet he afterwards shows this to be its object, (Exod. xxxi. 13, 14,) and that God commanded the people to rest on the seventh day with this intent. Moses then himself shows that the command had another object, which Ezekiel interprets for us; but the matter is made much clearer in the Gospel, since in Christ the truth and substance of this precept is set forth, which Paul calls the body. I have, then, sufficiently explained this object, namely, that the Israelites might know God to be their sanctifier. But if we desire to understand the matter better, we ought first to lay it down that the Sabbath was the sign of mortification. God, therefore, sanctifies us ; because when we remain in our natural state we are there mixed with others, and have nothing different from unbelievers : hence, therefore, it is necessary to begin by dying to ourselves and the world, and by exercising self-denial ; and this depends on the grace of God. But I perceive that I cannot complete the subject to-day : so I shall put it off till to-morrow.

PRAYER.

Grant, Almighty God, since thou hast not only deigned to bestow upon us a rule for living rightly, but hast so shown thyself our Father in Christ as to be prepared to engrave thy law in our inward parts : Grant, I pray thee, that we may not cast away that inestimable boon through either ingratitude or sloth; but may we offer up ourselves to thee as a sacrifice : and then do thou so pardon us that our infirmities may not hinder us from finding thee always propitious whenever we fly to thy mercy in Christ, thine only-begotten Son.—Amen.

Lecture Sixty-Second.

WE said in yesterday's lecture, that God's Church was separated from the profane nations that he might regenerate it by his Spirit: we said also, that the Sabbath was a proof of this favour; but now a confirmation of this teaching must be added. This is easily gathered from the institution of the Sabbath, when God is said to have rested from his work on the seventh day. (Gen. ii. 2; Exod. xx. 11, and xxxi. 17; Deut. v. 14.) Now there is no doubt that he wished to bring the faithful to imitate his example: it follows, then, that rest was enjoined upon the ancient people, that they should each rest from their works, and so conform themselves to God's example. For we are said to rest from our works when we are dead to ourselves; and allow ourselves to be governed by God's Spirit, when we live in him, and he in us. Now, therefore, we see that the grace of regeneration was promised to the ancient people when God consecrated the seventh day; and the Apostle also shows this in the Epistle to the Hebrews, where he treats of the true and lawful use of the Sabbath, and refutes the gross supposition with which the Jews were imbued, that God was properly worshipped by an outward rest. (Chap. iv. 5.) He shows them that it was only an outward symbol, and that it contained a spiritual mystery. It now follows, as I lately touched on it, that the Sabbath was a sacrament, since it was a visible figure of an invisible grace. And this also is expressed with sufficient clearness by the Prophet, when he says, *the Sabbath was given for a sign*. By this word, therefore, he shows that regeneration was promised to the ancient people; and if I may use the expression by a visible word, since God not only spoke, but wished some symbol or pledge or mark of his promise to be perpetual. The phrase *between me and you* must be noticed: from which we gather that there is a mutual agreement in the sacraments, by which God binds us to himself, and we mutually pledge our faith. And hence also their foolishness is refuted who think the sacraments nothing but marks of outward separation: for if the sacraments concern only the profession of faith, it is inconsistent with the Prophet's teaching that they are a mutual and reciprocal sign, as I may express it, since God requires faith on the part of his people; and he promises in return what he witnesses and prefigures by an outward sign. It now follows—

13. But the house of Israel rebelled against me in the wilderness: they walked not in my statutes, and they despised my judgments, which *if* a man do, he shall even live in them; and my sabbaths they greatly polluted: then I said, I would pour out my fury upon them in the wilderness, to consume them.

13. Et rebelles fuerunt in me[1] domus Israel[2] in deserto: in decretis meis non ambularunt, et judicia mea spreverunt: quæ qui fecerit homo vivet in ipsis: et Sabbatha mea violarunt valde: et dixi[3] effundere excandescentiam meam super eos in deserto ad consumendum eos.

14. But I wrought for my name's sake, that it should not be polluted before the heathen, in whose sight I brought them out.

14. Et feci propter nomen meum, ut non profanaretur in oculis gentium, sub quarum oculis eduxeram ipsos.

Here God pronounces that the sons were like their fathers; and that the people, after their deliverance from Egypt, were so obstinate in their wickedness as not to profit in any way. He had complained already before of their rejecting his grace: for it is equivalent to rejecting all offers to be corrupted by superstitions, and not to cleanse themselves from that defilement, although they knew it to be abominable before God. But after the law was promulgated, they then might have put away their perverse affections. And surely redemption ought to have conformed them to obey God; when they beheld his hand stretched out as it were from heaven, how was it that this spectacle did not avail to humble them, and to make them submissive to God? But in addition to the teaching of the law, God's promise was given, by which he bore witness to them, that if they sought from him the spirit of regeneration, the Sabbath would be really given them as a pledge and sign of it; and since all these things produced no effect, that was a proof of astound-

[1] Or, "were bitter against me."—*Calvin.*
[2] We have often spoken of this word.—*Calvin.*
[3] That is, "I have decreed."—*Calvin.*

ing contumacy. God says, therefore, that he obtained nothing more in the desert than he had formerly experienced from the people under their Egyptian tyranny: *then also*, says he, *the house of Israel exasperated me in the desert.* The circumstance of place must be noticed, because they were wonderfully rescued by God's incredible power, and they depended every moment on his good pleasure; for there they wanted food and drink: God daily rained down manna from heaven, and brought them water from the rock. (Exod. xvi. 14; Numb. xi. 9; Deut. viii. 15, 16.) Since, therefore, necessity compelled them every moment to look to God, was it not more than brutal stupidity to exasperate God? When men grow wanton, it arises from becoming intoxicated by prosperity, and forgetful of their lot through not feeling how much they need God's help. But when death is presented to our view, when terror hems us in on every side, when God is up in arms against us, what madness it is to despise him! We see, then, why the Prophet dwells so on this point.

He says too, *they did not walk in God's precepts, and they despised his judgments.* He confirms what was said yesterday, that they were not deceived through ignorance, but manifested utter contempt of God, since they knew well enough what was pleasing to him. Since, then, they had a sure rule which could not deceive them, we see how they wandered away after their own superstitions by deliberate wickedness. This is the reason, then, why Ezekiel says *that they despised God's judgments.* He repeats the promise which I expounded yesterday. For this reason also availed to exaggerate their crime, namely, the mildness of God in deigning to allure them: he did not command them, exactingly and imperiously, as he might have done, but he entered into a covenant with them, and testified that a reward was prepared for them if they kept the law. Since, therefore, they neglected this promise, we see that they were not only rebels, but ungrateful to God. He adds, *they had polluted his Sabbaths;* which I refer not only to the outward right, but rather to the inward spirit. It is true, indeed, that their impiety was sufficiently notorious as to outward desecration, as it appears from the seventeenth chapter of Jeremiah, when he says, that they carried their burdens on the Sabbath, and occupied themselves in common business. (Ver. 21, 22.) There is no doubt that they broke the Sabbath when they then promiscuously transacted their own business. But when it is added, *that they violated the Sabbath greatly* or grievously, we may understand that profanation is denoted in the mystery itself, since they struck off the yoke, and gave the rein to their own desires: for Isaiah also shows that the Sabbath was violated in this way, especially when the will of men is consulted. (Chap. lviii. 13.) For hypocrites think they have discharged every duty by abstaining from all work; but the Prophet replies, that this is a mere laughing-stock, since they fast on a Sabbath for strife and contention, and then that they gratify their will, which is opposed to self-denial. Hence God not only accuses the ancient people here for not hallowing the Sabbath, but also for neglecting its legitimate object and use. He now repeats what we saw yesterday. *I have determined, therefore, to pour out upon them mine anger in the desert to consume them.* If it is asked when this was done, it is sufficient to reply, that God's wrath was frequently inflamed by the people's wickedness. For although Moses does not verbally relate every event, yet there is no doubt that God often threatened the people with destruction, as we shall soon see with reference to their dispersion. It follows, *I did it for my name's sake, that it should not be profaned in the eyes of the Gentiles.* God repeats again that he was appeased, not because he pardoned them, but because he was unwilling to allow his name to become a laughing-stock among the nations. We said that in this way God's twofold pity is commended, as he had already gratuitously adopted the people: hence their redemption could only be ascribed to his sole and gratuitous liberality, since it flowed from the election or adoption which we have mentioned. But though this was one kind of mercy, yet it did not suffice to render the people worthy of the grace offered them. Hence it came to pass that the promise given to Abraham could not profit them, unless God conquered the nation's iniquity. This is the meaning of the Prophet when he says, that the people were preserved, although unworthy of it, since God saw that otherwise his name would be profaned among the nations. Without doubt he had respect to the covenant, since the Israelites had perished a hundred times over without any help from the name of God unless he had adopted them. It was necessary, therefore, that God should spare them, since their preservation was connected with his sacred name and regard for his covenant. It now follows—

15. Yet also I lifted up my hand unto them in the wilderness, that I would not bring them into the land which I had given *them*, flowing with milk and honey, which *is* the glory of all lands.

15. Atque etiam ego manum meam sustuli ipsis in deserto, ne inducerem eos in terram quam dederam ipsis fluentem lacte et melle, quæ desiderium est cunctis terris.[1]

God here shows that his threats were ineffectual, even when he inflicted severe punishment, yet the people were not broken down and subdued: and this is a sign of a most perverse disposition. The foolish are at length corrected with rods, but when those who are chastised become worse instead of repenting, they betray their desperate character. God therefore here signifies that the Israelites were of an abandoned disposition, because there were no means of bringing them back to good conduct. At first he enticed them by his mercy, then gave them the law, and added a sacrament, as we have seen; but this proved wholly useless: what remained then, except to terrify them partly by threats and partly by punishments? He tried both, for he threatened them when they sinned, without any advantage: then he showed them in reality that theirs was no vain terror, since all those died in the desert who had refused to go forward when he called them into the land of Canaan. (Num. xxxii. 10.) Since they were not bent by those signs of God's wrath, their contumacy appears so great, that they ought to perish a hundred times over: *I also,* says he, *raised my hand;* he doubtless means that he swore, as we gather from Moses and from the Psalms, I swore in my wrath if they should enter into my rest. (Ps. xcv. 11.) He says then *that he raised his hand;* we have explained whence the simile is taken, *that I would not bring them into the land which I had*

[1] Or, " is desirable."—*Calvin.*

given them. Here God emphatically shows how formidable that punishment was, as it deprived them of that sure heritage which he had bestowed on them: for before they were born they were lords of the land of Canaan—since four hundred years before it was promised to Abraham in their name. Since they cast themselves off from this inheritance, they plainly displayed their slothfulness: *I had given them an inheritance,* says he, for they compelled me to swear: *I swore* that they should not reach it. He adds, *a land flowing with milk and honey, desired by all nations.* By these words he enlarges upon the people's ingratitude, since they despised no mean benefit, but a land in which they might dwell happily. For God had so enriched it with his gifts, that they might have been as it were in paradise. Since then such fertility did not attract them to obey God, hence it appears, that they were in every way refractory. It afterwards follows—

16. Because they despised my judgments, and walked not in my statutes, but polluted my sabbaths: for their heart went after their idols.

16. Propterea quod in judiciis meis spreverunt:[1] in decretis meis non ambularunt et sabbatha mea polluerunt,[2] quia post idola sua[3] cor eorum ambulavit.

The reason of the oath of which mention has been made is expressed by Moses, because being frightened by a false report they wished to return to Egypt: but here a cause is assigned to their superstitions. (Num. xiii. 32, 33, and xiv. 1-3.) But it suits each case well, since if they had been sincerely obedient to God, they would never have refused to remove their camp, and fearlessly to proceed where he commanded them. But since they first detested the land, and then terror and despair seized their minds so that they rejected the inestimable blessing of God, it is clear that not a drop of piety existed in their hearts. Although therefore the special reason why they did not enter the land of Canaan was their refusing to obey the call of God, yet the Prophet adds also their superstitions. For impiety and contempt of God was the reason why they so boldly, proudly,

[1] That is, "they have despised my judgments and my decrees."—*Calvin.*
[2] Violated, profaned: the word חלל, *chelel,* is the same.—*Calvin.*
[3] Or, "filth, defilement," as I have elsewhere said.—*Calvin.*

and furiously rejected the grace of God, and wished even to stone Moses, and then when penitent they encouraged each other to return to live again under the tyranny of Egypt. We see, therefore, how the Prophet here lays down general causes from which that impious dislike of the land proceeded, as well as the rejection of the grace of God. He says, therefore, *because they had despised my judgments and had not walked in my statutes.* He here inverts the order: he had formerly said that they had not walked in his statutes and had despised my judgments; but now he begins with the contempt: *and have polluted my sabbaths, because their hearts went after their idols.* The sense is, that they always treated God deceitfully: and although they held that he was to be worshipped formally, yet they were always addicted to various superstitions: as also Stephen reproves them, (Acts vii. 40-43,) for he agrees entirely with our Prophet. As he puts sabbaths in the plural number, I do not interpret it so strictly as some do, thinking that the Prophet means sabbaths of years, and afterwards the jubilee: for there were three sabbaths among the Jews; that is, every seventh day was consecrated to God, and every seventh year, and every fiftieth. Although it is true that years were sabbatical as well as days, yet I do not think that the Prophet is making any subtle distinctions here: but I take sabbath to mean the seventh day. It now follows—

17. Nevertheless mine eye spared them from destroying them, neither did I make an end of them in the wilderness.	17. Et pepercit oculus meus super ipsos[1] ne perderem ipsos, et ne facerem ipsos[2] consumptionem in deserto.

This is added, because God often afflicted the people with heavy punishments, but he restrained himself, that he should not utterly destroy both their persons and their name. He says, then, *that he spared them* through respect for his own name, as he formerly said, *that he should not execute consumption on them;* that is, that he should not utterly blot out the memory of them. He did not spare them entirely to foster their depravity by his indulgence, but as we shall afterwards see, he withdrew his hand that he should not

[1] " My eye took no notice of them."—*Calvin.*
[2] " And I did not execute on them."—*Calvin.*

consume them, as he might most justly have done. It now follows—

18. But I said unto their children in the wilderness, Walk ye not in the statutes of your fathers, neither observe their judgments, nor defile yourselves with their idols:	18. Et dixi ad filios ipsorum in deserto, In decretis,[1] patrum vestrorum ne ambuletis, et judicia ipsorum ne servetis: et in idolis[2] ipsorum ne polluamini.
19. I *am* the Lord your God; walk in my statutes, and keep my judgments, and do them.	19. Ego Iehovah Deus vester, in decretis meis ambulate, et judicia mea servate, et facite ea.

After God has shown that the obstinate wickedness of the people was such that they profited by neither rigour nor clemency, he now says that the sons were altogether like their fathers. For when he says that he turned his discourse to their sons, he obliquely indicates that he was so broken down by their disgust, that he is unwilling to address the deaf. *I said*, therefore, *to their sons:* why not to themselves? because they had become obdurate in their impiety, and gave no hope of repentance. Since then God had experienced their utmost obstinacy, he says *that he turned his discourse to their sons; Do not walk in the statutes of your fathers, and do not observe their judgments.* Here God does not speak of bad examples and of plain and palpable crimes, but he uses words seemingly favourable—*judgments and statutes.* If he had simply said that their fathers were wicked, and hence the sons must take care not to imitate them, that would have been ordinary teaching; but by adaptation he uses honourable expressions, namely, *my statutes and judgments.* Meanwhile he forbids their posterity to conform to the statutes and laws of their fathers, meaning to their ceremonies and rites. Lest any should object that those statutes were to be observed which tend to a right end, he adds, *that ye pollute not yourselves with their filth and defilements.* Here the former language of accommodation is removed, and God as it were wipes away the colouring, that it may be clearly apparent that those statutes and precepts differed in nothing from thefts, robberies, and adulteries: this is the Prophet's meaning.

Besides, this passage is worthy of notice, because we may learn from it how frivolous is the excuse of those who boast

---

[1] Or, "statutes."—*Calvin.*   [2] Or, "pollutions."—*Calvin.*

of their fathers, and arrogantly predict that they will be pardoned if they conform themselves to their example. For God not only forbids us to imitate the gross and open wickedness of our parents, but their laws, statutes, and ceremonies, and whatever is apparently plausible, and seems to the common sense of mankind worthy of praise. And thus the foolishness of the papists is detected, who think that they lie safely concealed under the shield of Ajax, when they boast to us of the examples of their fathers, and the value of antiquity: we clearly see how plainly God's Spirit refutes them when he pronounces that they must obey his statutes and precepts, and not listen to open wickedness only, but not even to good intentions, as they say, and devotions, and the traditions of the fathers. But what is the worship of God in the papacy in these days but a confused jumble, which they have thrown together from numberless fictions? for whoever will examine all their triflings, will find them fabricated by the will of man; and they are not ashamed to oppose the traditions of their fathers to the word of God. Now, therefore, we see the whole papacy laid prostrate, and all the remarkable traditions of the fathers in which they boast, when the Prophet says, *walk ye not in the statutes of your fathers*. But since antiquity deserves some reverence, it would be gross and barbarous promiscuously to reject all the examples of the fathers: hence we need prudence and selection here, and God's Spirit suggests this to us when he adds *pollutions* or idols. Hence the traditions of the fathers must be examined; and it is a mark of prudent discretion to observe what they contain, and whence they proceed. If we discover that they have no other tendency than to the pure worship of God, we may embrace them; but if they draw us away from the pure and simple worship of God, if they infect true and sincere religion by their own mixtures, we must utterly reject them.

Let us proceed then. *I*, says he, *am Jehovah your God; walk ye in my statutes, and observe my judgments*. God confirms the former sentence, and at the same time provides a remedy for all corruptions when he says, *walk ye in my precepts, because I am your God:* for by these words he claims as peculiarly his own what men commonly arrogate to themselves. They do not dare, indeed, to despoil God of his authority, but they carry themselves as his allies, and infect his law with their commentaries, as if it was not sufficient for complete and solid wisdom. Here, therefore, God pronounces himself to be the only lawgiver. If, therefore, *I am your God, walk ye in my statutes.* Hence it follows, that we indirectly deny God when we turn aside even a little from his law. The passage is remarkable, if we only estimate the Prophet's language aright. For the two clauses must be read together, *because I am your God, therefore walk ye in my precepts,* and thus show that ye are my people. But if they are not content with God's precepts only, but mingle human comments with them, God indirectly teaches that he is not acknowledged, since they deprive him of a portion of his rights; for if God is one, he also is the only lawgiver. It follows—

20. And hallow my sabbaths; and they shall be a sign between me and you, that ye may know that I *am* the Lord your God.

20. Et sabbatha mea sanctificate, et erunt in signum inter me et vos, ad cognoscendum[1] quod ego Iehovah Deus vester.

What he had said generally concerning the commandments he now applies again to the Sabbath, and not without reason. For, as we said yesterday, God not only wished by that day of rest to exact from the people what was due to him, but he rather commands it for another purpose, namely, *that his Sabbaths should be sanctified.* But the manner of keeping it holy was formerly explained, since mere rest was insufficient. God was not satisfied by the people's resting from their occupations, but the inward sanctification was always the chief end in view. And for this reason he also repeats again, *that they may be a sign between me and you to show you that I Jehovah am your God.* In this passage God bears witness, that if the Jews rightly observed their Sabbaths they should feel the effects of that favour which he wished to be represented thereby. For we said that the Sabbath was a sacrament of regeneration: now therefore he promises the efficacy of his Spirit, if they did not shut the door by their own impiety and contempt. Hence we see that sacraments are

[1] That is, "that ye may recognise, or know."—*Calvin.*

never destitute of the virtue of the Spirit unless when men render themselves unworthy of the grace offered them. When papists speak of the sacraments they say that they are efficacious, if we only remove the obstacle of mortal sin: they make no mention of faith. If a person is neither a thief, nor an adulterer, nor a homicide, they say that the sacraments produce their own effect: for example, if any one without a single particle of faith intrudes himself at the table of Christ, they say that he receives not only his body and blood, but the fruit of his death and resurrection, and only because he has not committed mortal sin; that is, cannot be convicted of theft or homicide. We see how they are steeped in blindness, according to God's just judgment. We must hold, therefore, that there is a mutual relation between faith and the sacraments, and hence, that the sacraments are effective through faith. Man's unworthiness does not detract anything from them, for they always retain their nature. Baptism is the laver of regeneration, although the whole world should be incredulous: (Tit. iii. 5:) the Supper of Christ is the communication of his body and blood, (1 Cor. x. 16,) although there were not a spark of faith in the world: but we do not perceive the grace which is offered to us; and although spiritual things always remain the same, yet we do not obtain their effect, nor perceive their value, unless we are cautious that our want of faith should not profane what God has consecrated to our salvation.[1]

[1] At a period when the controversy concerning the efficacy of sacraments is revived with all its former virulence, and the authority of Calvin is often called in to decide between conflicting statements, the language of this passage is worthy of special notice. It would startle some of our modern critics to find Calvin calling the Sabbath "a Sacrament of regeneration." In treating this class of subjects, it is essential to ascertain the exact ideas of the medieval controversialists, and to perceive how very different they were from our own. For example, Protestants of the present day would pronounce any man unsound who allowed of more sacraments than two, while Romanists would require all men to admit them to be seven; yet Calvin would have no objection to the assertion that there are seventy. He used the word for what is now currently expressed by the phrase "the means of grace." All aids and helps to the cultivation of the life of God in the soul have been termed sacramental; and by using the word in a comprehensive sense, the assertion is strictly true. Sabbaths are to us, as well as to the Jews, means of grace, conducive to regeneration. Calvin also asserts that these means of grace are never destitute of the Holy

PRAYER.

Grant, Almighty God, since the doctrine of thy Gospel sounds daily in our ears, when thou invitest us so kindly by thy amazing clemency, and stretchest out thine hand by thine only-begotten Son,—Grant, I pray thee, that we may be of a teachable and flexible disposition, and that we may sincerely submit to thee: and since thy law contains so many dreadful examples of thy wrath, may we be moved by them, and may we walk with fear and trembling in obedience to thy word, that at length we may enjoy that inheritance which thou hast promised for us in thy heavenly kingdom, by the same Christ our Lord.—Amen.

Spirit's virtue, except we render ourselves unworthy of the grace which they contain. He differs from the papists, not with reference to what a sacrament is in itself, but as to the need of faith in the recipient for the personal advantage to be derived from it. The opinion is absolutely expressed, that they always retain their nature, on the principle that spiritual things always remain the same: man's unbelief is said to make no difference as to the reality of the grace inherent in the sacrament; it only affects our reception of it. The spiritual blessing is there: our want of faith is the only cause why the blessing does not pass by the appointed channel to the unworthy recipient. As the sentiments of our Reformer are sometimes quoted in support of views very different from this, the reader's attention is particularly directed to his commentary on this verse, since the greatest errors arise from interpreting controversial phrases by the modern meaning which the words have acquired.

The history of opinions which have formerly prevailed on subjects deeply interesting to ourselves is always serviceable towards the formation of accurate opinions. Hence we may here refer to Dr. Lawrence's Bampton Lectures for the year 1804, in which the lecturer has distinctly stated the different views taken by the Papists and the Schoolmen, the Lutherans and the followers of Zuingle and Calvin. In Sermon vi., p. 123, he makes the same statement with reference to the papists as Calvin does in his comment on this verse, viz., " asserting, among other extravagancies, that the Sacraments are in themselves efficacious by virtue of their own operation, exclusively of all merit in the recipient." In notes on Sermon iii., p. 276, he adds, " The Lutherans contended that the Holy Spirit was efficacious in baptism;" and quotes Calvin's letter to Melancthon, "...non inanes esse figuras sed reipsa præstari, quidquid figurant. In baptismo adesse spiritus efficaciam, ut nos abluat et regeneret." See also his opinion on the state of the children of Christians dying unbaptized. Instit., lib. iv. cap. 15, § 22. The view of Zuingle will be found in his *Declaratio de peccato originali*, Op., vol. ii. p. 118; and Epist. Urbano Regio, vol. i. p. 383; and of Bullinger, in his treatise *adversus Cala-baptistarum prava dogmata*, p. 57. It will not be expected that the admirers of Calvin will be satisfied with Dr. Lawrence's reasonings and conclusions; but the notes to his discourses form a most valuable digest of the views of the Schoolmen and the various Reformers of celebrity, selected with judgment from the voluminous disputations of those stirring times. See also the Dissertation on this verse at the end of this volume.

Lecture Sixty-Third.

21. Notwithstanding the children rebelled against me: they walked not in my statutes, neither kept my judgments to do them, which *if* a man do, he shall even live in them; they polluted my sabbaths: then I said, I would pour out my fury upon them, to accomplish my anger against them in the wilderness.

22. Nevertheless I withdrew mine hand, and wrought for my name's sake, that it should not be polluted in the sight of the heathen, in whose sight I brought them forth.

23. I lifted up mine hand unto them also in the wilderness, that I would scatter them among the heathen, and disperse them through the countries;

24. Because they had not executed my judgments, but had despised my statutes, and had polluted my sabbaths, and their eyes were after their fathers' idols.

21. Et rebelles fuerunt[1] me filii: in decretis meis non ambulaverunt, et judicia mea non servarunt, ut ea facerent: quæ qui fecerit homo vivet in ipsis: sabbatha mea profanarunt: et dixi[2] effundere iracundiam meam,[3] super eos ad complendum iram meam in ipsis in deserto.

22. Et retraxi[4] manum meam: et feci propter nomen meum, ne profanaretur in oculis gentium è quarum oculis eduxeram eos.

23. Etiam ego levavi manum meam ipsis in deserto[5] ad disjiciendos ipsos inter gentes, et spargendos per terras;

24. Eo quòd judicia mea non fecerunt, et statuta mea repudiarunt, et sabbatha mea violarunt, et post idola patrum suorum fuerunt eorum oculi.

I JOIN these four verses together, because they have been already explained, and I do not wish to burden you with useless repetitions. In short, God accuses the whole posterity, because they were by no means more obedient than their fathers. Again, he charges them with rebellion, since they neither obeyed his commands, nor were persuaded by mild promises; for, on the one hand, he demanded the worship due to him, and invited them softly by the promise of reward. He complains that neither plan succeeded. He adds, what we have already seen, that he proposed to scatter them through various quarters of the world, and utterly to dissipate them. He assigns as a reason for his moderation his unwillingness that his name should be profaned among the nations: he also announces that they had never restrained their impiety from bursting forth, and hence it was only through his own incredible patience and indulgence that they had not perished a hundred, nay, a thousand times. The rest may be gathered from the previous context. It follows—

---

[1] Or, "irritated," or, "exasperated me."—*Calvin*.
[2] That is, "I decreed."—*Calvin*.
[3] Or, "my burning wrath."—*Calvin*.
[4] "Still I drew back."—*Calvin*.
[5] Or, "against them."—*Calvin*.

| 25. Wherefore I gave them also statutes *that were* not good, and judgments whereby they should not live. | 25. Ego quoque dedi illis decreta non bona, et judicia in quibus non vivent. |

Here God announces that he had taken vengeance upon a people so hard and obstinate, by permitting them to endure another yoke, since they would not be ruled by the doctrine of the law; for we saw that, when God imposed the law upon the Israelites, they would have been extremely happy, had they only considered how honourable it was to be in covenant with God, who deigned to bind them to himself in mutual fidelity. This was a remarkable honour and privilege, since God not only showed them what was right, but promised them a reward which he by no means owed them. But what was the conduct of that unteachable nation? It threw off the yoke of the law; hence it deserved to experience a different government. *God, therefore, gave them laws that were not good,* when he suffered them to be miserably subjected to an immense heap of errors: such laws as these were not good. Some writers have violently distorted this passage, by thinking the law itself, as promulgated by Moses, "not good," since Paul calls it deadly; but they corrupt the Prophet's sense, since God is comparing his law with the superstitions of the Gentiles: others explain it of the tributes which the people were compelled to pay to foreigners. But, first of all, God does not speak here of only one age; nay, during the time of the Israelites' freedom his vengeance was nevertheless severe.

Thus, in the next verse, the Prophet confirms what I have briefly touched on, namely, that *the laws called not good* are all the fictions of men, by which they harass themselves, while they think that God is worshipped acceptably in this way: for we know how miserably men labour and distract themselves when Satan has fascinated them with his toils, and when they anxiously invent numerous rites, because there is no end of their superstitions; hence these statutes are not good: for when they have undergone much labour in their idolatry, no other reward awaits them than God's appearance against them as an avenger to punish the profanation of his own lawful worship. They indeed by no means look for this, but they utterly deceive themselves;

hence they must hope for no reward but what is founded on the covenant and promise of God; for all false and vicious forms of worship, all adventitious rites, which men heap together from all sides, have no promise from God, and hence they vainly trust to them for life. God began to show them this in the wilderness; but in succeeding ages he did not fail to exercise the same vengeance. We see how they fell in with the superstitions of the Moabites; and why so? unless God blinded them by his just judgments. (Numb. xxv. 1-3.) He had experienced their untamed dispositions, and so he set them free from control; and not only so, but afterwards gave them up to Satan, and so he says *that he gave them laws that were not good.* The Prophet might indeed have said, that they despised God's law through their own wisdom, that they foolishly and rashly legislated for themselves: this was indeed true; but he wished to express the penalty of which Paul speaks, when he says that the impious were delivered to a reprobate mind, and to obedience to a lie, (Romans i. 24-26,) since they did not submit to the truth, and did not suffer themselves to be ruled by God, and thus were given up to the tyranny of Satan and to the service of mere creatures. Now, therefore, we understand the Prophet's meaning, *I have given them also,* says he, *laws not good,* as if he had said that the people so threw themselves into various idolatries, that God desired in this way to avenge their incredible obstinacy; for if the Jews had calmly acquiesced in God's sovereignty, he had not given them evil laws, that is, he had not suffered them to be so tormented under Satan's tyranny; but when they were entangled in his snares, God openly shows them to be unworthy of his government and care, since they were too refractory. It follows—

26. And I polluted them in their own gifts, in that they caused to pass through *the fire* all that openeth the womb, that I might make them desolate, to the end that they might know that I *am* the Lord.

26. Et contaminavi ipsos in suis muneribus, trajiciendo quidquid aperit vulvam, ut perderem ipsos, ut quod, (*sed supervacuum est,*) ut cognoscant quod ego Iehovah.

There is no doubt that God here continues the same doctrine: hence we gather that injurious laws were given to the people when they adopted various errors and worshipped idols of their own fabrication instead of God: hence it is added, *I polluted them in their gifts.* This, then, was added by the Prophet, lest the Jews should object that they had not altogether rejected the worship of God ; for they mingled the ceremonies of the laws with the fictions of the Gentiles, as we saw before, and the Prophet will shortly repeat : in this way they thought they discharged their duty to God, though they added mixtures of their own. Here the Prophet meets them, and cuts off all occasion for turning aside, since they were polluted in their gifts, and nothing was pure or sincere when they thus corrupted God's precepts by their comments. However, they daily offered their gifts, and professed to present them to the true God ; yet they obtained no advantage, because God abominated mixtures of this kind, as we have previously said ; for he cannot bear to be worshipped by the will of men, but wishes his children to be simply content with his commands. Now, we perceive the meaning of the Prophet—*God pollutes them in their gifts ;* that is, renders their gifts polluting whenever they think that they discharge their duty ;—but how ? why, he says, *when they cause whatever opens the womb to pass through.*[1] Here the Prophet touches on only one kind of superstition, but, by a figure of speech, he means all kinds, by which the Jews vitiated God's pure worship ; for this superstition was very detestable, to pass their sons through the fire, and to consecrate them to idols. But in this passage God speaks only of the first-born, so as greatly to exaggerate the crime : that ceremony was indeed general ; but since God claimed the first-born as his own, and wished them to be redeemed at a fixed price, (Exod. xiii. 2, xxii. 29, and xxxiv. 19, 20,) and by this act wished the remembrance of their redemption to be kept up, since all the first-born of Israel, as well as of animals, had escaped, whilst those of the Egyptians perished, (Numb. iii. 13, and viii. 16,) was it not monstrous to pass through the fire, and to offer to idols those who were specially devoted and sacred to God ? We see, then, that the Prophet does not speak in vain of the first-born.

[1] Supply " the fire," as in the authorized version.

That I should destroy them, says he, *and they should know that I am Jehovah.* God here shows that he had proceeded gradually to the final vengeance; and for this reason the people were the more convicted of stupidity, since they never perceived God's judgments manifest. If God had suddenly and impetuously issued his vengeance from heaven, men's astonishment would not have been wonderful; but when he grants them space of time and a truce that they may weigh the matter at leisure, and admonishes them to repentance, not once only, but often; and then if they remain always the same and are not affected, they show themselves utterly desperate by this slothfulness, as the Prophet now asserts. But when he adds, *that they may know that I am Jehovah*, he means that as he was not acknowledged as a father by the Jews, he would be their judge, and compel them whether they would or not to feel the formidable nature of that power which they despised. Since we have treated this subject fully before, we now pass it by more lightly. Yet we must notice this, that God is recognised by the reprobate, since, when his fatherly goodness has been for a long time despised by them, he at length appears as a judge, and draws them against their will to his tribunal, and executes his vengeance, so that they cannot escape. It follows—

27. Therefore, son of man, speak unto the house of Israel, and say unto them, Thus saith the Lord God, Yet in this your fathers have blasphemed me, in that they have committed a trespass against me.

28. *For* when I had brought them into the land, *for* the which I lifted up mine hand to give it to them, then they saw every high hill, and all the thick trees, and they offered there their sacrifices, and there they presented the provocation of their offering: there also they made their sweet savour, and poured out there their drink-offerings.

27. Propterea loquere ad domum Israel, fili hominis, et dic illis, Sic dicit Dominator Iehovah: Adhuc in hoc contumeliosi in me fuerunt patres vestri prævaricando in me prævaricatione.

28. Nam introduxi[1] in terram pro qua sustuleram manum meam ad dandum eam ipsis: et viderunt omnem collem excelsum, et omnem arborem frondosam: et sacrificarunt illic sacrificia sua, et obtulerunt illic irritationem oblationis suæ, et posuerunt illic odorem bonæ fragrantiæ suæ, et fuderunt illic sua libamina.

He now descends to the wickedness of the people, by which God was provoked after they had taken possession of

---

[1] "For the copula ought to be resolved in this way."—*Calvin*.

the land of Canaan, since they despised God after being so carefully warned. He complains, therefore, that this was very disgraceful, since, after he had put them in possession of the land of promise, they had never desisted from purposely insulting him. ·This disgrace was intolerable, since he had profited nothing by them in the wilderness: this witnessing was sufficiently serious to stir them up. "Walk ye not in the decrees of your fathers : I am your God, observe ye my law." Since, therefore, God drew them under obedience to himself, what a mark of pride it was not to attend to that witness-bearing, but to pursue their own mad career? In truth, the crime was the more atrocious when at length they entered the land of Canaan, and had obtained so many victories, that they did not learn by experience how God declared his power for the very purpose of binding them closer to himself. For the numerous benefits which God had conferred upon them were but so many bonds by which they were bound more closely to him. This expostulation, then, is not in vain, when he reproaches them by saying, *when they dishonoured me,* or rebelled against me. This was not a single crime, or simple perfidy, but a continual delight in wantonly insulting him ; for גדף, *gedef,* signifies to reject, treat contumeliously, or disdain. God, therefore, by this word wishes to express the deliberate insolence of the people, while they rose so wickedly against him as if they would spit in his face. The full meaning is, that they were not only breakers of treaties and rebels when they contaminatèd the land of Canaan with their superstitions, but were so petulant that they professedly threw scorn upon God.

Hence, *after I had brought them into the land for which,* or concerning which, *I had lifted up my hand to give it them, they saw,* says he, *every high hill, and every green* or branching *tree, and there they sacrificed.* God wished to have one altar built for himself, and sacrifices to be offered in one place ; nay, before the people had any certain and fixed station, God was unwilling that any altar should be built to him of polished stones, that no trace of it should remain ; but a mound only was to be made of either turf or rough stones. (Exod. xx. 25 ; Deut. xxvii. 5, 6.) Now he says, whenever hills and branching trees were lying before them, there they found enticements to superstition. This, therefore, is the reproach which God now complains was offered to him. But this passage, like many others, teaches, that not only is God's worship corrupted when his honour is transferred to idols, but also when men heap up their own fictions, and contaminate God's commands by the mixture. We must remember, then, that there are two kinds of idolatries ; the one being grosser when idols are worshipped openly, and Moloch, or any Baal, is substituted for the living God : that is a palpable superstition, because God is in some sense cast down from his throne. But the other kind of idolatry, although more hidden, is abominable before God, namely, when, under the disguise of a name, men boldly mingle whatever comes into their minds, and invent various modes of worship ; as at present we see in the papacy statues adored, and dead men invoked, and God's honour violated in various ways. Hence, however, the papists chatter, they are self-convicted, and the wonder is that they are not utterly silenced, since their superstitions are so gross that even boys perceive them. But there are other superstitions more specious and refined ; for when they have invented many things in honour of God, they will not bring forward the names of either St. Barbara or St. Christopher, but the name of God covers all those abominations. But we see that this excuse is frivolous, when men assert that they have nothing else in their mind than the worship of God. Not only does God wish worship to be offered to himself alone, but that it should be without any dependence on human will : he wishes the law to be the single rule of true worship ; and thus he rejects all fictitious rites. Hence the Prophet deservedly excuses the Israelites, *because they turned their eyes towards every high hill and every branching tree, and there offered the provocation of their offering.* He calls it *the provocation of their offering,* since they not only foolishly poured forth much·money on those vitiated rites, but also provoked God to anger. We see, therefore, that men not only lose their labour when they decline from God's commands, and rashly fatigue themselves with their own superstitions, but they provoke God to a contest, because they snatch from him the right of a lawgiver: for it is in his power to determine how he ought to be worshipped; and when men claim this power to themselves, it is like ascending to the very throne of God. But if they follow the inventions of others, still it is setting them up as lawgivers, while God is degraded from his tribunal. Thus it is not surprising if God's wrath is provoked by any sacrifices, besides those which the law prescribes. And this is expressed very clearly by Isaiah, when God announces that he will do what will frighten them all as an unexpected prodigy: I will blind the eyes of the wise, says he, and I will take away prudence from the aged. (Chap. xxix. 14.) And why so? because they worship me by the precepts of men.

It follows, *And they offered their sweet odour,* or agreeable fragrance. These two things seem contrary to each other, that their offerings inflamed God's wrath, and yet their savour was sweet. But the Prophet speaks ironically when he says, *their incense was sweet-smelling.* By conceding this he derides them, since they falsely supposed God was appeased in this way, although he reproves them at the same time for defiling, by their corruptions, that incense which ought to have been of delightful fragrance. For the language of Moses is repeated: The scent shall reach God's nostrils, and he shall be appeased. (Deut. xxxiii. 10.) Since, then, the incense of the law was sweet-smelling, God here bitterly reproaches the Jews for infecting that good odour with their foulness. Hence the phrase is used in a sense contrary to its direct meaning. Lastly, he says, *they have poured out their drink-offerings there.* Here God reviews the various kinds of oblations which he had fully prescribed in the law, but he shows that the Jews were rebellious against them all; and he further detects their unbridled petulance, since they had not only violated the law in one point, but had left no part untouched by their superstitions. God had commanded sacrifices, but these they rendered polluting: he added various oblations, yet all these they defiled: he desired libations to be made, and wine to be poured out, but this part of the service was not kept pure from superstitions. Thus he shows that the people purposely took all means of declaring war against God, when they falsely pretended that nothing more was prescribed than to worship him as they pleased. It follows—

29. Then I said unto them, What *is* the high place whereunto ye go? And the name thereof is called Bamah unto this day.

29. Et dixi illis, ut quid[1] excelsum quod vos ingredimini?[2] et vocatum fuit nomen ejus excelsum usque ad hunc diem.

Although there is no ambiguity in the Prophet's words, yet the sentence seems frigid, and interpreters, in my judgment, have not understood the Prophet's meaning. It may seem spiritless, that God should ask, *what is the high place?* But it means that they were not deceived through ignorance, since he had often cautioned them against profaning the true and genuine worship, for he often endeavoured to draw them back again when he saw them wandering after their own superstitions. Hence they are continually rebuked by the prophets; and their obstinacy is the more apparent, since, nevertheless, they followed their own perverseness. But because all these reproaches were useless, God here enlarges upon their crime, since they were deaf. *I have said,* therefore; that is, by means of prophets. For we know how constantly the prophets discharged their duty, by urging them to worship at one altar only. For this reason the people's wickedness was greater; whence God says, What is this? and why do ye so greatly desire your high places when they displease me, and ye know my commands? your ears are deaf, and obstructed by wickedness. On the whole, he asks how could such madness seize upon them as to approach these high places, since he had pointed out a place where he was to be sought and invoked. My temple, says he, is neglected; meanwhile ye run to high places, and yet *it is known by the name of a high place.* There is no mystery in this word; but God means that no reproaches or threats of his prophets could prevent the people from worshipping on these high places. He says, then, *that the name was still used,* since the same dignity and religious regard for them still

[1] " Whither," or, " of what kind."—*Calvin.*
[2] Or, " why do ye go there?"—*Calvin.*

flourished, when their remembrance ought to be utterly abolished. If God had only once pronounced that those high places were not approved by him, all ought to have changed their course instantly : he exclaimed against them long and vehemently by his prophets, and yet the name "high places" was constantly in everybody's mouth ; it was famous among them, as if God ought to be sought there. Now therefore we see that the Jews were condemned for too much pride, because they not only failed to desert their high places when repeatedly admonished, but they pertinaciously wished to oppose those places to God's sanctuary, although they were so many pollutions. Hence we gather the condemnation of the people's obstinate malice, since fathers handed down the name to their sons, so that through a continued posterity they opposed these high places to the only sanctuary of God. It follows—

| 30. Wherefore say unto the house of Israel, Thus saith the Lord God, Are ye polluted after the manner of your fathers ? and commit ye whoredom after their abominations ? | 30. Propterea dic ad domum Israel, Sic dicit Dominator Iehovah, An in via patrum vestrorum vos polluti estis ? et post idola ipsorum[1] vos scortamini ? |

Now at length the Prophet openly attacks those by whom he was consulted. After showing that they sprang from impure fathers—which was sufficiently manifest from their never ceasing to provoke God in every age from the very beginning to the end—he turns their own language against them, and asks, *whether they were polluted after the superstitions of their fathers ?* The old interpretation is " truly ;" but ה, *he*, the mark of interrogation, does not allow of that. I am surprised at the rendering of some expositors, " are ye not polluted ?" as if the word were הלוא, *hel-va*, for in my opinion they pervert the Prophet's sense, for this would make him ask absurdly, *what ? are ye polluted in the way of your fathers ? and are ye gone astray after their idols ?* For when they were in exile, that disinheriting ought to subdue them although they had been endued with a more than iron pride : and then they pretended to piety, when they came to the Prophet and desired to receive some consolation from him. Since, therefore, they pretended to some modesty,

[1] Or, "filthiness."—*Calvin.*

God here asks them *how they could pollute themselves in the way of their fathers?* what could it all mean? the things are quite contrary: ye approach my servant as if you intended to submit your minds and your senses to my word; but when ye so feign yourselves to be attentive to my answers, *how does it happen that ye pollute yourselves in the way of your fathers?* This seems to me the Spirit's meaning. *Thou shalt say, then, are ye polluted in the way of your fathers?* that is, are ye so obstinate as not to reflect upon your course, and never to look back? for ye see how severely God was revenged on your obstinacy: ye now seek me in appearance, as if this were your only refuge; then how is it that *ye pollute yourselves in the way of your fathers? and why do ye commit fornication after their idols?* It now follows—

31. For when ye offer your gifts, when ye make your sons pass through the fire, ye pollute yourselves with all your idols, even unto this day: and shall I be enquired of by you, O house of Israel? *As* I live, saith the Lord God, I will not be enquired of by you.	31. Et offerendo dona vestra,[1] et trajiciendo filios vestros per ignem vos polluimini in omnibus idolis vestris usque hodie: et ego inquirar a vobis, domus Israel? Vivo ego dicit Dominator Iehovah, si inquirar a vobis.

He follows up the same sentiment, that it was a monstrous sin that they so pertinaciously remained fixed in the perverse imitation of their fathers: for they had been drawn off from their lusts by God's numerous chastisements, and then they pretended to be afterwards disposed to obedience: God therefore here says, *why, then, by offering your gifts, do ye make your sons pass through the fire, and pollute yourselves with all your idols even to this day?* For this question concerns what is quite incredible and worthy of the greatest surprise, since there was no way of reconciling the sufferings of the Israelites in exile with their remaining obstinate in their wickedness. But the Prophet here again deprives them of that vain pretence with which they covered themselves in offering their gifts: he concedes to them what was true, yet, at the same time, he objects, that *they passed their sons through the fire, and were polluted in all their idols.* He adds, at length, *shall I be inquired of by you?* I have elsewhere explained that clause, which is now for the third time

---

[1] "By tendering your oblations."—*Calvin.*

repeated. Many take it in a different sense, that God will not deign to answer them any more: but, in my opinion, he simply reproaches their perfidy, because, when they approached the Prophet, they wished to blind his eyes. *Shall I*, says he, *be inquired of you?* for דרש, *deresh*, means to seek, and to attain the end of our search, when the person asked answers, and the person sought presents himself. But here God simply shows that they do not come in a right mind, and that nothing else was imposed on them except seeking him. But because that was almost incredible, hence he swears that they were merely hypocritical in pretending to true piety in suppliantly applying to the Prophet for an answer in God's name, and then wantonly deriding it, and impiously and wickedly using his name, and thus profaning it.

PRAYER.

Grant, Almighty God, since thou dost not cease thy daily exhortations to repentance, but indulgest us, and bearest with us, while thou correctest us by thy word and thy chastisements, that we may not remain obstinate, but may learn to submit ourselves to thee: Grant, I pray thee, that we may not offer ourselves as thy disciples with feigned repentance, but be so sincerely and cordially devoted to thee, that we may desire nothing else than to progress more and more in the knowledge of thy heavenly doctrine, till at length we enjoy that full light which we hope for through our Lord Jesus Christ.—Amen.

Lecture Sixty-Fourth.

32. And that which cometh into your mind shall not be at all, that ye say, We will be as the heathen, as the families of the countries, to serve wood and stone.

33. *As* I live, saith the Lord God, surely with a mighty hand, and with a stretched-out arm, and with fury poured out, will I rule over you.

32. Et ascendit[1] super spiritum vestrum non erit, quia vos dixistis,[2] Erimus sicut gentes, sicut familiæ terrarum, ut serviamus ligno et lapidi.

33. Vivo ego, dicit Dominator Iehovah, Si non in manu robusta et brachio extento, et excandescentia effusa dominabor super vos.

Now God discloses what those old men had in their minds who, as well as the rest of the captives, came to the Prophet

[1] We must understand the relative, " that which arises."—*Calvin.*

[2] It is the participle, " ye say."—*Calvin.*

for the purpose of inquiry, namely, a feeling of despair, since they thought nothing would be more useful to themselves than to revolt utterly from God, and to form themselves after the manner and rites of the Gentiles; for they found themselves specially hated by the profane nations, because they worshipped a peculiar God. Since, therefore, the law separated them from all the rest of the world, that they might escape that hatred and envy, they encouraged the perverse intention of deserting God's worship and passing over to the Gentiles. For they hoped that those who had been formerly hostile would have shown themselves favourable. Now God not only announces that he would not suffer it, but he asserts with an oath, *what ye are thinking of shall not come to pass, since I will draw you back with a strong hand, and with an extended arm, and poured out wrath.* The meaning is, that although those miserable captives desired to throw off God's yoke and to mingle themselves with the profane nations, yet God would have respect to his covenant and not suffer them to be snatched away from him, just as a master fetches back his fugitive slave; or like a prince who might destroy the perfidious and rebellious, yet only chastises them that they may groan under a hard slavery: this is the complete sense.

But this passage is worthy of observation, since in the present day the same thought makes many anxious; for the name of sincere piety distresses them, and so they consult their love of ease, and satisfy both themselves and others by uniting with the rest of the world, and avoiding the hatred of mankind in consequence of their religion. Others again desire to escape in any way from God, because they feel him hostile to them, for the condition of the Church seems to them much worse than that of the world at large. And truly as God takes special care of it, so he chastises its faults more severely. We see then how he spares unbelievers and foreigners, as if he connived at their crimes: meanwhile his hand is always extended to chastise all who profess to be in the number of the pious. But some would desire to bid farewell to God, if they could choose for themselves. Hence I said we must observe this passage. The Israelites thought that nothing would be better than to be joined to the Gentiles and to become in all respects like them, since they imagined that in this way they would enjoy relaxation, since God was more lenient to the Gentiles than he had been to them, and because they perceived themselves exposed to many dangers and troubles, harassed by assaults and subject to daily threats. Hence that perverse deliberation which is here reproved;—*what arises in your mind,* says he, *shall not come to pass, because ye say we shall be as the nations and the families of the earth.* But we must also consider the end, because the people's folly was so great that they thought they would be free from God's chastisements, if they utterly rejected all religion. God therefore denies that he would suffer it. Now a clearer explanation follows : *As I live,* says he, *if I will not rule over you with a strong hand and a stretched-out arm;* in this sense—when they had removed all refuges he would yet be an avenger of his rights and empire, so as to compel them to return to him, as we have said, and thus violently to bring back the fugitives. We now see the great stupidity of the people in thinking the only remedy for their troubles to be in declining from true piety. Let us then be careful that we do not harden ourselves when God chastises us, and desire to withdraw from his power and dominion. Meanwhile God shows that he will rule, but in some other way; because we know with what humanity he treated his people, and what patience he exercised towards them, when they so often provoked his wrath. He now announces *that he would be the Lord, but with a strong hand and a stretched-out arm,* since he would forget his former clemency and subject them to perverse bondage. As when a master sees that he cannot obtain voluntary obedience from his slaves, he compels them to the galleys, or other laborious works, until they become half dead. God denounces that such will be the condemnation which he will use against them, since they never profited by either clemency or pardon. It follows—

34. And I will bring you out from the people, and will gather you out of the countries wherein ye are scattered,	34. Et educam vos e populis, et colligam vos e terris per quas fuistis dispersi, in manu valida,

| with a mighty hand, and with a stretched-out arm, and with fury poured out. | (*vel robusta,*) et brachio extento, et excandescentia effusa. |

He confirms the same sentiment, and at the same time marks out the manner of his dominion. For when the Jews were dispersed in captivity, they were like strangers to God's jurisdiction: they were mingled with the Gentiles, and their condition seemed very like an exemption from God's power. Now God signifies when he wishes to recover his right, that he had a place at hand, *since he will bring them out from the Gentiles, and gather them from the lands through which they were dispersed.* We are aware, as we have often said before, that it was a kind of abdication, when God expelled the ten tribes from the land of Canaan and a part also of that of Judah. Since then they were disinherited, they thought themselves free on their part, and they no longer regarded the authority of God, since they ceased to be his peculiar heritage when they were deprived of the promised land. Here God reminds them that although he had emancipated them for the time, yet they were in some sense under his hand, since he would collect them again, and so subdue them, that they should not escape his authority. *I will draw you back,* says he, *and gather you with an outstretched arm and with a strong hand.* But what he adds concerning the fury of his wrath does not seem consistent with this. For it was a sign of favour to collect them again, although hard and sorrowful slavery awaited them; yet they might perceive some taste of the divine goodness in gathering them from exile. For we know the bitterness of their captivity, especially under the Chaldæans, by whom they were subdued. But the phrase *wrath* may relate as much to the Gentiles as to the Israelites themselves: yet I explain it more willingly of the Israelites, because although God in reality shows that he did not altogether neglect them, yet he asserts his right as a master grievously offended. Just as a person who had lost his slave may afterwards receive him into his house, and yet that house may be like a sepulchre, because he is either thrust into a deep dungeon, or three or four times as much is exacted of him as he can bear. So therefore God pronounces, although he may gather the

Israelites again under his hand, yet they shall feel him to be displeased with them, since he nevertheless will require the punishment of their impiety; and this will be better understood from the context.

35. And I will bring you into the wilderness of the people, and there will I plead with you face to face.	35. Et introducem vos in desertum gentium, et judicabor vobiscum illic[1] facie ad faciem.
36. Like as I pleaded with your fathers in the wilderness of the land of Egypt, so will I plead with you, saith the Lord God.	36. Quemadmodum judicatus sum[2] cum patribus vestris in deserto terræ Ægypti, sic disceptabo vobiscum dicit Dominator Iehovah.

He specially marks this reason here, which is a medium between rejection and reconciliation to favour: for God's bringing the Israelites out of Chaldæa might seem a sign of favour, as if he were again their deliverer. But he here defines why he intended to bring them forth, *namely, to plead with them in the desert as with their fathers.* We know that when the people came out of Egypt they did not possess the promised land, because they shut the door against themselves by their ingratitude: but if there had been no hope left, it was better for the people to spend their time under the tyranny of Egypt than to pine away in the desert. For it was a kind of life scarcely human to wander in a wilderness and to behold nothing pleasant or agreeable; a mere solitude instead of cultivated fields, and nothing but discomfort instead of beautiful flowers and trees and undulating ground: and besides this, to feed on nothing but manna, to taste no wine, to drink only water from the rock, and to endure heat and cold in the open air. Such freedom then was by no means agreeable, unless they had hoped to become possessors of the land of Canaan. But a whole generation was deprived of that advantage through their ingratitude. God therefore appositely compares them to their fathers, who had gone forth into the wilderness, and he says, *I will make you pass into the desert of the nations.* Here he compares the desert of Egypt to that of the Gentiles. Although the passage from the land of Canaan to Chaldæa is partly across an arid and unfruitful wilderness, yet I do not doubt that

---

[1] That is, " I will plead with you by right."—*Calvin.*
[2] That is, " I have pleaded."—*Calvin.*

God here metaphorically points out the state of the people after their return from exile.

The complete meaning is, as he surrounded their fathers throughout their whole life in the wilderness, so after they were brought back from Chaldæa their life should be as solitary as if they were banished to an obscure corner of the world, and to a miserable and deserted land. Here, therefore, another region is not intended, but the state of the people when dwelling in the land of Canaan; although he speaks not only of that small band which returned to their country, but of the liberty promiscuously given to all. He calls that state *a desert of the Gentiles*, to which all were subjected, whether they remained in distant regions or returned home. We must hold, then, that God would be so far the deliverer of the people that the benefit would reach only a few, since, when the multitude wandered in the desert, they perished there, and did not enjoy the promised inheritance. We now see how God established his sway over the Israelites, when he did not suffer them to be perpetually captive, and yet did not show himself appeased when he brought them back, since he still remained a severe judge. *I will bring you,* therefore, *into the desert of the nations;* this is the heat of anger of which he had spoken, *and I will judge you,* or plead with you, *face to face.* He signifies by these words, that although their return to Judæa was evident, yet he was not propitious, since he met them as an adversary. *There,* says he, *I will meet with you face to face,* as when contention is rife, adversaries become opposed, and contend hand to hand: thus God here points out the extremity of rigour when he says, *that he will dispute with them face to face.* But he says, that *he was a pleader in the desert of Egypt,* and the sense extends to the future; not that it ought to be understood that God descended to plead a cause, and place himself at another's tribunal; still it was a kind of pleading when the people were compelled to feel that their impiety and obstinacy was not excusable; and also when experience at the same time taught them that God was by no means appeased, since his wrath was again stirred up. Isaiah's language is slightly different: Come ye, says he, let us reason together, I will plead with you. (Chap. i.) He is there prepared to argue his cause, as if with an equal. But the case is soon closed and the sentence passed, since it is evident that the people are deservedly punished by God on account of their sins. Thus he pleaded with their fathers in the Egyptian desert when he deprived them all of entrance into the promised land. And afterwards he often punished them for their murmurs, perverse cravings, lusts, idolatries, and other crimes. Hence, let us learn that God is pleading with us whenever any signs of his anger appear; for we cannot derive any advantage from obstinate resistance: and hence nothing remains but to accuse ourselves for our faults. It follows—

37. And I will cause you to pass under the rod, and I will bring you into the bond of the covenant.

37. Et transire faciam vos sub virga, et adducam vos in vinculo fœderis.

He follows up the same kind of instruction, that the people were not permitted to perish because they belonged to him, as if he had said that they should be always his, whether they liked it or not. And yet he seems to promise here what was very agreeable, that he would always esteem them as his flock. This is the meaning of *to pass under the rod;* for שבט, *shebet*, does not mean a sceptre here, nor a staff by which a delinquent is struck, but it means a shepherd's crook. It is, then, a simile taken from a shepherd who numbers and marks his flock; and this phrase often recurs. It means, because God has once acquired the people as his own, he cannot be rightly deprived of them. The exiles, indeed, had imagined themselves free if they could blot out of their minds and memories the name of the true God, and pollute themselves with the defilements of the Gentiles. But God, on the other hand, pronounces, that as a shepherd notices his sheep, and counts their number, and makes them pass under his staff, like a king reviewing his army, so he would reckon up his people, and not suffer any one to snatch them from him, since he claims authority over them all without exception. Now, therefore, we understand the sense of the words: whence we gather again, that abandoned men gain nothing by their obstinacy, but God's really showing that the dominion which he has once assumed cannot by any means be snatched away from him. So this passage teaches us the kind of reward which awaits all apostates who think themselves emancipated when they brutally indulge in impiety, because *God at length will make them pass under the rod,* that is, he will call and compel them to render an account, as if their profession of faith was like a brand burnt in to their hearts.

He says, *in the bonds of a covenant,* but in a different sense from what Hosea denominates a bond of affection. (Chap. xi. 4.) He is there treating of reconciliation ; but in this passage God pronounces that he will no longer be entreated by the Israelites. Hence, *the bond of the covenant* means the constancy of his covenant, as far as he is concerned : and the simile is suitable, because God had bound his people to himself, on the condition that they should be always surrounded with these bonds. Hence, when they petulantly wandered like untamed beasts, yet God had hidden bonds of his covenant : that is, he persevered in his own covenant, so that he collected them all again to himself, not to rule over them as a father, but to punish their revolt more severely. Here is a tacit comparison between the Israelites and the Gentiles; for the Gentiles, through their never approaching nearer to God, wandered away in their licentiousness without restraint. But the state of the elect people was different, since the end of their covenant was this, that God held them bound to him, even if the whole world should escape from him. It follows—

38. And I will purge out from among you the rebels, and them that transgress against me: I will bring them forth out of the country where they sojourn, and they shall not enter into the land of Israel; and ye shall know that I *am* the Lord.

38. Et purgabo[1] e vobis rebelles et perfidos in me : e terra habitationum suarum educam impios, et ad terram Israel non ingredientur : et cognoscetis quod ego Iehovah.

He continues the discourse which he had commenced, namely, that God would not suffer the exiles to withdraw themselves from him from the time he had adopted them. Then, since they were bound by the blessing of redemption,

[1] Or, " I will choose."—*Calvin.*

although they thought themselves far removed from the sight of God, after they were cast into exile, he says he would be present *to gather them from the land of their dwellings;* that is, wherever they were dispersed to bring them out. Some suppose the phrase to include a promise of favour, because it is said, I will purge you ; but the word to choose, as I prefer to render it, or to discern, means, that God will drag to light those who think they have obtained hiding-places in which they can escape his eyes. Although, therefore, they promise themselves complete exemption from God's authority, he, on the other hand, pronounces them deceived, since he would collect them all together *from the land of their habitations*, although they were dispersed in different places. God's threatenings are sufficiently evident from the second clause of the verse, *they shall not come*, says he, *into the land of Israel, and ye shall know that I am Jehovah.* He confirms what we saw before, that when liberty was granted them, they did not on that account become God's Church, since he had another reason for ruling over them, namely, to chastise them severely for their wickedness. *They shall not come*, therefore, *into the land of Israel;* that is, they shall remain, and grow corrupt in the desert, as we know that to be a most severe punishment, when God swore, that except two persons, Caleb and Joshua, no one should enter the land of Canaan. (Numb. xiv. 23, 24.) So also in this passage, I will free you, that is, when your return to your country shall be evident, a new light shall seem to have shone forth, but yet reflect on what happened to your fathers ; for although redeemed, they perished in the desert, and never possessed the land of Canaan. The same thing shall happen to you also, since your return is only a prelude to my favour : but ye shall never return to the land of Israel. But this is extended to those who returned and dwelt in their native land. But we said that Judæa was a place of exile since the course of God's favour was broken off, and God begun to plead with them afresh, even when he had led them from their captivity at Babylon. *And ye shall know that I am Jehovah*, as we said yesterday, God is recognised by the reprobate, while they are compelled to acknowledged a judge whose fatherly clemency they had despised. It follows—

39. As for you, O house of Israel, thus saith the Lord God, Go ye, serve ye every one his idols, and hereafter *also*, if ye will not hearken unto me: but pollute ye my holy name no more with your gifts, and with your idols.	39. Et vos domus Israel, sic dicit Dominator Iehovah, Quisque idolis suis ite servite, postquam non auditis me, et nomen sanctitatis meæ,[1] ne profanetis amplius in muneribus vestris, et idolis vestris.

Now again God expressly bears witness that he rejects the Israelites because they infected the pure worship of the law with their mixtures; for we said that they were deceived by a vain imagination when they thought God pleased with their obedience, while they worshipped him only half-heartedly. When they heaped up their fictions, they thought this diligence would be pleasing to God, because they professed to acknowledge the true God as their redeemer. Here again he announces that he rejects all half-worship, since he wished to have the entire affections, and to admit no rival: *Now*, says he, *O house of Israel, thus saith Jehovah, Go each of you and serve your idols*, just as if he would cast them off from his family. And yet we see that they were always under his dominion; and thus some kind of inconsistency arises when God rejects them from his sway, and yet retains them as his right. But the liberty which is now granted is to show them that it is in vain to worship God by halves.

This passage is peculiarly remarkable, since at this time many are deceived, while they rest upon their own inventions, and think that they best discharge their duty towards God when they partially obey his commandments, and then pile up a great heap of superstitions, partly received from their fathers and partly fabricated by themselves. Again, scarcely one in a hundred will be found who does not think it better partially to worship God than entirely to devote themselves to idols; and this indeed is true as far as man is concerned; for the impiety is more foul and detestable when men openly reject God, and divorce themselves from him, and devote themselves to idols, than if they partly worshipped God and partly idols. But in the meantime, we

---

[1] Verbally, meaning " my holy name."—*Calvin.*

see that God pronounces that he cannot bear this profanation; and we must diligently notice the reason which is added; for when gross and palpable impiety is indulged in, God's name is not so profaned as when clever men reconcile the pure worship of God with superstitions: and for this reason, that monstrous INDECISION[1] was in God's sight worse than the papacy; and why so? for although the papists profane God's name, yet their madness is at present so detected, that it openly appears that they are idolaters; but that invention mingled darkness with light, and infected the pure doctrine with its leaven. But God here exclaims that he could not endure this deception when men profess to worship him, for they defile themselves with superstitions, since profaneness is added to impiety, and both are the result of hypocrisy. The rest to-morrow.

PRAYER.

Grant, Almighty God, since thou hast once redeemed us by the death of thine only-begotten Son, that we may not interrupt the course of thy favour by our ingratitude; but may we so proceed in obedience to thy Gospel, that we may be brought at length to the perfection of that grace which is commenced within us, and may proceed more and more every day in true piety, till at length we are gathered into thy heavenly kingdom, and enjoy the inheritance promised and obtained for us by the same Christ our Lord. —Amen.

Lecture Sixty-Fifth.

WE yesterday saw the reason why God prefers that men should be entirely devoted to their superstitions rather than mingle them with the resemblance of true piety, since this is but a profanation of his holy name. He wishes to be kept separate from all idols. Hence it is not surprising that he loosens the reins from the Israelites, that they should cast themselves entirely on their idolatries; and he repeats again what he had said, *that his name was profaned by gifts and*

---

[1] Calvin's language is here rather remarkable. He calls the clinging to the worship of God, while bowing down to idols, *illud prodigiosum* INTERIM, which is in the French translation *ce beau monstre* d'INTERIM. The same idea is also expressed by the word *commentum*, translated *ceste belle invention ainsi forgee*.

idols, since the unbelievers pretended to worship him, but at the same time transferred his glory to idols. Hence he does not suffer himself to be trifled with in this way; so wherever offerings and idols occur, we should notice that all mixtures by which the pure simplicity of lawful worship is corrupted are condemned. It now follows—

40. For in mine holy mountain, in the mountain of the height of Israel, saith the Lord God, there shall all the house of Israel, all of them in the land, serve me: there will I accept them, and there will I require your offerings, and the first-fruits of your oblations, with all your holy things.	40. Quia in monte sanctitatis meæ, in monte excelso Israel, dicit Dominator Iehovah, illic colent me tota domus Israel, tota inquam in terra, illic propitius ero illis:[1] et illic requiram oblationes vestras et primitias donorum vestrorum in omnibus sanctificationibus vestris.

God now directs his address to the elect, or the remnant in whom he wished his Church to survive. Thus far he has spoken of the whole body of the people: he says, although he should free them from the hand of the Gentiles, yet that redemption would be but partial, because they should perish in the desert, and never enjoy the promised land. On the whole, he shows that those to whom a free return to their own country was given were no less strangers than if they had been exiles at the time, and always remained outlaws, since their impiety prevented their restoration. God now addresses the true Israelites, who were not only naturally descended from their fathers, but were genuine and spiritual children, as Paul distinguishes between those sons of Abraham born according to the flesh and to promise. (Rom. ix. 7-9.) For this reason also it is said in Psalm lxxiii.— And surely God is good to Israel—to those who are upright in heart: for the Prophet here asserts that God is gracious towards the Israelites; but since many hypocrites boast themselves to be members of the Church, for the sake of correcting them, he restricts the sentence, and does not reckon any as true Israelites except the upright in heart. So the same thing is repeated in Psalms xv. and xxiv.—Who shall ascend into the mount of the Lord? But the perfidious and the wicked did mingle themselves with the sincere worshippers; yet the Prophet excludes them from the list of the faithful, since he says that none should have a fixed

[1] Or, "I will embrace them with my favour."—*Calvin.*

station in God's sanctuary unless the sound in heart and the clean in hand. In the same sense also the Prophet formerly taught, that although hypocrites proudly boasted themselves to be God's people, yet their names were not written in the secret catalogue of the righteous. (Ezek. xiii. 9.) We now see how well those things which seem inconsistent agree together, namely, that the Lord's redeeming Israel from the tyranny of the Gentiles would not profit them, and yet that they should come into the mountain of Israel and worship him sincerely. Israel is here placed before us in a twofold light, for many were Israelites in name; but here the Prophet is treating of the elect, whom Paul calls a remnant of grace. (Rom. xi. 5.)

In the mountain, says he, *of my holiness, in the lofty mountain of Israel.* He does not call the mountain high, because it was loftier than others, for we know that there were many lofty mountains in the land of Judæa; and Zion was but a small hill; but we have elsewhere seen that it was preferred to lofty mountains, because it excelled in dignity. Here our Prophet does not regard the height of Mount Zion, but the singular glory with which it was adorned; as if he had said that God resided there, and his glory shone forth over all the loftiness of the world. Meanwhile I do not doubt that this epithet is obliquely opposed to the high places, which were consecrated everywhere, as we saw before. Since, therefore, the people had erected altars in all elevated places of all kinds, here God opposes one lofty mountain to all these, whose height had deceived those wretched men who thought themselves when there, nearer to heaven. This, therefore, is the reason why he calls it a high mountain. He says, *there shall the whole house of Israel worship me, the whole,* I say, *in the land.* It is not surprising that the whole house of Israel is placed here without exception, because, as I have said, the Prophet does not comprehend all those who boasted in that title, but he only means the pure worshippers of God, who were the spiritual children of Abraham. But here God describes the agreement in faith among all the faithful, as if he had said that the people would be fresh, and would not follow various speculations, as they formerly wandered, each after his own superstitions, but there should be one common rule for all. So we are taught by this passage that our worship does not please God except we are bent upon a simple agreement of faith, and the celebration of his name with our mouth. The impious often subscribe to different modes of belief, but they have no regard to God: but here we must hold the principle, that God cannot be worshipped unless the doctrine of his law flourishes. *The whole house of Israel*, I say, *in the land*. He signifies by these words that the whole land of Israel, so long contaminated by much filth, should be so sacred that the pure and perfect worship of God should alone be beheld there. *In the land*, then, purged from all defilements by which it was before polluted, he adds a promise, *there will I be propitious to you*. We formerly saw that all the people's sacrifices were rejected, and that for one reason, because they mixed them with their own inventions. Now, God pronounces that he would be propitious to them, because he will be purely worshipped, and his service shall no longer be vitiated by the perverse comments of men. We here see, therefore, that God's complacency or favour is accompanied with a detestation of all superstitions, as we have often mentioned previously. As, therefore, God abominates whatever is added to the simple teaching of the law, so he asserts that he will be propitious where he is purely worshipped according to the law. He adds, *and there will I require your oblations:* the person is changed, but the sense flows on readily: he says, *I will require your oblations:* he puts one kind of oblation, but he includes them all, as will be seen at the end of the verse. Although I confess that two different kinds of offering are signified by the words תרומה, *theromeh*, and תנופה, *thenopheh*, yet they are often taken for any kind of offering when used separately, a part being put for the whole, as I have said. He says, then, that the offerings were grateful to him, and he implies that by the word requiring, because we have seen that the people's gifts were refused when corrupted by foreign superstitions, and God is said to exact the gifts which he approves. *And the first-fruits of your gifts*, he says, that is, the flower or excellence of your gifts, *in all your sanctifications*, that is, in all my worship. It signifies, on the whole, when the Israelites betake themselves to the simple doctrine of the law, their obedience is so grateful to God, that their gifts please him, their offerings are taken into account, and their whole worship is accepted. It now follows—

41. I will accept you with your sweet savour, when I bring you out from the people, and gather you out of the countries wherein ye have been scattered; and I will be sanctified in you before the heathen.	41. In odore bonæ fragrantiæ propitius ero vobis cum eduxero vos e populis, et collegero vos ex terris, per quas dispersi eritis, et sanctificabor in vobis in oculis gentium.

He continues the same sentiment, namely, that the people's worship would be acceptable, when those who had formerly been deceived by their superstitions had bidden them farewell, and follow the law only. He uses the word " savour," according to the customary legal form, not because incense was pleasing to God, but because external ceremonies were no vain discipline for the people when they retained the truth. For surely incense of itself is of no consequence, but God wished in a palpable manner to testify that he did not reject the sacrifices which he had commanded. Hence, by these forms of speech, the Holy Spirit signifies that God was truly appeased when men approach him with sincere faith and repentance, and desire to be reconciled, and suppliantly pray for pardon by ingenuous confession of sin, and look up to Christ: this is the savour which Moses everywhere teaches was sweet to God. But as the incense of the law was always sweet, so all others were offensive, as we have already seen. The Prophet, therefore, adds nothing new here, but confirms his former teaching, that God delights in the pure and sincere worship of the faithful, when they try nothing but by his law. *Afterwards,* says he, *I will lead you out from the people, and will collect you from the lands through which ye have been dispersed.* He repeats the same words which were formerly used, but with another sense and purpose; since, while he redeems alike the hypocrites and his elect, the offered liberty does not profit the hypocrites: because, wherever they might dwell, their station was in the wilderness; and even in the very bosom of the land of Canaan they were exiles, and their life was erratic, and they were without any enjoyment of the promised inheritance, but wandered in the desert, and through distant regions. For although they dwelt in the midst of a crowd, yet such was their condition that God had deservedly threatened them with remaining in the wilderness of the Gentiles even till death. But now, when he speaks of the elect and the faithful, he makes a difference between them and the hypocrites. For a question might otherwise arise, since all were apparently alike, What was the tendency of the promise, that some should be exiles and others return to their inheritance? For Daniel never returned to his country, and there is no doubt that other pious worshippers of God were at the same time held back: but we know how sinful a multitude returned to Judæa when the edict of Cyrus permitted them. For all were afterwards attentive to their own private business: the temple was neglected; God was defrauded of his first-fruits and offerings; they married strange wives; and mingled polygamy with their sacrifices. (Hag. i. 4.) We have already seen how sharply and severely the three last prophets inveigh against them. Since many returned into the land of Canaan in their unchanged state, and who had better remained in Chaldæa: for this reason the Prophet directs his discourse to the elect, and says that they should not only be brought back, but when restored, as if by stealth, their worship would be pleasing to God in the land. *When, therefore, I shall have brought you forth, I shall be sanctified in you before the eyes of the Gentiles.* God was in some sense sanctified in the wicked, because they became an illustrious specimen of his power when the Chaldæans were slain, and his temple erected a second time. But here the Prophet, as I have said, separates the elect from the reprobate, since God was sanctified in them in a special manner, when a new church emerged again, in which piety, true religion, and holiness of life flourished. When, therefore, such a spectacle was offered to the eyes of the Gentiles, then God asserted his glory among his faithful ones. Lastly, these passages are to be read conjointly, *that he will be propitious to them, and will be pleased with their first-fruits and offerings, and he will be sanctified in the eyes of the Gentiles:* as it is said in Ps. cxiv. 2, When Israel went out of

Egypt, Israel was God's power, and Judah his sanctification, or sanctity. It follows—

42. And ye shall know that I *am* the Lord, when I shall bring you into the land of Israel, into the country *for* the which I lifted up mine hand to give it to your fathers.	42. Et cognoscetis quod ego Iehovah, cum vos introduxero in terram Israel, in terram[1] pro qua levavi manum meam, ut darem ipsam patribus vestris.

For the sake of frightening them, he threatened that he would be conspicuous to the reprobate, saying, *ye shall know that I am Jehovah,*—meaning, that he would be their judge: hence he was known to the reprobate by proofs of his anger or wrath. But now another kind of knowledge is denoted, namely, that which brings a sweet taste of paternal love: *ye shall know,* says he, *that I am Jehovah your God, when I shall have brought you in again.* He here shows his full and complete benefit towards the faithful, which we saw before was withheld from the reprobate. For they were brought back, because, without exception, all were permitted to return to their country; for then the yoke of an imperious tyranny was broken when they were freed from the dominion of the Chaldees, and the king of the Medes had permitted them to build the temple, and to dwell in the land of Canaan. All were set at liberty, as I have said; but that was the only favour conferred upon the wicked, since they all perished in the desert of the Gentiles: but God's elect were led by the hand to the land of Israel, and there they really possessed the promised inheritance, since they dwelt there as sons and lawful heirs. The hypocrites returned, as I have said, but they never possessed the land by right of inheritance, for they wandered hither and thither in the desert, and although they resided at home, were always wandering exiles. We see, then, that a singular privilege is intended when it is said, *I will be known by you, when I shall have brought you back from the nations and the lands through which you were dispersed, into the land concerning which I sware that I would give it to your fathers.* Here a mark is inscribed, that the faithful may know that this promise was not common to all: for the dwelling in the land of Canaan of itself was not a matter of much consequence, but here a

---

[1] He had used אדמה, *admeh,* before, but he now uses ארץ, *aretz.*—*Calvin.*

value is expressed, that they should arrive at that land as God's heirs, and succeed their sacred fathers, to whom the inheritance was promised. As *God swore that he would give the land to Abraham, Isaac, and Jacob,* this ought not to be restricted to them personally, as we very well know; and yet they were its true heirs and lords, as their sepulchres bear witness. They suffered vexation by constantly changing their settlements, and were never at rest in one residence. During life they were strangers, but their sepulchre was a proof of true and lawful dominion: and in this way they transmitted the hope of the promised inheritance to their posterity. Now, therefore, we see with what intention the Prophet here says that the land was promised to their fathers, that its value might raise the minds of the faithful to consider the magnitude of the benefit. It follows—

43. And there shall ye remember your ways, and all your doings, wherein ye have been defiled; and ye shall loathe yourselves in your own sight for all your evils that ye have committed.

43. Et recordabimini illic viarum vestrarum, et omnium operum vestrorum, in quibus polluti estis: et eritis excisi[1] in faciebus vestris, in cunctis sceleribus vestris quæ perpetrastis.

Here God shows that he would at length be propitious to his elect when they repented. Thus he signifies that there was no other means of reconciliation than by the intervention of repentance. And we must carefully remark this, as I have previously mentioned. For we know with what security all men usually indulge themselves, nor are the pious themselves affected with grief sufficiently serious, when God invites them to the hope of safety and at the same time offers pardon. They embrace indeed greedily what they hear, but meanwhile they bury their sins. But God wishes us to taste his goodness, that the remembrance of our crimes should be bitter, and also that every one should judge himself that he may obtain pardon from him. Now, therefore, we understand the Prophet's intention. We saw a similar passage in Jeremiah: this teaching occurs throughout the Prophets, *there,* says he, *ye shall remember me.* The circumstance of place is to be noticed, because the Prophet means that after the elect shall have returned to God's favour, and he shall

[1] Or, " abominable."—*Calvin.*

account them as true members of his Church, then they ought to be mindful of their former life and to repent of their sins. As if he had said, as long as God afflicts you and ye remain under the tyranny of the Gentiles in exile, the sense of your evils will compel you to groan, so the remembrance of your sins should return, since, whether ye will or not, their punishment will ever be before your eyes, since they would be easily persuaded that their sentence was usual and common. But he shows them that the sons of God were not only mindful of their sins, when they feel themselves chastised by him, and experience shows his hostility, but when received into favour and in the enjoyment of their inheritance, they live under God's wings, and he cherishes them as a tender offspring: when, therefore, the faithful are treated so humanely by God, yet the Prophet shows that in their condition they ought to be mindful of their sins, *and of all your works in which ye have been polluted,* says he. He now shows to what purpose they were to be mindful. For the wicked are compelled to call their sins to remembrance when God, by forcibly turning their attention to them, draws them to consider what they desire to bury in oblivion. But it is here said, *ye shall be confounded in your own sight.* Since the Hebrew word קוט, *kot,* signifies to cut off, many interpreters take it for " ye shall be cut off;" that is, ye shall judge yourselves worthy of destruction among those whom God will cut off and blot out of the earth. But this seems forced. Since the same word sometimes signifies to litigate, and to become abominable, I willingly take this meaning, *that they shall be abominable,* or contemptible, *in their own sight:* that is, they shall be so ashamed, as willingly and fully to acknowledge themselves utterly disgraced. Hence Ezekiel means that the faithful should suffer voluntary disgrace, that they may glorify God by the pure and genuine confession of their shame. If any one prefers to expound it, ye shall be condemned or convinced, that sense will suit well enough ; but I have already brought forward what seemed more simple. For I said that this was the fruit of penitence, when we lie confounded before God and are vile and despicable in our own eyes, and when we not only suffer ourselves to be condemned by others, but inwardly reflect upon our own disgrace, and so of our own accord prostrate ourselves before God. This then is the fruit of penitence, this is true humility, flowing from genuine shame. At length it follows—

44. And ye shall know that I *am* the Lord, when I have wrought with you for my name's sake, not according to your wicked ways, nor according to your corrupt doings, O ye house of Israel, saith the Lord God.	44. Et cognoscetis quod ego Iehovah, cum fecero vobiscum propter nomen meum, non secundum vias vestras malas, et secundum opera vestra corrupta, domus Israel, dicit Dominator Iehovah.

Here at length God pronounces that his glory would be chiefly conspicuous in the pity which he bestowed upon those who were desperate and abandoned, gratuitously and solely with respect to his own name. Hence Paul so specially celebrates the grace of God in the first chapter of the epistle to the Ephesians, as that mercy by which God deigns to call his own elect in a peculiar sense—his glory; for his glory extends further than his pity. (Ver. 6, 12, 14.) As thy name, so thy praise is extended through all lands, (Ps. xlviii. 10;) for God deserves no less glory when he destroys the wicked than when he pities his own people. But Paul calls that gratuitous favour glory *par excellence*, by which God embraced his own elect when he adopted them. So also it is said in this passage, *then ye shall know that I am Jehovah, since I shall deal with you on behalf of my name, and not according to your sins.* But when God wishes his glory to shine conspicuously in gratuitous pity, hence we gather that the enemies of his glory were too gross and open, who obscure his mercy, or extenuate it, or as far as they can, endeavour to reduce it to nothing. But we know the teaching of the papacy to be that God's gratuitous goodness either lies buried or enfolded in dark obscurity, or utterly vanishes away: for they have invented a system of general merits which they oppose to God's gratuitous favour. For they distinguish merits into preparations, good works acquiring God's favour, and satisfactions, by which they buy off the penalties to which they were subjected. Afterwards they add what they call the suffrages of the saints; for they fabricate for themselves numberless patrons, and various reasonings are concocted for the purpose of obscuring God's glory, or at least of allowing only a few sparks to be visible. Since therefore the whole papacy tends that way, we see that they professedly oppose God's glory, and those who defend such abominations are sworn enemies of God's glory.

For ourselves, then, let us learn that we cannot otherwise worship God with acceptance unless we adopt whatever pleases him as pertaining to our salvation. For if we wish to come to a debtor and creditor account, or to consider that he is in the slightest degree indebted to us, we in this way diminish his glory, and as far as lies in our power we despoil ourselves of that inestimable privilege which the Prophet now commends. Hence let us desire to acknowledge God in this way, since he treats us with amazing clemency and pity out of regard for his own name, and not according to our sins. And since that was said to his ancient people because they returned to the land of Canaan, how much more ought God's gratuitous goodness to be extolled by us, when his heavenly kingdom is at this day open to us, and when he openly calls us to himself in heaven, and to the hope of that happy immortality which has been obtained for us through Christ?

PRAYER.

Grant, Almighty God, since we have already entered in hope upon the threshold of our eternal inheritance, and know that there is a certain mansion for us in heaven after Christ has been received there, who is our head, and the first-fruits of our salvation: Grant, I say, that we may proceed more and more in the course of thy holy calling until at length we reach the goal, and so enjoy that eternal glory of which thou affordest us a taste in this world, by the same Christ our Lord.—Amen.

PRAISE TO GOD.

AFTER finishing this last LECTURE, that most illustrious man, JOHN CALVIN, the Divine, who had previously been sick, then began to be so much weaker that he was compelled to recline on a couch, and could no longer proceed with the explanation of EZEKIEL. This accounts for his stopping at the close of the Twentieth Chapter, and not finishing the work so auspiciously begun. Nothing remains, kind Reader, but that you receive most favourably and graciously what is now sent forth to the world.

NOTES AND COMMENTS
BY THE EDITOR.

THE PROMISED CONTRIBUTION TOWARDS A COMPLETE APPARATUS CRITICUS HAS BEEN ARRANGED AS FOLLOWS—(*See Translator's Preface*, VOL. I. p. xxxi.)—

SECTIONS I., II., AND III., BEING INDEXES, ARE PLACED AT THE END OF THE VOLUME.

SECTIONS IV., V., VI., AND VII., NOW FOLLOW ONE ANOTHER.

SECTION VIII. IS PRECEDED BY ITS OWN "LIST OF CONTENTS."

IV.—A COMPLETE SYNOPSIS OF THE CONTENTS OF THE WHOLE OF EZEKIEL'S PROPHECIES.

I. THE PROPHET'S COMMISSION.
II. THE PROPHET'S UTTERANCES.
III. THE PROPHET'S CONSOLATIONS.

I. The Prophet's Commission.
Chaps. i.-iii.

Sect. 1. Its Allegoric Character—the Whirlwinds—the Four Living Creatures—the Wheels—the Firmaments—the Throne and the Human Appearance seated thereon, ... chap. i.
— 2. The Address—the Roll—the Abounding Lamentation, ... ii.
— 3. The Rebellion of the People—the Motion of the Living Creatures—the Charge as a Watchman—the Hand of Jehovah by the river Chebar, iii.

II. The Prophet's Utterances.

α. AGAINST THE JEWS, . . . iv.-xxiv.
β. AGAINST GENTILES, . . . xxv.-xxxii.

The Utterances against the Jews are divisible into those against Jerusalem—the Mountain and Land of Israel—the King—the False Prophets—the Elders of the People, with various repetitions, under different images.

Sect. 1. The Emblem of the Siege upon the Tile, ch. iv. 1-3
—that of Lying on the right and left side, iv. 4-8
—that of Taking Food by Measure, . iv. 9-12
The Explanation, ... iv. 13-17
— 2. The Emblem of the Razor, . . v. 1-4
The Explanation, ... v. 5-17
— 3. Against the Mountains of Israel, . vi. 1-15
— 4. Against the Land of Israel, . . vii. 1-27
— 5. The Vision of the Image of Jealousy, . viii. 1-11
The Chamber of Imagery, . . . viii. 12-16
The Explanation, ... viii. 17, 18
— 6. The Vision of the man with the slaughter weapon, ... ix. 1-11
— 7. The Vision of the Cherubim—their description and their motions, . . . x. 1-22
— 8. The Emblems of the Caldron and the Flesh, and its application to Jerusalem, . . xi. 1-25
— 9. The Emblem of the Prophet's removing his Goods, and its Interpretation, . . . xii. 1-16
— 10. The flattering Proverb of Israel rebuked, xii. 17-28
— 11. The Utterance against the False Prophets, both male and female, ... xiii. 1-23
— 12. Against the Elders of the People, . xiv. 1-23
— 13. The Emblem of the Vine used for Fuel, xv. 1-8
— 14. The Emblem of Israel as an Outcast infant nurtured by the Almighty, . . xvi. 1-14
Married, and yet committing Adultery, xvi. 15-34
This Wickedness denounced and punished, xvi. 35-59
The Almighty's merciful relenting, xvi. 60-63
— 15. The Emblem of the Eagle and the Cedar, xvii. 1-10
The Explanation, referring to Zedekiah, Nebuchadnezzar, and Pharaoh, . . xvii. 11-24
— 16. A Vindication of the Divine Justice, and Confutation of Israel's Proverb, . . xviii. 1-32
— 17. The Emblem of the Lioness and her Whelps, xix. 1-9
— 18. The Emblem of the Vine plucked up and consumed, ... xix. 10-14
— 19. The Elders of Israel rebuked for their sins, xx. 1-32

Sect. 20. The Divine Promises of Restoration, xx. 33-44
— 21. The Word dropped toward the South, xx. 45-49
— 22. The Prophet's face set toward Jerusalem, xxi. 1-7
— 23. The Sharp Sword and the Great Slaughter, xxi. 8-27
— 24. The Sword drawn against the Ammonites, xxi. 28-32
— 25. The Sins of Jerusalem and God's Vengeance, xxii. 1-22
— 26. The Woes uttered against False Prophets, xxii. 23-31
— 27. The Adulteries of the People, . xxiii. 1-49
— 28. The Parable of the Boiling Pot, . xxiv. 1-14
The Prophet's severe Affliction, . xxiv. 15-27

β. *The Utterances against Gentiles.*

Sect. 1. Against the Ammonites, . . xxv. 1-7
— 2. Against the Moabites, . . xxv. 8-11
— 3. Against the Edomites, . . xxv. 12-14
— 4. Against the Philistines, . . xxv. 15-17
— 5. Against Tyre, through chapters xxvi., xxvii., and xxviii. to ver. 19.
— 6. Against Zidon, ... xxviii. 20-26
— 7. Against Pharaoh, . . . xxix. 1-7
— 8. Against Egypt, ... xxix. 8-21
— 9. Against Ethiopia, . . . xxx. 1-5
— 10. Against the Upholders of Egypt, . xxx. 6-19
— 11. Against Pharaoh, . . . xxx. 20-26
— 12. Assyria as a Cedar of Lebanon, . xxxi. 1-9
— 13. Its Fall and Destruction, . . xxxi. 10-18
— 14. A Bitter Lamentation over Egypt, xxxii. 1-21
— 15. A Bitter Lamentation over Assyria, xxxii. 22, 23
— 16. A Bitter Lamentation over Elam, xxxii. 24, 25
— 17. A Bitter Lamentation over Meshech and Tubal, xxxii. 26-28
— 18. A Bitter Lamentation over Edom, xxxii. 29-32

These Utterances are all most vividly and graphically pourtrayed. Allegories, Metaphors, and Parables are most appropriately interspersed with fiery Denunciations and awful Threatenings in consequence of gross iniquities.

III. The Prophet's Consolations.

A Series of Exhortations and Promises of Deliverance under Cyrus, a Description of the Temple, and a View of the Future Divisions of the Land under the Prosperous Reign of Messiah.

Sect. 1. The Prophet's duty as a Watchman, xxxiii. 1-16
— 2. A Vindication of God's equity, . xxxiii. 17-33
— 3. A Reproof to the Shepherds of the People, xxxiv. 1-10
— 4. The Almighty the Good Shepherd, xxxiv. 11-31
— 5. The Desolation of Mount Seir, . xxxv. 1-15
— 6. The Destruction of the Heathen, xxxvi. 1-7
— 7. The Blessings on Israel, . . xxxvi. 8-38
— 8. The Vision of the Dry Bones, . xxxvii. 1-14
— 9. The Rods of Judah and Ephraim, xxxvii. 15-20
— 10. The Future Reign of David the King, xxxvii. 21-28
— 11. Prophecies against Gog and Magog, xxxviii. 1-23
— 12. Judgments upon Gog, . . xxxix. 1-16
— 13. The Great Sacrifice on the Mountains, xxxix. 17-20
— 14. Israel Restored from Captivity, xxxix. 21-29
— 15. The Vision of Measuring the Temple, xl. 1-49
— 16. The Measures and Ornaments, . xli. 1-26
— 17. The Priests' Chambers and the Outer Court, xlii. 1-20
— 18. The Returning Glory of Jehovah, . xliii. 1-9
— 19. The Whole Fashion of The House, . xliii. 10-12
— 20. The Measurement of The Altar, . xliii. 13-17
— 21. The Sacrifices on The Altar, . . xliii. 18-27
— 22. Various Ordinances for the Priests, xliv. 1-31
— 23. The Apportionment of the Land, . xlv. 1-8
— 24. The Duties of the Priests, . . xlv. 9-25
— 25. The Duties of the Prince and of the People, xlvi. 1-24
— 26. The Vision of the Rising Waters, . xlvii. 1-12
— 27. The Divisions and Limits of the Land, xlvii. 13-23

Sect. 28. The Portions for the Tribes and the Priests,
xlviii. 1-29
— 29. The various Gates of the City, xlviii. 30-35

These closing Visions and Consolations are singularly striking, and afford scope for copious illustration; but as our COMMENTATOR did not live to expound them, it would ill become his Translator to obtrude on the reader his own researches into these deep things of the Spirit of God.

A minute description of *The Temple Scenery* has been attempted by a learned Jew, SOLOMON BENNETT, R.A. of Berlin, (Edit. London, 1834.) His work contains a most elaborate account of every interesting particular. Chapters xl., xli., and xlii. are explained verse by verse; and a ground-plan and bird's-eye view are subjoined.

These chapters are also explained by FRY on *The Second Advent,* vol. i. sec. 13, pp. 556-587.

V.—A TRANSLATION OF THE FIRST TWENTY CHAPTERS OF THE PROPHECIES OF EZEKIEL, AS MODIFIED BY THESE COMMENTARIES.

CHAPTER I.

1 Now it came to pass in the thirtieth year,[1] in the fourth month, on the fifth day of the month, as I was among the captives by the river Chebar, that the heavens were opened, and I saw visions of God. 2 In the fifth day of the month, in the fifth year of the captivity of King Jehoiakim, 3 the word of Jehovah came to Ezekiel, son of Buzi the priest, in the land of the Chaldæans, near the river Chebar, and the hand of Jehovah was upon him there.

4 And I looked, and, behold, a tempestuous wind coming from the north; a great cloud, and a fire folding round itself, and a brightness was round about it; and out of the midst there was, as it were, the appearance of Hasmal in the midst of the fire. 5 And in the middle of this, was the likeness of four living creatures, and their aspect was the likeness of a man: 6 they had each four faces and four wings, 7 their feet were straight, and the sole of their feet like that of a calf's foot, (or round, vol. i. p. 70, note,) and they cast forth sparks

---

[1] *The thirtieth year.* The date at which this reckoning commences is doubtful. Calvin dates from a Jubilee, (vol. i. p. 52,) but Jerome from the 18th year of King Josiah, when the book of the law was found. Origen, Hom. I., understands it of Ezekiel's age; and so does Gregory, Hom. II. Maldonatus interprets it of the captivity, and quotes the authority of Theodoret. Pradus, as quoted by Rosenmüller, agrees with Jerome. The Editor refers his readers once for all to the valuable commentary of Rosenmüller on this Prophet for all kinds of valuable critical information; while the English student will find the notes to Archbishop Newcome's version very judicious.

like the appearance of polished brass : ⁸ and they had human hands under their wings on their four sides; and they had four faces and wings. ⁹ And each wing was connected with the next wing: when they moved they did not turn back : each animal went forward in the direction of his face. ¹⁰ As to the likeness of their faces, these four had the face of a man and the face of a lion on the right side; and on the left, these four had the face of an ox and the face of an eagle. ¹¹ Their faces, then, and their wings were extended[1] from above, and each wing was bound to its neighbour, and two covered their body. ¹² And each walked in the direction of its face; and wheresoever the spirit (or will, p. 77) proceeded, they proceeded : they did not return in their course. ¹³ As to the likeness of the living creatures, their aspect was like coals of burning fire, like the appearance of lamps passing up and down between the living creatures: and the fire was bright, and lightning issued from it. ¹⁴ And the living creatures ran and returned like lightning.

¹⁵ While I was beholding the living creatures, behold one wheel on the earth, near each living creature, at right angles,[2] at the face of each. ¹⁶ The appearance of the wheels and their workmanship was like chrysolite : and they were all alike : and their appearance and their form were like one wheel within another. ¹⁷ When they moved forward, they went upon their four sides : they did not turn back when they proceeded. ¹⁸ And I beheld their circumferences, and their size, and their terribleness; and their strakes were full of eyes, round about these four. ¹⁹ And when the living creatures walked, the wheels moved beside them; and when the living creatures were raised from the earth, the wheels were raised with them.[3] ²⁰ Whithersoever the spirit led the living creatures, thither it also led the wheels: the wheels

---

[1] Or, " divided." See vol. i. p. 75, note. The MSS. vary slightly. Calvin has translated very literally; and the Prophet's language being so elliptical, it is almost impossible to present a perfectly accurate representation of " a cherub" to a modern inquirer.

[2] Explained in a note, p. 82, vol. i. See Jerome in Comment. ad Hoseam, cap. 12, and Chrysos. Orat. 35, p. 448, ed. Morell...Rosen. in ver.

[3] Alexander Knox, who beautifies whatever he touches upon, has applied this verse most happily in illustration of the " exquisitely regular" movements of the Almighty, and the " attendant machinery" of Providence."—*Remains*, vol. i. p. 230.

were raised up also with the living creatures, because their spirit was in the wheels also. ²¹ When the animals moved forward, the wheels did the same : they both were stationary and both elevated together ; because the spirit of the animals was in the wheels. ²² Above the heads of the living creatures was the likeness of a firmament, as the appearance of terrible crystal stretched over and above their heads.

²³ And under the firmament their wings were straight, each towards its neighbour: and each living creature had two wings, which covered their bodies on this side and on that. ²⁴ And I heard the voice of their wings, like the voice of mighty waters, and like the voice of God : the voice of their speech was like the sound of an army when they moved forward ; and when they stood, they let down their wings. ²⁵ And there was a voice from the firmament over their heads when they stood and let down their wings.

²⁶ And above the firmament over their heads was the likeness of a throne, like the vision of a sapphire stone: and above the likeness of the throne was an image like the aspect of a man upon it. ²⁷ And I saw, as it were, the colour of amber, like the appearance of fire round about within it : from the appearance of his loins, both upwards and downwards, I saw the aspect of fire, and a brightness all round about him. ²⁸ Like the appearance of a bow in a cloud on a rainy day, such was the aspect of his brightness round about. This was a vision of the similitude of Jehovah's glory : and I gazed at it, and fell upon my face, and heard a voice speaking unto me. And he said unto me,—

CHAPTER II.

¹ Son of man, stand upon thy feet, and I will speak unto thee. ² And the Spirit came to me when he addressed me, and placed me upon my feet : and I heard him address me ; and he said unto me—

³ Son of man, I send thee to the children of Israel,
To revolting tribes who have rebelled against me :

They and their fathers have acted perfidiously against me,
Even to this very day.
⁴ They are children of a hard face, and of a stiff heart.
Therefore I send thee unto them;
And thou shalt say to them—
Thus saith the LORD JEHOVAH.
⁵ And they, whether they will hear, or whether they will not,
For they are a rebellious house,
Yet shall know that a Prophet has been among them.
⁶ And thou, son of man, be not afraid of them;
Fear not their words, though they are rebellious,
And are thorns towards thee, and thou dwellest with scorpions.
Be not afraid of their language;
Be not dismayed at their looks,
Since they are a rebellious house.
⁷ And thou shalt utter my words unto them,
Whether they will hear, or whether they will forbear;
For they are rebels.
⁸ And thou, son of man, hear what I say unto thee:
Be not thou rebellious like that rebellious house;
Open thy mouth, and eat what I put before thee.
⁹ Then I looked up, and, behold, a hand extended to me;
And lo! a roll of a book was in it:
¹⁰ Then he spread it before my face;
And lo! the roll was written behind and before,
And the writing was lamentations, and mourning, and wo.

CHAPTER III.

¹ After that he said to me,
Son of man, eat completely what thou hast found; namely, this roll,
And go and speak to the house of Israel.
² So I opened my mouth, and he fed me with that roll.
³ And said to me, Son of man,
Feed thy belly, and fill thy bowels with this roll which I give thee.
So I ate it, and it was in my mouth

Like honey for sweetness.
4 Then he said to me, Son of man!
Go to the house of Israel and address them in my words,
5 Since thou art not sent to a people profound in lip and hard of speech,
Thou art sent to the house of Israel:
6 Not to many peoples profound in lip and heavy in speech,
Whom thou canst not understand;[1]
Had I sent thee unto them, they would have hearkened unto thee.
7 But the house of Israel will not hear thee;
Because they will not hear me;
Since the whole house of Israel are hard of front and stout of heart.
8 Lo! I have made thy face hard against their faces,
And thy forehead hard against their forehead.
9 As an adamant, harder than flint,
Have I made thy forehead: fear them not:
Be not broken down at their presence,
For they are a house of rebellion.

10 Moreover, he said to me, Son of man!
All my words which I shall speak to thee,
Receive in thine heart and hear with thine ears:
11 And go—get thee to the captives, to the children of thy people,
And speak unto them and tell them,—
Thus saith the Lord Jehovah,
Whether they will hear, or whether they will not.

12 Then the Spirit raised me up: and I heard behind me
A voice of mighty rustling, which said,
Blessed be the glory of Jehovah from his place!
13 I heard also the sound of the wings of the living creatures,
Each kissing that of its companion,
And the noise of the wheels beside them—the sound of a mighty shaking.
14 Then the Spirit raised me, and took me away,

---
[1] See vol. i. p. 131, note.

And I set forth in bitterness and indignation of spirit,
And the hand of Jehovah was strong upon me.

15 Then I came to the captives at Thel-abib,
    They were seated by the river Chebar: there they sat:
    And I also sat there seven days desolate in the midst of them.
16 Then it happened at the end of the seven days,
    That the word of Jehovah came to me, saying,
17 Son of man! I have appointed thee a watchman over the house of Israel;
    Hence thou shalt hear words from my mouth,
    And shalt warn them from me.
18 When I say unto the wicked, Thou shalt surely die:
    And thou warnest him not, and speakest not unto him;
    And warnest him not from his wicked way to save his life:
    That wicked man shall die in his iniquity;
    But his blood will I require at thy hand.
19 Yet if thou warn the wicked, and he turn not from his impious and evil way,
    He shall die in his iniquity;
    But thou hast freed thine own soul.
20 If a just man shall turn from his righteousness, and commit iniquity:
    And I put a stumbling-block before his face, he shall die:
    Because thou hast not warned him, he shall die in his sins,
    The righteousness which he has done shall not be remembered;
    But his blood will I require at thy hand.
21 Then if thou warn the righteous that he sin not,
    And he doth not sin, he shall surely live, because he is warned,
    Thou also hast delivered thine own soul.

22 Then the hand of Jehovah was upon me, and he said to me,
    Arise, go unto the plain, and there I will speak to thee.
23 Then I arose, and went to the plain, and lo!
    The glory of Jehovah stood there,
    As the glory which I had beheld by the river Chebar:

²⁴ And I fell upon my face, and the Spirit entered into me,
And placed me upon my feet, and addressed me, and said,
Go—shut thyself within thine house.
²⁵ And now—son of man!—lo! they shall put chains upon thee,
And shall bind thee with them, and thou shalt not go forth into the midst of them:
²⁶ Then I will make thy tongue cleave to thy palate,
And thou shalt be dumb, and be no longer a reprover to them:
Because they are a house of rebellion.
²⁷ But when I shall speak to thee, and shall open thy mouth,
Thou shalt say unto them, Thus saith the Lord Jehovah,
He who hears, may hear: he who forbears, may forbear;
Since they are a house of rebellion.[1]

CHAPTER IV.

¹ Thou also, son of man! take thee a tile,
And put it before thy face,
And paint upon it the city Jerusalem:
² Lay siege against it, and build a tower against it:
Cast a mound against it, and set a camp against it:
Set battering-rams against it all round.
³ Then take an iron pan, and set it for a wall between thee and the city;
Strengthen thy face against it, and it shall be besieged,
And thou shalt besiege it. This is a sign to the house of Israel.

⁴ Lie thou also on thy left side, and place the iniquity of the house of Israel upon it;
According to the number of the days during which thou shalt lie upon it
Thou shalt bear their iniquity.
⁵ For I have appointed unto thee the years of their iniquity,
According to the number of the days, three hundred and ninety days:

[1] See vol. i. p. 168, note.

Thus shalt thou bear the iniquity of the house of Israel.
6 And when thou hast finished those days,
Then again thou shalt lie on thy right side,
And thou shalt bear the iniquity of the house of Judah forty days;
Each day for a year, as I have appointed thee.
7 Then thou shalt direct thy face toward the siege of Jerusalem,
And thine arm shall be uncovered,
And thou shalt prophesy against it.
8 Lo! I have put cords upon thee,
And thou shalt not turn from side to side
Until thou hast fulfilled the days of thy sieges.

9 Take thou also wheat and barley, and beans, and lentiles, and millet, and fitches,
And put them in one vessel, and make it into bread for thee,
According to the number of the days on which thou shalt lie on thy side:
Three hundred and ninety days shalt thou eat it.
10 And the food which thou shalt eat by weight,
Shall be twenty shekels a day: from time to time shalt thou eat it.
11 And water shalt thou drink by measure, the sixth part of a hin:
From time to time shalt thou drink it.
12 Then thou shalt eat barley cake, and shalt bake it
With human dung before their eyes: And Jehovah said,
13 Even thus shall the children of Israel eat their defiled bread
Among the Gentiles whither I have driven them.
14 Then I said, Alas, O Lord Jehovah!
Lo! my soul has not been polluted,
And from my youth up never have I eaten
What died of itself, or was torn to pieces;
And abominable flesh has never entered my mouth.
15 Then he said, See! I have given thee

The dung of oxen for that of men,
And thou shalt cook thy bread with this.[1]

16 Moreover, he said to me, Son of man!
Lo! I break the staff of bread in Jerusalem;
And they shall eat bread by weight and with fear;
And shall drink water by measure and with astonishment,
17 So that bread and water shall fail them,
And they shall be astonished one with another,
And consume away in their iniquity.[2]

CHAPTER V.

1 And thou, son of man! take thee a sharp sword,
Take thee a barber's razor, and pass it over thy head and
  thy beard:
Then take thee a just balance and divide the hair.
2 A third part thou shalt burn in the midst of the city,
When the days of the siege are fulfilled;
A third part shalt thou smite about with the sword;
And another third shalt thou scatter to the wind;
And I will unsheathe the sword after them.
3 Then thou shalt take a few of them,
And bind them in thy skirts.
4 Then take some of them, and cast them into the fire,
And burn them; for thence shall fire go forth
Upon all the house of Israel.
5 Then saith the Lord Jehovah, This is Jerusalem:
In the midst of the nations and of the surrounding countries
Have I placed her.
6 And she has changed my judgments into wickedness
Beyond all the nations, and my statutes beyond all the
  surrounding people:
They have despised my judgments,
And have not walked in my statutes.
7 Therefore, thus saith the Lord Jehovah,
Because of your multiplication more than the nations round
  about you,

[1] See vol. i. p. 186, note.   [2] See vol. i. p. 187, note.

And your not walking in my statutes, and not keeping my judgments,

And your not acting like the nations around you,

8 Wherefore, thus saith the Lord Jehovah,

Behold, I am against thee, even I:

And I will execute my judgments in the midst of thee

Before the eyes of the Gentiles.

9 And I will execute against thee what I never yet have done,

Nor will ever do in future,

On account of all thine abominations.

10 Therefore fathers shall devour their sons,

And sons their fathers, in the midst of thee:

I will execute judgments against thee,

And disperse all thy remnants to all winds of heaven.

11 Because I live, saith the Lord Jehovah,

Since thou hast polluted my sanctuary[1]

With all thy detestable and abominable things,

Therefore I will break thee in pieces:

My eye shall not spare, neither will I pity thee.

12 A third part shall die of the pestilence,

And be consumed by famine in the midst of thee;

A third part shall be consumed by the sword round about thee;

A third part will I disperse towards every wind,

And will draw out a sword after them.

13 Thus shall mine anger be accomplished,

And I will cause my burning anger to rest upon them;

And I will enjoy consolation; and they shall know that I am Jehovah,

Who have spoken in my zeal, when I shall have accomplished my fury on them.

14 Moreover, I will lay thee waste,

And make thee a reproach among the nations around thee

In the eyes of every passer by.

15 So thou shalt be a reproach and a reviling,

---

[1] The rendering according to note, vol. i. p. 205.

A chastisement and an astonishment to the nations round about thee,
While I shall execute judgments against thee
In anger and burning, and furious rebukes.
I Jehovah have spoken it.
16 When I shall send upon them the evil arrows of famine
For their destruction, which I shall dart upon them to destroy them;[1]
Then will I add famine against them,
And will break their staff of bread.
17 Then will I send against you famine and wild beasts,
And they shall bereave you: and pestilence and blood shall pass through thee;
And I will cause the sword to come upon thee.[2]
I Jehovah have spoken it.

CHAPTER VI.

1 The word also of Jehovah came to me, saying,
2 Son of man! set thy face towards the mountain of Israel,
And prophesy against them, and say,
3 Ye mountains of Israel, hear the word of the Lord Jehovah:
Thus saith the Lord Jehovah to the mountains and the hills,
To the rivers and the valleys:
Behold! I will bring the sword against you, and destroy your high places;
4 And your altars shall be desolate,
Your idols shall be broken;
And I will cast down your slain before your idols.
5 Then I will place the carcases of the sons of Israel
Before your idols; I will scatter them before the idols.
I will sprinkle your bones round about your altars.
6 In all your habitations cities shall be desolate,[3]
And high places shall be reduced to devastation,
That your altars may be wasted and desolated,
And your idols may be broken up and abolished,

---

[1] See vol. i. p. 213, note.   [2] See vol. i. p. 215, note.
[3] Explained by Calvin, vol. i. p. 224, note.

And your images cut down, and your works blotted out.
7 Then the slain shall fall in the midst of you,
And ye shall know that I am Jehovah.
8 Still, I will leave a remnant, that ye may have some
Who shall escape the sword among the nations,
When ye shall be scattered through the countries.
9 And the remnant shall remember me among the nations,
Among which they shall become captives,
Because I am broken down with their adulterous heart,
Which has departed from me, and with their eyes,
Which are full of lust after their idols;
And they shall loathe themselves for all the evils
Which they have committed in all their abominations.
10 Then they shall know that I Jehovah said not in vain,
I will cause them to suffer this evil.[1]

11 Thus saith the Lord Jehovah,
Strike with thy hand, and stamp with thy feet,
And say, Alas! for all the evil abominations of the house of Israel,
For they shall fall by the sword, and famine, and pestilence.
12 He who shall be afar off shall die by the pestilence;
He who shall be near shall fall by the sword;[2]
He who shall remain and be besieged shall die through hunger;
And I will fulfil my indignation upon them.
13 And ye shall know that I am Jehovah,
When their wounded shall be among their idols round about their altars,
Upon every high hill, on all the heads of the mountains,
Under every green tree and every thick oak,
In the place where they offered the incense of sweet fragrance to all their idols.
14 So I will stretch out my hand upon them,
And I will make the land desert and desolate—
More than the desert of Diblathah, in all their dwellings;
And they shall know that I am Jehovah.

[1] For Calvin's sense of "evil," see vol. i. p. 232, note.
[2] For another rendering, see vol. i. p. 235, note.

CHAPTER VII.

¹ Then the word of Jehovah came to me, saying,
² Thou also, son of man, thus saith the Lord Jehovah
Concerning the land of Israel, An end, an end is come
Upon the four quarters of the land.
³ Now an end is come upon thee,
And I will send my indignation against thee,
And I will judge thee according to thy ways,
And I will put upon thee all thine abominations.
⁴ Then mine eye shall not spare thee, nor will I pity thee;
Because I will recompense thy ways upon thee,
And thy abominations shall be in the midst of thee,
And ye shall know that I am Jehovah.

⁵ Thus saith the Lord Jehovah,
Lo! evil, and only evil, shall come.[1]
⁶ An end is come—an end is come;
It has watched against thee; behold! it is come.
⁷ The morning is come upon thee, O dweller in the land;
The time is come; the day of tumult is near, and not the clamour of the mountains.
⁸ Now I will shortly pour out my indignation upon thee,
And I will accomplish my anger against thee,
And I will judge thee according to thy ways,
And I will put upon thee all thine abominations.
⁹ Mine eye shall not spare, neither will I pity;
According to thy ways will I put upon thee,
And thine abominations shall be in the midst of thee;
And ye shall know that I Jehovah am smiting thee.
¹⁰ Behold the day: behold it is come;
The morning has advanced, the rod has flourished;
¹¹ Pride has flourished: violence has sprung up into a staff of impiety:
None of them, nor yet their opulence, shall remain:

---

[1] Another reading proposed, vol. i. p. 245, note. Archbishop Newcome adopts the reading of the note, which is supported by more than twenty MSS., " Lo! evil cometh after evil."

There shall be no noise nor any lamentation for them :
12 The appointed time is come ; the day has approached :
The buyer shall not rejoice; the seller shall not be sorrowful;
Because indignation shall be on all their multitude :
13 Since the seller shall not return to his merchandise,
And their life is yet among the living ;
Because the vision is concerning the whole multitude,[1]
It shall not return ; and no man shall strengthen his soul in his iniquity.

14 They have blown the trumpet; they have prepared all things;
But none is gone out to battle, because my wrath
Is upon the whole multitude.
15 The sword abroad ; pestilence and famine at home.
He that is in the field shall die by the sword ;
He that is in the city shall be consumed by famine and pestilence.
16 And the escapers of them shall escape,
And shall be upon the hills like doves of the valleys,
All mourning,[2] every one in his iniquity.
17 All hands shall be loosened ; all knees shall flow like water.
18 And they shall gird themselves with sackcloth,
And dread shall cover them,
And shame shall be upon all faces,
And baldness upon all heads.
19 They shall cast their silver into the street,
And their gold shall be an unclean thing :
Their silver and their gold shall not deliver them
In the day of Jehovah's wrath :
They shall neither satisfy their souls nor fill their bellies,
Because it was the stumbling-block of their iniquity.
20 As to the beauty of their ornaments, they turned it to pride,
And they made the images of their abominations
And of their defilements out of it (*i.e.*, gold) ;[3]
Therefore I have cast it from them.
21 And I will deliver it into the hand of strangers for a prey,

---

[1] See another rendering, vol. i. p. 255.
[2] See vol. i. p. 259, note.
[3] See vol. i. p. 264.

And of the wicked of the land for a spoil;
And they shall profane it.
²² My face also will I turn from them,
For they will profane my secret place:
And robbers will enter into it and profane it.

²³ Make a chain:—for the land is filled
With a judgment of bloods,
The city, too, is full of violence.
²⁴ For I will bring on it the wicked among the Gentiles;
And they shall possess their houses:
I will also cause their pride to cease,
And their sanctuaries shall be polluted.
²⁵ Destruction is come: and they shall seek peace when there is none.
²⁶ Calamity shall come upon calamity, and rumour upon rumour;
Then they shall seek a vision from a prophet;
But the law shall perish from the priest,
And counsel from the aged.

²⁷ The king shall mourn, and the princes shall be clothed with desolation,
And the hands of the people of the land shall be troubled:
According to their ways will I act towards them,
According to their judgments will I judge them:
And they shall know that I am Jehovah.

CHAPTER VIII.

¹ And it happened in the sixth year, in the sixth month, in the fifth day, I was sitting in my house, and the elders of Judah were sitting before my face, and there the hand of the Lord Jehovah fell upon me.

² I looked, and behold a likeness as the appearance of fire:
From the appearance of its loins downwards, fire;
And from its loins upwards, as the appearance of brightness,

Like the figure of Hasmal.
3 And he sent the likeness of a hand,
And raised me by a lock of my head;
And the Spirit lifted me up between earth and heaven,
And led me to Jerusalem in the visions of God,
To the door of the inner gate looking towards the north;
Where was the seat of the idol jealousy, causing jealousy.
4 Then lo! there was the glory of the God of Israel,
According to the vision which I saw in the plain.

5 And said to me, Son of man, lift up thine eyes now
To the way of the north:
So I raised my eyes towards the north,
And lo! towards the north at the gate of the altar,
That idol—jealousy—at the entrance.
6 And he said to me, Son of man, seest thou their deeds?
The great abominations which the house of Israel perpetrate here,
That I should depart far from my sanctuary?
But turn thee yet again, and thou shalt see greater abominations.
7 Then he led me to the door of the court,
And I looked, and lo! an opening in the wall.
Then he said to me, Son of man, dig now into the wall;
And I dug in the wall, and behold a door.
8 Then he said to me, Enter and see the evil abominations which they do.
9 Then I entered and beheld, and lo! every likeness of a reptile,
10 And abominations of animals, and all idols of the house of Israel,
Were depicted on the wall round about.
11 And seventy men of the elders of the house of Israel,
And Jazaniah, son of Saphan, stood in the midst of them,
Who stood before them, and to each a censer in his hand,
And a thick cloud of incense ascended.
12 Then he said to me, Hast thou seen, son of man,
What the elders of the house of Israel do in darkness,
Each in the hidden places of his imagery?

Who say, Jehovah does not see us; Jehovah has deserted the land.
¹³ Then he said to me, Turn thee again,
And thou shalt see the great abominations which they do.
¹⁴ Then he brought me to the door of the gate of Jehovah's house,
Which looks to the north: and lo! there sat women
Lamenting for Thammuz.
¹⁵ Then he said to me, Son of man, turn thee again,
And thou shalt see greater abominations than these.
¹⁶ Then he led me to the inner court of Jehovah's house,
And lo! at the gate of Jehovah's temple, between the entrance and the altar,
About five and twenty men, with their backs towards Jehovah's temple,
And their faces towards the east, worshipping the rising sun.
¹⁷ Then he said to me, Hast thou seen this, son of man?
Is it a light thing to the house of Judah
To do these abominations which they have done there?
Because they have filled the land with violence,
And have returned to provoke me,
And lo! they put the branch to their nose.
¹⁸ I also in return will deal in my fury:
Mine eye shall neither spare nor pity;
And when they cry in mine ears with a loud voice
I will not hear them.

CHAPTER IX.

¹ He cried also in mine ear with a loud voice, saying,
Let the rulers of the city approach,.
Every one with his weapon of destruction in his hand.
² And lo! six men coming from the way of the higher gate, which is towards the north,
And each had his slaughter-weapon in his hand;
And one man in the midst of them clothed in linen,
With a writer's inkhorn at his side:

Then they went in and stood near the brazen altar.
³ Then the glory of the God of Israel ascended from the cherubim
Above which it rested, to the threshold of the house,
And cried to the man clothed in linen, with the inkhorn at his side;
⁴ Then Jehovah said to him,
Pass through the midst of the city, through the midst of Jerusalem,
And make a sign upon the foreheads of the men who sigh
And cry for all the abominations which they suffer in the midst of it.
⁵ But to the others he said in my hearing,
Go ye after him through the city, and smite;
Let not your eye spare, and do not pity:
⁶ Old and young, girl, boy, and woman slay to the death;
Yet approach not any who bears the sign,
And begin from my sanctuary.
Then they began at the elders who were in front of the house.
⁷ And he said to them, Pollute the house, and fill the altars with the slain:
Go ye forth. And they went forth, and made a slaughter in the city.
⁸ And it happened while they were slaying that I was left:
Then I fell upon my face, and cried out and said,
Aha! Lord Jehovah, wilt thou slay all the reliques of Israel
By pouring forth thine anger upon Jerusalem?
⁹ Then he said to me, The iniquity of the house of Israel and Judah
Is great beyond measure, and the land is full of blood,
And the city is full of perversity: because they said,
Jehovah has deserted the land: Jehovah regardeth it not.
¹⁰ As for me also, mine eye shall not spare them,
I will not pity them: their ways will I recompense on their heads.
¹¹ And lo! the man clad in linen, who had the inkhorn by his side,

Returned and made his report, saying,
I have done as thou didst command me.

CHAPTER X.

¹ Then I looked, and lo! above the firmament, which was above the head of the cherubim,
As it were a sapphire-stone,
Like the appearance of a throne which was seen above them.
² Then he spake to the man clad in linen garments, and said,
Go in to the midst of the wheels under the cherub,
And fill thy palms with coals of fire from the midst of the cherubim,
And scatter them over the city. And he went in my sight.
³ And the cherubim stood on the right of the house when the man came.
And a cloud filled the inner court.
⁴ Then the glory of Jehovah was raised above the cherub towards the threshold of the house;
And the house was filled with cloud,
And the court was filled with the brightness of Jehovah's glory.
⁵ Then the sound of the wings of the cherubim was heard to the outer court,
Like the voice of the Omnipotent God when he speaketh.
⁶ And it happened when he had commanded the man clothed with linen,
Saying, Take fire from between the wheels, from the midst of the cherubim;
Then he went in and stood beside the wheel.
⁷ And one cherub stretched his hand from the midst of the cherubim,
To the fire which was in the midst of the cherubim,
And he took it, and put it into the palms of the man clothed in linen;
Then he took it and departed.
⁸ And there appeared in the cherubim themselves,
The likeness of a man's hand under their wings.

⁹ Then I looked, and lo! four wheels near the cherubim,
One wheel by one cherub, another wheel near another cherub:
And the appearance of the wheels was like the stone tharsis.
¹⁰ And as for their aspect, the appearance of each was the same,¹
As if a wheel was in the midst of a wheel.
¹¹ When they moved, they went on their four sides;
They did not return in going forward,
Since they moved towards the direction of their head;
They did not return as they went.
¹² And their whole body, and backs, and hands, and wings,
The four wheels, indeed, themselves were full of eyes all round.
¹³ He cried to the wheels in my hearing, O wheel!

¹⁴ And each living creature had four faces:
The face of the first that of a cherub;
The face of the second that of a man;
Of the third that of a lion; and the fourth an eagle's.
¹⁵ And the cherubim were raised up.
This is the living creature which I saw by the river Chebar.
¹⁶ Then when the cherubim moved, the wheels moved near them;
And when the cherubim raised their wings aloft
From the earth,
The wheels did not turn away from the side of them.
¹⁷ When the living creatures stood, they stood;
When they were lifted up, the wheels also were raised:
Because the spirit of the living creature was in them.

¹⁸ Then the glory of Jehovah went forth from the threshold of the house,
And stood over the cherubim.
¹⁹ Then the cherubim raised their wings, and went up from the earth in my sight:
When they went forth, the wheels also went before them,

---
¹ See note on p. 330, vol. i.

And each stood above the threshold of the east gate of
  Jehovah's house;
And the glory of the God of Israel was above them.
20 It is the very living creature which I saw
  Under the God of Israel by the river Chebar;
  And I knew them to be cherubim.

21 Each had four faces apiece, and four wings;
  And the likeness of the hands of a man under their wings.
22 And the likeness of their faces was that which I saw at
    the river Chebar,
  Both their appearance and themselves:[1]
  Each moved towards his own face.

CHAPTER XI.

1 Then the spirit raised me up, and brought me
  To the eastern gate of Jehovah's house; and lo!
  At the threshold of the gate, five and twenty men;
  Then I saw in the midst of them Jaazaniah, son of Asur;
  And Pelthiah, son of Benaiah, princes of the people.
2 Then he said to me, Son of man, these men divine vanity,
  And plan perverse counsel in this city;
3 Who say, It is not near; let us build houses:
  The city is the caldron, and we are the flesh:
4 Wherefore, prophesy against them, prophesy, son of man.

5 Then the Spirit of Jehovah fell upon me, and said to me,
  Say, Thus saith Jehovah, Thus have ye spoken, O house
    of Israel,
  The mountings of your spirit, I know them:
6 Ye have multiplied your slain in this city,
  And ye have filled its streets with the slain.
7 Wherefore, thus saith the Lord Jehovah, Your slain,
  Whom ye placed in the midst—they shall be the flesh,
  And the city the caldron; and I will cast you forth from
    the midst of it:

[1] Vol. i. p. 345, note.

8 Ye have feared the sword, and I will bring the sword upon you, saith the Lord Jehovah:
9 And I will cast you out of the midst of it,
And will deliver you into the hand of strangers,
And will exercise judgments against you.
10 Then ye shall fall by the sword: in the border of Israel
Will I judge you; and ye shall know that I am Jehovah.
11 It shall not be your caldron,
And ye shall not be in the midst of it for flesh;
In the border of Israel will I judge you.
12 And ye shall know that I am Jehovah;
Because ye have not walked in my statutes,
And have not executed my judgments;
But ye have done according to the judgments of the nations around you.
13 And it happened, while I prophesied,
That Phalatias, the son of Benaiah, died:
Then I fell upon my face, and cried with a loud voice, and said,
Ah! Lord Jehovah! wilt thou consume the remnant of Israel!
14 Then the word of Jehovah came to me again, saying,
15 Son of man, thy brethren, thy brethren,
Thy kindred, and all the whole house of Israel,
To these the inhabitants of Jerusalem have said,
Depart ye far from Jehovah, the land is given as an heritage to us.
16 Wherefore say, Thus saith the Lord Jehovah,
Because ye have been cast far away among the Gentiles,
And dispersed through the lands,
Therefore will I be to them a sanctuary of fewness[1]
In the lands to which they have come.

17 Wherefore thou shalt say, Thus saith the Lord Jehovah,
I will gather you out of the peoples, and collect you out of the lands
To which ye have been driven, and I will give you the land of Israel.

[1] See vol. i. p. 362, note.

¹⁸ And they shall come there, and take away all its idols,
And all its abominations out of it.
¹⁹ Then I will give them one heart, and will put a new Spirit within them;
And I will take away the stony heart from their flesh,
And will give them a heart of flesh:
²⁰ That they may walk in my statutes,
And keep my judgments, and do them:
Then they shall be my people, and I will be their God.
²¹ Then I will repay on their own head the way of those
Whose heart walks after a heart of foulness[1] and grossness,
Saith the Lord Jehovah.

²² Then the cherubim raised their wings, and the wheels beside them,
And the glory of the God of Israel was over above them.
²³ And the glory of Jehovah ascended out of the midst of the city,
And stood over the mount on the east of the city.
²⁴ Then the spirit raised me, and brought me to Chaldæa,
To the captivity,
In a vision, in the Spirit of God.
Then the vision which I saw went up from me.
²⁵ And I spoke to the captivity
All the words of Jehovah which he had shown me.

CHAPTER XII.

¹ The word of Jehovah came also unto me, saying,
² Son of man, thou dwellest in the midst of a rebellious house:
They have eyes to see, and they see not;
They have ears to hear, and they hear not,
Because their house is revolting.
³ And thou, son of man, make thyself vessels for removal,
And remove in the day-time before their eyes:
Then thou shalt move from thy place to another in their sight,

---

[1] See vol. i. p. 382, note.

Since perhaps they may consider, for they are a rebellious house:
4 And bring forth vessels like vessels for removal
In the day-time in their sight :
And thou shalt go forth at even in their sight,
Like a departure into captivity.
5 In their sight thou shalt dig thyself a wall,
And carry out (thy goods) by it :
6 In their eyes upon thy shoulder shalt thou carry (them) ;
In darkness shalt thou go forth :
Thou shalt cover thy face, and not look upon the ground,
Because I have placed thee as a sign to the house of Israel.
7 Then I did as I was commanded :
My vessels I carried forth like vessels for captivity
In the daytime ;
Then in the evening I dug through the wall by my hand ;[1]
In the darkness I led them forth,
Upon my shoulder I carried them in their sight.

8 Then in the morning the word of Jehovah came to me, saying,
9 Son of man, has not the house of Israel, the rebellious house, said to thee,
10 What doest thou ? Say to them,
Thus saith the Lord Jehovah :
This burden[2] relates to the prince in Jerusalem,
And to all the house of Israel in the midst of them.
11 Say unto them, I am your portent :
As I have done, so shall it be done to them :
They shall be taken away and led into captivity.
12 Then the prince in the midst of them
Shall carry on his shoulder in the darkness,
And go forth through the wall,
Through which they have dug for carrying out by it :
He shall cover his face so as not to look upon the ground.
13 Then I will spread my net over him, and he shall be taken in my snare :

[1] See vol. i. p. 396, note: "for myself."
[2] See vol. i. p. 395, note; where Calvin explains the word "burden."

Then I will lead him away to Babylon in the land of
  Chaldæa;
Yet he shall not see it, though he shall die there.
¹⁴ And all who are about him to help him, and all his garrison,
  Will I scatter to every wind, and I will unsheath my sword
  after them.¹
¹⁵ Then they shall know that I am Jehovah,
  After I shall have scattered them among the nations,
  And shall have dispersed them through their lands.
¹⁶ And I will make the remnant of them but few
  By the sword, and famine, and pestilence;
  That they may narrate all their abominations
  Among the Gentiles to whom they come;
  And they shall know that I am Jehovah.

¹⁷ Moreover, the word of Jehovah came to me, saying,
¹⁸ Son of man, eat thy bread with trembling, and drink thy
    water
  With tumult and anxiety: And thou shalt say to the
    people of the land,
¹⁹ Thus saith the Lord Jehovah to the dwellers at Jerusalem,
  And on the land of Israel, They shall eat their bread in
    torture,²
  And shall drink their water in desolation,
  That the land may be spoiled of its fulness,
  On account of the violence of all its inhabitants.
²⁰ And inhabited cities shall be reduced to solitude,
  And the land laid waste; and ye shall know that I am
    Jehovah.
²¹ Then the word of Jehovah came to me, saying,
²² Son of man, What is this proverb of yours in the land of
    Israel, saying,
  The days are prostrated, and all prophecy has ceased?
²³ Wherefore thou shalt say to them, Thus saith the Lord
    Jehovah,
  I will make this proverb cease,
  And they shall no more use this proverb in Israel;
  But rather say to them, The days are at hand,

¹ Vol. i. p. 402, note.   ² See vol. i. p. 406, note.

And the word of every vision.
24 Because there shall no longer be any lying vision,
Nor any flattering divination in the midst of the house of Israel.
25 Since I Jehovah will speak:
And the word which I shall speak, I will also perform;
It shall no longer be prolonged:
Since in your days, O exasperating house,
The word which I shall speak, I will perform, saith the Lord Jehovah.

26 Then the word of Jehovah came to me, saying,
27 Son of man, behold the house of Israel say,
The vision which he saw is extended to many days,
And he prophesieth for times afar off.
28 Wherefore thou shalt say to them, Thus saith the Lord Jehovah,
It shall not be put off any longer;
All the words which I have spoken, even every word,
Will I fulfil, saith the Lord Jehovah.

CHAPTER XIII.

1 And the word of Jehovah came to me, saying,
2 Son of man, prophesy against the prophets of Israel
That prophesy, and say unto them that prophesy out of their own hearts,
Hear ye the word of Jehovah;
3 Thus saith the Lord Jehovah, Wo unto the foolish prophets,
Who walk after their own spirit, and have seen nothing![1]
4 Like foxes in the deserts, are thy prophets, O Israel.
5 Ye have not gone up to the broken places,
Nor repaired the hedge around the house of Israel,
To stand in the battle in the day of Jehovah.
6 They have seen vanity, they have divined a lie,
Saying, Jehovah saith, and Jehovah has not sent them;
And they caused men to hope for the confirmation of their word.

---
[1] See vol. ii. p. 9, note.

⁷ Have ye not seen a vision of vanity, and spoken a divination of lies?
And yet ye say Jehovah says it, and I have not spoken it.
⁸ Wherefore thus saith the Lord Jehovah,[1]
Because ye have spoken vanity, and have seen a lie,
Wherefore behold! I am against them,
Saith the Lord Jehovah.
⁹ And my hand shall be against the prophets who see vanity and divine a lie:
They shall not be in the counsel of my people,
And shall not be written in the catalogue of the house of Israel,
And they shall not return to the land of Israel;
And ye shall know that I am the Lord Jehovah.
¹⁰ Because, even because, they have deceived my people,
By saying, Peace, and there was no peace:
And one built up a wall, and, behold, others daubed it with untempered mortar:
¹¹ Say to those who daub it with untempered mortar,
It shall fall:
There shall be an inundating shower:
And I will send hailstones;
And the breath of whirlwinds shall rend it.
¹² Lo! the wall shall fall: shall it not be said to you,
Where is the daubing with which ye have daubed it?
¹³ Besides, thus saith the Lord Jehovah, I will make it fall:[2]
There shall be the breath of tempests in my wrath,
And an inundating shower in my anger,
And hailstones in my fury to consume them.
¹⁴ Then I will overthrow the wall which ye have daubed with untempered mortar,
And I will bring it down to the ground;
Then its foundation shall be discovered when it shall fall,
And ye shall be consumed in the midst of it;
And ye shall know that I am Jehovah.
¹⁵ I will also satisfy mine indignation upon the wall
As well as upon its daubing, and will say to them,
The wall is gone, and the daubers of it are no more.

---

[1] See vol. ii. p. 14, note.   [2] See vol. ii. p. 22, note.

¹⁶ The prophets of Israel prophesied concerning Jerusalem,
And saw a vision of peace for it;
Yet there is no peace, saith the Lord Jehovah.

¹⁷ Son of man, do thou set thy face against the daughters of thy people,
Who prophesy out of their own heart, and prophesy against them,
¹⁸ And thou shalt say, Thus saith the Lord Jehovah,
Wo to those who sow pillows to all armholes,
And make coverings for the head of every stature,
To hunt souls! Will ye hunt the souls of my people?
And will ye preserve your own souls alive?
¹⁹ Will ye profane me before my people for handfuls of barley and pieces of bread,
To slay the souls that were not dying,
And to give life to the souls that were not alive,
By deceiving my people who listen to your lies?

²⁰ Because thus saith the Lord Jehovah, Behold!
I am against your pillows by which ye there hunt souls for their escape;
And I will tear them from your arms,
And set free the souls which ye have hunted, that they may escape.
²¹ I will also rend your coverings, and deliver my people out of your hands;
They shall no longer be a prey in your hands;
And ye shall know that I am Jehovah.
²² Because ye have grieved the heart of the just by falsehood,
And I have not grieved him;
And ye have strengthened the hands of the wicked,
So that he should not be converted from his evil way
²³ For saving his life: wherefore ye shall not see a lie
Nor divine a divination any more;
For I will rescue my people from your hands:
And ye shall know that I am Jehovah.

CHAPTER XIV.

¹ Then men came to me from the elders of Israel,
And sat before my face.
² Then came the word of Jehovah to me, saying,
³ Son of man, these men have set their idols up in their heart,
And have put a stumblingblock of iniquity before their face:
Shall I verily be inquired of by them?
⁴ Wherefore speak unto them, and say, Thus saith the Lord Jehovah,
Every man of the house of Israel, who setteth up his idols in his heart,
And has put the stumblingblock of his iniquity before his face,
And has come to the Prophet; I Jehovah
Will answer him according to the multitude of his idols;[1]
⁵ That I may seize the house of Israel in their own heart,
Because they have entirely separated themselves from me by their idols.
⁶ Therefore say unto the house of Israel,
Thus saith the Lord Jehovah, Turn ye,
Even turn yourselves from your idols;
And turn your faces from all your abominations.
⁷ For every one of the house of Israel, or of the strangers sojourning in Israel,
Who is separated[2] from following after me,
And has set up his idols in his heart,
And put the stumblingblock of his iniquity before his face,
And cometh to the Prophet to inquire of me through him;
I Jehovah will answer him for myself.
⁸ Then will I set my face against that man,
And set him for a sign and a proverb,
And I will cut him off from the midst of my people;
And ye shall know that I am Jehovah.
⁹ And when a prophet is deceived in uttering his speech,

---

[1] See vol. ii. p. 47, note.   [2] See vol. ii p. 51, note.

I Jehovah have deceived that prophet;
   And I will stretch forth my hand upon him,
   And will blot him out of the midst of my people Israel.
10 They shall also bear their iniquity;
   As the iniquity of the inquirer, so shall be the iniquity of the prophet;
11 That the house of Israel may stray from me no more,
   Neither be polluted any more with all their wickedness;
   That they may be my people, and I may be their God, saith the Lord Jehovah.

12 Then the word of Jehovah came to me, saying,
13 Son of man, when a land has acted wickedly against me,[1]
   And I shall stretch out my hand upon it,
   And shall break the staff of its bread,
   And shall send famine upon it, and cut off from it man and beast:
14 Though these three men were in it, Noah, Daniel, and Job,
   They shall deliver but their own souls in their righteousness,
   Saith the Lord Jehovah.
15 If I cause an evil beast to pass through the land,
   And it bereave it and lay it waste,
   So that no man can pass through on account of the beast:
16 Though these three men were in it, as I live, saith the Lord Jehovah,
   If they shall deliver their own souls,
   They alone shall be delivered, and the land shall be laid waste.
17 Or if I make a sword pass through that land,
   And I say to the sword, Pass through the land,
   So that man and beast may be cut off from it:
18 And these three men are in the midst of it,
   As I live, saith the Lord Jehovah,
   They shall not deliver their sons and their daughters,
   Since they alone shall be set free.
19 Or if I shall send a pestilence upon that land,
   And pour out my wrath upon it in blood,
   To destroy from it man and beast:

   ---
   [1] " By prevaricating prevarication," vol. ii. p. 67, note.

20 And Noah, Daniel, and Job were in the midst of it,
   As I live, saith the Lord Jehovah,
   They shall not deliver either son or daughter;
   They shall free their own soul in their righteousness.
21 Therefore thus saith the Lord Jehovah,
   How much more when I send my four grievous judgments against Jerusalem,
   The sword, and famine, and evil beast, to destroy from it man and beast?
22 And lo! the remnant that is left in it,[1]
   The remnant of those who go forth, namely, sons and daughters,
   They shall go forth unto you:
   And ye shall see their ways and their works,
   And ye shall console yourselves for all the evil
   Which I have brought upon Jerusalem,
   Yea, all that I have brought upon her.
23 Then shall ye be comforted when ye shall see their ways and their works:
   And ye shall know that I have not done in vain
   Whatever I have done in it, saith the Lord Jehovah.

CHAPTER XV.

1 Then came the word of Jehovah unto me, saying,
2 Son of man, What is the wood of the vine
   Better than any branching-tree among the trees of the wood?
3 Shall wood be taken from it to form any work?
   Or will it make a peg to hang any vessel thereon?
4 Behold, it it is cast into the fire for burning;
   The fire devoured both ends of it, and its middle is burnt.[2]
   Is it useful for any purpose?
5 Lo! when it was entire, it was not used for any purpose:
   How much less when the fire has consumed it,
   And it is burnt up, shall it be useful for any purpose?

---

[1] See vol. ii. p. 79, note.
[2] See vol. ii. p. 84, note.

⁶ Therefore thus saith the Lord Jehovah,
  As the wood of the vine among the trees of the forest,
  Which I have cast into the fire for fuel,
  So have I given the inhabitants of Jerusalem :
⁷ Then will I set my face against them ;
  They shall pass through fire, and fire shall consume them;
  And they shall know that I am Jehovah,
  When I have set my face against them.
⁸ Then will I make the land desolate,
  Because they have transgressed with transgression,¹
  Saith the Lord Jehovah.

CHAPTER XVI.

¹ Then the word of Jehovah came unto me, saying,
² Son of man, lay open to Jerusalem her abominations.
³ Thus shalt thou say, Thus saith the Lord Jehovah unto Jerusalem,
  Thy source and thy birth-place was the land of Canaan ;
  Thy father was an Amorite, thy mother a Hittite.
⁴ Then as to thy nativity, in the day of thy birth ·
  Thy navel was not cut : thou wast not washed with water
  To supple thee : thou wast not salted with salt,²
  Nor wrapped in swaddling clothes.
⁵ No eye pitied thee, to do unto thee any one of these things,
  In considering thee ; and thou wast cast forth
  On the surface of the field, to the disgrace of thy person,
    in the day of thy birth.
⁶ Then I passed near thee and saw thy defilements,
  And I said to thee in thy bloods, Live ;
  Yea, I said to thee in thy bloods, Live.
⁷ Then I made thee grow as a germ of the field,
  And thou didst increase and flourish ;
  Thou becamest remarkably beautiful ;³
  Thy breasts became prominent and thine hair profuse,
  Yet thou wast naked and bare.

¹ See vol. ii. p. 91, note.   ² See vol. ii. p. 96, note.
³ See vol. ii. p. 100, note.

⁸ Then I passed by and saw thee: and lo! the time, the time for love:
Then I stretched out my skirt over thee,
And covered thy nakedness; and I swore to thee,
And made a covenant with thee,
And thou wast mine, saith the Lord Jehovah.
⁹ Then I washed thee with water, and cleansed thy blood from thee,
And anointed thee with oil, and clothed thee in a Phrygian robe;
¹⁰ Then I shod thee with badgers' skin, and dressed thee in fine linen;
Then I arrayed thee in silk, and adorned thee with ornaments,
¹¹ And put bracelets on thy hands, and a chain round thy neck.
¹² Then I put a ring through thy nose,[1] and ear-rings in thine ears,
And a crown of comeliness on thy head.
¹³ I adorned thee with gold and silver, and clothed thee with fine linen,
And silk and broidered work: thou didst eat fine flour, and honey, and oil;
And thou wast beautiful exceedingly,
And thou didst proceed prosperously to thy kingdom.
¹⁴ Then thy fame went forth among the nations for beauty,
Because thou wast perfect in the beauty
Which I caused unto thee, saith the Lord Jehovah.
¹⁵ But thou didst trust in thy beauty, and commit fornication through thy renown,
And didst pour out thy fornications to every passer by;
¹⁶ His it was.—Then thou hast taken of thy garments,
And made thee high places sprinkled with spots,
And hast committed fornication upon them:
They do not come, and it shall not be.[2]
¹⁷ Thou hast also taken vessels of thy beauty of my gold

[1] Vol. ii. p. 105, note.
[2] The meaning of this clause is doubtful. See Calvin's Commentary, vol. ii. p. 113. Newcome very judiciously translates, " whither thou shouldst not have come, neither should it have been done."

And of my silver which I had given thee;
And thou hast made for thyself images of men,
And hast committed fornication with them.
18 Then thou hast taken of thy variegated garments,
And hast clothed them: and my oil and mine incense
Hast thou set before them.
19 My bread also which I gave thee, fine flour and oil,
And honey with which I fed thee,
Thou hast set it before them for a sweet savour;
And so it has happened, saith the Lord Jehovah.
20 Then thou hast taken thy sons and thy daughters which thou hast borne to me,
And hast slain them to be devoured:
Are then thy fornications a small thing?
21 Then thou hast slain my sons, and caused them to be thrown to idols.[1]
22 And in all thine abominations and thy lewdness
Thou hast not remembered the days of thy youth,
When thou wast naked and bare, and defiled in thy bloods.
23 So after all thy wickedness it hath happened to thee,
Wo! wo! unto thee, saith the Lord Jehovah.
24 Then thou hast built a high place for thyself,
And hast made thee a raised spot in every street.
25 At the head of every way thou hast built thy high place;
Then thou hast made thy beauty abominable,
And hast spread thy feet to every passer by,
And hast multiplied thy lewdnesses.

26 Thou hast also committed adultery with the Egyptians
Thy neighbours, great of flesh: and over and over again
Hast committed lewdness to irritate me.
27 Then lo! I stretched out my hand over thee,
And I diminished thy portion, and delivered thee up
To the lust of the daughters of the Philistines, who hated thee,
And were ashamed of thine abandoned ways.
28 Then thou hast committed adultery with the sons of Ashur,
Since thou wast not satisfied, thou hast been lewd with them;
Yet even then thou wast not satisfied.

---

[1] See vol. ii. p. 121, note.

²⁹ Then thou hast increased thy lewdnesses
In the land of Canaan unto Chaldæa;
And even this did not satiate thee.
³⁰ How soft is thine heart, saith the Lord Jehovah,
Since thou doest all the work of a bold abandoned woman!
³¹ Since thou hast raised thine high place at the head of every way,
And hast made thy lofty place in every celebrated spot;
And hast not been like a harlot in scorning hire.[1]
³² An adulterous woman receiving strangers instead of her husband!
³³ To all harlots men give a reward;
But thou hast given thy gifts to all thy lovers,
And thou hast hired them to come to thee from all sides
³⁴ For thy fornications—for in thy lewdness
Thou hast inverted the custom of other women;
Since there is no fornication like thine:
Because thou hast given instead of receiving a gift,
Then thou hast acted contrary to others.

³⁵ Wherefore, O harlot, hear Jehovah's word!
³⁶ Thus saith the Lord Jehovah,
Because thy shamelessness is poured out,
And thy baseness detected in thy lewdness towards thy lovers,
And towards all the idols of thine abominations,
And in the bloods of thy children whom thou hast given to them;
³⁷ Wherefore lo! I will assemble all thy lovers
Whom thou hast attracted, and all whom thou hast loved and hated;
I will assemble them from all around thee,
And I will lay bare thy nakedness before them,
And they shall behold all thy turpitude.
³⁸ Then will I judge thee with the judgment of adulteresses,
And of those who pour out blood; and I will give thee

---

[1] Calvin in his comment explains the sense in which "scorning" is used, vol. ii. p. 135; but Newcome justly supposes the original word to be the Chaldee for "to gather."

The blood of fury and of jealousy.
39 And I will give thee into their hand,
And they shall pull down thy high place,
And destroy thy raised places, and shall spoil thee of thy robes;
They shall also take the vessels of thy glory,
And send thee away naked and bare.
40 Then they shall stir up a crowd against thee,
And stone thee with stones, and thrust at thee with swords.
41 Then they shall burn thy houses with fire,
And shall execute judgments against thee in the eyes of many women:
Then will I cause thee to cease from fornication,
Neither shalt thou offer a gift any more.
42 And I will cause my fury towards thee to rest,
And my jealousy shall depart from thee,
And I will rest and be no longer angry.
43 Because thou hast not remembered the days of thy youth,
But hast provoked me in all those things;
I will even recompense thy way upon thine head,
Saith the Lord Jehovah; since thou hast taken no thought
For all thine abominations.[1]

44 Lo! every user of proverbs shall use this proverb against thee,
Saying, As the mother is, so is the daughter.
45 Thou art the daughter of thy mother, who hast cast away her husband and her sons;
And the sister of thy sisters, who loathe their husbands and children;
Your mother was a Hittite, and your father an Amorite:
46 And thine elder sister is Samaria, and her daughters those who dwell at thy left hand;
And thy younger sister, who dwells at thy right hand, is Sodom and her daughters.
47 Yet thou hast not walked in their ways,
And thou hast not done according to their abominations,
As if it had been a very small thing,

[1] See vol. ii. p. 148, note.

And thou hast been more corrupt than they in all thy ways.

⁴⁸ As I live, saith the Lord Jehovah,
If Sodom thy sister and her daughters have done
As thou and thy daughters have done!
⁴⁹ Lo! this was the iniquity of Sodom thy sister,
Pride, fulness of bread, and security of ease
Belonged to her and her daughters: and she did not lay hold
Of the hand of the poor and needy; but she was haughty,
⁵⁰ And did abomination before me,
Hence I took them away as it pleased me.¹

⁵¹ And Samaria hath not committed half of thy sins;
But thou hast multiplied thine abominations beyond them,
And hast justified thy sisters in all the abominations which thou hast done.
⁵² Bear thou, then, thy disgrace by which thou hast pleaded for thy sister,
By thy crimes which thou hast committed beyond them;
They are justified more than thou: be thou then ashamed,
And bear thy disgrace, since thou hast justified thy sisters.
⁵³ Yet will I turn the captivity, yea, the captivity of Sodom and her daughters,
And the captivity of Samaria and her daughters,
And the captivity of thy captivities in the midst of them,
⁵⁴ That thou mayest bear thy reproach, and mayest be ashamed
Of all that thou hast done in consoling them.
⁵⁵ And thy sisters Sodom and her daughters shall return to their former state,
And Samaria and her daughters shall return to theirs,
And thou and thy daughters shall return to yours.
⁵⁶ Then thy sister Sodom was not mentioned by thee,
In the day of thy pride, before thy wickedness was detected;
⁵⁷ As in the time of thy reproach from the daughters of Syria,
And from all around of the daughters of the Philistines,

¹ See vol. ii. p. 156, note.

Who despised thee round about.
58 As for thy depraved thoughts and abominations,
Thou hast borne them, saith Jehovah.
59 For thus saith the Lord Jehovah,
I will also do to thee as thou hast done,
Who hast despised the oath and broken the covenant.
60 Yet I will remember my covenant with thee
In the days of thy youth, and I will establish a perpetual covenant with thee.
61 Then thou shalt remember thy ways and be ashamed,
When thou shalt receive thy sisters, both elder and younger than thyself;
And I will give them unto thee for daughters,
But not by thy covenant.
62 For I will establish my covenant with thee,
And thou shalt know that I am Jehovah.
63 That thou mayest remember and be ashamed,
And not open thy mouth any more because of thy disgrace,
When I am propitious to thee for all thy deeds,
Saith the Lord Jehovah.

CHAPTER XVII.

1 Then the word of Jehovah came to me, saying,
2 Son of man, put forth an enigma and utter a proverb to the house of Israel;
3 And say, Thus saith the Lord Jehovah,
A mighty eagle, with great wings, long feathers, and full of plumage,
Of various colours, came to Mount Lebanon,
And took the highest branch of a cedar;
4 He cropped off the top of its young twigs,
And carried it into the land of the merchant;
He planted it in a city of merchants.
5 He took also of the seed of the land,
And put it in a fruitful field;
He planted it near many waters, like a willow.[1]

[1] Newcome adopts the rendering of the Septuagint and Cocceius, "with much care," *curatio, observatio*, but quotes Dathe and Golius, p. 1362, for the Arabic, in the same sense as Calvin, "a willow."

⁶ Then it grew and became a luxuriant vine, low of stature,
So that its branches turned towards the eagle,
And its roots were under him ; and it became a vine,
And brought forth branches, and sent out boughs.
⁷ There was also another large eagle,[1] of great wings and of copious plumage,
And lo ! this vine bent its roots towards him,
And sent forth its branches towards him,
That he might water it from the beds of his plantation.
⁸ In a good soil near many streams was it planted,
That it should produce leaves and bring forth fruit,
So as to be a magnificent vine.

⁹ Say thou, Thus saith the Lord Jehovah, Shall it prosper ?
Shall not one pluck up its roots and cut down its fruits,
And dry up all its branches, that it may wither ?
Then it shall not be for a great arm or much people
To take it[2] away from its roots.
¹⁰ Yet, behold, when planted, shall it prosper ?
Shall it not completely wither when the east wind has touched it ?
Upon the beds of its plantation shall it wither.

¹¹ Then the word of Jehovah came to me, saying,
¹² Say, I pray thee, to the rebellious house, Know ye not what this means ?
Say, Lo ! the king of Babylon is come to Jerusalem,
And has taken away its king and its elders, and carried them with him to Babylon ;
¹³ Then he took from the royal seed, and struck an agreement with him,
And made him descend to an oath ;
Then he took also the mighty of the land ;
¹⁴ That the kingdom should be low, and not raise itself up,
And keep its agreement and stand in it.
¹⁵ But he rebelled against him, by sending his ambassadors
To Egypt, that horses and much people might be given him :

[1] See vol. ii. p. 192, note.   [2] See vol. ii. p. 193, note.

Shall he who doeth these things prosper and escape?
Shall he who breaks the treaty get off?

¹⁶ As I live, saith the Lord Jehovah, if he shall not die
In the place of the king who made him reign,
Whose oath he has despised, and whose treaty he has made vain,
In the midst of Babylon.

¹⁷ Neither with a mighty army nor a great host
Shall Pharaoh meet with him in battle,
By throwing up a mound and by building a tower, to cut off many souls.

¹⁸ Through breaking the covenant he has despised his oath,
And, behold, he has stretched forth his hand,
And has done all this, and shall not escape.

¹⁹ Besides, thus saith the Lord Jehovah, As I live,
If I do not recompense on his own head
My oath which he has despised, and my covenant which he has broken,

²⁰ Then I will stretch my net over him, and he shall be taken in my snare;
And I will lead him to Babylon, and will plead with him there,
Concerning the transgression which he has transgressed against me.

²¹ And all his fugitives, with all his forces, shall fall by the sword;
And the remnant shall be scattered to every wind;
And ye shall know that I Jehovah have spoken.

²² Thus saith the Lord Jehovah, I will take from the top of the lofty cedar,
And I will tear off a tender branch from its twigs and will set it:
And I will plant it on a lofty and elevated mountain;

²³ On a lofty mountain of Israel will I plant it;
And it shall bring forth a bough and bear fruit, and shall be a tall cedar;[1]
Then every bird shall dwell under it;

---

[1] See vol. ii. p. 208, note.

Every winged thing shall shelter itself under the shadow
of its branches.
24 Then all the trees of the field shall know that I am
Jehovah,
Who humble the high tree and raise aloft the low tree;
I dry up the green tree, and make the dry tree fruitful:
I Jehovah have spoken, and have done it.

CHAPTER XVIII.

1 Then the word of Jehovah came to me, saying,
2 What mean ye by using this proverb[1] about the land of
Israel,
Saying, The fathers have eaten sour grapes,
And the children's teeth are set on edge?
3 As I live, saith the Lord Jehovah, Ye shall not hereafter
Use this proverb any more in Israel.
4 Behold, all souls are mine; as the soul of the father,
So the soul of the son is mine. The soul which has sinned
shall die itself.
5 But if a man have been just, and done judgment and
justice,
6 And have neither eaten upon the mountains, nor raised
his eyes
To the idols of the house of Israel, and have not polluted
His neighbour's wife, nor approached a female when separated;
7 If he have not afflicted any one, and have restored to the
debtor his pledge,
Have not seized the prey, have given his bread to the
hungry,
And have covered the naked with a garment:
8 Have not given upon usury, and have taken no increase,
Have withdrawn his hand from iniquity,
And have done justice faithfully between man and man;

---

[1] Saying or apothegm; note, vol. ii. p. 213.

⁹ Have walked in my statutes, and kept my judgments, to do the truth ;¹
He is just, he shall surely live, saith the Lord Jehovah.
¹⁰ But if he beget a son, who is a robber and a shedder of blood,
And who doeth to his brother² any one of these things,
¹¹ And hath not done all these precepts of the law,
But hath eaten on the mountains, and defiled his neighbour's wife ;
¹² Hath oppressed the poor and needy, hath spoiled by violence,
Hath not restored the pledge, hath lifted up his eyes unto idols ;
¹³ Hath done abomination, hath given on usury and taken increase ;
Shall he live ? He shall not live ; he hath done all these abominations ;
He shall surely die : his blood shall be on him.

¹⁴ And lo ! if he beget a son, and he see all the wickedness which his father has committed,
And feared, and hath not done according to them ;
¹⁵ Hath not eaten upon the mountains, and hath not raised his eyes
To the idols of the house of Israel, and has not defiled his neighbour's wife ;
Hath oppressed no one, hath not taken a pledge,
¹⁶ Hath not spoiled by violence, hath given his bread to the hungry,
And hath covered the naked with a garment ;
¹⁷ Hath withdrawn his hand from the poor,
Hath not received increase and usury, hath done my judgments,
Hath walked in my decrees ; he shall not die
Through the iniquity of his father ; he shall surely live.

¹⁸ His father,—because by oppressing he has oppressed,
And has snatched the prey from his brother,

¹ Conduct himself faithfully; note, vol. ii. p. 219.
² See vol. ii. p. 231, note.

And has done that which is not good in the midst of the people,—
Behold, he shall die in his iniquity.
19 And ye say, Why? shall not the son bear his father's iniquity?
Because the son has done judgment and justice,
And hath kept all my statutes and hath done them,
Therefore shall he surely live.
20 The soul which has sinned, that shall die.
The son shall not bear the father's iniquity,
And the father shall not bear the son's iniquity;
The righteousness of the righteous shall be upon him,
And the impiety of the impious shall be upon him.
21 Then, if the wicked man shall withdraw from all the wickedness which he has done,
And have kept all my sayings, and have done justice and judgment,
He shall surely live—he shall not die.
22 All the transgressions which he has committed
Shall not come into memory to him;
But in his righteousness which he has done shall he live.
23 Do I earnestly desire the death of the wicked, saith the Lord Jehovah?
Do I not desire that he turn from his evil ways and live?

24 Then, if a just man turn aside from his justice,
And do iniquity, according to all the abominations
Which the wicked man has done, shall he live?
All his righteous deeds shall not come into remembrance?[1]
In the transgression which he has transgressed,
And in the wickedness which he has wickedly done,
In them shall he die—yet ye have said—
25 The way of the Lord is not upright. Hear ye then,
O house of Israel, is not my way upright?
Are not your ways perverse?[2]
26 If the just man has turned aside from his justice,
And has done iniquity, and has died in it,

[1] See vol. ii. p. 249, note.
[2] Accurately balanced: note, vol. ii. p. 252.

In his own iniquity which he has committed shall he die.
27 And if the wicked man has turned aside from the wickedness which he has done,
And has done judgment and justice, he shall preserve his soul alive.[1]
28 Then, if he have seen and have turned away from all the wickedness
Which he has done, he shall surely live—he shall not die.
29 Yet the house of Israel have said, The way of the Lord is not upright.
Are not my ways upright, O house of Israel?
Are not your ways perverse?
30 Wherefore I will judge each of you according to his ways,
O house of Israel, saith the Lord Jehovah.
Turn ye, and depart from all your transgressions,
And let not iniquity be your snare.
31 Cast away from you all your iniquities whereby ye have transgressed;
And make you a new heart and a new spirit:
For why will ye die, O house of Israel?
32 Since I do not delight in the death of the dying,
Saith the Lord Jehovah—wherefore turn ye, and live.

CHAPTER XIX.

1 Wherefore take thou up this mournful strain against the princes of Israel,
2 And say, Why did thy mother—a lioness—
Lie down among lions? she brought up her whelps
In the midst of lions.
3 Then she bore one of her whelps, and he was made a lion:
Then he learnt to seize his prey, and he devoured men.
4 Then the Gentiles heard of him; he was taken in their pit,
And they led him in chains into the land of Egypt.
5 Then she saw what she had hoped for, and how her hope had perished;
And she took another of her whelps, and made him a lion.
6 Then he walked in the midst of lions, and became a lion;

---
[1] See vol. ii. p. 256, note.

And he learnt to seize the prey, and devoured men.
7 Then he harassed their palaces and destroyed their cities;
And the land was rendered desolate, and all its fulness,
By the voice of his roaring.
8 Then the nations set themselves against him
From all sides and regions, and spread their net over him.
He was taken in their pit-fall: and they put him in ward,
9 And brought him in chains to the king of Babylon.
They led him into strongholds, that his voice
Might be no longer heard in the mountains of Israel.

10 Thy mother, when she bore thee,[1] was planted like a vine near the waters:
She was fruitful and branching beside many waters.
11 And the rods of her strength were for sceptres for rulers,
And her stature was elevated, and appeared aloft
In the multitude of her branches.
12 Then she was torn in fury, and cast on the ground;
And the east wind dried up her fruit;
Her strong rods were broken off and dried up;
The fire consumed them; and now she is planted
13 In the desert, in a land of dryness and thirst.
14 Then a fire went forth from the rod of her branches, and devoured her fruit;
And there was not a rod of strength in her—a sceptre for ruling.
This is the lamentation, and shall be for a wailing.

CHAPTER XX.

1 It occurred in the seventh year, the fifth month, the tenth day of the month,
Men from the elders of Israel came to consult Jehovah,

---

[1] Calvin translates with the authorized version *in tuo sanguine*, "in thy blood," and explains it as above, *dum peperit*. Capellus and Pradus, by a slight alteration of the Hebrew letters from בדמך, *bedemek*, to כרמן, *keremen*, translate "like a pomegranate." Doederlein, in his Annotations on Grotius, prefers this sense; but Jerome, Rab. Solomon, and Rab. David, take it as Calvin does. Both Rosenmüller and Newcome discuss the point with ability.

And sat before my face. And the word of Jehovah
2 Came to me, saying, Son of man, speak to the elders of Israel,
3 And say unto them, Thus saith the Lord Jehovah,
Are ye come to inquire of me? As I live,
If I will be sought by you, saith the Lord Jehovah,
4 Wilt thou judge them, wilt thou judge them, son of man?
Explain to them the abominations of their fathers;
5 Then thou shalt say unto them, Thus saith the Lord Jehovah,
In the day on which I chose Israel, and lifted up my hand
To the seed of the house of Jacob, and was known to them in the land of Egypt,
Then I raised my hand to them, saying, I am Jehovah your God:
6 In that day I lifted up my hand towards them,
To bring them from the land of Egypt into a land which I espied for them,
Flowing with milk and honey, desirable beyond all lands.
7 Then I said to them, Cast ye away every one the abominations of his eyes,
And pollute not yourselves with the idols of Egypt:
I Jehovah am your God; and they rebelled against me,
8 And were unwilling to hear me: they did not cast away
The idols of their eyes: they did not desert the idols of Egypt:
Then I said that I would pour out my wrath upon them;
To fill up my fury against them in the midst of the land of Egypt.
9 But I acted for my name's sake, that it should not be profaned in the eyes of the nations,
In the midst of which they were; in whose sight I was known to them,
By bringing them forth from the land of Egypt.
10 Then I led them out from the land of Egypt, and brought them into the desert.
11 And I gave them my decrees, and made known my judgments unto them,
Which if a man do, he shall live in them.

¹² Moreover I gave them my sabbaths for a sign between me and them,
That they might know that I am he who sanctifieth them.
¹³ But the house of Israel rebelled against me in the desert:
They walked not in my decrees,
And despised my judgments,
Which if a man do, he shall live in them.
And my sabbaths they greatly violated: Then I said
I would pour out my wrath in the desert to consume them.
¹⁴ Then I acted for my name's sake, that it should not be profaned
In the eyes of the nations, in whose sight I led them out.
¹⁵ Yet I lifted up my hand to them in the desert,
That I should not lead them into the land which I had given them,
Flowing with milk and honey, the desire of all lands,
¹⁶ Because they despised my judgments, and walked not in my decrees,
And polluted my sabbaths; because their heart walked after their idols.
¹⁷ Then mine eye spared them, so that I did not destroy them,
And did not consume them in the desert.

¹⁸ Then I said unto their sons in the desert,
Walk ye not in the decrees of your fathers,
And keep not their judgments, and pollute not yourselves with their idols:
¹⁹ I Jehovah am your God, walk ye in my decrees,
And keep my judgments, and do them:
²⁰ And hallow my sabbaths; and they shall be a sign between me and you,
That ye may know that I Jehovah am your God.
²¹ Then these sons became rebels against me:
They walked not in my decrees, and kept not my judgments
To do them, which if a man do, he shall live in them;
They profaned my sabbaths: and I said
That I would pour out my wrath upon them,
To accomplish my fury against them in the desert.

²² Then I withdrew my hand, and acted for my name's sake,
That it should not be profaned in the eyes of the nations,
Before whose sight I led them out.

²³ I also lifted up my hand to them in the desert
To scatter them among the nations, and disperse them through the lands;
²⁴ Because they did not perform my judgments,
And despised my statutes, and violated my sabbaths;
And their eyes were after their fathers' idols.
²⁵ I therefore gave them decrees that were not good,
And judgments by which they could not live;
²⁶ And I contaminated them in their gifts,
By casting away every first-born offspring,
To destroy them, that they may know that I am Jehovah.
²⁷ Wherefore, speak to the house of Israel, son of man, and say to them,
Thus saith the Lord Jehovah, Hitherto your fathers
Have dishonoured me in this by prevaricating greatly against me:
²⁸ For I introduced them into the land, for which I raised my hand to give it them;
And they saw every high hill, and every branching tree:
Then they sacrificed there their offerings,
And offered there the irritation of their oblation,
And placed there the odour of their sweet fragrance,
And poured out there their libations.
²⁹ Then said I unto them, What is the high place to which ye approach?
For its name is called "Lofty" unto this day.
³⁰ Wherefore, say unto the house of Israel, Thus saith the Lord Jehovah,
Are ye polluted after the way of your fathers?
And do ye commit adultery after their idols?
³¹ For in offering your gifts, and in passing your sons through the fire,
Ye pollute yourselves in all your idols unto this day:
Then shall I be inquired of by you, O house of Israel!

As I live, saith the Lord Jehovah, if I shall be inquired of
    by you.

³² That also which comes into your mind shall not happen,
    Since ye say, We will be as the nations, as the families of
        the lands,
³³ To serve wood and stone. As I live, saith the Lord Jehovah,
    If I will not rule over you with a strong hand, and an extended arm, and in fury poured forth.
³⁴ And I will lead you out from the people, and collect you
        from the lands
    Through which ye were dispersed, by a strong hand, and
        with an extended arm,
³⁵ And with fury poured forth. Then I will lead you into
        the desert of the Gentiles,
    And will plead with you there face to face.
³⁶ As I pleaded with your fathers in the desert of the land
        of Egypt,
    So will I dispute with you, saith the Lord Jehovah.
³⁷ Then I will make you pass under the rod,
    And bring you within the bond of a covenant:
³⁸ Then will I purge out from among you the rebels,
    And the transgressors against me: from the land of their
        habitation
    Will I bring the impious, and they shall not enter the
        land of Israel;
    And ye shall know that I am Jehovah.

³⁹ As for you, O house of Israel, thus saith the Lord Jehovah,
    Go ye, let each serve his idols, since ye do not hear me,
    And the name of my sanctity profane no longer
⁴⁰ With your gifts and your idols, since in the mountain of
        my sanctity,
    In a lofty mountain of Israel, saith the Lord Jehovah,
    There shall the whole house of Israel worship me;
    All, I say, in the land: there will I be propitious to them;
    And there will I require your oblations,
    And the first-fruits of your gifts in all your purifications.

⁴¹ In the odour of sweet fragrance will I be propitious to you,
When I shall have brought you from the people,
And gathered you from the lands through which ye will be dispersed;
And I will be sanctified in you in the eyes of the nations.
⁴² Then shall ye know that I am Jehovah,
When I shall have brought you back into the land of Israel,
Into the region about which I raised my hand to give it to your fathers.
⁴³ And there I will remember your ways, and all your works,
In which ye were polluted; and ye shall be confused in face[1]
Through all your wickednesses which ye have committed.
⁴⁴ Then shall ye know that I am Jehovah, when I shall have done among you
According to my name, not according to your evil ways,
Nor according to your corrupt doings,
O house of Israel, saith the Lord Jehovah.

※ As CALVIN's LATIN TRANSLATION ends here, so the version by the Translator comes naturally to a close. It has not been thought necessary to re-translate from the original the remainder of EZEKIEL, as the previously-quoted labours of Newcome and Rosenmüller are sufficiently accessible and explanatory.

[1] See vol. ii. p. 342, note.

VI.—A LIST OF THE CHIEF INTERPRETERS, ANCIENT AND MODERN.

I. Jewish Commentators.

SCHELOMOH JARCHI BEN JIZCHAK, commonly called Solomon Jarchi, son of Isaac, known to the Jews by the word *Raschi*, made up of the initials of רבי שלמה ירחי, *Rabbi Schelomoh Jarchi*, was an eminent commentator on the whole of the Old Testament. He was born at Troyes, in Champagne, a province of France, and died A.D. 1180. His chief value arises from his having collected the best traditionary interpretations of his ancestors from the earliest times.

DAVID KIMCHI, son of Joseph, known to the Jews by the name of *Radak*, from the initial letters of רבי דוד קמחי, *Rabbi David Kimchi*, was a Spaniard. Though he lived so lately as the twelfth century, his interpretation is much valued by both Jews and Christians for its *grammatical* accuracy. His commentary on Ezekiel is found in the Rabbinical Writings, edited by Buxtorf, A.D. 1618. Basil, 2 vols.; and also 1724, Amsterdam.

ISAAC ABARBANEL, a Portuguese Jew, born at Lisbon, A.D. 1437, and died in Apulia, A.D. 1508. His comments on Ezekiel appeared first at Pesaro, in Italy, A.D. 1520; and then again at Amsterdam, A.D. 1641. He is highly esteemed for his extensive erudition and his clear style.

SHELOMOH BEN MELECH, a Spaniard, who lived at Constantinople in the middle of the sixteenth century. Under the title, *The Perfection of Beauty*, he wrote an elaborate commentary on the Old Testament, Constantinople, A.D. 1554. It was reprinted at Amsterdam, A.D. 1661 and 1685, fol., with the additions of Jacob Abendana. Tympius and Danzius have illustrated the manner in which he has improved upon or misunderstood D. Kimchi, according to Wolf, Bibliothec. Hebr., vol. iv. pp. 989, 991.

These references to Jewish interpreters will enable the reader to judge how far their opinion on the sense of a passage is decisive. It must be remembered that they all lived more than a thousand years after the Christian era, and that consequently they are not to be esteemed of decisive authority.

Further information may be obtained from Jo. Christ. Wolf's Bibliotheca Hebræa, vol. ii. p. 368, and elsewhere. Le Long and Boerner's Bib. Sac. ab. A. G. Masch, pt. i. p. 135; and De Rossi's Annal. Heb. Typ., Parmæ, 1795, p. 131; and Hartwell Horne, vol. ii. part ii., where he has chiefly followed Carpzov.

II. The Early Fathers.

ORIGEN (between A.D. 185 and 254) appears to have commented very voluminously on Ezekiel, as, from the fragments which remain, it appears that the twentieth volume only reached to chap. xi. Jerome has translated fourteen homilies of Origen's on Ezekiel into Latin, which are found in his works. *Edit.*, Vallarsii, Venet. 1736, tom. v. p. 877; and in *De La Rue's* collected edition of Origen's Works, vol. iii. p. 325.

EPHREM of Edessa, who lived about A.D. 370, wrote a Commentary on this Prophet in Syriac, which is found in vol. ii. of his works, as edited by Pet. Benedict, in Syriac and Latin, at Rome, 1740, fol.

EUSEBIUS HIERONYMUS—the well-known Jerome—wrote fourteen books of Comments on Ezekiel. See his works, edit. Martiani, vol. iii., and Valarsii, vol. v. Rosenmüller esteems his interpretations highly, and often quotes them at length. Smith's Biographical Dictionary, Art. Hieronymus, p. 465, states, that the fourteen books of his Comments on this Prophet were written at intervals, between A.D. 411 and 414, having been commenced immediately after his Comments on Isaiah, but repeatedly broken off. See also the prolegomena to the 126th Epistle to Marcellinus, &c.; the Benedictine edition, vol. iii. p. 1072.

THEODORET, Bishop of Cyrus, in Syria, who lived about A.D. 420, wrote a Commentary on Ezekiel, found in his works, edited by Jac. Sirmond, vol. ii. p. 300; and in the edit. Halen., vol. ii. part ii.

III. Commentators of the Sixteenth and Seventeenth Centuries.

JO. ŒCOLAMPADII Commentarius in Ezekielem. Argentorati, 1534, 4to; Basileæ, 1548, fol.

VICTORINI STRIGELII Ezechiel Propheta ad Ebraicam veritatem recognitus, et argumentis atque scholiis illustratus. Lipsiæ, 1564, 1575, 1579, 8vo.

HECTORIS PINTI Commentarius in Ezechielem. Salmanticæ, 1568, fol.; Antverp, 1570, 1582; Lugduni, 1581, 4to; Ibid. 1584, fol.; Colon., 1615, 4to.

PHIL. HEILBRUNNER Ezechielis Prophetæ vaticinia illustrata. Lavingæ, 1587, 8vo.

HIERON. PRADI et JO. BAPT. VILLALPANDI, in Ezechielem Explanationes. Romæ, 1596, 3 vols. fol.

This work is much praised and quoted by Rosenmüller. The first volume contains the Comments of Pradus on the first six-and-twenty chapters: he died before it was published; so that his coadjutor edited it, and compiled the two latter volumes. They had access to a *Catena Patrum Græcorum in Ezechielem*, preserved in the Vatican Library, which they inserted, translated into Latin by a member of their own order; and they enriched their work with valuable illustrations of the city and temple at Jerusalem. A full description of the work will be found in *den Nachrichten von einer Hallischen* Bibliothek, pt. viii. p. 18, and foll.

AMANDI POLANI a POLANSDORF Commentaria in Ezechielem. Basileæ, 1601, 4to; and 1608, 4to.

A digest of public lectures delivered in the old Academy at Basil.

FRANC. JUNII Commentaria in Ezechielem Prophetam. Genevæ, 1609, fol.; and 1610, 8vo.

Jo. MALDONATI Commentarii in Ezechielem. Moguntiæ, 1611, small 4to.

This work, by a learned Jesuit, is very explanatory. The Latin translation is good, and the Jewish interpretations freely used. Many Hebrew words we have found well explained.

GASPAR SANCTII Commentarius in Ezechielem. Lugduni, 1612, 1619, fol.

JAC. BRANDMÜLLERI Commentarius in Ezechielem. Basil. 1621, 4to.

An Exposition of the Prophecy of Ezekiel. By GEORGE GREENHILL. London, 1645. 5 vols. 4to.

Doctrinal and practical lectures delivered to a congregation at Stepney by the writer, a member of the Westminster Assembly of Divines. Excellent of its kind, but not critical. Various editions, originally published at different times, from 1645 to 1658.

Jo. COCCEII Commentarius in Ezekielem. Lugd. Batav. 1668, 4to.

IV. Later Commentators.

GEORG. CALIXTI Scholæ Propheticæ ex Prelectionibus in.... Ezekielem collectæ. Quedlinburgi, 1715, 4to.

Das Zeugniss Iesu aus dem Propheten Ezechiel durch den Geist der Weissagung dargethan von WILHELM PETERSEN. Francofurti, 1719, 4to.

Jo. FRID. STARCKII, V.D.M., Francofurtani, Commentarius in Prophetam Ezechielem. Francof. ad Mœn., 1731, 4to.

A laborious, useful, and practical Commentary.

GEORG. COSTARD Dissertationes II. Critico-Sacræ quarum prima explicata Ezech. ch. xiii. 18. Oxon. 1752, 8vo.

Ezechiel aufs Neue aus dem Hebraischen übersetzt, und mit kurgen Anmerkungen für unstudirte Leser begleitet von JOH. CARL. VOLBORTH. Goett. 1787.

For an account of this work, see Eichhorn's Allgem. Biblioth. der Bib. Lit., vol. i. p. 807.

An Attempt towards an Improved Version, a Metrical Arrangement, and an Explanation of the Prophet Ezekiel. By WM. NEWCOME, D.D., Bishop of Waterford, and afterwards Archbishop of Armagh. Dublin, 1788, 4to.

This is an invaluable work to the mere English reader of this Prophet. Tegg, in his edition of 1836, 1 vol. 8vo, pp. 294, has rendered it very accessible: it is safe, sound, and judicious, with excellent notes. See also Eichhorn Bibl., vol. ii. p. 131; and J. D. Michaelis Neue orient. u. exeget. Bibli., pt. vi. p. 87.

HERMANNI VENEMA Lectiones Academicæ ad Ezechielem. Pt. i. usque ad cap. xxi. Edidit. Jo. Hen. Verschuir. Leovard, 1790, 4to, 2 parts. See again, Eich. Bibl., vol. iii. p. 694.

Jo. GODOFR Eichhorn die Biblischen Propheten, vol. ii. and iii. Ezekielis Vaticinia. Gotting. 1818, 1819.

The Temple of Ezekiel; viz., an Elucidation of the 40th and following Chapters. By SOLOMON BENNETT, R.A., of Berlin. London, 1824. 4to.

EM. F. ROSENMÜLLER'S Scholia in Ezekielem. 2 vols. 8vo, 2d edition. 1826. Lipsiæ.

Invaluable. The Editor is much indebted to it for many references to other valuable works.

HAVERNICK'S Introduction to Ezekiel, translated from the German by the Rev. F. W. Gotch, M.A. See Kitto's Journal of Sacred Literature, No. 1, January 1848; also the Article "Ezekiel"—Kitto's Cyclopædia of Biblical Literature.

VII.—A NOTICE OF THE ANCIENT VERSIONS AND CODEXES WHICH CONTAIN EZEKIEL'S PROPHECIES.

THE ARABIC VERSION OF EZEKIEL. It was made from the Septuagint, and is contained in the London Polyglott. It agrees throughout with that Greek text which exists in the Alexandrine Codex, now in the British Museum. It was executed from Hesychius's edition of the Septuagint, and is valuable for the comparison of cognate words and phrases with the Hebrew.

THE CHALDEE VERSION, said to have been made by Jonathan, the son of Uzziel, is found in the London Polyglott, and is praised in Buxtorf's Rabbinical Commentaries.

THE ALEXANDRINE CODEX is esteemed the most ancient MS. existing, written probably in the fourth century, though some authorities place it much later.[1] The book of Ezekiel was translated for this version during the reign of Ptolemy Philometer. Of all the prophets, Jeremiah seems the best executed: then Amos, and Ezekiel, and Isaiah the worst of all, except Daniel. Edited by Jo. Ern. Grabe, 1707-1720. 4 vols. fol. Oxon.

THE CODICES OF KENNICOTT AND DE ROSSI. Only some of them contain Ezekiel; that formerly belonging to the learned Reuchlin (No. 154) contains this Prophet, with a Targum also. The Codex Norimburgensis, (No. 198,) written about A.D. 1290, is noticed here only for the order in which Ezekiel

[1] See Hartwell Horne's Introduction, &c., vol. ii. pt. i. p. 116, edit. 6th, where full information on this and kindred subjects is to be found.

is placed : it is neither that of the Masorites nor the Talmudists. Again, in Codex No. 224, the order is Jeremiah, Ezekiel, Isaiah.

THE CODEX ROMANUS OR VATICANUS is of great antiquity. A fac-simile of this MS. was made for Dr. Grabe in 1704, and Horne has given an accurate specimen of Ezekiel, chap. i. 1-3. This fac-simile is among the MSS. of the Bodleian Library. Cardinal Anton. Carasa executed an edition under the auspices of Pope Sixtus V. Rome, 1587. Fol.

THE SYRO. ESTRANGHELÆ Version is a translation into Syriac of Origen's Hexaplar edition of the Septuagint. A MS. exists in the Ambrosian Library at Milan. It contains Scholia of the Greek and Syrian fathers, and various valuable annotations. Matth. Norberg edited from it the Prophecies of Ezekiel and Jeremiah, in 1787, 4to, Londini Gothorum; giving it the title of *Codex Syriaco-Hexaplaris Ambrosiano-Mediolanensis.* See Eichhorn's account of it in his Allgem. Bib. der Bibl. Lit., vol. i. p. 837, and foll.

THE VULGATE VERSION needs mention here only to point out the differences in rendering Ezekiel between the editions of Sixtus V. and Clement VIII. In chap xiv. 22, the former has *egredientur*, which is correct, and the latter *ingredientur*.

AMONG THE FIVE GOTHIC MSS. discovered by Ang. Maï, in the Ambrosian Library at Milan, amidst the CODICES RESCRIPTI, the homilies of Gregory the Great on this Prophet were found written over various portions of St. Paul's Epistles. These homilies were executed before the eighth century.

VIII.—DISSERTATIONS ON IMPORTANT SUBJECTS, TREATED OF IN THESE LECTURES.

- I.—On the Cherubim. Chap. i. ver. 1.
- II.—Calvinus Judaizans an Orthodoxus?
- III.—Calvin's Severity towards the Jews.
- IV.—The Figurative Expressions of Ezekiel.
- V.—On Eating the Roll. Chap. iii. α. ver. 1.
  - The Great Rushing. β. ver. 12.
  - On Tel-Abib. γ. ver. 12.
- VI.—Jerusalem Painted on a Brick. iv. α. ver. 1.
  - The Three Hundred and Ninety Days. β. ver. 5.
- VII.—The Septuagint Order. vii. 3-13.
- VIII.—The Image of Jealousy. viii. 1-14.
- IX.—The Man in the Linen Garment. ix. 2.
- X.—The Coals Scattered over the City. x. 2.
- XI.—The Five-and-Twenty Evil Counsellors. xi. 1.
- XII.—The False Prophets. xiii. α. ver. 1.
  - On the Principle of Accommodation. β.
  - On the Phrase Prostituerunt Deum. γ. ver. 19.
- XIII.—Israel an Adulteress. xvi. α. ver. 1.
  - Captive Israel and Papal Rome. β. ver. 20.
  - On the Word Nephesh, Soul. γ. ver. 27.
  - The Primitive Church and the New Testament. δ. ver. 61.
- XIV.—The Great Eagle. xvii. α. ver. 3.
  - The Lofty Branch of the Tall Cedar. β. ver. 22.
- XV.—The Eating Sour Grapes. xviii. α. ver. 1.
  - Usury and Interest. β. ver. 8.
  - Perplexing and Thorny Questions. γ. ver. 20.
- XVI.—The Sabbath a Sacrament and a Mystery. xx. 13, 14.

Dissertation First.

ON THE CHERUBIM.

THE Visions recorded in the first and tenth chapters of this Prophet have received much illustration, and yet remain involved in great obscurity. It seems desirable to supply some information, even at the risk of being tedious and minute. The living creatures of the first chapter are called in the ninth and tenth—*cherubim*. The derivation of the word is a point of some importance. Castell, in his elaborate Lex. Hept., connects it with the Chaldee root כרב, *kereb*, signifying "to plough," and quotes Ezek. i. 10, where "an ox" occurs, "a strong animal, of great labour, especially in ploughing; and being used for the expiation of sins, becomes a type of Christ, who is there perhaps to be understood; for as the ox is the leader of the herd, so Christ is the head of the faithful." Josephus says they were animals never seen by any one. (Antiq., lib. iii. chap. 6, and lib. viii. chap. 2.) The Arabic root of the same three letters, *kereb*, signifies anxiety and oppressive labour, *anxit animum, invertit aratio terram;* while the cognate forms of the Syriac signify ploughing and laborious effort. "The most probable," says Gesenius, "among the many derivations of this word which have been proposed, is that from the Syriac, *potens, magnus fortis.*" Professor Lee writes, in evident despair, "It would be idle to offer anything on the etymology: nothing satisfactory having yet been discovered. Castell, Simonis, Gesenius, &c., may be consulted by those who wish to see what has been said on this subject."

The cherubic form has been fully pourtrayed by our Commentator; and by engravings in *the Cyclopædia of Biblical Literature* we are enabled to compare Egyptian and Persian winged symbols with those of the Hebrews. A sculptured bas-relief of a winged human figure as it existed before the time of Moses, and placed by the Egyptians over their sacred arcs, is worthy of comparison with the descriptions of Scripture. The Persian bas-relief at Moung-Aub, is a human figure arrayed in an embroidered robe, " with such quadruple wings as the vision of Ezekiel ascribes to the cherubim, with the addition of ample horns, the well-known symbols of regal power." The opinions of divines relative to their design and signification are very diversified. Among the ancients Philo supposed them to signify the two hemispheres, the flaming sword showing the motion of the planets, and the lion and the man being Leo and Aquarius, the signs of the Zodiac. Irenæus (Adv. Heres. iii. 11) treats them as emblems of the four elements, the four quarters of the globe, the four gospels, and the four covenants. Tertullian (Apolog. cap. xlvii.) referred them to the torrid zone, while Justin Martyr treats Ezekiel's figures as relating to Nebuchadnezzar eating grass like the ox, with his hand like a lion's, and his nails like the claws of a bird, (Quæst. et Respons. xliv. p. 325, edit. Heidelbergæ, 1593;) and that they were consolatory to the captive Israelites by setting before them the prospect of their own return, and their oppressor's downfal. The analogy to the four gospels, as presented to us by Irenæus, is peculiarly ingenious, and worthy of perusal. Spencer, in his Ritual Observances of the Hebrews, has ingeniously explained their form and description. (*Lib.* iii. *Dissert.* v. cap. iii. and iv. sect. 2.) Grotius considers them to represent " the properties of God, and his actions towards his people," (*Annot. in Vet. Test.*;) and Doederlin, while conceding the praise of ingenuity to the conjectures of his author, yet treats his speculations as the abortion rather than the legitimate offspring of a luxuriant fancy. (Vogel's edit. Grot. continued by Doeder., vol. ii. p. 247.) Further information as to the views of ancient writers has been collected by Rosenmüller, on chap. i. 10, pp. 68, 69, edit. sec. Lipsiæ, 1826. The translation of Houbigant may be consulted, and Spencer on the Laws and Ritual of the Hebrews, lib. iii. Dissert. 5, chap. 1, and foll. The various readings on which different translations are founded are rendered very accessible to the English reader by the simple and comprehensive notes of Archbishop Newcome.

It is interesting to observe the way in which the learned Jesuit Maldonatus comments on this first chapter. He interprets the four visions separately: first, the tempest; next, the figure of the four animals; the third, the form of the wheels; and the fourth, the firmament, and the man sitting on the throne. He objects to the allegorical interpretation of Origen and his school, and considers that the tempest signifies the calamities which the Chaldæans caused to the Jews and their city. By the whirlwind, the nearness of the calamities is pointed out; and by the north wind, its rapidity and destructive force. Some, he says, refer it to Babylon, making it symbolize the manners of the Chaldæans, which were rough and boisterous. The great cloud seems to him to signify the army of the king of Babylon; and the fire, his wrath and fury: the surrounding brightness is an indication of the divine majesty, and the amber colour is an image of God himself. Jerome takes the amber as a symbol of pity, since amber has an attractive power, and by placing it in connexion with the army of the king of Babylon, it implies that God directed every event concerning the captivity. Gregory and others interpret the amber of Christ.

THE SECOND VISION he considers more difficult; he first gives the views of other interpreters, and then brings forward his own formed *divino beneficio, meditando, legendo, orando.* Origen (*Hom.* I. *in Ezek.*) takes the four living creatures for the four affections of man's nature: the man representing the reasoning faculty, the lion the inflamable passions, the ox concupiscence, and the eagle, as it soars upwards, the divine spirit within us. St. Ambrose (Lib. iii. *de virginibus*) refers them to prudence, fortitude, temperance, and justice. Jerome and Gregory understand them of the four evangelists; and the details respecting the wheels, the wings, and the sparks of fire, are consistently interpreted. Catina Syrius refers them to the camp of Israel in the desert: the face of a man meaning all Israel, that of a lion the tribe of Judah, that of an ox the tribe of Levi, and that of an eagle God looking down from above, and taking vengeance on the people. Theodoret (*Comment. in loc.*) considers them to represent the majesty and glory of God resident in these cherubim. It appears that in his day the opinion of Jerome was most popular; and it was necessary to give many reasons why the four evangelists were not signified by this vision. Philosophical interpreters also existed, no unworthy predecessors of the German rationalists. They supposed all things indiscriminately signified by these representatives of animated nature, while some preferred the changes of the events of providence to the manifestations of external nature. His own opinion he records as follows: that the cherubim represent four heathen kingdoms, Chaldæan, Assyrian, Egyptian, and Tyrian. He supposes them placed under the firmament, and under the sapphire throne, to indicate the supreme power of the Almighty over all things. The wings are the human guards by which kings protect themselves; the hands represent human industry, strength, and labour; the fire indicates the Spirit of God in kings; and the various motions forwards and backwards show the changes in governments and the perturbations of empires, all under the control of a supreme governor. This scheme is well fortified by passages of Scripture, and has the merit of great exactness and ingenuity.[1]

We now turn to a very different interpreter—Œcolampadius. His comments of this chapter is essentially spiritual. He sees in it a representation of God judging the world through Christ. The great truths of revelation he sees obscurely shadowed forth under carnal and Jewish images; and he is anxious to point out the spiritual reign of Christ as promulgated by these outward and visible representations of God's glory. He refers these visions, first of all, to the Jews and their captivity; but he claims for them the office of tangibly illustrating the abiding glory of the universal

[1] Maldon. in Ezek. chap. i. p. 327, &c., edit. Moguntiæ 1611. Here the reader may see the Jewish comments of Rabb. David, Solomon, and the Chaldee paraphrast; also R. Moses, lib. iii. cap. 6.

assembly of the faithful. "The universal Church," he says, "has three parts: first, its head is Hasmal, represented as an old man seated on a throne: next, animals, the just or living members, are those more perfect in the Church, adorned with a variety of gifts : the wheels are the weaker and more ordinary members, which belong to the body, and form the common herd of believers, who belong to the more solid parts of the Church, since they are under the influence of the same Spirit, although they have not attained that fulness of which St. Paul speaks, and have not drunk into the peculiar and interior spirit of the Gospel."[1] He then confesses the great difficulty of ascertaining the correct interpretation : he rejects all Jewish comments, and approves of the spiritualizing method of referring it to the coming kingdom of Christ. The whirlwind, for instance, he asserts to be a figure of the devastation which preceded Christ's first coming, and shall also signalize his second advent: the great cloud expresses God's judgments on the world, and the fire the process of trial through which all things are to pass. Hasmal he regards as the name of an angel or fiery living one speaking, and blames Jerome for following the Septuagint, and translating it *electrum*.

This spiritually-minded reformer has furnished a valuable exposition of the mystery contained in the vision recorded in the tenth chapter, which is worthy of notice. The likeness of a man upon the throne he assumes to be our Saviour, whose reign is supreme "in the consciences of his elect." Most properly is he called Hasmal, " quod de eo admirabunda taciturnitate, et per cogitationes arcanas magnifica loquamur, opus dei in illo admirantes." The cherubim are beneath him, because he is adored by angels, and has spirits for his messengers and attendants. The firmament, he says, is grace offered through Christ, which strengthens the hearts of the elect by being infused within them. The living creatures, their wheels and machinery for motion, represent the progress of the Church, suffering as yet under corruption, but waiting and groaning for the redemption of the body. In each living creature all qualities are bound together ; for

[1] Comment. in om. lib. Proph. p. 5, Ez. : Genev. 1558.

the four faces represent the spiritual endowments of advancing Christians; the same animal is a man in judgment, a lion in patient endurance, a calf in usefulness and guileless sincerity, and an eagle in prompt and cheerful obedience to its lord: the wings are faith and divine love, which veil the face, which is conscience, and of this there are four kinds corresponding to the human, the leonine, the infantile, and the aquiline appearances. "It is the property of a good conscience to be raised upwards towards God when confirmed in grace, and, forgetful of things past, to be more and more anxious to reach the firmament of grace." The hands under each wing represent those good works by which living faith and active love manifest their divine power; while the wheels signify the inferior members of the Church, who, though not attaining to the same righteous standard, are animated by a similar spirit. The feet being straight and equable, and turning easily and constantly in all directions, are said to signify the messengers of God proclaiming his salvation throughout the world, and "bearing all things to all men, that they may bring many profitably to Christ." The sound produced by the motion of the wings means the fame of salvation arriving at distant regions; and when the Prophet hears the voice exhorting the wheels, it seems to him to say, "O wheels, follow with alacrity the spirit of the living creature within you; let nothing delay you; let nothing tear you from the fourfold figure, which is the body of Christ; for if ye cleave to this, even in its lowest part, ye shall be raised up together with it." The motion of each animal, in the direction of its face, signifies every Christian acting according to his conscience; and although there are differences of gifts, and each exercises his own independently, yet all follow one common leader, being animated by a common spirit. Thus the companion of Zuingle spiritualizes the passage with much consistency and at great length, affording a singular example of the method of throwing the light of matured Christian experience upon a scene so exclusively Jewish. To enable us to decide whether the view of Calvin or Œcolampadius is the correct one, we must state some general principles, which will be found in the following section.

Dissertation Second.

CALVINUS JUDAIZANS AN ORTHODOXUS?

"CALVINUS JUDAIZANS" was the title of a work published at Wittemberg, A.D. 1595, by Ægidius Hunnius. It contained a sharp censure for applying to the temporal state and circumstances of the Jews those prophecies which were supposed to refer spiritually to the Christian Church. The year, however, did not pass away before David Pareus replied, under the title of "Calvinus Orthodoxus." And all who have perused his comments on this Prophet must vindicate him from the charge of favouring Judaism, and applaud him for wisely neglecting all allegorical significations and mystical expositions. While it will be impossible to discuss the whole question of prophetic interpretation, it will be necessary to state some general views by which we ought to be guided.

The prophecies of the Old Testament were in many instances a divinely provided introduction to the events of the New. In them we may see the outlines of the process by which God was ever educating man for ultimate restoration to His image. They contain a suggestive method of instruction by palpable signs and wonders, which addressed the soul through their influence on the senses. Their value to the Jew was very different from that to the Christian. To the former they were the highest revelation attainable, while for us they do not reveal a single attribute or purpose of Deity which is not more fully made known through the Gospel dispensation. The Hebrew visions stand to us in the relation of porch to temple, and of dawn to day. They are to the Christian a divine first lesson-book, and contain a series of condescending instructions suited to a low stage of religious and mental life. They were specially appropriate to the people to whom they were bestowed, and of a structure and material in accordance with the dispensation to which they ministered. They were prefigurative and preformative throughout. They were preparatory and thus far excellent, but not "chiefest of all," because not permanent. Like the scaffolding, the growing blade, the finished portrait, they fail in comparison with the stately building, the ripened corn, the living person. Now Calvin avoids the extremes of the merely literal system and of the mystical allegories of the double sense. The former system treats the Old Testament as if it were all written at the same time, and every part of it addressed equally to all men. It excepts the ceremonial observances, and then considers that every sentence is reconcilable with all the rest by a spiritual process of traditionary reasoning. It is sternly opposed to all discrimination between the records of different eras; it admits of nothing gradual, variable, or local. Of the latter system we have an excellent example in the quotation just made from the comparison of Zuingle. He sees Christ and justification by faith everywhere. Not only must Hasmal—a mere colour—be an emblem of the Son of God, but all who cannot receive this are branded as unenlightened. The truths which he has received through the gospel are so vividly impressed upon his soul and so thoroughly leaven his spirit, that he sees everything scriptural by this bright light of his inner man. His deficiency is of judgment, not of grace. The question ought not to be, what series of Christian doctrine can be grafted upon the cherubic emblem, but what truths it was intended to convey to the soul of the Prophet and the people,—surely not those of the Augsburgh Confession of Faith. We have to guard against a twofold error: on the one hand, a merely critical and rationalistic interpretation which never proceeds beyond the surface; and, on the other, against a fanciful exposition of figurative language, as if in every case the doctrines, the graces, and the experiences of the New Covenant were intended to be revealed to Hebrew prophets.

Apposite, indeed, was the exclamation of the Jew, when he said of Ezekiel, "Doth he not speak parables?" He had to take a tile and draw a city upon it; to shave his head, and divide the hair into three significant parts; and the Jew might fairly ask, How is all this to benefit his soul? It could only do so by appealing to the spiritual principle in man's soul. As the Prophet must eat the roll, so we must try to comprehend the meaning of divine emblems, that they may become to us the bread of life. There is a husk around many a spiritual fruit, and oftentimes a stone within it, which seems devoid of nutriment; but still this is the way in which it pleases our heavenly Father to nourish us. All signs, emblems, and sacraments of any true religion are beneficial to us only when we spiritually perceive their inward and animating grace. All that is outward in form and ceremony and machinery is only the vehicle, not the substance, of our support as God's children, and our growth in his likeness. This foundation truth must be laid firmly as a basis for every portion of the superstructure. The carnal mind never did and never can comprehend the things of the Spirit of God. The power of understanding the meaning must come from the same Deity who sends the vision. On this broad rock of truth we may build every sound interpretation of all the figurative language of Scripture. This principle we may gather from the way in which the early Christian writers explain the symbols of Holy Writ. St. Chrysostom, for instance, treats clearly the lesson we should learn from the seraph's taking the coal from the altar and touching the Prophet's lips with its hallowed fire.[1] St. Ambrose seems scarcely satisfied with the image—bread of life: he must "eat life." "Whoso then," says he, "eateth life cannot die. How should he die whose food is life?"[2] "and this bread," he adds, "is the remission of sins." St. Augustine speaks of "angels feeding on the eternal word," and of "men eating angels' food."[3] Language like this implies the struggle of the spiritual mind to express itself fully through the medium of carnal lan-

[1] Hom. v. sec. 3, and compare the Litany of St. James, Ass. Cod. Lit. v. 56.
[2] In Ps. cxviii. Lit. 18, sec. 28, 48.
[3] In Ps. xxxiii. En. i. sec. 6, and Ps. lxxviii. 26.

guage; and what were the Shechinah and the Seraphim, the Urim and the Thummim, the live goat and the slain goat, but symbols receiving all their significance from the Divine truths which they conveyed to the soul? The worship of the one God through the appointed Mediator was ever the same in its hidden essence, and ever must be, while it is ever varying in its form, according to the divers needs of our frail humanity. It is flexible exceedingly to the eye and the ear, and unchangeable only in its living spirit. All nature, organic and inorganic, has been used to illustrate it and communicate it, but this never has made, nor can make, the unseen visible. Still the question will recur, Where must we draw the line between the human and the divine in these prophetic visions? No man can draw such a line with accuracy except for himself. Let all who doubt this assertion try to divide mind from matter in the living man. Many have attempted it, and their failures remain to mark the narrow limits of their knowledge and the assumed regions of their ignorance. The matured Christian instincts of the cultivated worshipper will be every man's best guide under the promised teaching of the Holy Spirit. An infallible interpreter is not for us in the flesh; the interpreting Spirit must dwell within us, otherwise we shall see nothing but the outward aspect of the gorgeous vision. The inspiration within must harmonize with that without, which is not verbal but ideal. The heaven-wrought ideas of the Hebrew Prophets protect themselves.

We do not require either a verbal or literal *theopneustia*: the truths themselves by their own imperishableness defeat the mortality of the language with which they are associated. They reverberate and percolate through all the pages of the mighty record; they hide themselves obscurely in one chapter only to emerge more clearly in another; they diverge in one book only to recombine in another; so that to the sympathizing soul Scripture is ever a self-sufficing interpreter. Hence we are not careful to defend Calvin's interpretations as faultless: theology as a science has advanced rapidly during three hundred years; and while some of his expositions have become antiquated, we still uphold him as "orthodoxus." The law of development operates in the moral as well as in the physical universe. " Draw a *cordon sanitaire*," says a modern reviewer, " against dandelion or thistle-down, and see if the armies of earth would suffice to interrupt this process of radiation, which yet is but the distribution of weeds. The secret implications of the truth have escaped at a thousand points in vast arches above our heads, rising high above the garden wall, and have sown the earth with memorials of the mystery which they envelop."[1]

A second principle which we must bear in mind is, that every prophetic revelation was expressly adapted to the capacity of its original recipients. The extrinsic agency is always transitory. We of later generations learn enough if we profit by the latent and permanent essence. Hence the interpretation of the cherubim by the four evangelists is utterly untenable: and all such suppositions are indexes of a state of mind wholly incompetent to unfold prophetic mysteries. The very occurrence of hundreds of crude guesses like this, implies the necessity of submitting the prophetic emblems to some general laws of exposition. The highest criticism and the profoundest scholarship should be applied to them, that we may at once ignore all traditions which are proved to be corruptions. These prophecies presuppose a moral responsibility in the people to whom they were addressed; and hence they were fitted to awaken this feeling when dormant, to frighten it when morbidly perverted, and to animate it when righteously sensitive. Calvin's assertion that the living creatures and the wheels imply that God by his angels guides the physical motions of the earth, the air, and the sea, (vol. i. p. 89,) is altogether untenable. Revelation does not teach anything which human philosophy can discover. It manifests its whole aim and essence to be moral, lying in that region of our nature which is under the sway of the conscience, and the will rather than of the intellect. These emblematic visions appeal to the affections and aspirations of soul, to the energies of reverence and faith, of wonder and of love. They have to do with what is

[1] Review of " Vindication of Protestant Principles."—*Tait's Mag.* p. 758. 1847.

infinite and unseen, the immeasurable and the unattainable. Hence they are rather divine agencies for quickening, stimulating, and directing man's highest nature. They assist us towards attaining a true idea of God, they show us our own insignificant vileness and littleness, and suggest the possibility of an at-onement of these two. They stir up our attention to the threatenings and the promises of an Invisible Person, which can influence us only by being believed, and enforce the commands of ineffable wisdom, which can benefit us only by being obeyed. They present to our thoughts the idea of condescending mediation, the infinitely holy condescending to purify and to abide with the morally unclean. They may further imply the general providence over the chosen race, as well as the special guidance of individuals; the moulding into its preordained shape all their future history, and yet not sensibly controlling the will of agents left responsible for their every action. No discoveries of science can ever interfere with such an interpretation as this, and those who adopt it need never fear the necessity for changing it when the progress of physical knowledge must lead us to alter our views of other interpretations. It belongs to a region of our nature completely separable from that which comprehends either the niceties of language, or the laws of the physical universe. There is a wide gulf, deep and impassable, between the moral and the intellectual departments of our nature. The imperfect state of physical science at the time of the Reformation is a sufficient apology for the mistakes of reformers; but their ignorance is not pardonable in us. We need not Judaize, and yet we may be apt scholars in all Hebrew lore, and orthodox interpreters of the Sacred Word of the Most High.

Dissertation Third.

CALVIN'S SEVERITY TOWARDS THE JEWS.

IN addition to the charge of Judaizing, our author has been accused of dwelling too copiously on our Prophet's severity towards the Jews. And if we can read the signs of the times in modern publications, there is reason to fear that various delusions are abroad on this subject. There are those who treat the Jews as in the present day, so peculiarly favoured by God, that they invest them with the halo of a special sanctity. Reverencing as Christians ought the designs of the Almighty in past ages, they entertain far too exalted ideas of the personal holiness of the agents by whom those designs were accomplished. Old Testament characters are too often treated as "saints," when they have few moral or religious qualities which entitle them to that sacred appellation. And regarding the people as a body, it is scarcely possible to find anywhere worse specimens of moral culture. If we estimate responsibility according to the amount of light and guidance and privilege, then, indeed, Tyre and Sidon were far less culpable than Hebron and Jerusalem. How opposite, for instance, is their history to what might have been expected from reading the book of Deuteronomy. Instead of binding their written law "as frontlets between their eyes," no ancient nation were so careless of its sacred books. The Hindoos cling tenaciously to their shasters, while Israel utterly neglected their Mosaic code. One would have supposed that they would have been superstitiously careful of the five books of their inspired leaders. Why should they not have multiplied copies of them? Why not have constituted the Levites the authorized guardians and expounders of them? From the time of Joshua to David there is no notice of the existence of any sacred books which now belong to us: and more than this, reference is made to other records not now existing. And after Solomon's temple was solemnly dedicated, how soon ten of the tribes relapsed into the grossest idolatry; and even in Judah, how remarkable is the occurrence in Josiah's time. The very priests seem to have been ignorant of the existence of a written copy of the law. The unexpected discovery of one has such an effect upon the king and the people, that it led to a thorough restoration of the national worship; and yet we find a command that every king should write for himself a copy of the law from that preserved by the priests. Both kings and priests seem to have neglected their duty; and even the prophets do not charge them with this crime among others. The loss of the original autographs is never mentioned; nor have we the slightest hint of what became of the second original of the two stone-tables. During the short period of their captivity they lost their spoken language and the characters in which it was written, so that on their return they were obliged to read Hebrew through an interpreter. Was not this an unmatched instance of want of reverence for the will of Jehovah? When a nation could act with such deliberate carelessness and irreverence at various epochs, can we be surprised at their falling into the grossest depths of immoral profanity? When the divine records have been thus despised, all folly and all wickedness is possible for such a people, and both are generated with a fearful rapidity. How different, then, is their real history from what one might expect of a people chosen by the Almighty as his earthly representatives of religion before the heathen! They were miraculously trained to typify and receive the Messiah, and yet they constantly appear to be frustrating the very purpose of their choice. If we speak of the mass of the nation, they seem in every respect to have thrown away their privileges, and to have studiously incurred God's anger, and to have determined to brave his vengeance. Under such a view of the ancient people, no language of Calvin's can be too strong; and it is only to obviate the consequences of modern erroneous suppositions that it becomes necessary to defend him. In stimulating the compassion of the Christian Church towards the salvation of Jews at present existing, the most fallacious views are sometimes presented of their past history and their loveliness in God's sight. To be beloved for their fathers' sake by no means implies any innate moral loveliness in the conduct of those fathers; and every erroneous view of Jewish history, and every false interpretation of Jewish prophecy, does but Judaize the Christian Church, and prevent it from going onwards to perfection, by keeping it in trammels to either exploded prejudices or to unwise innovations. False views of the Jewish history are now so very common, that they naturally create a distaste for that emphatic condemnation of their conduct which prevails through these Lectures.

Dissertation Fourth.

ON THE FIGURATIVE EXPRESSIONS OF EZEKIEL.

THE most cursory observers of Ezekiel's peculiarities must notice the highly figurative character of his visions. The princes of Israel are whelps, their mother a lioness. A great eagle comes down with one fell swoop upon the mountains of Lebanon, and plucks off the topmost boughs of its lofty cedars. Here we have to connect what logicians call the *protasis* with the APODOSIS, and out of the sensible similitude to ascertain the mystical explanation. The canon laid down by Glasse is of constant utility:—" In parabolis, si integre accipiantur, tria sunt : *radix, cortex,* et *medulla* sive *fructus. Radix* est scopus in quem tendit parabola. *Cortex* est similitudo sensibilis, quæ adhibetur, et suo sensu literali constat. *Medulla* seu fructus est sensus parabolæ mysticus, seu ipsa res ad quam parabolæ fit accommodatio, seu quæ per similitudinem propositam significatur." Philologia Sacra, lib. ii. pars. i. tr. 2, sect. 5, canon 3 : Lipsiæ, 1725. Not only is it necessary to ascertain the literal meaning of the figurative expression, but we must always proceed one step farther before we can profit by the metaphor. The medulla—the *res ipsa*—is still to be discovered, and this alone it is which brings profit to the soul. We must not only comprehend the figure and its literal interpretation, but we must take one step beyond this, and comprehend what divines call the mystical sense. We may attain to the "science of correspondences" without adopting the fancies of Emmanuel Swedenborg; but what he diligently and erroneously sought we must endeavour to find. With Van Mildert, in his Bampton Lectures, we use the word mystical in its true and classical rather than in its present and popular meaning ; and though we have no special affection for the word, we contend earnestly with the lecturer for the idea which it expresses. This inner sense will not, from its very nature, be crippled by the details of the natural allegory. The very essence of spiritual thought is mobility and indefiniteness. The great master of Roman eloquence has wisely observed—" Non enim res tota toti rei necesse est similis sit: sed ad ipsum, ad quod conferetur, similitudinem habeat, oportet."[1] The same idea is expressed by Saurin in his Historical Discourses—" Non seulement il n'est pas necessaire que chacun de leur membres ait une veu particulière, qui se rapporte directement au but de celui qui la propose : il faut même que ce but soit en quelque sort cachè sous des images étrangères destinées à l'enveloper."[2] As the correct elucidation of these points is of the greatest importance, every light which can be thrown on them has its value. Bishop Warburton, for instance, in the midst of his elaborate and ill-digested paradoxes, is led to discuss the nature of types and symbols, visions and figures, and he treats them with clearness, precision, and ability. He lays the foundation for their use in the compound nature of man. He shows how the Egyptians, Mexicans, and Chinese, communicated ideas through the senses by signs, hieroglyphics, and picture-writing of all kinds. He quotes Ezekiel chap. xxxi. as a striking instance of well-applied metaphor : " for men," says he, " so conversant in matters, still wanted sensible images to convey abstract ideas."[3] He adduces chap. xxiv. as an instance of a parable purposely used " to throw obscurity over the information," just as the tropical hieroglyphic was turned into the tropical symbol. He treats the " dark saying" of chap. xvii. 2, as a riddle more involved than a parable ; " for the nature of God's dispensations required enigmas, and the genius of those times made them natural." The course of his argument leads him to comment at full length on the celebrated vision of the dry bones in

---

[1] M. T. Cicero ad Herennium. Edit. Bipont, vol. i. p. 122.
[2] Vol. iii. p. 405.   [3] Div. Leg., lib. 4, sect. 4.

chap. xxxvii,[1] and to discuss the logical value of the assertion, " All words that are used in a figurative sense must be first understood in a literal." Perhaps it may be better to say, All figures of speech are intended to convey to the mind an image of something real, and they are useless to us unless we thus apprehend their literal meaning. But Warburton did not see the next step in the process of deriving spiritual instruction from the visions of the Holy Spirit of God. He was not spiritually enlightened, and failed to do more than expound the letter of Scripture. We need, besides this, the divine teaching of the Holy Spirit, that we may apprehend what Bishop Van Mildert calls, in his celebrated Bampton Lectures, *the mystical sense.* " The importance," says Bishop Horne, in his preface to the Psalms, " of the mystical interpretation can hardly be called in question ;" " without it, the spirit and power of many passages will almost wholly evaporate." The learned Rambach, in his Sacred Hermeneutics, (p. 81,) has adduced several instances in confirmation of these observations. The spiritual man only can thus pierce through the letter, and grasp the very marrow of God's word: the carnal mind is in this respect utterly blind, for these things are only spiritually discerned. The word *mystical* may seem fanatical to some, but, taken in its scholastic sense, it is easily appreciable by all who know anything of profound criticism. Rambach has justly laid it down—" Est regula theologorum, sensum mysticum non esse argumentativum." (Just. Herm. Sac., p. 72.) It appeals not so much to the intellect as to the conscience—not to the mental comprehension, but to the heaven-born life of the soul; and if this be wanting, all argument on the point is thrown away. The spiritual interpretation may be abused, like all other good things. Cocceius, for instance, affords a remarkable instance of this error, as well as some of the Puritan Divines ; but no sensible man denies the value of a possession because some are foolish enough to misuse it.[2]

---

[1] Div. Leg., lib. vi. sect. 2.

[2] For Cocceius, see Mosheim, Ecc. Hist. Cent. xvii. sect. ii., p. 2; and for cautions against over spiritualising, see Rev. J. J. Conybeare's Bampton Lectures for 1824; and Bishop Van Mildert's Bampton Lectures, p. 241, and following.

On all sides we have to tread with the utmost caution, and may well listen to the voice of Jerome on Galatians i. : " Nec putemus in verbis Scripturarum esse Evangelium, sed in sensu. Non in superficie, sed in medullâ : non in sermonum foliis, sed in radice rationis." But even this view, truthful as it seems, may be abused ; for in our own day we find the anti-materialism of the universe denied. Who would suppose, that at the close of the first half of this nineteenth century we should hear of a publication, bearing the ominous title, " The Anti-Materialist: Denying the reality of Matter, and Vindicating the Universality of Spirit ?"[1] If this were the whole title, it would not concern us here ; but when it is added, " proved chiefly by a reference to Holy Writ," with another sentence, implying that such speculations can settle the points in dispute between those who affirm and those who deny the orthodoxy of Established Churches, such assumptions cause us to sigh over the endless follies of our nature. Such reasoners first of all assume *what is* Holy Writ, and then apply their own previously-conceived notions to distort and derange it. The very title of such a work implies the greatest possible irreverence for the Divine Oracles ; the most unjustifiable assumptions, and the most unfair contrasts. " The universality of spirit " is strictly and essentially co-existent with "the reality of matter." Every word which we have uttered in this short epilogue is intended to uphold and illustrate such a proposition : it is only necessary to append to it, that through material existences—as trees, cities, food, and clothing—we become capable of comprehending the wants, the nourishment, and the nature of our spiritual manhood.

Suitable in every respect is the judicious reasoning of Origen, which sixteen centuries have rather confirmed than confuted. "If ever, in reading Holy Scripture, thou encounter an idea which becomes to thee a stone of stumbling or a rock of offence, accuse only thyself: doubt not that this stone of stumbling and rock of offence has an important meaning : νοήματα—food for thy mind. Begin by believing, and thou shalt soon find, under this imaginary source of

[1] By John Dudley, Clerk. 1 vol. 8vo.

offence, abundant utility." He then compares the skilful interpreter of Scripture to an intelligent botanist, knowing the different uses and properties of various plants, and shows how every "holy and spiritual botanist of the word of God" will find the virtue of the word, without esteeming the slightest portion of it either redundant or superfluous.[1] The preceding Lectures are a good illustration of the sagacious wisdom of these remarks.

[1] Hom. xxxix., in Jer. xliv. 22.

Dissertation Fifth.

a. ON EATING THE ROLL.
Chap. iii. 1.

This method of conveying instruction is peculiarly Oriental. Jarchi, for instance, writes: "*Parabolica est locutio, ac si dicat: attende aurem tuam et audi.*" The Septuagint translate, מגלת־ספר, *megleth-sepher*, *volumen libri* by κεφαλὶς βιβλίου, which does not seem sufficiently accurate. Both Fuller, in his *Miscell. S.S.*, book 2d, chap. x., and Vossius *de Sept. Int.* agree with Jerome in remarking the inaccuracy. *Pro involuto libro*, he says, LXX. *capitulum libri* transtulerunt; capitulum intelligamus exordium. The opinion of J. H. Maii, Jun., is preferred by Rosenmüller, viz., that מגלה, *menleh*, signifies the roller on which the volumes of the Ancients were rolled, as we learn from Maimonides, in his ספר תורה, *sepher-toreh*, chap. ix. 2, 14. The writing on both sides was very uncommon: the Greeks call it ὀπισθόγραφον, which is illustrated by Juvenal, Sat. I. 5, 6.

—— aut summi plene jam margine libri
Scriptus, et in tergo, necdum finitus Orestes?

The Chaldee paraphrast explains the sense of eating the roll correctly—" anima tua saturabitur ;" and in this way the Prophet was to be strengthened to become literally "firm of forehead, and hard of heart," for contending with "peoples deep of lip and heavy of tongue." This firmness is represented by the gem, שמיר, *shemir*, which Bochart terms *smiris*, adamant according to Jerome, since the corresponding Arabic word is *samoor*. See also Schindler's Lex. Pentag. col. 1897, and R. Sal. Jarchi in loc., who gives the view of the Jerusalem Targum.

β. THE GREAT RUSHING.
Chap. iii. 12.

The physical disturbances accompanying the prophetic visions are worthy of notice. It is impossible to reduce them to any class of natural phenomena. The Prophet is suddenly removed by the Spirit into the midst of the exiles; *in extasi*, says Rosenmüller—" the mind was separated from the body by a divine instinct." Œcolampadius considers that " he seemed to be seized as by a wind," and " thought he heard the voice of a great tumult." " The glory of the Lord," he adds, " came out of its place, and left the temple and the people," " and the Church and heavenly Jerusalem praise the Lord for this act of his grace." He then comments most spiritually on this removal of the visible glory from the natural temple, taking it as an instance of *populus credentium*, being at all times *locus Dei*. Maldonatus takes the same view when he writes, " I seemed to be seized by the Spirit, or an angel, and to be transferred to Jerusalem." He considers it too Rabbinical to treat the Spirit as if it were merely wind, and the voice only thunder, as R. David and Jonathan do. He prefers the opinion of Jerome to that of the Jewish interpreters. R. Sal. Jarchi implies that the Spirit really raised him: " Deus præcepit Spiritui ut eum portaret ad locum ubi Judæi exules degebant." As to the last word in this verse, ממקומו, *memkomo*, it seems to refer to the place where the vision was seen: scil. personent ejus laudes per mundum universum, uti Mal. i. 5. If the whole scene is treated simply as a vision offered to the Prophet's mind through his senses, it becomes very intelligible and impressive.

γ. ON TEL-ABIB.
CHAP. iii. 15.

We notice these words simply to caution the reader against over-allegorizing. There can be no doubt that it is the name of a place; as תל חרשא, *tel chersha*, and תל מלח, *tel melech*, in Ezra and Nehemiah. Syrian villages often have the name of *tel*, which simply means hill or mountain. Burckhardt (Travels in Syria, p. 149) observes this: but Jerome and Cocceius, who adopt the allegorizing system, are not content with this. The former takes the words for "a heap of new fruits," which is symbolical of the state of the Israelites: the latter translates "the time of new fruit;" both interpretations being systematically erroneous. As the Chebar runs into the Euphrates from Mount Masius, the captives were situated up the river to the north of Babylon. A various reading, too, in this verse has been the source of some perplexity. The common text (*chetib*) has ואשר, *vasher*, derived from שרא, *shera, habitavit, commoratus est*; but some MSS. adopt ואשב, *vasheb*, "and I sat" (*keri*); according to Kennicott and De Rossi, "etiam Hispanici, Soncinensis Bibliorum editio, Brixiensis et Complutensis." The Septuagint adopts the former reading; and Vogel, in his edit. of Capell. Crit. Sac., p. 231, adopts the latter. The sense will then be, "And I dwelt, since they dwelt there, I even dwelt." Both Dathe and Rosenmüller reject this, and agree with Calvin's version. His critique on the word שמם, *shemem*, vol. i. p. 146, is quite in accordance with the English version, and with foreign comments. Newcome paraphrases thus: "Astonished at the commission with which I was entrusted; and affected by the overpowering splendour of the visions." The Chaldee has שתק, *shethek*, "silent." Maldonatus adds, "so that I could not speak for seven days."

Dissertation Sixth.

α. JERUSALEM PAINTED ON A BRICK.
Chap. iv. 1.

BISHOP WARBURTON (book iv. sec. iv. of his *Divine Legation*) has ably discussed the Oriental and Egyptian methods of symbolical writing. He explains Ezekiel's method of hieroglyphics, vol. ii. p. 57, edit. 1837. Œcolampadius comments very practically on this exercise of the *ars σκιογραφίκη*. "The Church is besieged by its enemies, because it is a despiser of God's word. Heretics erect the towers of human traditions, and oppose the tower and doctrine of David, since it is not defended by any shield. They set up human righteousness, and are not subject to that of God." The whole passage is worthy of perusal, and is in striking contrast with the sober and unimaginative comment of Calvin. The custom of writing on bricks is thus noticed by Pliny: "Epigenes informs us that the Babylonians had inscribed their observations on the stars for 720 years on burnt bricks, *coctilibus laterculis*." Hist. Nat., b. viii. sec. 57. The chief point of interest in this narrative is its visionary character. The best commentators agree that none of these actions were real: the lying on the left side for 390 days was only in a vision: the left hand is supposed to refer to the ten tribes, as Samaria was situated to the left of Jerusalem. In the 4th verse, "thou shalt bear the punishment of their iniquity," is correctly interpreted by Newcome, "thou shalt pre-signify the punishment which they shall bear." This is the only sense which similar passages can have—St. Paul having shown us that the picture-writing of the Jewish law had its real fulfilment in the work of Messiah.

β. THE THREE HUNDRED AND NINETY DAYS.

CHAP. iv. 5.

There is a difference in the number of days between the Hebrew text and that of the Septuagint. The latter assigns but 190 days to the kingdom of Israel, and yet agrees with the Hebrew in assigning forty days to the kingdom of Judah. Theodoret, in his comment on the passage, explains the Septuagint as follows : Although in the reign of Rehoboam the people were divided, yet they are considered as one nation, being separate, and yet conjoined. When, therefore, the Prophet had assigned 150 days to Israel and 40 to Judah, he combines them again, and makes 190 days. These forty days represent the forty years which remained of the original seventy. Thirty years of captivity were now passed : for Ezekiel began to prophesy in the thirtieth year of the captivity ; and Jeremiah shows us, that in the thirty-seventh year of the captivity of Jeconiah, Evilad-marodach raised his head and led him from his prison-house in the first year of his reign. Then came Baltasar, and Darius the Mede ; whence the forty days of Judah signify the forty remaining years : and the 150 concerning Israel indicate the 150 years after the building of the city, and its becoming filled with inhabitants. This happened in the twentieth year of Artaxerxes, the son of Xerxes, in the time of Nehemiah. Beginning, then, at the fifth year of Jeconiah's captivity, we shall find it forty years to the first year of Cyrus the Persian, then twenty-nine years for the reign of Cyrus, seven for Cambyses, thirty-five for Darius Hystaspes, twenty for Xerxes, and nineteen for Artaxerxes, since in the next year the walls were built. The Israelites participated in this return : for though formerly distinct from the tribe of Judah, they were afterwards united, and all inhabited their common metropolis together.

Jerome also notices this difference of numbering, being surprised that the common reading in his day was 190 years ; while the Hebrew text, and Aquila, Symmachus, and Theodotion, all read 390 years, and even those copies of the Septuagint which are not vitiated. Some, he adds, compute it from the baptism of our Saviour to the end of the world; others again from the destruction of Jerusalem, in the reign of Vespasian, to a period of prosperity for the once favoured nation. The events of history have shown the fallacy of these computations. Ephrem, in his comments on this passage, speaks of the 430 years as beginning with the reign of Solomon, and as extending to the eleventh year of King Zedekiah.

Jerome's method of computing this period is worthy of notice. He dates its commencement from the reign of Pekah, the son of Remaliah, (2 Kings xv. 29,) and its close during the reign of Artaxerxes Mnemon, who is the Ahasuerus of the book of Esther. He reckons the length of the reign of each king in succession, and satisfies himself that he has computed the number which he finds in the prophets, since he reckons this historical period to consist of 389 years and four months. The sleeping on the right side for forty days he interprets, from Nebuchadnezzar's carrying away Jehoiakim to Babylon, to the first year of the sway of Cyrus, under whom the Jews obtained their freedom. The writers on Biblical Chronology do not acquiesce in this computation. J. G. Frank commences the period with the revolt under Jeroboam, and concludes it with the destruction of Solomon's temple. Jeroboam's first year agrees with the year 3215 of the Jubilee period, and the destruction of the kingdom of Israel in 3470. "If, therefore," says he, "you add 390 years to 3214, the date of Jeroboam's revolt, you will obtain 3604 Jub. per., corresponding to the destruction of Solomon's temple."[1]

The Hebrew commentators, R. Solomon and David, do not suppose that a time of punishment for sin is represented, but the time during which it was committed, and so they date the beginning of the period during the early judges, and close it in the reign of Hosea. Œcolampadius adopts this comment with approval, but Maldonatus pronounces it to be erroneous, "for the Prophet is not speaking of their sins, but of their punishment." Grotius supposes it to represent

[1] See Nov. Syst. Chronol. Fund., lib. i. chap. iv. sect. 92, p. 165.

the time of God's patient endurance of the sins of the people. The settlement of this question depends upon the use of the phrase עָוֹן נָשָׂא, *nasa ghon,* to bear iniquity, or the punishment of iniquity. The word is used in both senses; it occurs in Gen. iv. 13, and xix. 15; Ps. lxix. 27, where the authorized version and the marginal readings imply that our translators were aware of the twofold use of the word. The idea of "punishment" seems most suitable here; and the adoption of this translation would cause us to neglect the Jewish interpretation, and to count the years forward from the times of Ezekiel, and to seek for the fulfilment of the prophecy in those events of Israel's history which were then future.

Dissertation Seventh.

THE SEPTUAGINT ORDER.
Chap. vii. 3-13.

These verses are much confused in the Septuagint, and this seems to have been the case in Jerome's time. The Greek Codexes of the Alexandrian version do not agree, as we find from Theodoret and the Arabic version. Theodoret and the Chaldee paraphrast follow the Hebrew order; and the latter, from עיני, *gnini*, "my eye," puts מימרי, *mimri*, "my word," for the sake of avoiding "these anthropomorphic phrases." The thirteenth verse evidently refers to the year of jubilee. Both Theodoret and the Vulgate translate correctly, and Jerome explains it satisfactorily. There is a difference in reading between the Hebrew and the Septuagint here also; the last clause is sufficiently important to note these differences. Jerome explains it thus: "Non proderit homini iniquitas sua, nec ei præbebit aliquam similitudinem." The translation of the Syriac is, "et vir iniquitate sua non conservabit vitam suam;" and of the Chaldee paraphrast, "quisque sibi in peccatis suis sibi placet, et dum viri permanent, pœnitentiam non apprehendent." The Syriac reading makes the sense as follows: "Neither shall any strengthen his life by his iniquity."

Dissertation Eighth.

THE IMAGE OF JEALOUSY.
CHAP. viii. 1-14.

THE singularity of the Vision of this chapter renders it worthy of special notice. It illustrates very strikingly the difference between the worship of Judaism and of the Gospel. The contrast is so remarkable, that every inference from it respecting Christian obligation must be most indirect. These "visions of God" occurred to the Prophet in the place of his captivity. Jerusalem and its temple, and its chambers of imagery, are all brought rapidly before his mind. Theodoret and Jerome maintain that the Prophet was not removed to Jerusalem, but that the scene was presented to his mind in a trance. Newcome continues the trance to the twenty-fourth verse of chap. xi. The appearance of fire in the second verse is supposed by some to be better changed to "man," by reading איש, *aish*, for אש, *eesh*, with various codexes of the Septuagint, the Complutensian edition of the Arabic version; but in the second clause, זהר, *zohar*, signifies the brightness of a star, just as *zoharat*, in Arabic and Amharic, means the planet Venus. In the Complutensian and Aldine editions of the Septuagint it is translated "breeze," or "light air," according to the view of Theodotion. The best translation seems to be, to take the first clause as "the appearance of a man," and the second as "the appearance of brightness."

This remarkable vision is a singular instance of the manner in which the Almighty instructed his prophets. The sixth year of (ver. 1) is to be understood of the reign of Jeconiah. "The appearance of fire" ought most probably to be "of a man;" (ver. 2) for אש, *ash*, "fire," may have been substituted for אִישׁ, *aish*, "a man." The Septuagint, Theodoret, the Complutensian and Arabic versions, all take it so; but the De Rossi does not find it in any of the codexes; and only one of Kennicott's (No. 89) has אִישׁ, *aish*. Still the best modern critics prefer it.

Ver. 3. When the Prophet is taken by a lock of his hair, Kimchi supposes it to signify the violence by which the exiles of Judah would be treated; but all modern writers suppose that this was only a vision: οὐ τοίνυν σωματικὴ ἦν μετάθεσις, οὐδὲ τῶν τῆς σαρκὸς ὀφθαλμῶν ἡ Θεωρία: "there was no bodily change of place, nor any real view by the eyes of the flesh," says Theodoret. The first object presented to the visionary eye of the Prophet was an idolatrous image, metaphorically denominated "jealousy," from the provocation which the idolatries of the people occasioned. The derivation of the word "Tammuz" (ver. 14) is obscure. It is supposed to refer to Adonis, as worshipped by the Syrians. Lucian *de Dea Syria*, vol. iii., and Macrobii *Saturnalia*, chap. xxi., illustrate this point; but what "The IMAGE of JEALOUSY," which rivalled Jehovah and provoked his anger, really was, cannot be determined; most probably it was a statue of Moloch or Baal. Selden "*on the Syrian Deities*" enters at large on the subject.[1] The whole of this scenery Bishop Warburton pronounces to be Egyptian, and versed as he was in Egyptian antiquities, his judgment is deserving of notice. "They contain," says he, "a very lively and circumstantial description of the so celebrated mysteries of Isis and Osiris."[2] The rites were celebrated in a subterraneous place by the Sanhedrim or elders of Israel, and the paintings on the wall correspond with the descriptions of the mystic cells of Egypt. The woman "weeping for Tammuz" (ver. 13) he treats as a Phœnician superstition, while the worship of "the sun towards the east" (ver. 15) is a Persian custom. "When the Prophet is bid to turn from the Egyptian to the Phœnician rites, he is then said to look towards the north, which was the situation of Phœnicia with regard to Jerusalem: consequently, he before stood southward, the situation of Egypt with regard to the same place. And when

[1] Synt. ii. cap. i. p. 195. [2] Div. Leg., lib. iv. sect. 6.

from thence he is bid to turn into the inner court of the Lord's house, to see the Persian rites, this was east, the situation of Persia. With such exactness is the representation of the whole vision conducted." He sees " these three capital superstitions" pourtrayed again in chapter xvi., when the Egyptians are described as " great of flesh." This phrase Warburton considers to apply to Egypt, because it was " the grand origin and invention of idolatry." The " mark upon the forehead," in verse 4 of chap. ix., he treats as an expression of God's special and particular providence. Jehovah was their Tutelary Deity, and their sin was immeasurably heightened by the theocratic privileges which they preeminently enjoyed. Hence this learned writer is enabled to press into his service chap. xiv. 13, and chap. xxv. 8, while he forcibly illustrates both the language and the idea of the Prophet. His view is confirmed by a passage in Diodorus Siculus, who, in lib. i. p. 59, edit. Wess., records : " Round the room in Thebes where the body of King Osymanduas seemed to be buried, a multitude of chambers were built, which had elegant paintings of all the beasts sacred in Egypt." Notices of the worship of the Persians will be found in Perronius's Itinerary, p. 665, and D'Auquetil's Voyages, tab. iii. n. 3, 4. Hebenstreit has written a dissertation on the rites of Bacchus to illustrate this chapter ; and Hyde's Religion of the Ancient Persians, lib. i. chap. xxvii. edit. Oxon., 1760, may be consulted with advantage.

Dissertation Ninth.

THE MAN IN THE LINEN GARMENT.
Chap. ix. 2.

CALVIN (vol. i. p. 302) does not altogether reject the idea that this person prefigured Messiah. Theodoret's view seems judicious. " The dress of the seventh person was that of a priest: for he did not belong to those who punished, but to those who redeemed those worthy of preservation." In Jerome's day it was thought to represent the Saviour, "who is a priest," says he, and quotes Ps. cx. 4, very appropriately. C. D. Michaelis has remarked the customary method of carrying the inkhorn in the East in the present day. *Syl. Com. Theol. Edit. Pott.*, vol. ii. p. 75. The fourth verse explains the reason why it was carried. Calvin's allusion to the use of the mark תו, *tho*, (vol. i. p. 305,) is fully explained by Origen, as quoted by Montfaucon in his notes to the Hexapla. The invention which Calvin calls "puerile" is recorded by Jerome, who made good use of Origen, and added other conjectures. Rosenmüller has quoted in full the passages to which Calvin merely alludes. Pradus and Vitringa have also amply illustrated the point.

On ver. 9, Calvin translates correctly "filled with bloods." (Vol. i. p. 316.) Although this is the common reading, it is not without exception. חמס, *chemes*, "violence," has been found instead of דמים, *demim*, "bloods." A Jewish critic of some note, R. Sal. Norzi, published a critical commentary in 1742, at Mantua, and states that the reading "violence" is found in one accurate and ancient MS., and in one ancient edition. Kimchi attests the same thing; but neither De Rossi nor Kennicott were able to verify the statement. This destruction was to begin at the sanctuary, or, as the

CHAP. IX. 2.   THE MAN IN THE LINEN GARMENT.   443

Septuagint and Theodoret understand it, with the holy ones, (ἀπο τῶν ἁγίων αὐτοῦ,) meaning the priests, who were the leaders in the desecration of the temple worship. Pradus agrees with Calvin in the reason given for the slaughter of the priests and elders first. (Vol. i. p. 310.) Although the person mentioned in ver. 11 is clothed as before, yet the Septuagint omits the word "linen," using simply ποδήρη : Theodotion is satisfied with the Hebrew word *Baddein*, and Aquila has *stola*. There is a marginal reading, too, suggested by the Masoretes ; but most of the codexes of Kennicott and De Rossi support the received text, as well as the Soncine and Complutensian editions, and the Babylonian Talmud. Calvin's translation and interpretation of this chapter is in accordance with the researches of modern critics. Maldonatus may be consulted for the opinions of Jewish writers on important words and phrases.

Dissertation Tenth.

THE COALS SCATTERED OVER THE CITY.
Chap. x. 2.

Jerome explains this scattering of the coals over the city as a symbol of its punishment and cleansing by fire, and quotes Isaiah x. 17, in support of his interpretation; and in accordance with Ps. cxx. 3, he calls them "hot burning coals," the penalty of "the false tongue"—remedium linguæ atque mendacii, and justifies his idea of purifying by Isaiah vi. 8. Jarchi explains as follows: "Sanctus ille Benedictus dixit Gabrieli, qui petiit a cherubino, ut ille sibi daret prunas quo illi paululum refrigescerent leviusque efficerentur decretum pœnæ quoad Judæos sive urbem Hierosolymam;" and refers to the commentary of Abarbenel, fol. 170, col. 4 med. Maldonatus supposes the coals to indicate not the cleansing but the destruction of the city; and their collection by the angel at the command of God, and "from amidst the wheels," implies that this burning did not arise by chance and by man's design, but by God's providence and commandment. At p. 346, vol. i., we have already referred to Œcolampadius, but as his comments are most spiritual, and very inaccessible to the ordinary student of prophecy, we shall quote a few explanatory passages here. The sprinkling of the coal, he thinks, to be an image of the burning city, "quod ex neglecto aut certe male administrando cultu." Hasmal he supposes to represent "those celestial tabernacles into which the Great High Priest entered once by his own blood, after procuring eternal redemption." In the whole vision he sees "Christ the head of his body, in which the law and spirit of life is included," and "how the golden consummation of the elect turns its face towards Christ. For the arc of the Church contains all its parts most elegantly (elegantissime)." He sees Christ in all parts of the Scriptures, as their end, scope, and spirit; and especially the man clothed in linen he says is " Christ acting in this dispensation on the outside of the eternal tabernacles which he at length entered with his blood." The third verse refers to "that judgment which Christ as man shall exercise by God's authority." The voice of the wings signifies " horrenda vox mali ingruentis," and the motion of the wheels " summa in administratione concordia." To us these comments seem very fanciful, as it is obvious that any writer may put forth similar guesses according to his own private though fallible judgment. The cherubim on the right side Jerome considers as representing those holy and exalted beings who dwell at God's right hand, while evil spirits dwell on his left hand. Michaelis, however, with less display of fancy, takes a simpler view, not dwelling on approaching punishment, but upon the departure of God's glory from the temple and city. See Syllog. Com. Theol., vol. v. p. 134; Eichhorn die Bibl. Proph., part ii. p. 456; and Pradus in loc. especially on ver. 20.

Dissertation Eleventh.

THE FIVE-AND-TWENTY EVIL COUNSELLORS.
Chap. xi. 1.

It is very probable, says Pradus, that as there were twenty-four rulers, and as many regions into which Jerusalem was divided, and a chief over them all, so the magistracy of the city is here brought before us. He recognises the analogy to the twenty-four elders in the Apocalypse. But there seems to be no authority for this division of the city into twenty-four "regions" or wards. See on this point Jahn Bibl. Arch., pt. ii. vol. ii. sect. 187. The conduct of these evil counsellors is well pourtrayed by Theodoret. Some commentators take this third verse as a question, so do the Arabic and Syriac versions, " Is it not near?" but Calvin's view is the best, and he is supported by good authorities. Jarchi understands the prophetic denunciations to be intended, " illa mala de quibus prophetæ vaticinantur nec in propinqua est pœna."

The death of Pelatiah (in ver. 13,) as well as the 12th verse, are omitted in the Roman and Alexandrian codexes; and in the Arabic version of the London and Paris Polyglotts. See Walton's Proleg. xiv. 21. There are some minor variations in the readings of Theodoret, the Complutensian edition, and the Syriac version. From the concluding verses of the chapter, the old commentators understand that the prophets were not bodily transferred to either Jerusalem or Chaldæa. The whole scene is called an " extasy." The Spirit of God acting on that of the Prophet, and enduing him with this celestial eye sight.

Dissertation Twelfth.

α. THE FALSE PROPHETS.
Chap. xiii. 1.

THE very existence of such a chapter as this suggests some instructive reflections. It may first remind us of the great moral difference between the position of the Jew and our own. The existence of prophets implies the corresponding possession of miraculous witness. A new prophet was a new herald of a fresh truth; and before he could claim attention he was called upon to show his new credentials. The false prophets had in reality no such proofs that they were sent of God, and yet by speaking smooth things they succeeded in deluding the people. If surprised at the possibility of such complete success, we may be reminded of similar instances in the practice of medicine in our own day among the uneducated. How blindly they rush to any clever impostor who settles among them with no better credentials than his ready skill and his audacious pretensions. The more unenlightened men are the more they catch at any prophet who asserts roundly and audaciously his mission from God. Now the Jew was called upon not to inquire first into the doctrine taught, but into "the sign" worked by the teacher—his first inquiry was to be not what God had revealed, but whom he has commissioned to teach it. Our position is rather the reverse. St. Paul assures us, that if an angel from heaven were to teach any other gospel than that taught by him we are to reject it. We, then, the readers of the Old Testament prophecies, are not to find in them a revelation of the Gospel, but a pointing to the coming Author of the Gospel. " Search the Scriptures," but for what? " they testify *of Me*." Types are fulfilled in the great Antitype—shadows become substance, and dimness splendour. This chapter of Ezekiel makes the teacher and his authority the subject of questioning, not the matter of his instructions. His coming in his own name is his first and all absorbing sin. However smooth his after communications, this is the great test of his unholy imposture.

The Reformers, in the earnestness of their zeal, often applied such chapters as these directly to themselves and their enemies. This led them to deal forth the wrath of God with too indiscriminating a haste, and has given rise to the assertion that their system was a compound of " Moses and the Inquisition."[1] Œcolampadius, for instance, designates the false teachers of his day, "*philauti, indocti, stulti, somniatores, cæci, vulpes dolosæ, rapaces, in desertis et in neglectis locis agentes, timidi, et canes muti.*"[2] Whenever there is a strict parallel between true and false teachers in our own times, such language may be justifiable, but where the right of private judgment is so largely exercised by ourselves, it is but consistent to allow others an equally extensive sphere for its operation. Contending earnestly for the faith and the truth is possible, without the accumulation of strong epithets on the heads of others.

β. ON THE PRINCIPLE OF ACCOMMODATION.
Chap. xiii.

Our Commentator, in various passages throughout this Prophet, finds it necessary to introduce the principle of accommodation. And as this necessity has been so largely insisted on by succeeding interpreters, we may well attempt to discover the true method of applying so elastic a principle. For instance, in this thirteenth chapter, on ver. 9, he says— " Ezekiel here accommodates his language to the common usage of mankind," *attemperat sermonem;* and also, "*pro modulo et ruditate mentis nostræ;*" on the 16th verse he asserts that false prophets are so called " *improprie,*" not

---

[1] See Spectator, January 19, 1850. Review of T. H. Dyer's "Life of John Calvin."
[2] Com. in chap. xiii. 5.

implying any want of propriety in using the name; but showing that the name only is intended, and that the reality is not asserted. The formidable list of German writers on this important point, collected by Wegscheider in his *Institutiones Theologicæ*, p. 99, Hal. 1826, shows it to be worthy of our attentive notice; for when once we permit ourselves to resolve everything into " dictio gnomica et parabolica," we may refine away the force and meaning of the prophecies altogether. While we confine ourselves to the topic immediately before us, a few general suggestions may be here thrown out. 1. In judging of the correctness of Calvin's language, we should remember the peculiar intellectual tendencies of the Reformers, in consequence of their religious antagonism to the prevailing doctrines of their day. They saw all around them the grossest superstitions; they lived among a people who believed in a real and permanent moral efficacy, proceeding from sacred rites and ceremonies. They naturally supposed an analogy to exist between the false teachers of Rome then rampant, and of Israel once beloved. The majority of the divines of the day were in all their habits of thought and reasoning—*realists;* that is, they treated abstract religious ideas as if they were undoubted realities. "Grace," for instance, must be something infused, and must be received only through one holy rite, and communicated fresh and fresh, in union with the elements of another. The schoolmen, who taught that our nature was actually stained and polluted by the propagation of original infection, held also that the laver of regeneration actually washed away this original depravity: if, in after life, fresh pollution was incurred, then through penance and the eucharist, fresh grace was transfused by actual and corporal union with the real body and blood of Christ. The language of Dr. M'Hale in the present day states the peculiarity of a sacrament to be, that it impresses an indelible character.[1] Chateaubriand speaks of those "who receive their God" at the altar, "while each incorporates with his own flesh and blood the flesh and blood of his God."[2]

[1] The Evidences and Doctrines of the Catholic Church, p. 402.
[2] Génie du Christianisme.

This is Realism run to seed: and against all this the Nominalist contended, not by denying the spiritual realities, but by looking for them in the right places. In the fourteenth century the University of Paris was famous for its learning, its resources, and influence over the mind of Europe. The majority in power and rank were Realists. At length William Occam, an English friar, assailed their philosophy, and damaged their religious influence. Himself a disciple of the great Scotus Erigena, he gathered around him a band of devoted adherents, and became in philosophy what Luther and Calvin afterwards were in religion. He succeeded sufficiently to attract the notice of the reigning pope, John XXII., who was sharp-sighted enough to see that if Nominalism spread Romanism must perish. Hence by his command in 1339, the University of Paris publicly condemned and denounced the philosophy of Occam.[1] As usual, when the man is denounced, the principles take root and flourish. In another age, Luther and Melancthon own him as their master and their guide. The former calls him "*Carus magister meus;*" the latter "*Deliciæ quondam nostræ.*"[2] The next century finds the disputes at Paris as fierce as ever. The famous Gerson and his persevering disciples caused their enemies to respect their mental sway, till Rome again interfered. In 1743, the Bishop of Avranches felt the philosophy of the schools, on which the false doctrines of Rome were built, in danger, and then he persuaded Louis XI., the ruling monarch of France, to order their writings to be seized and their persons imprisoned. But as time passed on, the king relented, for about eight years afterwards he revoked his edict, and restored the party to their former philosophical position. The Reformers lived amidst this perversion of ideas on religious subjects, and their writings show them to be unconsciously tinged with the sentiments of the Realists. The schoolmen, for instance, still argued for a corporeal propagation of what was termed *fomes* or *concupiscentia*, calling it a *qualitas corporis*, derived

[1] Boulay Hist. Acad. Par., vol. iv. p. 257; and v. p. 708.
[2] See Admon. ad Eccl. ap. Cœlest., p. 261; et Orat. pro M. Luth. Opera, vol. ii. p. 58.

either from *contagione pomi,* or *afflatu serpentis.*[1] While the Lutherans took one step in the right direction, the Zuinglians added another: and the influence of the prevailing opinions of their day is very perceptible in the tone in which the Reformers comment on the prophets. Calvin, for instance, is remarkable for his sound common-sense view of difficulties: if an apparent inconsistency occurs, he is ready at once with his phrases, *forma loquendi, per concessionem, ironice,* καταχρηστικῶς, *improprie,* all implying his own right to use his private judgment in solving a difficulty according to his pleasure. He often finds it necessary to exercise it. In chap. xx. 28, (vol. ii. p. 321,) he ventures to suppose a phrase used in a sense directly contrary to its obvious meaning; and in verses 5-8, (vol. ii. p. 293,) he treats the Prophet's words as "translatitiæ locutiones." His desire to identify the prophetic teaching with the law of Moses on the one side, and with the precepts of the gospel on the other, leads him to invent these varying schemes for avoiding the literal meaning. The inexperienced student will learn wisdom by allowing the Law, the Prophets, and the Apostles, to speak their own separate language, and gradually to develop the designs and the character of God without either confusion or distortion. Still, the use of the word *improprie* must not mislead us; it does not signify "improperly" in the ordinary sense, but is used as *in* and *proprie* in Latin. It implies that a phrase does not bear the meaning which it seems to have: it denies the Realist's view of a question, and asserts that of the Nominalist. For instance, righteousness infused is the doctrine of one school; righteousness imputed that of the other: the text of the fifty-fifth lecture speaks the language of the former; the comment of Calvin that of the latter. The Reformers have taught us to look for spiritual realities where only they can be found, and to deny their necessary connexion with outward observances and tangible elements, whether under the temple rites, or the prophetic visions, or the apostolic ordinances.

---

[1] See Apol. Confess. ap. Cœlest., p. 2, and Scotus, lib. ii. distinct. 32.

γ. ON THE PHRASE "PROSTITUERUNT DEUM."

CHAP. xiii. 19. VOL. ii. p. 33.

The remarks of the last article apply directly to Calvin's language respecting the Almighty: he says that the wicked "defile his glory," "corrupt his justice," and "prostitute even God himself," (ver. 19,) and then "drown in the lowest abyss of hell the whole world when disappointed of their gains." This is the language of Realists, who suppose it possible for men thus to treat either the Almighty or their fellow-creatures. The anathemas of the Council of Trent are founded on the same fallacious basis, and the strong language of the vulgar savours of the same innate belief. The modern reader at once supplies the word "name" after the offensive verb "to prostitute." Calvin probably understood it so, but he did not write it so. His phraseology is largely tinctured with the errors of his times, though he has written enough to be correctly interpreted by himself. When we moderns think on the subject for a moment, we admit that no man can defile God's glory, or corrupt his justice, or devote his fellow-sinner to the lowest abyss: we take any such expressions as simply denoting the views of the speakers or writers about matters immeasurably beyond them. If we more thoroughly understood the teaching of Locke and the continental Nominalists respecting abstract ideas, we should live without any fears of the success of those who unchurch all sects but their own, and who assert the cleansing efficacy of suffering, and the possibility of discovering the whole body of Catholic tradition. With us, for instance, altars are not only prohibited, but impossible. They are now a mere name: their reality is confined to the one altar, the Cross. It is equally as impossible to prostitute God as to erect an altar.

The reader of these Commentaries must have observed that Calvin's idea of God is rather more familiar than infinite: he introduces his name into the minutest concerns, and thinks of him not as acting by general and settled laws, but as personally and constantly intervening between the conduct and the destinies of men. He naturally transfers the conceptions and instincts of morality and holiness which he finds within himself to the Almighty—he clothes his idea of an awful Spirit with the attributes of a human conscience: he imagines his Deity a divine man, purified, exalted, and unlimitedly endowed. Our acquaintance with the physical sciences leads us to see the Great Supreme acting through the visible universe by fixed and undeviating laws: so we expect that revelation will unfold to us laws of similar harmony, although apparently disturbed by the anomaly of rebellion and the mystery of sin. But Calvin without hesitation supposes him to interfere perpetually with the ordinary processes of our animal nature. For instance, in the 14th verse of this chapter, he supposes the Almighty to withdraw from the ordinary bread of this life its usual nourishment by way of punishing the wicked. He is said to break the staff of bread by puffing it up, and depriving it of its power of affording aliment to the body. He repeats this singular comment as the correct explanation of the language of Moses in Deut. viii. 3. (See vol. ii. p. 71.) It may be perfectly true, that "unless God breathes into the bread the virtue of nourishment the bread is useless;" but where is the proof that he withdraws this nourishing power when the bread is tasted by the ungodly? The ignorance of the Reformers of those physical laws by which it pleases the Almighty that the natural universe should be governed, was very injurious to them as commentators on sacred writ: they were constantly in danger of being like men who write on glass with diamonds, and thus obscure light with scratches. And not only so, when Calvin speaks of " a secret virtue infused into the bread," he adopts the language of the Realists: he assumes the existence of a quality which is philosophically incorrect. A disciple of Locke will be aware that this supposed virtue is only an abstract idea existing in the mind of man and not in the bread, and that it is only an admissible form of speech when it is understood as a general term for the aggregate of those chemical agents and properties which are realities. If God then withdraws this " infused virtue," it is only a form of saying that he withdraws or suspends certain chemical agencies: and who will now confidently assert this to be his method of interfering with the never-ceasing operations of his creation? So in ver. 14, the action of Phinehas, Numbers xxv., is said to be *infectum aliquo vitio*. This again is the language of the Realists, and is erroneous. His work could not be infected morally either way: it must have been his mind or his affections. The language erroneously transfers moral attributes to the *deed* instead of to the *man*.

And here it may appositely be stated, that a correct exposition of the prophecies never requires any violation of either physical or moral truth. Faith in the unity and supremacy of truth is one form of faith in God. The prophecies are rather illustrated than obscured by our increasing knowledge of the material universe. No true success in prophetic interpretations can be attained without a hearty reliance on the unity and majesty of all truth, without a calm confidence that contradictions are only apparent, and if we cannot explain them now, they will become clear hereafter. Reason, in its calmest and clearest vision, can be superseded only by being surpassed; feeling, in its tenderest mood, must still be ennobled by trust; and conscience must witness audibly and reverently to our need of the Spirit's mysterious guidance "into all truth."

Throughout the Prophet Ezekiel, Calvin is nobly consistent in pleading for God's justice. There is no instinct more deeply seated in the human soul than this,—the Godlike must be just: nothing can be permanently opposed to this essential principle. It must sooner or later be vindicated, and bring a certain measure of retribution, which must follow hard upon its transgression. Still many traditional modes of thought concerning the Almighty occur in these Commentaries, which modern information has very largely modified. God's handwriting is now legible in many ways, where of old it was a blank. If his interposition is not now recognised in cherubs, and wheels, and burning flame, we are more conscious of the natural wonders developed in the dewdrop and the flower. Our age believes so many things of which the Reformers were ignorant, and disbelieves so much on which they laid stress, that we are in danger of overlooking the existence of great primeval truths, which constitute the essential religious life in man in all ages unchangeably. Veneration for what we believe God to be must be at the foundation of all piety; and imitation of what we believe God to do must ever be the substance of all duty. The first qualification for perusing Ezekiel with advantage is the spiritual purification of self; and in this attainment Calvin materially assists us, by setting before us large conceptions of the Almighty's character, and mature judgments of his purposes.

Dissertation Thirteenth.

a. ISRAEL AN ADULTERESS.
Chap. xvi. 1.

The allegory which runs through this chapter is by no means an unusual one in the Prophets. The beginning of verse 3 has occasioned some variety of remark. Œcolampadius takes מכורה, *mekoreh*, meaning "birth," "origin," for מגורה, *megoreh*, meaning "dwelling;" as Calvin translates it *habitationes*. Houbigant derives it from כרה, *kereh*, "to dig," which Newcome prefers: it may come from מכר, *meker*, "to sell," and thus means "dealings;" but this is not so appropriate here. Rosenmüller reviews these derivations, adding as another, viz., *formationes*; but approves of the sense "origin," *effossiones*, from כור, *cor*, "to dig." This is clearly the best, the Jews having constantly before them the digging out of a rock—as in Isaiah li. 1. Both Theodoret and Jerome explain verse 3 with precision: the former has—ἀραῖς γὰρ ὁ Χαναὰν ὑπεβλήθη, καὶ δουλείαν ὑπὸ τοῦ προπάτορος Νῶε κατεδικάσθη; the latter writes—Cham quippe, pater Chanaan, princeps fuit gentis Ægyptiæ.... radicem Ierusalem terram Ægypti esse dicemus. In verse 4 the salting and swaddling the body is said to represent the Almighty's care of the people when under Egyptian bondage. The custom of throwing the skirt over the female is alluded to by Theocritus Idyll. xviii. 19; and a fragment of Euripides preserved by Stobæus. This cleansing from pollution is explained by the Chaldee paraphrast to mean the deliverance from Egypt. Those who are curious in the various articles of clothing in verses 10 to 14 may consult Schrœder de Vestitu Mul., chap. xiv. p. 221; Bochart Hieroz., pt. i. lib. iii.; Jablonskii Opuscula, t. i. p. 290, &c.; and J. D. Michaelis in Suppl., p. 1565. " The images of men," (ver. 17,) Jerome interprets of the idols of Bel, Chemosh, and Ashtoreth, which were made out of the sacred gold and silver of the temple. The passing through the fire, (ver. 21,) the Vulgate renders *consecrans illos;* but Aquila, Symmachus, and Theodotion take the same view as Calvin. Theodoret interprets the 26th verse of the grossness of the Egyptian idolatry in worshipping the ibis, the cow, and the crocodile. The punishment of the Jews (verses 36-43) is figuratively predicted by similar language, which Theodoret clearly illustrates—οὐ γυναῖκας τὰς γυναῖκας ὀνομάζει, ἀλλὰ τροπικῶς τὰς πόλεις οὕτω καλεῖ, ἐπειδὴ καὶ αὐτὴν πόλιν οὖσαν δίκην γυναικὸς εἰς τὸ δικαστήριον εἰσάγει. The comment of Œcolampadius on verses 20 and 23 is copious and instructive.

β. CAPTIVE ISRAEL AND PAPAL ROME.
Chap. xvi. 20.

In commenting on this verse, Calvin draws a striking comparison between the Jews of Ezekiel's day and the Romanists of his own. And as the controversy with Rome is at present a subject of absorbing interest, it is very important to ascertain the exact views of the Reformers as to that giant apostacy. The parallel between them seems to our Reformer most complete. He allows both to be true Churches, while he condemns them as breakers of God's covenant. Both Israel and the Papacy are still said to be under covenant with God; so that " our baptism requires no renewal :" (ver. 20,) yet still the devil reigns in the Papacy without quite extinguishing God's grace. The Church is there amidst all its corruptions; otherwise Antichrist could not sit in God's temple. The papal priests are said to imitate the Jewish in all things, even to the material of which the surplice is made. The priests of Rome are called " papales sacrifici"—the language of the Realists; which is erroneous, because it admits too much. It asserts that they offer a sacrifice: the Protestant denies the fact, and disallows the term. In the controversy with Rome, we should be more careful than even Calvin in the terms we employ. To allow the analogy here pointed out, is to allow too much. While we assert, that the pretence to sacrificial functions is a gross imposture, we must at the same time refuse their claim to be acknowledged as priests. We must instantly erect the standard of nominalism, showing that there is but one High Priest, but one sacrifice, and one altar in the religion of Christ. This is real—all the rest mere accommodation. On this ground, too, Calvin's view of the covenant actually remaining among them, and of their being such a temple that Antichrist can be seated therein, is very questionable. It is necessary that the reader should see the consequences of allowing too much to the advocates of the papacy: there are many reasons, on which we cannot enter here, for believing that St. Paul did not refer in any way to Papal Rome by the phrase, "the temple of God:" and if this be conceded, then Calvin's argument concerning Antichrist falls to the ground. It is very important to be aware of the tinge which the theological language of the sixteenth century gave to all the writings of that stirring age.

γ. ON THE WORD "NEPHESH," SOUL.

Chap. xvi. 27.

Calvin expresses himself rather hastily when he says (vol. ii. p. 131,) this word נפש, *nephesh*, means "lust," or desire, "appetite." It occurs eighteen times in these twenty chapters of Ezekiel; and in every case except this, when our version reads "will," it is properly translated "soul," or "person." As the word is in itself exceedingly important, and occurs some hundred times throughout the Old Testament, it is desirable to ascertain how far it admits of so many various meanings. We ought to lay it down as a general rule, that the usual sense of a word is not to be departed from without extreme necessity; and there seems none here for deviating from the ordinary meaning. Both

Castell and Shindler, in their Lexx., give all the various uses of the word at full length; and both Gesenius and Lee fall into the error of stating too great a variety of meanings without giving the reasons for such discordant senses. Its original meaning is " breath ;" and as " life" was supposed to reside in the breath, hence it expresses anything that has life, any living energy or mental activity, so that " the soul" is said to hunger and thirst, to fast and become cold. (See Proverbs, Psalms, and Job.) Schrœder *de Vestitu Mulierum,* and Gesenius, both give the sense of " fragrance" on Is. iii. 20. The Rabbis distinguish three kinds of *nephesh* in man, the vegetative, the brutal, and the intellectual. This description is philosophically correct, since it is now ascertained that " the life" of man strictly partakes of the elements of vegetable and animal vitality, together with the intellectual power and the moral sentiments, usually termed," soul," in modern divinity. Connecting this word with לב, *leb,* " heart," we observe that Gesenius agrees with Calvin on ver. 30, (vol. ii. p. 134,) that it signifies "the seat of intelligence." The Hebrews supposed that the human heart " was actually the seat of the affections ;" these are now known to act through the brain, and hence the old phraseology of " giving the heart to God" should be allowed to become obsolete. There is no proof that the word *nephesh* implied this immortal principle in man; the hunting souls, and slaying them, as in the thirteenth chapter, refer to the destruction of life. In the time of the translators, and in the distant counties of England at this day, the word " soul" is used where more refined speakers use the word " person." For instance, in chap. xviii., " the soul that sinneth it shall die," may be reduced to modern English by saying, " the person who sins shall die himself." It is by no means necessary, in this 27th verse, to deviate, with Calvin and our translators, from the ordinary sense ; it is readily rendered, " and delivered thee up to the persons who hate thee, viz., the daughters," &c. Thus two English words only are required as the correct equivalent for *nephesh* throughout Ezekiel—a point on which we ought to insist, as giving certainty and definiteness to any version of the Prophet's language.

δ. THE PRIMITIVE CHURCH AND THE NEW TESTAMENT.

Chap. xvi. 61.

It is worthy of notice, that in Calvin's time, as in our own, appeals were frequently made to the teaching of "the primitive Church." The Reformers were especially anxious to ascertain what the primitive Church really taught, and to compare it with Holy Scripture: they did not repose implicitly on its dicta, because they looked upon the phrase as an idea rather than a reality. Here again the necessary collision between realism and nominalism arises. There is no such thing as the primitive Church in the sense in which it was used in Calvin's day, and has been revived in our own. The words stand for an abstract idea, comprehending many single churches, and stating what is held to be common to all. For instance, the Church at Antioch was in reality the primitive Gentile Church; its doctrines, discipline, and worship, were realities, and, could they be ascertained accurately, would present to our minds a distinct and definite object; but any representation of doctrines and ceremonies said to be common to many churches, and thus spoken of as appertaining to the primitive Church, is a mental deduction after the process of selection and assortment has been carried on. We have to guard against the erroneous view of the Realist, lest we should look to the primitive Church " to reveal what is to be believed, rather than to teach what has been revealed." See an admirable letter of the Archbishop of Canterbury to Rev. W. Maskell.

Although Calvin's language throughout this chapter is precise and correct, yet he inadvertently falls now and then into that of the Realist. On verse 29 he uses the phrase "guttam pietatis in animis"—the erroneous language of his Romanist adversaries. Piety, he knew well enough, was not a thing infused into man—righteousness infused is the doctrine of realism—righteousness imputed is nominalism: the former has of late been revived and systematized by Newman and Ward; while the latter has the inspired sanction of the Pauline Epistles.

In his comments on this verse, our Reformer uses the word "testament" and "covenant" for the same idea. It is better to avoid this partial confusion. The word "testamentum" should properly be applied to the record, which informs us of the "fœdus." Grotius has expressed the difference accurately: with him "testamentum" is equivalent to "libri fœderis," and, as accuracy in theological expressions is most desirable, it is wiser to translate $\delta\iota\alpha\theta\acute{\eta}\kappa\eta$ in every instance by "covenant," and to confine the word testament most strictly to the written record. This will aid us in keeping before our minds the covenant between the Almighty and his living Church; we shall appreciate our position as children of the New Covenant, and avoid the error of regarding the Old Testament, with its laws, and ceremonies, and sacrifices, as binding upon us, who are no longer "children of the bond woman, but of the free."

Dissertation Fourteenth.

α. THE GREAT EAGLE.
Chap. xvii. 3.

The allegory of "The Great Eagle" is well sustained throughout this chapter. A golden eagle with extended wings was the standard of the king of Persia in the time of Cyrus, (*Xenoph. Cyrop.*, lib. vii. chap. 1,) and it was probably adopted from the Assyrian empire. The length of its wing is supposed by Grotius to apply to the widely-extended empire of Nebuchadnezzar. Kimchi interprets "the variegated colour like a peacock" of the majesty and dignity of his kingdom; but Michaelis agrees with Calvin. The interpretation of Lebanon, to which Calvin objects, is adopted by Jerome and Theodoret; but Rosenmüller agrees with our Author. He also takes the word כנען, *ken-gnen*, (ver. 4,) exactly in Calvin's sense, quoting Prov. xxxi. 24, " quod incolæ ejus terræ, utpote maris accolæ, mercaturæ erant deditissimi." See also Dathe's edit. of Glass. Phil. Sac., p. 1184. The sense which Calvin disapproves is adopted by the Septuagint, the Roman Codex, the Arabian version, Theodoret, and the Chaldee paraphrast. The criticism in the note to verse 8 is correct; and the interpretation generally is in accordance with the explanations of Jarchi, Kimchi, Jerome, Michaelis, Grotius, and other critics ancient and modern. Newcome has noticed some various readings, and others are easily gathered from De Rossi, and the different versions and codexes; but they are not of sufficient interest to need further detail.

β. THE LOFTY BRANCH OF THE TALL CEDAR.

CHAP. xvii. 22.

The interpretation of the 22d verse is worthy of remark. Kimchi and Grotius think that Zerubbabel is intended here, but Rosenmüller agrees with Calvin in referring it to Christ. The Chaldee paraphrast and Jarchi apply it to "King Messiah." (See Talm. Schabbat, fol. 30, and Cholin, fol. 139, b., and R. Abendana ad Michlal Jophi.) Calvin's supposition, however, that where the prophets speak of "this hope of freedom to the elect," it should be dated from the rebuilding of the temple, and continued to the end of Christ's kingdom, is incorrect. It causes him to date this kingdom from the rebuilding of the temple, in forgetfulness of the many disasters which happened to the people between the times of Ezra and of our Lord. The building of the second temple was not an event of any immediate spiritual import to the Jews: it was followed by overwhelming temporal disasters; so that the reign of Messiah did not commence till the Mediator of the New Covenant was revealed, and "the new kingdom of the heavens" fully heralded into the world at large.

Dissertation Fifteenth.

THE EATING SOUR GRAPES.

Chap. xviii. 1.

THE proverb of the fathers eating sour grapes and the children's teeth being set on edge, requires a few remarks, in consequence of the conjectures of some modern writers on sacred subjects. Andrew Norton, in his elaborate notes on "The Genuineness of the Gospels,"[1] has attempted to show a discrepancy between Ezekiel and the Pentateuch. He compares this proverb with the language of Exodus, chap. xx., where God is said to visit the iniquity of the fathers on the children: he then quotes the Talmud as objecting to Ezekiel's prophecies as contradictory to the Pentateuch: and thus he insinuates that the two passages cannot be reconciled. If this be so, it is further implied that the Divine authority of either Exodus or Ezekiel is doubtful. But there seems no reason to conclude these two passages to be contradictory. The circumstances under which they were spoken give the tone and meaning to each. Moses enunciates a general law of God's moral government, which we see carried out every day before our eyes. Let the parent of a family, by honest industry and religious conduct acquire for himself the esteem and respect of his fellow-men, then it follows by an established law of God's providence, that his family gain honourable advantages by their parent's reputation. But let a parent by intemperance and dishonesty bring disgrace and poverty on himself, and it is equally a

[1] Vol. ii., p. cxl.

law of providential government that his children will suffer by his misconduct. The wickedness of the father will often fall dreadfully on his unconscious offspring. This is an undeviating, an irreversible law applicable at all times, and daily operating before us in ten thousand instances. But the Jews attempted to excuse their own sins by throwing them on their fathers. The generation which Ezekiel addressed were personally blameworthy; the language of this passage was *theirs:* it is the language of a false excuse—an attempt to charge the Almighty with unfairness, that they might throw the blame from themselves. No argument, then, can be drawn from its occurrence contrary to the Divine authority of the Pentateuch. Ezekiel records the language and chastises it, thereby upholding the authority of the law, and vindicating rather than destroying the unity of the Divine records. The instruction to be received from the chapter has been well pointed out by the present Archbishop of Canterbury, in his " Apostolic Preaching."—Sixth edit., p. 69.

A translation of a work of the Professor of Biblical Criticism at Heidelberg having been published in London, it becomes desirable to notice the result of his critical labours on this chapter of our Prophet. G. L. Bauer, in his " Theologie des alten Testaments," has the following comment: " The whole book of Ezekiel is an illustration of the Judaic belief, that Jehovah is the King and Governor of his people Israel. He rewards and punishes them: blesses them with prosperity, and afflicts them with adversity. Ezekiel teaches (in direct opposition to the Mosaic doctrine that God will visit the sins of the fathers upon the children unto the third and fourth generation), that the son shall not bear the iniquity of the father: that moral conduct will ensure to the individual length of days: that the righteousness of the righteous shall be upon him, and the wickedness of the wicked shall be upon him, and that the soul that sinneth he shall die. The eighteenth chapter is the most beautiful and the most useful in the book, but it has reference exclusively to God's conduct towards his own people." Here we have the usual mixture of Neologian wisdom and folly. There is no real contrast between Moses and this Prophet. Moses states a general law of God's moral government of mankind, and Ezekiel protests against an abuse of that doctrine. The Jews of his day wished to throw all the blame on their fathers, and to charge the Almighty with unfairness in punishing them for the faults of their ancestors. They forgot their own personal share in rebellion against the Most High. Nor is it the slightest objection that " it has reference exclusively to God's conduct towards his own people." Here the Jews are specially addressed, and the principle is readily applicable to all mankind as soon as it is shown that they are under similar relations to the Almighty as the Jews. The writer who cannot see how easily Moses and Ezekiel are reconciled has but very slight pretensions to occupy a divinity chair; he may make hasty assertions, and give shrewd guesses; but his opinion ought to be well weighed before it is reckoned either valuable or trustworthy. Bauer's criticisms on various passages of this Prophet are by no means so objectionable as those on the other Old Testament writers; though he is open to the charge of exercising that " fertile imagination"[1] which he brings so irreverently against Ezekiel.

A question of still larger import arises naturally out of their own defence of this eighteenth chapter; namely, what degree of authority have the laws of the Old Covenant over us, the children of the New? If, on the one hand, the reasonings of Professor Norton, as contained in the notes to his second volume of his " Evidences of the Genuineness of the Gospels" are unsound, the following assertion of a writer, in reply to the Queen's Professor of Modern History at Cambridge is unwise—" One inspired declaration is all that is needed, and whether it be found in the Old Testament or in the New, is all one to us Christians; it is God's word, and God's word cannot deceive."[2] It is clear enough that the Old Testament is God's word—but is it so to us? Is its authority the same " to us Christians" as that of the New?

[1] See Edit. London. Eng. trans., p. 125.
[2] See a Pamphlet by the Rev. W. B. Hopkins, in reply to Sir James Stephen, LL.D., Professor of Modern History in the University of Cambridge, sect. ii., p. 37.

He who would avoid Judaizing must answer in the negative: he who best understands the nature of our New Covenant in Christ Jesus will distinguish carefully between the authority of the inspired records of the two covenants over the conscience of the disciples of the new kingdom of the heavens. When we speak of Holy Writ collectively, as contrasted with all uninspired compositions, it is emphatically the Word of God; but when we are attempting to define the relation in which each Testament separately stands to ourselves, we must not hastily adopt the mere popular language of the day. By doing so, we are unable to repel the assaults of the worldly wise, and are in danger of lowering the value of the Sacred Oracles in the eyes of the scientific inquirers of our times.

To the scholar who is acquainted with the difficulties which are reviewed by Professor Norton, the following observations will appear elementary; but as there are some simple-minded believers who may be perplexed by the specious arguments of the sceptic, a few remarks may be instructive. First of all, we should not treat the Old Testament as one book all written at the same time. It should be divided into various portions corresponding to the periods in which each book was written. The Pentateuch, for instance, should be studied separately from the Prophets; while the interval of nearly 1000 years, between the death of Moses and the visions of Ezekiel, should be constantly borne in mind. The Pentateuch, but not exactly as we have it, was the Word of God for Jews—its authority as a law to Christians was never admissible. St. Paul's whole life was a protest against this going back again to Moses, instead of going forward to Christ. The ministration of death was exchanged for a dispensation of life: while God's moral law remains unchangeable, its authority rests on other grounds to us than the thunders of Sinai and the tables of stone. Thus, again, the prophetic announcements were direct and special for Israel and Judah; but they contain guidance and warning for us only when we are placed in a similar position morally before God. Ezekiel, for instance, is a watchman to us only so far as it can be shown that our sins, needs, and responsibilities are similar to those of the Hebrews. It must be uttered again and again that we are discipled into the New Covenant of which St. Paul was a chief herald unto us Gentiles; and our highest attainment is to stand fast in the liberty wherewith our Redeemer has made us free. Wherever there is a spiritual analogy between our state and that of the captives at Chebar, Ezekiel is for us; his stirring voice is for our reproof and instruction in righteousness; but wherever the difference of condition is so great that this analogy fails, then Ezekiel is only indirectly our monitor from heaven. The light from heaven is reflected directly *upon us* through Jesus and his Apostles, and only obliquely through Moses and the Prophets.[1]

By the expression of this view of the value of the Old Testament to us, we do but give form and voice to the feelings which exist in the minds of many earnest and thoughtful Christians. They cannot receive all that is in the Old Testament as equally binding on them with what is revealed in the New. They cannot sympathize with the antagonist of the Queen's Professor of History: they feel that many proposed solutions of acknowledged difficulties are superficial and evasive rather than self-evident and satisfactory. Such obstacles are not necessarily connected with the Christian verities, they are not essential portions of our religion: we may safely confess ourselves ignorant of the true solution, without endangering a single particle of " the faith once delivered to the saints." By upholding the Pentateuch as the Word of God to the Jews of former ages, we defend and enforce its inspiration and suitability for its original time and purpose; by treating the prophecies of the era of the Captivity as spoken originally to the people *alive at the time,* we vindicate the Divine inspiration of the Prophet, and we prepare our own minds to receive intelligently any indirect instruction which may be applicable to ourselves. The integrity of the Jewish canon is thus acknowledged and preserved, while we are free to inquire how far its sacred books are instructive for all times and all nations. The whole life

---

[1] See Augustine De Civit. Dei, lib. xviii. chap. xxxviii. p. 836. Ed. Paris. 1838.

and ministry of St. Paul taught one invariable truth on this important question, and its significant witness was clear and emphatic to our higher privileges and nobler aims under the NEW COVENANT in Christ Jesus our Lord.

β. USURY AND INTEREST.
CHAP. xviii. 8.

The manner in which this subject is treated illustrates our remarks on the non-application of the Jewish law to Christian duties. Calvin is evidently at a loss how to distinguish between lawful and unlawful interest. He does not clearly say that one law was applicable to the Jew and another to us. Usury may be sinful, but not because it was forbidden to Israel of old. The comment on this verse is not based upon principles in accordance with the New Covenant. It may fairly be stated that this eighteenth chapter is not law to us; our duties depend upon another foundation. The law which is to decide what is "interest" and what "usury," must rest upon the golden rule of doing unto others as we would that they should do unto us. If we be formed after the image of Christ, we shall educate conscience, and cultivate justice and mercy, and decide these points by a different standard from that of the Jewish law; and when Calvin states "in lege ea est perfectio ad quam nihil possit accedere," he does not state the sense in which he uses "lege," and seems to confine it to the Mosaic precepts. This instance is sufficient to show the true use which we are to make of the Old Testament, and to guard us against a misapplication of its statements.

A singular instance of the fallacy of applying the Old Testament directly to the events of the world in the present day occurs in the State Trials in the reign of James the Second. In the case of the East India Company *v.* Sandys, a question arose respecting the right of the King's subjects to trade with nations eastward of the Cape of Good Hope without the King's license. Holt, afterwards the celebrated Chief-Justice, argued his point with more zeal than discretion. He gravely cites the doctrine of Lord Coke, that "infidels are perpetual enemies;" and then, in the same breath, quotes the book of Judges, to show by analogy, that as the Jews were restrained from merchandise with the Canaanites, so Christians ought to be restricted in their dealings with Pagans.[1] One instance out of many may suffice to remind us, that the assumption that Christians are in all cases to act according to God's commands to the Jews, is the basis of modern Judaism; and the frequency of such reasonings, though supported at times by the writings of some of our venerable Reformers, calls loudly for the voice of another Paul to proclaim, "Stand fast in the liberty wherewith Christ has made you free."

The imprudent manner in which some commentators have connected the incidents of the Old Testament with the doctrine of the New is readily illustrated by a passage in the first epistle to the Corinthians by Clement of Rome. In quoting the narrative of Rahab receiving the spies before the destruction of Jericho, he adverts to their suggesting the hanging out a scarlet thread from her house, and then adds directly, "making it manifest that by the blood of the Lord redemption shall be to all those who believe and trust upon God. Ye see then, beloved, that there was not only faith, but prophecy in the woman."[2] If this method of illustration be considered as allegorical, and as only suggestive of a remote comparison, it is tolerable; but if it be intended to imply any typical connexion between the accident of the scarlet colour and the redemption through Messiah, it is irreverent and inappropriate in the extreme. The learned Wotton defends Clement by the example of his master, Paul, and quotes Justin Martyr, who treats the same event "as a symbol of the blood of Christ."[3] Guided by such illustrious names, the Reformers often adopted the same "spiritualizing" system. The sounder and soberer criticism of later days has instructed us not to adopt the imaginations of men as if they were inseparably bound up with the supreme word of God.

[1] See State Trials, 10, 519, and Lord Campbell's Lives of the Chief-Justices, vol. ii. p. 126.
[2] See Wotton's Edit., 1718, Cantab., chap. xii. p. 54.
[3] Dial. cum Tryphone.

The following extract is worthy of notice, as illustrating the principles for which we contend :—

"The same freedom of thought [as that of Luther] on topics not strictly theological formed a prominent feature in the character of Calvin. A curious instance of it occurs in one of his letters,[1] where he discussed an ethical question of no small moment in the science of political economy, 'How far it is consistent with morality to accept of interest for a pecuniary loan?' On this question, which, even in Protestant countries, continued till a very recent period to divide the opinions both of divines and lawyers, Calvin treats the authority of Aristotle and that of the Church with equal disregard. To the former he opposes a close and logical argument not unworthy of Mr. Bentham: to the latter he replies, by showing that the Mosaic law on this point was not a moral, but a municipal prohibition—a prohibition not to be judged of from any particular text of Scripture, but upon the principles of natural equity."[2]

γ. PERPLEXING AND THORNY QUESTIONS.
Chap. xviii. 20.

In this and the following verses Calvin pronounces rather too dogmatically upon matters which are beyond human comprehension. He strives to reconcile statements apparently contradictory, and in doing so enunciates principles which cannot be positively determined. For instance, the will of an infant, before its birth, is said to be "perverse and rebellious against God," vol. ii. p. 241. Although we are reminded (in ver. 23, vol. ii. p. 247) that God's secret counsels are inscrutable to us, yet the assertion is hazarded that he "has devoted the reprobate to eternal destruction, and wishes them to perish." Some effort is made to reconcile the freeness of this will with the certainty of the destruction—the knot is said to be "easily untied;" but the expe-

---
[1] See also his views expressed in his Tracts.
[2] Prof. Dugald Stewart's Preliminary Dissertation to the Encyc. Britt.

rience of nearly three centuries has proved that these exciting disputes have not been satisfactorily settled : they are still what they are called on p. 255, " perplexing and thorny questions," and must remain so till the promise is accomplished, that faith shall be exchanged for sight. It does not seem desirable to enter upon these abstruse points when commenting upon a Hebrew Prophet : the revelation to Ezekiel was far different in its subject-matter from that to St. Paul : there is no necessity for supposing either that the evangelical doctrines were fully made known to the Prophets, or that their language is verbally binding upon us—the offspring of the far-off Gentiles.

In these "Dissertations" we only venture to suggest some general principles of correct interpretation, and to point out some errors into which our Reformer has fallen, partly through the infirmity natural to man, and partly through the philosophical systems and the false divinity current in his times. While he so evidently surpassed his own age in stern and devoted piety, and avoided the fanciful conjectures in which many of the Reformers indulged ; Calvin is at times open to the charge of teaching dogmatically questions which have never been decided by Revelation. Let us bear with him on this point, while we profit by his judicious and instructive lectures ; remembering that within the fringes of his shadow his modern revilers are not worthy to tread.

Another instance of perplexity occurs on p. 335, vol. ii. The "Indecision" refers to the decree of the Emperor Charles V. called " The Interim." Calvin's hatred of it was sincere but injudicious. It was a first step to better things. See Mosheim, cent. xvi. sect. 1, and the authorities quoted in Maclaine's note.

Dissertation Sixteenth.

THE SABBATH A SACRAMENT AND A MYSTERY.
CHAP. xx. 13, 14.

WE have already cautioned the modern reader of Calvin not to be startled at his assertion, that "the Sabbath is a Sacrament." We have in these days become so thoroughly imbued with the notion that there can be but two Sacraments, that we reject at once the possibility of a third. This causes us again to call the reader's attention in detail to the principles expressed in the note to the 20th verse of this chapter.

A number of words occur in theological discussions which are not met with in Holy Scripture. Among these are the words *Sacramentum, Persona, Trinitas, Unitas.* If these were merely translations of equivalent Greek words found in the New Testament, all difficulty would cease; but they are not: although they express the ideas of the Apostles correctly, if taken in the sense in which they were originally used. The Protestant of these later times, if he would understand them aright, should study their use in the Schoolmen, and by the leading writers of the Church of Rome, and then approach the writings of the Reformers. Lawrence's Bampton Lectures have already been mentioned: besides these, Bishop Davenant's *Determinationes* of theological questions, when Margaret Professor of Divinity at Cambridge, are a valuable specimen of the subject-matter of theological dispute in the days immediately preceding his own. (See edit. 1634, and also 1639, in Lib. of Queen's Coll., Cam.) The greatest mistakes have been committed by English writers on Theology in consequence of their unconscious subjection to a traditional phraseology. It may fairly be called a slavery to words. They have lost sight of realities, through anxiety for a verbal orthodoxy. This has led them to look for spiritual realities where they are not to be found. In tracing the cause of this, we find it to arise from our receiving so many of our theological expressions through the Latin Vulgate. And not only are the words, but the ideas, of the Reformers tinctured by their education under the religious philosophy which they rejected. Calvin, for instance, in verse 16, vol. ii. p. 307, uses the phrase "*guttam pietatis ;*" in verse 20, "*guttam fidei ;*" and in verse 19, "*suis commentis inficiunt legem ipsius,*" vol. ii. p. 311 : the two former expressions implying that piety and faith are qualities within the soul, measurable by quantity : and the latter, that the fictions of man can in any way affect the purity of the law of God. Instances of this kind are here pointed out, that we may be aware of the principle on which Calvin's expressions on many interesting points frequently rest. Other words as well as *sacramentum* are used by Calvin in a sense rather different from their modern meaning. For example, *virtus* and *virtutes*, *doctrina* and *religio*, occur throughout these Lectures, and sometimes need a circumlocution for their English equivalents. In the 29th verse of this chapter *religio* occurs for respect paid to idols, vol. ii. p. 323 : and "*mysterium*" must be taken rather in its classical than its familiar meaning. The Greek μυστηριόν was translated "*sacramentum*" in the copies used by Tertullian, Cyprian, and Ambrose. Tertullian accordingly calls the doctrines of the Trinity and of our Lord's Incarnation "*sacramenta.*" Prudentius uses it for "the whole Christian doctrine," as St. Paul does the word μυστηρίον. 1 Cor. iv. 1. It is sufficient to point out this difference in the use of terms, that no reader may judge Calvin hastily, but rather be led to discover the error or the unsoundness in himself. Those Reformers who were more strenuous Nominalists than Calvin, did not deny the realities of the faith : but they sought for them *where they are only to be found :* not in rites, and words, and creeds, and ceremonies, but in the inner soul of man ; in our moral and spiritual nature ; in the character and revelation of God ; in the teachings and guidings of the Holy Spirit ; and in the renewed lives and peaceful deaths of all who are new-created in Christ Jesus their Lord.

I.—A COPIOUS INDEX OF WORDS, PHRASES, AND THINGS OCCURRING IN THE PRECEDING LECTURES.

A

ABDICATION of the people, i. 108.
Abominations, i. 282; ii. 93, 231, 285, &c.
Abraham, i. 175; Christ the seed of, i. 98; called, ii. 94; his obedience and faith, ii. 118; father of the faithful, ii. 93, 117, &c.
Absalom, his incest, i. 204.
Abundance of bread, i. 187.
Abyss, deep, i. 273.
Accommodation, language of, i. 125, 139, 333; ii. 223, 293, 448, &c.
Accuser, conscience an, i. 157.
Actions, divine, how regulated, i. 106.
Adam, fall of, i. 378, &c.; ii. 217, 241, &c.
Adamant, i. 136, 137.
Admonitions, why necessary, i. 153, 157; ii. 93.
Adonis or Venus, i. 292.
Adoption and regeneration, their effects, i. 159; ii. 300; symbol of, ii. 121.
Adulterers, their baseness, ii. 222, 456.
Adulterous heart, i. 230, &c.
Affectation, frigid, ii. 73.
Affections of the prophets, i. 153.
Ahaz, sufferings in time of, ii. 169.
Allegory, ii. 187.
Altars, i. 219; lofty, i. 221, 225; desolate, i. 222; profane, i. 238; brazen, i. 300, 302; ii. 452.
Ambassador, i. 117, 155; ii. 195.
Amber, colour of, i. 103, 277.
Ambiguity, ii. 322.
Amorite father, ii. 93.
Ancients of Israel, i. 285, 308.
Angels God's ministers, i. 56; their wings, i. 69; their motions, i. 77; human form, i. 302, &c.

Angelic motion, i. 321, 328, 346; righteousness, ii. 264.
Animals, four, their meaning, i. 65; cherubim, i. 69, 304, 309, 324, &c.
Annals, computation of, i. 52.
Antichrist, ii. 121.
Apostolic authority, i. 121.
Apostates, their punishment, ii. 54, 64, 161.
Appearance, i. 81, 95, 277.
Area of the temple, i. 311.
Arc of heaven, or rainbow, i. 104; ii. 53.
Arguments, fallacious, of the people, i. 350.
Ark of the Covenant, i. 65, 341.
Arm extended, ii. 36, 325, 326, &c.
Armholes and pillows, ii. 27, &c.
Armoury of God, i. 155.
Arrows, evil, i. 213.
Aspect, of God, what sense, i. 106; bold, i. 135.
Asperity of prophetic language, i. 122.
Assembly, ii. 15.
Assurance of faith, ii. 41.
Assyrians, ii. 131, 132, 138, &c.
Astonishment, i. 187, 211.
Authority, apostolic, i. 121; of prophets, i. 352; of God, ii. 260.
Auxiliaries to religion pernicious, ii. 142; human, profitless, ii. 196.

B

BABE, new-born, ii. 109.
Babylon, exile in, i. 52; city of merchants, i. 400, &c.; ii. 183, &c.
Backslider, i. 160; ii. 252.
Badger's skin, ii. 107.
Baldness, i. 260.
Bamah, lofty, ii. 322.
Baptism, its efficacy, i. 171; the laver of regeneration, ii. 312.

GENERAL INDEX.

Barley cakes, i. 184 ; handfuls of, ii. 32.
Battle, i. 258 ; of the Lord, ii. 10.
Beard, head, and hair, i. 190.
Belly filled, i. 263.
Benefits to the ungrateful, i. 195 ; their legitimate use, i. 373 ; illustrated by allegory, ii. 106.
Beryl stone, i. 329.
Birth, ii. 93.
Bishops, false, of the papacy, i. 148.
Bitter people, i. 133; spirit, i. 145.
Bitterness of spirit, i. 144.
Blandrata, George, i. 100.
Blasphemy, i. 141, 413.
Blindness of the reprobate, i. 389.
Blood filling the land, i. 316 ; plural, ii. 98, 105, &c.
Blood of lamb, i. 306.
Blossom-pride, i. 250.
Blow, deadly, i. 169.
Bombarding, ancient art of, i. 170.
Bond of a covenant, ii. 331.
Bones, scattered, i. 223.
Book, roll of, i. 127 ; of life, ii. 17.
Border of Israel, i. 355.
Bow in the cloud, i. 103.
Bracelets, ii. 105.
Branch, i. 296.
Brass, burnished, i. 70.
Brazen-front, i. 117.
Breach, ii. 11, 19.
Bread defiled, i. 184 ; staff of, i. 187, 213 ; ii. 67, 70 ; its secret virtue, ii. 71 ; fulness of, ii. 155.
Break the covenant, ii. 195.
Brethren, i. 363.
Brick, i. 171.
Briers and thorns, i. 120.
Brightness, i. 63, 277, 325.
Broidered work, ii. 105.
Bud-pride, i. 250.
Builder of a wall, ii. 19.
Bundle of twigs, ii. 91.
Buoyed up, ii. 159.
Burden of the prince, i. 395.
Buyer, i. 253.
Buzi, son of, i. 60.
Byssus fine linen, ii. 107.

C

CAKES, barley, i. 184; handfuls of, ii. 32.
Caldron, the city, i. 348.
Caleb and Joshua, ii. 333.
Call of Abraham, ii. 94.
Calling of the Gentiles, ii. 67, 89.
Calumnies of God's enemies, i. 121.
Camp, i. 170.
Captivity, meaning of, i. 51, &c.
Carefulness, i. 406.
Causes, providential and proximate, ii. 204.
Cedar, lofty, ii. 207, 463, &c.
Celestial hierarchy, ii. 37.
Censer, i. 285.
Ceremonies, sinful and vain, i. 284 ; ii. 30.
Chain, i. 268 ; ii. 267.
Chaldæans, i. 205 ; ii. 138, &c.
Chambers of imagery, i. 189.
Charity, its source, ii. 224, 234.
Chastity of soul, i. 231 ; ii. 112, 169.
Chebar, i. 146.
Cherubim, i. 69 ; wings of, i. 91, 304, 319, 324, &c. ; departure of, 325.
Christ, Abraham's seed, i. 98 ; his reign supreme, i. 125 ; ii. 175 ; the end of the law, ii. 176 ; new creatures in, ii. 180 ; grace of, ii. 181; kingdom of, ii. 207, 208 ; grace of, ii. 212, 298 ; immortality of, ii. 345.
Christopher, St., ii. 320.
Chrysolite, i. 83.
Church, its authority, i. 121; Catholic, i. 125 ; preservation, i. 363, 368 ; its restoration, i. 369 ; ii. 185 ; how preserved and defended, ii. 58 ; its life and safety, ii. 99 ; the primitive, ii. 176 ; ancient, ii. 178 ; salvation of, ii. 296 ; hypocrites in, ii. 336.
City besieged, i. 177, 299, &c.
Claims of the Pope, i. 152, 352.
Cloud, i. 103, 325.
Coals, scattered, i. 322.
Colour of amber, i. 63, 103, 277 ; hasmal, i. 68.
Commission of the prophets, ii. 348.
Confidence inspired by God, i. 137.
Conscience, i. 119; ii. 41 ; an accuser, i. 157.
Consolation, ii. 83, 348.
Conspiracy of papists against God, i. 125.
Controversy, i. 396.
Contumacy of the Jews, i. 55, &c.
Conversions of the world, i. 76.
Co-operation with God, i. 377.
Corners of the land, i. 241.
Counsel, i. 270, 347 ; ii. 15.
Court, i. 324, 325 ; of the temple, i. 294, 310, &c.
Covenant with Abraham, i. 178 ; ark of the, i. 65, 341, 367, 369, &c.; ii. 176, 289 ; perpetuity of, ii. 180 ; bond of a, ii. 330 ; New, ii. 173, &c.
Creeping things, i. 285.
Crop off, a twig, ii. 188, 207.
Cross among Samaritans and Papists, i. 305.
Crown, ii. 105.

Crystal, i. 90.
Curses of the law, i. 122 ; ii. 70, 243.
Cushions, ii. 37. See *Pillows*.
Cyrus and Darius, ii. 207.

D

DANIEL, Job, and Noah, ii. 69, 72, 75.
Darius, ii. 207.
Darkness, i. 247, 279 ; sparks in, i. 376 ; ii. 182.
Daub a wall, ii. 19, 23, &c.
Daughters of the people, ii. 27, 75, 77, 118, 129, 150, &c.
David, ii. 163, 183, 209, &c.
Day for a year, i. 174 ; of tumult, i. 248 ; prolonged, i. 409 ; of youth, ii. 172.
Dead, without lamentation, i. 253 ; carcases, i. 223 ; daily, ii. 81.
Dearth. See *Famine*.
Death of sinners, ii. 268.
Debauchery, i. 293.
Debtor, pledge restored, ii. 219, 223, 231, 303, &c.
Deceive, my people, ii. 35 ; a prophet, ii. 55, &c.
Defile the house, i. 310 ; ii. 133.
Deity of the Son, i. 100.
Departure of cherubim, i. 325 ; of God from the temple, i. 326, 341 ; of those going forth, ii. 81.
Desert, foxes in, ii. 9 ; dry, ii. 279.
Desolate, the prophet, i. 146 ; cities, i. 225 ; land, i. 406 ; ii. 316.
Detestable things, i. 205, 369, 382.
Devastation, i. 407.
Diblathah, i. 239.
Die in his iniquity, i. 157 ; there, 400.
Dig through a wall, i. 371.
Disciple, i. 134 ; ii. 45.
Discipline, instruction by, i. 211.
Divination flattering, i. 411 ; lying, ii. 13, 40.
Divinity of Christ, i. 101.
Docility of Jews and heathen, i. 133.
Doings, corrupt, ii. 344.
Door of inner gate, i. 279 ; eastern gate, i. 340.
Doctrine, its effects, i. 114 ; despised, i. 119 ; false, ii. 63 ; of false prophets, ii. 25 ; sound, ii. 29.
Doves of the valleys, i. 259.
Dumb, Ezekiel, i. 146, 166.
Dung, i. 184, 365.
Duties, the prophets', i. 111 ; ii. 263.
Dwelling-place, desolate, i. 224 ; of God, i. 311, 340, 399 ; ii. 79 ; among scorpions, i. 121.

E

EAGLE, i. 333 ; ii. 188, 193, 462.
Ear, i. 139, 298, 389.
Earth and heaven, i. 279 ; wicked of the, i. 265.
Ease of the reprobate, ii. 157.
East gate, i. 340, 346 ; wind, ii. 193.
Eat a roll, i. 129, 202 ; bread, i. 407.
Edification, a desire of, ii. 29.
Edge, set on, ii. 213, 215, &c.
Edom, sons of, ii. 146.
Elders of Judah, i. 276 ; seventy, i. 288 ; five-and-twenty, i. 347 ; their hypocrisy, ii. 44, 282, &c.
Elect, as used by Jerome, i. 68 ; excepted from punishment, i. 299 ; tried and afflicted, i. 307 ; promise to, i. 368 ; preserved finally, i. 376 ; ii. 17 ; mercy to, ii. 68 ; escape imposture, ii. 39, 251, &c.
Election twofold, ii. 121, 255.
End, i. 241, 243, 246 ; full, i. 360 ; of the law, ii. 230 ; of the people, ii. 308.
Enter within the wheel, i. 323 ; into the land, ii. 14, 332 ; into a covenant, ii. 102, &c.
Enticements, vain, i. 412.
Entry, i. 281.
Error of false prophets, ii. 46, 57, 315.
Escape, some left, ii. 81.
Essence of God, Christ, i. 100, 101.
Establish a covenant, ii. 178.
Estate, ii. 166.
Eternal life, ii. 52.
Examples, evil, of fathers, ii. 232, 310.
Excess, i. 122 ; ii. 139.
Exile in Babylon, i. 52 ; of Zedekiah, i. 367, 401 ; ii. 191, 279, &c.
Existence, wretched, ii. 81.
Expanse of heaven, i. 321.
Expansion, or firmament, i. 89, 91, 95, 319, 343.
Expiation by Christ, ii. 185.
Eye, i. 281, 308 ; not spare, i. 318 ; full of, i. 331, 389, 398, &c.
Ezekiel a priest, i. 59 ; styled "son of man," i. 107 ; rude in speech, i. 133 ; in bitterness of spirit, i. 144 ; at Tel-Abib, i. 146 ; dumb, 146, 166 ; with the elders of Judah, i. 276 ; and ii. throughout.

F

FACE of living creatures, i. 69 ; direction of, i. 82, &c. ; of wheels, i. 82, &c. ; strong against, i. 136 ; to set against, i. 170, 217 ; ii. 53, 91 ; turn

from, i. 266; fell upon, i. 312; four, i. 333; the same, i. 345; withdraw, ii. 51; to face, ii. 330.
Failure of man, i. 162.
Faith, i. 131; assurance of, ii. 41, 177; justifying, what, ii. 238, 298 ; in sacraments, ii. 312.
Faithful, safety of, i. 256; adorned, i. 306 ; depend on God, ii. 103, &c.; Abraham, father of, ii. 177.
Fall of Adam, i. 378 ; ii. 217, 241.
Fallacies, i. 348 ; of Satan, ii. 39, &c., 291.
False prophets and teachers, i. 150, 195, 233; ii. 25, 40, 57, 119, &c.
Fame, ii. 110.
Families of the courtiers, ii. 325.
Famine, i. 187, 213, 234, 258, 404, &c.; ii. 71, 79, &c.
Fanatics, ii. 9.
Fathers transgressed, i. 109 ; their example, i. 115, &c.; evil example, ii. 232, 310; Amorite, ii. 93 ; soul of, ii. 213 ; their sins, ii. 240, &c.
Feathers, full of, ii. 188, 189.
Feeble, all hands, i. 260.
Feet, i. 108, 164, &c. ; ii. 124, 126, &c.
Field, bud of, ii. 100 ; uncultivated, ii. 145; fruitful, ii. 191.
Figures, to excite wonder, i. 71 ; to instruct, i. 78 ; illusory, i. 110.
Filthiness of the people, ii. 139.
Fire, splendour of, i. 68, 171, 278 ; i. 102, &c.; ii. 84, 86, &c.
Firmament, i. 89, 91, 95, 319, 343.
First-born, ii. 202, 317.
Flame of God's wrath, ii. 184.
Flash, i. 348, 355.
Flattering divination, i. 411.
Flattery, i. 412.
Flour, fine, ii. 106, 115.
Fly, souls, ii. 36.
Foolish prophets, i. 5, &c. ; ii. 37, &c.
Forbear, i. 168.
Forehead, i. 302, 306 ; sign on, ii. 81.
Foresight, ii. 265.
Forest, ii. 86.
Fornications of the Jews, ii. 110, &c.
Fort, i. 170 ; ii. 199.
Fortitude, i. 117.
Fortune, blind, i. 67.
Foundation, ii. 23, 265.
Foxes in the desert, ii. 9.
Freewill, i. 109, 373, 375 ; ii. 262.
Free gift, i. 377.
Fruit, ii. 192, 261.
Fugitives, ii. 206.
Fulness of bread, ii. 155.
Furrows, ii. 193.

Fury of God, i. 208, 211, &c. ; ii. 23, 146, 287, 303, &c.

G

GAIN, to corrupt truth for, ii. 83 ; unlawful, ii. 225.
Gate, inner, i. 279 ; porch of the, i. 280 ; of the altar, i. 281 ; of the Lord's house, i. 292; higher, i. 300; east, i. 340, 346.
Garments, to deck high places, ii. 113; broidered, ii. 115, 219, 232.
Gentiles, i. 114, 185, 229, &c. ; calling of, ii. 67, 89; tyranny, ii. 337, &c. See *Heathen*.
Gift, God's, i. 211 ; ii. 111, 261; free, i. 377 ; to lovers, ii. 137 ; of Holy Spirit, ii. 243, 262 ; polluted, ii. 316.
Globe, all regions of, i. 69.
Glory of God, i. 106, 141, 164, 281, 304, 325, 340, 345, 384, &c. ; ii. 123, 211, 344 ; of all lands, ii. 287, 306.
Gold and silver, i. 262 ; ii. 114.
Gospel, chief end of, i. 154 ; insipid to whom, ii. 37 ; with law and prophets, ii. 247, 248.
Grace of God, i. 377 ; of Christ, ii. 181; of Holy Spirit, i. 378 ; remnant of, ii. 65 ; rejected, ii. 184, 291; embraced, ii. 185.
Grape, sour, ii. 213, 215, 464.
Gratuitous pardon, ii. 73 ; favour, ii. 84 ; reconciliation, ii. 174 ; adoption, ii. 287 ; opposed by the papacy, ii. 344.
Green tree, i. 237 ; ii. 319.
Grief, i. 261; ii. 181.
Groan and cry, i. 306.
Ground, not see, i. 398; undulating, ii. 329.
Guard, off our, ii. 251.
Guilt of infants, ii. 242 ; blotted out, ii. 245.

H

HAIL, ii. 23.
Hair of head and beard, i. 190.
Hammer of the word, i. 113.
Hand, instrument of action, i. 71; of the Lord, i. 161, 163, 279, &c. ; ii. 54.
Hardness of the people, i. 136.
Harlot, the Jews a, ii. 110, 112, 131, &c.
Harshness to Jews, none, i. 141.
Hasmal, a colour, i. 68.
Heart, hard or strong, i. 63, 117, 132, 135, 213, 370, 373, &c. ; ii. 145 ; adulterous, i. 230, &c. ; one, i. 370; new, i. 375 ; ii. 260, &c.

Heathen, i. 135, 362, &c. ; ii. 314, 325, 339, &c. See *Gentiles.*
Heaven, arc of, or rainbow, i. 104 ; the third, ii. 29 ; God at rest, ii. 235.
Hedge, ii. 10.
Heresy and blasphemies of Servetus, i. 97.
Hierarchy, celestial, ii. 37.
High places, ii. 135, 143, 323, &c.; priest, ii. 9.
Hill, high, i. 237, &c. ; ii. 318, &c.
Hire, ii. 135, 145.
History, sacred, ii. 59.
Hittite mother, ii. 93.
Holds, ii. 275.
Hole in the wall, i. 285.
Holiness, mountain of, ii. 337.
Holy place, i. 269.
Home, happy, ii. 137.
Honey, i. 130 ; ii. 106, 109, 115, 116, 287, 289.
Honour, worthy of, i. 161 ; of false gods, ii. 142 ; God's, profaned, ii. 293.
Hope, ii. 12 ; no remnant of, ii. 24 ; of escape, ii. 69 ; of gain, ii. 139; well, ii. 167; of safety, ii. 182, 250 ; futile, ii. 271.
Horn of pride, ii. 156.
Host, noise of, i. 92.
Hostility to God, ii. 254, 276.
Human form of Christ, i. 99, 101, 344; race corrupt, ii. 218 ; instincts, ii. 223 ; race perishing, ii. 241; comments, ii. 311.
Humility of the prophet, i. 81.
Hungry, ii. 219.
Hunter, i. 401.
Hypocrites perish wilfully, i. 119 ; not profit, i. 176 ; abuse God's goodness, i. 244, 399 ; ii. 7, 17, 53, 55, 181, 336, 339, 341.

I

IDOL, i. 222, 224, 237, &c. ; multitude of, ii. 48, &c.
Idolatry, hateful, i. 223, &c. ; ii. 320, &c.
Ignorance, of false prophets, ii. 21 ; of men, ii. 265.
Image of jealousy, i. 279.
Imagery, chambers of, i. 289.
Immortality of Christ, ii. 345.
Impiety, i. 410; ii. 31, 334, &c.
Impious men, scourges, i. 266 ; ii. 47 ; rites, i. 359 ; ii. 59.
Impostors, ii. 7, 11, 59.
Imposture, ii. 44, 57.
Impudence, i. 414 ; ii. 258.

Incense, i. 285 ; ii. 321.
Incentive, to perseverance, i. 124.
Incest of Absalom, i. 204.
Increase, ii. 219.
Incredulous, ii. 35.
Indecision, its nature, ii. 335.
Indignation, of God, i. 234, &c., 294.
Infants, subject to death, ii. 218 ; guilt of, ii. 241 ; blotted out, ii. 245.
Ingratitude, of the Jews, i. 200, 233 ; ii. 63, 131, 161, 171, 175, 307.
Inheritance, of God, ii. 155, 330, 341.
Iniquity, dying in, i. 157.
Inkhorn, i. 300, 302, 319.
Inner court, i. 324.
Instruction, by discipline, i. 211.
Intelligence, of living creatures, i. 89, 373 ; ii. 241, 264.
Intentions of papists, i. 231 ; of the Prophet, i. 383, 408 ; ii. 30.
Interest, for money, ii. 225, &c.
Interim, worse than papacy, ii. 335, 472.
Intoxicate, by false imaginations, ii. 156, 158.
Iris, i. 104.
Iron, wall of, i. 170.
Isaiah, his testimony, i. 101, compared with, i. 139.
Israel, ancients of, i. 285, 308.

J

JAAZANIAH, i. 285.
Jacob, i. 106.
Jealousy, image of, i. 281 ; ii. 142, 147; provocations to, i. 286 ; ii. 318.
Jeconiah, King, i. 218, &c. ; ii. 190, &c.
Jehoahaz, King, ii. 269.
Jehoiakim, King, i. 53 ; ii. 272, 275, &c.
Jeremiah, i. 53, 60, 203 ; ii. 81, &c.
Jeroboam, i. 175, 222 ; ii. 161.
Jerome, i. 103, 175, 182, 201, 252 ; ii. 140, &c.
Jesse, house of, ii. 209.
Jewels of gold, ii. 114.
Jews, their contumacy, i. 55, &c. ; their fornications, ii. 110, &c. ; a harlot, ii. 110, 112, 131, &c. ; no harshness to, i. 141 ; mercy to, ii. 67; unsatiable, ii. 131.
Job, Noah, and Daniel, ii. 69, 72, 75.
Jobel, i. 53.
John the Baptist, i. 58.
Josiah, i. 177 ; ii. 233 ; passover under, i. 53.
Joshua and Caleb, ii. 333.
Jubilee, i. 52.
Judah, elders of, i. 276 ; seventy, i. 288 ; five and twenty, i. 347 ; their

hypocrisy, ii. 44, 282, &c.; Ezekiel with, i. 276, and ii. *passim.*
Judge, ii. 163; just, ii. 260.
Judgment, of God, i. 198, 213, 242, 275, 359, 374, &c.; four sore, ii. 79, 263, &c.
Juno, i. 104.
Jupiter, imaginary, ii. 202.
Just, ii. 220.
Justice, or righteousness, i. 130, 159; shadow of, ii. 233; solid rule of, ii. 236.
Justification, ii. 162; of papists, ii. 182; the true doctrine of, ii. 162, 237, 238, 244.

K

KERCHIEFS, as veils, ii. 27, 38.
Kindred, men of, i. 362.
King, i. 176; ii. 186, 187, 195, 199, &c.
Kingdom, of God, i. 127; of Christ, ii. 207, 208, 212.
Knife, i. 170.
Knowledge, experimental, i. 403; salutary, i. 404; heavenly, ii. 63; of God, ii. 291, 341.
Knot, indissoluble, ii. 18; hard, ii. 155; untied, ii. 248.

L

LAMB, blood of, i. 306; ii. 268, 280.
Lamentation, i. 127.
Lamp, i. 78, 80.
Land, deserted, i. 316, 366, &c.; of traffic, ii. 188.
Language, hard, i. 131; aright, ii. 311.
Lapse, of the faithful, ii. 250.
Lasciviousness, ii. 123.
Laughingstock, i. 121, 349, 403; to Gentiles, ii. 169, 294, 305.
Laver of regeneration, ii. 312.
Law and prophets, i. 100, 359, &c.; and gospel, ii. 37, 248; perpetual, ii. 47; and testimony, ii. 165, 451.
Leaves, wither, ii. 193.
Lebanon, ii. 188, 189, &c.
Legislators implacable, ii. 35.
Lewdness, ii. 148, 170.
Licence, ii. 7.
Lie, to see, ii. 14, 43; hear, ii. 32; embrace a, ii. 57.
Life, save, i. 151, 165; of man, ii. 266, 297, 299; eternal, ii. 52; holy, ii. 256.
Light, intense, i. 375; ii. 247.
Lightning, i. 81.
Likeness, of a man, i. 69, 99; one, i. 330.

Linen clothing, i. 302, 327; robes, ii. 107; byssus or fine linen, *ib.*
Lion, i. 333; ii. 267.
Lions, princes compared to, ii. 271.
Lioness, Israel's mother, ii. 267.
Living creatures, i. 78, 88, 143, 336, 339.
Lock of the head, i. 279.
Loins, i. 277.
Losses of the people, ii. 170.
Love, time of, ii. 103.
Lovers, ii. 137, 140.
Lust, and cruelty, i. 401; of the flesh enticing, ii. 129; driven about by, ii. 205; renounced, ii. 246; impelled by, ii. 292.
Luxury, i. 365; its evil effects, ii. 111.
Lying divination, ii. 13, 40.

M

MADNESS, of the wicked, i. 225, 229, 293; ii. 253, 255, 257.
Magnitude, of the sun, i. 58; its wonders, 90.
Maledictions, or curses of the law, i. 122; ii. 70, 243.
Man, failure of, i. 162.
Manasseh, i. 176, 177.
Mandates of God, i. 388.
Manslayer pardoned, ii. 35.
Mark, i. 305, 308; of God's children, ii. 17.
Marriage, i. 231; bond, ii. 103, 136.
Mattaniah, King, ii. 186.
Mercy of God, withdrawn, i. 298, 315; to the wicked, ii. 66; to the Jews, ii. 67; to the elect, ii. 268; alone, ii. 239.
Merits opposed to election, ii. 288.
Message of peace, i. 128; ii. 20, 116.
Metaphorical language, i. 93, 297; ii. 211, 266.
Micaiah, ii. 59.
Milk and honey, ii. 106, 287, 289.
Ministers placed on watch-towers, i. 148; false, ii. 150; true, ii. 153; responsible, i. 156; Satan's, ii. 7.
Ministry, ordinary, i. 16.
Miracles, freeing the people, ii. 289.
Misery of mankind, ii. 247.
Misfortune, ii. 200.
Mixtures abominated, ii. 317.
Moderation, i. 153; ii. 284.
Modesty, i. 137, 316; ii. 266.
Month, i. 51, 276.
Monosyllable, ii. 297.
Mortal sin, i. 152; ii. 40, 312.
Mortar untempered, ii. 19, &c.
Mother, Hittite, ii. 93.

Motion, inspired by God, i. 67.
Mountain, addressed, i. 217, 220; lofty, ii. 210 ; eat upon, ii. 221 ; of holiness, ii. 337.
Mouth, of God, i. 139 ; opened, i. 129 ; ii. 183 ; roof of, i. 166.
Mystery, great, i. 97; ii. 305.

N

NAKED, and bare, ii. 144, &c., 219, 232.
Nakedness, i. 269.
Name of God, i. 123, 131, 388 ; ii. 13, 71 ; abused, ii. 31, 32.
Nathaniel, i. 59.
Nation, revolting, i. 109, 113, 211.
Nativity, ii. 96.
Navel, ii. 96, 97.
Nazareth, i. 59.
Neglect, in prophets, i. 157.
Net, spread, ii. 204, 274, 400.
New creatures in Christ, ii. 180.
Noah, with Daniel and Job, ii. 68, 72, 75.
Nod, of God, i. 403.
Noise, of the host, i. 92, 143.
Nominalists, ii. 450, &c.
North, whirlwind from, i. 63.
Nose, with branch, ii. 296.
Nostrils, i. 297.
Nuptial rite, ii. 104.

O

OATH, despised, ii. 171, 199 ; reason of, ii. 307.
Obedience, true, i. 165 ; ii. 135, 327.
Oblation, ii. 321, 338.
Obscene, language, ii. 189 ; men, ii. 209, 273.
Obstacle, i. 113, 137, 385 ; ii. 312.
Obstinacy, i. 135, 207, 247, 347, 409 ; ii. 130, 214, 286, 303.
Obstinate wickedness, i. 113, 409 ; ii. 309, 324.
Offence, i. 155.
Offerings, ii. 118, 320, 338, 339.
Offspring, of God, ii. 119 ; accursed, ii. 243.
Oil, ii. 115.
Oracles, i. 267 ; ii. 29.
Organ of the Spirit, i. 213, 352.
Original sin, ii. 217, 241.
Ornaments, i. 263, 302, 365 ; ii. 113, 123.
Osiris, i. 292.
Overflowing shower, ii. 19, 21, 23.
Ox, face of, i. 74.
Oxen, horned, i. 117, 281.

P

PAINTED city, i. 181.
Painting, i. 286, 290.
Palate, i. 167, 307.
Papacy, its impiety, i. 291 ; its pomps, i. 364 ; its corruptions, ii. 35; priests, ii. 107, 457.
Papists, their conspiracy against the Church, i. 125 ; their rage, i. 273 ; anger, i. 365 ; free-will, i. 375 ; boast, i. 377 ; satisfactions, ii. 182; fathers and antiquity, ii. 308 ; foolishness, ii. 310; views of a sacrament, ii. 312 ; idolatry, ii. 320.
Parables, their use, ii. 185.
Paradise of God, ii. 168.
Pardon, promise of, i. 208, 298 ; no hope of, i. 347 ; ii. 13, 73, 247, 249.
Passover, under Josiah, i. 52.
Pastor, i. 149, 157.
Peace, message of, i. 128 ; ii. 20, 116.
Penitence, its nature, i. 230 ; ii. 13, 259.
People, abdication of the, i. 108 ; their hardness, i. 136 ; daughters of, ii. 27, 75, 77, 118, 129, 150, &c. ; end of the, ii. 308 ; their filthiness, ii. 139 ; losses of, ii. 170 ; princes of, i. 347, 349 ; ii. 194 ; compared to lions, ii. 271.
Perpetual succession, i. 365 ; ii. 16.
Perpetuity of the covenant, ii. 180.
Perseverance, i. 156.
Persians, their worship, i. 295.
Pestilence, i. 215, 234, 405.
Phalatias, his death, i. 360, 361.
Phinehas, ii. 11, 74.
Pictures, religious use of, i. 286.
Piety, true, i. 371 ; seed of, i. 403 ; ii. 10, 111, 125, 325.
Pillows, armholes and, ii. 27, &c.
Pledge, external, i. 367 ; received and taken, ii. 223, 234 ; restored, ii. 219, 223, 231 ; ii. 303.
Plenty, i. 215, 407.
Poison, i. 216.
Polluted gift, ii. 316.
Pomp, i. 269.
Pope, his claims, i. 152, 352 ; thunders, ii. 42.
Power of God, i. 219, 379.
Prayer, heard, i. 299 ; ii. 11.
Precepts, not in vain, ii. 230, 321.
Precious stones, amber, i. 103, 277 ; beryl, i. 329 ; chrysolite, i. 83 ; sapphire, i. 95, 319, 321.
Presence of God, i. 164.
Prevarication, ii. 69, 92, 205.
Pride, i. 250, 269 ; ii. 89, 212.

GENERAL INDEX.

Priest, Ezekiel, a, i. 59 ; high, ii. 9.
Primitive church, ii. 176.
Princes of the people, i. 347, 349 ; ii. 194 ; compared to lions, ii. 271.
Prodigy, ii. 14.
Promise, to the elect, i. 368; of the law, ii. 239.
Prophetic language, its asperity, i. 122.
Prophet, his office, i. 51, 56 ; instructed, i. 78 ; dazzled, i. 103 ; fed with a roll, i. 129 ; lying on his side, i. 173, &c. ; false, ii. 7, 35, 53, 55, &c.
Prophets, affections of, i. 153 ; their commission, ii. 368 ; duties of the, i. 111 ; ii. 263.
Proverb, i. 409, 410 ; ii. 54, 55, 151.
Providence of God, i. 94, 333, 402.
Provocation, to jealousy, i. 286, 319 ; ii. 318.
Punishment, of the wicked, i. 173, 357, &c. ; ii. 61, &c., 64; on children, ii. 242, 293.

Q

QUAKING, i. 406.
Questions, perplexing and thorny, ii. 471.
Quiet, odour of, ii. 117.

R

RAINBOW, or arc of heaven, a sign, i. 104 ; ii. 53.
Razor, i. 191.
Realists, ii. 449, &c.
Reason, the faculty of, i. 373.
Rebukes, burning, i. 213.
Recompense, ii. 201,
Reconciliation, ii. 21, 43, 117, 179, 239, 342.
Redemption, ii. 303.
Regeneration, i. 159, 300, 373, 381 ; described, ii. 237, 251, 263 ; promised, ii. 302.
Reign of Christ supreme, i. 125 ; ii. 175 ; when, ii. 207, 212.
Remission of sins, ii. 250.
Remnant, of the citizens, i. 207, 314 ; of grace, ii. 65, 122, 165, 337.
Renovation, God's gift, ii. 250, 262.
Repentance, exhortation to, i. 169 ; portion of, i. 232 ; fruit of, i. 233 ; its sign, i. 372 ; two parts, ii. 263 ; needful, ii. 342, &c.
Repetition, necessary, i. 337.
Reproach, i. 211 ; ii. 166.
Reprobate, their punishment, i. 306 ; their ease, ii. 157 ; blindness, i. 389 ; ruin, ii. 47, 64, 157, 250, &c.

Riblah, ii. 199, 205.
Riddle, ii. 195.
Righteousness, i. 159, 160 ; twofold, ii. 237, 298.
Rings, i. 85.
Roaring, ii. 272.
Robbers, i. 267 ; ii. 11, 231, 269.
Rod, blossomed, i. 250, 303; for sceptre, ii. 275, 280.
Root, plucked up, ii. 193.
Ropes, to bind, i. 166.
Rumour, i. 211.

S

SABBATH, meaning of, ii. 300 ; sign, ii. 301 ; sacrament, ii. 302, 304 ; polluted, ii. 307.
Sackcloth, i. 261.
Sacraments, not vain signs, i. 110, 170, 171 ; ii. 303, 311 ; faith needed, ii. 312, 473.
Sacred history, ii. 59.
Sacrifices, ii. 117, 221, 318, 340.
Sacrilege of false teachers, i. 150, 195, 233 ; ii. 119.
Salvation, gratuitous, i. 381; ii. 47, 217, 238, 265.
Samaria, ii. 150, 152, 166, 268, &c.
Sanctification, ii. 301.
Sanctuary, polluted, i. 206, 269, 311 ; small, i. 366, 368.
Sapphire stone, i. 95, 319, 321.
Satan, i. 124, 168, 303, &c.; perverts truth, ii. 58, 59, 159, &c. ; his ministers, ii. 7.
Savour, sweet, ii. 115, 339.
Scorpions, dwelling-place among, i. 120.
Scourges, three, i. 234; four, ii. 80, 179, &c.
Seal of adoption, ii. 121.
Season, in and out of, i. 153.
Secret, of my people, ii. 14.
Seed, of Abraham, Christ, i. 98; of piety, i. 403 ; ii. 10, 111, 125, 325.
Seller, and buyer, i. 253.
Servetus, his blasphemies and heresy, i. 97.
Shoulder, i. 372, 394.
Shower, overflowing, ii. 19, 21, 23.
Siege, i. 173.
Signs, the rainbow, i. 104 ; ii. 53 ; sacraments, ii. 311.
Silence, a preparation, i. 146.
Silver and gold, i. 262 ; ii. 114.
Sins, remission of, ii. 250.
Sinners, i. 316 ; the death of, ii. 248.
Snare, ii. 205.
Sodom, ii. 150, 152, 166, 268.

GENERAL INDEX. 483

Solomon, ii. 187.
Son, the Deity of the, i. 100.
Son of man, Ezekiel, i. 107.
Souls, to slay, ii. 31 ; hunted, ii. 36 ; ii. 216, 458.
Sparks in darkness, i. 376 ; ii. 182.
Spirit, of God, i. 352, 386, &c. ; ii. 7, &c. ; of living creatures, i. 88, &c. ; its meaning, ii. 9 ; Holy, grace of, i. 378.
Splendour, of fire, 168, 171, 278.
Spouse, of Christ, i. 125.
Stature, ii. 27, 30, 275.
Statutes, i. 195 ; ii. 229, 245, 303, 308.
Stoics, ii. 205.
Stone, heart of, i. 213, 373 ; ii. 145 ; polished, ii. 319.
Strangers, i. 265.
Street, ii. 123, 135.
Stumblingblock, i. 216, 263 ; ii. 46.
Stupor, brutal, i. 293.
Succession, perpetual, i. 365 ; ii. 16.
Sun, its magnitude, i. 58 ; its wonders, i. 90.
Superstition, ii. 112, 161, 221, 269, 303, 307, 315, 321, 359, &c.
Swear, God, ii. 288.
Sweetness, odour of, ii. 116, 321.
Sword, i. 215, 217, &c. ; ii. 75, 77, &c.
Symbol, i. 171 ; of adoption, ii. 121.

T

Taunt, i. 211 ; ii. 55.
Teachers, of the Church, i. 148 ; false, i. 150, &c.
Teeth, set on edge, ii. 213, 215.
Temple, God's place, i. 142, 340 ; courts of the, i. 294, 310, &c. ; departure of God from the, i. 326, 341 ; false confidence in, i. 269 ; area of, i. 311 ; the second, i. 342 ; ii. 352.
Testament, New, ii. 173, 176, 460.
Testimony and law, ii. 165, 236.
Thammuz, i. 292, 293.
Tharsis, i. 83.
Thel-abib, i. 146.
Threats, i. 154, 217, 233 ; ii. 167.
Threshold, i. 325, 341.
Throne of God, i. 95, 321 ; ii. 45, 198, 321.
Thunder, i. 402.
Thunders of the Pope, ii. 42.
Tongue, i. 167, 172, 307.
Tower, ii. 200.
Traitor, ii. 251.
Transgressors, ii. 245.
Treaty, broken, ii. 201.
Tree, green, i. 237 ; ii. 319.
Trembling, i. 379.

Trespass, ii. 91, 204.
Tribunal of God, ii. 165, 321.
Triumph of the Prophet, i. 233.
Truth, to corrupt for gain, ii. 83.
Tumult, day of, i. 248 ; ii. 186.
Twig, crop off a, ii. 188, 207.
Tyranny, of the Gentiles, ii. 337, &c.

U

Uncircumcised, ii. 287.
Uncultivated fields, ii. 145.
Unsatisfied, the Jews, ii. 131.
Untempered mortar, ii. 19, &c.
Usury condemned, ii. 219, 225, 226, 469, &c.
Utterances, the Prophet's, ii. 348.

V

Vain enticements, i. 412.
Valley, i. 217, 221 ; doves of the, 259.
Vanity, ii. 44.
Vengeance, of God, i. 142, 153, 167, 269, &c.
Venus, or Adonis, i. 292.
Vessel, for moving, i. 390.
Vice, ii. 245.
Vine, ii. 83, 85, 193, &c. ; planted by waters, ii. 275, 277.
Violence, ii. 239.
Vision, i. 58, 279, &c.
Voice, of God, i. 92, 326 ; of wheels, i. 143 ; ii. 99, 275.
Void, make covenant, ii. 201.
Volume, of a book, i. 127.

W

Wailing, i. 252.
Wall, hole in the, i. 285 ; digging through, i. 287 ; builder of, ii. 19, 23, 25, &c. ; daubing, ib.
War, i. 235 ; ii. 199.
Warning, ii. 151 ; ii. 169.
Watchman, i. 148.
Watch-towers, ministers placed on, i. 148.
Weakness of man, ii. 87.
Weapon, destroying, i. 299 ; four, ii. 79.
Wheel of living creatures, i. 82, &c., 329, &c.
Whelp, lion's, ii. 267.
Whirlwind, from the north, i. 63 ; ii. 21.
Wicked, of the earth, i. 265 ; their madness, i. 225, 229, 293 ; ii. 253, 255, 257 ; mercy to, ii. 66 ; their punishment, i. 173, 357 ; ii. 61, 64 ; on children, ii. 242, 293, 357.

Wickedness, obstinate, i. 103, 409 ; ii. 309, 324.
Wilderness, ii. 279, 303, 314.
Will, free, i. 109, 373, 375 ; ii. 262.
Wine, ii. 187.
Wing, of the cherubim, i. 91 ; of eagle, ii. 188 ; of God, ii. 343.
Wives, strange, ii. 340.
Woe, mourning and, i. 127.
Women, ii. 27, 133, 145.
Wonders of the sun, i. 90.
Word of God, i. 108, 220, &c.
Work of the Spirit, i. 108 ; abolished, i. 224.
Worship of God, i. 198 ; idolatrous, i. 294, 361 ; ii. 55 ; impious, ii. 117 ; continued, ii. 161 ; pure, ii. 317, 322, 334, 337.

Wrath of God, i. 209, 253, 258 ; flame of, ii. 184, 321, 341.

Y

YEAR, day for a, i. 174.
Years, i. 174 ; ii. 101 ; seventy, 283.
Youth, i. 308, 309 ; ii. 100, 123, 241 ; perish, ii. 243 ; day of, ii. 172.

Z

ZEAL, i. 210 ; holy, ii. 285.
Zedekiah, exile of, i. 367, 398, 400 ; ii. 181, 191, 279, &c.
Zion, Mount, i. 57, 369, 384 ; ii. 337.
Zuingle, ii. 313.

II.—INDEX TO PASSAGES OF SCRIPTURE QUOTED AND EXPLAINED.

GENESIS.

Chap.	Ver.	Vol.	Page
i.	6	i.	90
	6,7,8	i.	321
ii.	2	ii.	302
iv.	9	i.	232
vi.	3	ii.	285
	7	ii.	109
vii.	1	ii.	73
ix.	13	i.	104
x.	19	ii.	152
xi.	5	ii.	266
xii.	3	ii.	178
xiii.		ii.	6
	10	ii.	168
	15	i.	369
xiv.	13, 14	ii.	128
xv.	6	ii.	177
	13, 14	ii.	103
xvi.	11	ii.	266
xvii.	7	ii.	300
	8	i.	369
xviii.	18	ii.	178
xix.	2, 3	i.	99
	24	ii.	243
	25	ii.	152
xxi.	9	ii.	16
	27-32	ii.	128
xxii.	9, 10	ii.	118
	17	ii.	300
xxvii.	34	i.	299
xxxii.	30	i.	106
xlix.	9	ii.	268

EXODUS.

Chap.	Ver.	Vol.	Page
i.	16-22	ii.	97
iii.	2, 3	i.	78
	7	ii.	99
	17	ii.	106
iv.	2	ii.	295
	22	ii.	155

Chap.	Ver.	Vol.	Page
v.	21	ii.	292
ix.	24	i.	68
xii.	22, 23	i.	306
	37	ii.	101
xiii.	2	ii.	317
	21, 22	ii.	106
xv.	20	ii.	28
xvi.	14	ii.	304
	15, 16	ii.	106
xvii.	6	ii.	106
xix.	4	i.	79
	6	ii.	104
			155
xx.	3, 4	ii.	299
	5	i.	79
		ii.	241
	11	ii.	302
	25	ii.	320
xxii.	25	ii.	106
	29	ii.	317
xxv.	18,19	i.	65
	20	i.	328
xxvii.	20	ii.	161
xxviii.	20	i.	83
xxxi.	13,14	ii.	301
	17	ii.	302
xxxii.	6	ii.	221
	25	ii.	11
xxxiv.	7	ii.	241
	19, 20	ii.	317
xxxv.	23	ii.	107
xxxvi.	19	ii.	107
xxxvii.	7, 8	i.	65
	9	i.	328
xl.	34, 35	i.	325

LEVITICUS.

Chap.	Ver.	Vol.	Page
ii.	1, 2	ii.	116
iii.	9, 13, 17	ii.	117
v.	3	i.	185

Chap.	Ver.	Vol.	Page
vi.	12, 13	i.	323
vii.	21	i.	185
xi.	2	i.	186
xv.	13	ii.	103
xviii.	5	ii.	266
	19	ii.	223
xx.	18	ii.	223
xxv.		i.	52
	13-15	i.	255
xxvi.	6	ii.	157
	26	i.	187
		i.	215
		ii.	172

NUMBERS.

Chap.	Ver.	Vol.	Page
iii.	13	ii.	317
vii.	89	i.	65
viii.	16	ii.	317
ix.	15	i.	325
xi.	9	ii.	304
	16	i.	288
xiii.	33, 34	ii.	307
xiv.	1, 2, 3	ii.	307
	18	i.	244
	18	ii.	13
	23, 24	ii.	333
xv.	15, 16	ii.	52
xvi.	11	i.	151
xx.	11	ii.	106
xxv.	1-3	ii.	316
	7, 8	ii.	74
xxxii.	10	ii.	306

DEUTERONOMY.

Chap.	Ver.	Vol.	Page
iv.	7	ii.	104
v.	7, 8	ii.	299
	9	i.	179
		ii.	241
	11	ii.	299

Chap.	Ver.	Vol.	Page
v.	14	ii.	302
	33	i.	359
vi.	4	i.	101
viii.	3	i.	188
			215
	3	ii.	56
			71
	15, 16	ii.	304
xi.	10	ii.	192
xiii.	3	ii.	6
xiv.	1	i.	261
xvii.	3	i.	294
xviii.	15-18	ii.	14
	18	ii.	282
	22	ii.	26
xxiv.	6	ii.	224
xxvii.		ii.	172
	5, 6	ii.	320
xxviii.	37	ii.	55
	53, 55	i.	203
xxix.	29	ii.	267
xxx.	12-14	ii.	283
	15-19	ii.	266
		ii.	297
	19	i.	199
xxxii.	8, 9	ii.	288
	11	ii.	132
	15	i.	198
	21	i.	280
	30	ii.	130
	47	ii.	266
xxxiii.	10	ii.	321

JOSHUA.

Chap.	Ver.	Vol.	Page
xxiv.	2, 3	ii.	94

JUDGES.

Chap.	Ver.	Vol.	Page
ii.	2	i.	174
iv.	4	ii.	28

INDEX TO PASSAGES OF SCRIPTURE.

1 SAMUEL.

Chap.	Ver.	Vol.	Page
xv.	22	i.	222
		ii.	135

2 SAMUEL.

Chap.	Ver.	Vol.	Page
vi.	2	i.	304
			341
xii.	12	i.	204
xvi.	21, 22	i.	204

1 KINGS.

Chap.	Ver.	Vol.	Page
vi.	5	i.	290
viii.	10, 11	i.	325
	64	i.	302
xi.		ii.	251
xii.		i.	222
		ii.	161
	20	i.	175
	28	i.	175
xiii.	2	i.	219
xxii.		ii.	59

2 KINGS.

Chap.	Ver.	Vol.	Page
xvi.	7-9	ii.	132
		ii.	169
xix.	15	i.	304
	35	i.	323
xxii.		i.	177
	14	ii.	28
xxiii.	23	i.	53
	30-36	ii.	269
	36	i.	53
xxiv.	8	i.	53
	15	ii.	186
xxv.		i.	192
			357
	4, 5	i.	400

2 CHRONICLES.

Chap.	Ver.	Vol.	Page
xviii.		ii.	59
xxviii.	18	ii.	170
xxxiv.	14	i.	53
xxxv.	18	i.	52
xxxvi.	10	ii.	186
	16	ii.	204
	17	ii.	269

EZRA.

Chap.	Ver.	Vol.	Page
ii.	2	ii.	209

JOB.

Chap.	Ver.	Vol.	Page
i.	6	i.	303
xxii.	14	i.	291

PSALMS.

Chap.	Ver.	Vol.	Page
ii.	4	ii.	59
iii.	5	i.	299
xi.	4	i.	143
xiv.	1, 2	ii.	217
xv.	1	ii.	336
	2	ii.	17
	4	ii.	203
	5	ii.	226
xviii.	8-15	i.	79
	12	i.	325
xix.	12	ii.	251
xxii.	3	i.	299
xxiv.	3	ii.	336
	4	ii.	17
xxvii.	5	i.	267
xxix.	5, 6, 9	i.	93
xxx.	5	ii.	13
xxxii.	1	i.	381
	3	i.	299
xxxiii.	12	i.	382
xxxvi.	6	i.	93
		ii.	58
			61
	9	ii.	243
	13	ii.	59
xxxvii.	3	ii.	183
xl.	3	ii.	183
	8	i.	128
xlviii.	10	ii.	344
li.	5	ii.	242
	12	ii.	261
	15	ii.	183
lxviii.	20	ii.	99
lxix.	10	i.	807
	28	ii.	17
lxxiii.	1	ii.	39
			336
lxxiv.	9	i.	168
			272
			341
lxxix.		i.	341
lxxx.	2	i.	327
	9, 10	ii.	85
	11, 12	i.	93
lxxxix.	37, 38	i.	313
			343
xc.	1	i.	367
xci.	11, 12	i.	306
xcv.	11	ii.	306
c.	3	i.	377
cii.	1	i.	313
	18	ii.	179
ciii.	8	i.	244
		ii.	13
	19	i.	143
	20, 21	i.	339
civ.	4	i.	77
cvi.	4	ii.	18
	23	ii.	11

Chap.	Ver.	Vol.	Page
cvi.	30	ii.	11
	31	ii.	74
cx.	1	ii.	175
cxi.	10	ii.	234
cxiv.	2	ii.	340
cxxx.	6	ii.	241
cxxxii.	14	i.	311
			340
			342
cxxxvii.	1	i.	58
	6	i.	307
	7	ii.	146
	9	ii.	243
cxxxviii.	8	i.	78

PROVERBS.

Chap.	Ver.	Vol.	Page
i.	7	ii.	234

ISAIAH.

Chap.	Ver.	Vol.	Page
i.	9, 10	i.	115
		ii.	331
ii.	2, 3	ii.	210
	3	ii.	175
iii.		ii.	108
	10	ii.	235
v.		ii.	85
	12	ii.	168
vi.	1	i.	101
	2	i.	66
	9, 10,	i.	112
viii.	12, 13	i.	125
	16	i.	115
			134
		ii.	165
	18	i.	125
			393
ix.	20	i.	215
x.	15	i.	403
	22	ii.	39
xi.	1	ii.	209
xiii.	22	ii.	273
xxviii.	1-8	i.	179
	11-13	i.	134
	15	i.	358
xxix.	11	i.	134
	11, 12	ii.	188
	14	ii.	321
	15	i.	290
xxx.	21	i.	359
		ii.	266
xxxi.	2	i.	348
xxxiii.	22	i.	109
xxxvii.	16	i.	304
	36	i.	323
xlv.	9	ii.	253
		i.	351
	23	ii.	254
xlviii.	22	ii.	398

Chap.	Ver.	Vol.	Page
li.	2	ii.	128
lii.	7	ii.	21
liii.	3	ii.	272
lv.	8, 9	ii.	179
	11	i.	256
lvii.	3	i.	115
	21	i.	358
lviii.	13	ii.	305
lix.	20	ii.	180
lx.	7	i.	342
lxiv.	3	i.	351
lxvi.	1	i.	143
			340

JEREMIAH.

Chap.	Ver.	Vol.	Page
i.	2	i.	54
	13	i.	349
			354
	19	i.	137
ii.	10, 11	i.	200
	21	ii.	85
	28	i.	224
	30	ii.	131
v.	3	ii.	261
vii.	2	i.	168
	4	i.	270
			341
	17	i.	277
ix.	1	i.	313
xi.	7	i.	168
	13	i.	224
xii.		i.	315
xv.	1	ii.	68
			73
	2	i.	191
	16	i.	126
			130
	20	i.	137
xvii.	21, 22	ii.	305
xviii.	18	i.	273
	6	ii.	216
xx.	2	i.	290
			315
	7	ii.	58
xxii.	10	ii.	81
	15	ii.	273
xxv.	12, 15	ii.	283
xxvii.	17	ii.	202
xxviii.		i.	56
xxix.	21, 24	i.	54
	10	ii.	283
xxxi.	15	ii.	72
	31	ii.	176
	32	ii.	177
	33	i.	381
		ii.	180
			237
			262
	34	ii.	178

INDEX TO PASSAGES OF SCRIPTURE.

Chap.	Ver.	Vol.	Page
xxxii.	2	ii.	245
xxxiv.	5	ii.	206
xxxv.	14	i.	168
xxxvi.	30	ii.	273
xxxvii.	1	ii.	186
xxxix.	4, 5	i.	400
	7	ii.	199
	10	i.	309
			357
xliii.	2-4	i.	309
xliv.	15, 16	i.	309
	17-19	i.	277
xlviii.	10	ii.	77
lii.	11	ii.	199

LAMENTATIONS.

iv.	10	i.	203
	20	i.	399

EZEKIEL.

i.	1, 2	i.	51
	10	i.	335
	28	i.	97
ii.	5, 8	i.	155
vii.	19	i.	215
viii.	12	i.	317
	15	i.	285
x.	14	i.	74
	20	i.	65
xi.	1	i.	360
	19	i.	360
		ii.	262
xiii.	9	ii.	337
	18, 19	i.	152
xiv.	3	ii.	284
xvi.	3	i.	115
		ii.	120
	6	ii.	277
	49	ii.	234
	63	ii.	216
xxvi.	27, 29	i.	56
xxix.		i.	56
	20	ii.	77
xxxvi.	25-27	i.	381
	26	ii.	237
	26, 27	ii.	262
			263

DANIEL.

iv.	8, 9	ii.	210
	17	ii.	210
			212
vi.	10	ii.	342
vii.	9, 10,		
	13	i.	98

HOSEA.

Chap.	Ver.	Vol.	Page
i.		i.	114
	9	ii.	176
ii.	4	ii.	95
	5	ii.	123
	23	ii.	66
iv.	10	i.	215
v.	11	i.	176
xi.	4	ii.	332
xiv.	9	ii.	254

JOEL.

ii.	28	ii.	28
	32	ii.	67

AMOS.

v.	18	i.	279

MICAH.

ii.	11	ii.	6
iv.	2	ii.	175
v.	2	ii.	211
vi.	14	i.	215
	16	i.	179
vii.	19	ii.	181

HABAKKUK.

i.	2	i.	315
	12	ii.	67

ZEPHANIAH.

iii.	9	i.	372

HAGGAI.

i.	4	ii.	340
	14	ii.	209
ii.	9	i.	342

ZECHARIAH.

ii.	13	ii.	183
viii.	23	ii.	175
xi.	1	ii.	190
	9	ii.	38
xii.	10	i.	358

MATTHEW.

iii.	8	ii.	259
	16	i.	58

Chap.	Ver.	Vol.	Page
iv.	4	i.	188
vii.	11	ii.	112
	6	ii.	285
x.	12, 13	i.	158
	29	i.	189
			339
xi.	24	ii.	163
xiii.		ii.	188
xv.	14	ii.	63
xviii.	18	ii.	34
xxiii.	32	ii.	287
xxiv.	13	i.	160
		ii.	249
	27	i.	81
	43, 44	ii.	153

MARK.

iv.		ii.	188

LUKE.

i.	78	ii.	247
iii.	8	ii.	259
iv.	4	i.	188
viii.		ii.	188
x.	5, 6	i.	158
xi.	13	ii.	112
xii.	16	i.	89
	39, 40	ii.	153
xvi.	15	i.	225
xvii.	10	ii.	244

JOHN.

i.	5	i.	376
iii.	16	i.	100
v.	17	i.	94
			339
xii.	41	i.	97
xiv.	10, 11	i.	101
xv.	1-7	ii.	87
	18	i.	135
xvi.	8	ii.	247

ACTS.

ii.	21	ii.	67
vii.	6, 7	ii.	103
	14	ii.	101
	40, 43	ii.	308
	51	ii.	287
	56	i.	58
xiv.	17	i.	105
xix.	24	ii.	29
xx.	28	i.	101
	31	i.	154

ROMANS.

Chap.	Ver.	Vol.	Page
i.	16	ii.	266
	24, 26	ii.	316
ii.	1-3	ii.	163
	12	i.	119
	13	ii.	236
iii.	1	ii.	89
	3, 4	ii.	120
	9	ii.	178
	19	ii.	183
			216
iv.	3	ii.	177
	15	ii.	297
vi.	12	i.	160
	19-21	ii.	182
		ii.	236
vii.	14	ii.	376
viii.	9	i.	376
	7	ii.	336
	13	ii.	240
ix.	6, 9	i.	382
	7, 8	ii.	121
	9	ii.	235
			336
	25	ii.	67
x.	5	ii.	237
			298
	6, 8	ii.	283
	13	ii.	67
	15	ii.	20
xi.		ii.	236
	5	ii.	38
	5, 6	ii.	39
			65
			122
			172
			337
	16-18	ii.	175
	29	i.	159
		ii.	250
xiv.	10, 11	ii.	254

1 CORINTHIANS.

i.	25	i.	171
iv.	20	i.	127
	21	i.	154
vi.	18	ii.	223
vii.	11	ii.	184
	14	ii.	122
	29-31	i.	253
ix.	16	i.	157
x.	3, 4	i.	335
	7	ii.	221
	12	ii.	249
	16	ii.	312
xi.	19	ii.	7

INDEX TO PASSAGES OF SCRIPTURE.

Chap.	Ver.	Vol.	Page
xi.	31	ii.	12
xii.	10	ii.	10
xiii.	12	ii.	61
			248

2 CORINTHIANS.

ii.	15, 16	i.	112
		ii.	34
iii.	5	ii.	236
v.	14	i.	145
vi.	8	i.	122
vii.	8	ii.	41
	9	ii.	174
	10, 11	ii.	184
x.	5-7	i.	155
		ii.	34
xi.	14	ii.	20
xii.	4	i.	102
		ii.	29

GALATIANS.

iii.	10, 13	ii.	239

EPHESIANS.

i.	4	ii.	265
	6, 12, 14	ii.	344
ii.	2	ii.	243
ii.	3	ii.	109
			242
			262

Chap.	Ver.	Vol.	Page
ii.	8	ii.	177
	10	i.	377
		ii.	249
	16	ii.	34
iii.	10	i.	66
	12	ii.	41
iv.	19	ii.	43
	22, 23	ii.	259

PHILEMON.

i.	23	i.	145
ii.	7	i.	99
		ii.	212
	12, 13	i.	379
iii.	18	i.	154
iv.	7	ii.	45

COLOSSIANS.

i.	16	i.	66
			328
ii.	16, 17	ii.	301
	23	ii.	8
iii.	15	ii.	45

1 THESSALONIANS.

v.	2	ii.	153
	4, 5	i.	247

2 THESSALONIANS.

ii.	4	ii.	120

Chap.	Ver.	Vol.	Page
ii.	11, 12	ii.	57
iii.	10	ii.	218

1 TIMOTHY.

i.	5	ii.	230
iii.	16	i.	101
	26	i.	97
vi.	16	i.	278

2 TIMOTHY.

ii.	19	i.	367
		ii.	250
iii.	9, 13	ii.	21
iv.	2	i.	153

TITUS.

iii.	5	ii.	312

HEBREWS.

i.	7	i.	77
ii.	13	i.	125
iv.	5	ii.	302
	12	ii.	49
vi.	13	ii.	76
			155
x.	7	i.	128
xi.	7	i.	257
			410
	19	ii.	118

JAMES.

Chap.	Ver.	Vol.	Page
i.	5	ii.	111
	17	i.	109
iv.	12	i.	109
			152

1 PETER.

i.	23	i.	159
ii.	9	ii.	183
iii.	14	i.	125
iv.	11	i.	132

2 PETER.

i.	19	i.	247
ii.	7	i.	307
iii.	8	i.	413

1 JOHN.

ii.	19	i.	159
		ii.	250
iii.	7	ii.	236
	9	i.	160
v.	18	ii.	238
	20	i.	101

JUDE.

i.	7	ii.	156

REVELATION.

iv.	3	i.	104

III.—A LIST OF THE SACRED AND PROFANE AUTHORS QUOTED BY CALVIN, WITH REFERENCES.

SACRED.

	Vol.	Page
AUGUSTINE De Bon. persev., &c.,	i.	378
Augustine, Hom. on John 89, book 19, against Faust,	i.	387
Augustine in John, chap. xx. 16,	ii.	250
Augustine, Epist. 24,	ii.	264
Dionysius,	ii.	37

PROFANE.

	Vol.	Page
Cicero in Orat., pro L. Muræna,	i.	390
Dionysius Halicarnassus,	ii.	119
Horace, Ode vi. lib. iii.,	ii.	215
Livy, lib. i. ch. xxxii.,	ii.	30
Ovid Metaph., lib. i.,	i.	70
Pliny the Younger, lib. x.,	i.	289
Virgil, Eclog. i.,	ii.	167
„ Georg. ii.,	i.	86

LIST OF HEBREW WORDS EXPLAINED.

THE ORDER OF THE PAGING HAS BEEN OBSERVED UNDER EACH LETTER.

VOL. I.

א
Page
איש 72
אביב 147
אם־לא 133
אם 133
אפיק 220
אחר 245
אחת 245
אף 297
אנך 306
אנה 306
אתות 393

ב
בוז 81
ברך 81
בקעה 281
במאך 314
בהפיצי 403

ג
גם 60
גוים 114
גלל 127
גם 201
גדופה 211
גלולים 223
גאון 264
גדלות 285

ד
דמות 278
דבר 411

ה
הגה 128
הי 128
המנכם 198
המה 198
הרעים 214
הר 247, 248
הר 248
הידד 248

Page
המון 252
הזמורה 297

ז
זהר 154

ח
חזקי 116
חתת 121
חרפה 211
חרב 225
חלל 266
חמס 296, 408

כ
כאמת 133
כי 138
כרים 171
כלה 208

ל
לאעמי 114

מ
מרד 113
מרדו 114
מורדים 120
מגלת 127
מאזנים 191
מרה 195, 196
מוסר 211
מאלה 285, 295
משבית 290
מאד 314
מעט 367
מופתים 393

נ
נשא 88
נטוי 90, 91
נטה 91
נקש 143
נה 252
נהה 252

Page
נדה 262
נפץ 301

ע
ענל 70
עבותים 166
עת 248
עריו 264
עין 278

פ
פגול 186
פליטיכם 228
פקדות 300
פלט 362
פלימם 362

צ
צפירה 247
צבי 264

ק
קשי 116
קט 231
קרוב 268
קנאה 281

ר
רקיע 90, 91

ש
שם 60
שדי 93
שמם 146, 187
שלח 213
שממה 239
שמה 239

ת
תל 147
תלל 147
תליל 147
תועבות 285
תו 305
תורה 305

LIST OF HEBREW WORDS EXPLAINED.

VOL. II.

א
	Page
אֲתָרִי	124
אַל	133
אֲחוֹתִיךְ	150
אֵלֶה	172
אֲשֶׁר	185
אֶדֶר	192
אֲדָמָה	341
אֶרֶץ	341

ב
בָּא	47
בָּהּ	47
בָּמוֹת	113
בָּעִיר	190
בְּאַלְמְנוֹתָיו	273

ג
גָּאוֹן	168
גָּאוֹנַיִךְ	168
גִּלּוּלִים	222
גָּזַל	224
גּוּף	319

ד
דָּרַשׁ	282, 284, 325

ז
זוּר	51
זְמוֹרָה	86
זִמָּה	150, 170

ח
חֵטְא	69

Page
חִידָה	187
חָלָל	307

ט
טַלְאוֹת	113

כ
כָּזָב	35
כּוּן	101
כְּנַעַן	188
כַּלָּה	293

ל
לְאֵמִי	66
לְכָל	185

מ
מַעֲלִי	52
מָשָׁל	55
מַעַל	67
מָשָׁל	187
מָלֵא	189

נ
נָבָל	8
נְבָלָה	8
נָזַר	51
נוֹצָה	189
נָשַׁךְ	225
נָתַן	274

ס
סוֹד	15

ע
	Page
עָנָה	47
עֶדְיִי	101
עַל	140
עָשִׁית	185
עוֹנוֹת	192

פ
פֶּרֶק	36

ק
קִנְאָה	148
קִינָה	268
קוֹט	343

ר
רִקְמָה	107
רֵעֲךָ	124
רָגַם	145
רָנַן	149
רָב	189
רְכֻלִּים	190

ש
שְׁלוֹת	157
שֶׁקֶט	157
שָׁאַט	170
שָׁמוּ	190
שֵׁבֶט	331

ת
תָּפֵל	19
תַּרְבִּית	225
תֹּכֶן	252
תְּנוּפָה	338
תְּרוּמָה	338

www.ingramcontent.com/pod-product-compliance
Lightning Source LLC
Chambersburg PA
CBHW071221290426
44108CB00013B/1249